DON'T BE AFRAID

VOLUME ONE

POLLY HARDER

DON'T BE AFRAID
ISBN 0-9772460-7-8

R.H. Publishing
P. O. Box 6207
Lincoln, NE. 68506
www.dontbeafraid.info

R.H. Publishing capitalizes certain pronouns from Scripture which refer to God the Father, Jesus Christ, His Son, and the Holy Spirit.

Although this is grammatically incorrect, R.H. Publishing does not acknowledge or dignify the name satan, devil or other related names by capitalizing them.

ACKNOWLEDGEMENTS

This book has been rewritten many times over a four year period. During this time, I wondered whether it was really intended for publication or was God simply wanting to make sure fear had no place in my own life. However, because of what God has shown me, I believe it is intended for everyone.

The completion of this book is not only the fruit of my labor, but also that of my family. No one could have supported me more, these past four years, than my mother, Marjorie Jeambey. She has always been there for me, as well as the other members of my family. She is a pillar of strength and an absolutely amazing woman. Thank you, Mom. I love you, and I pray God continues to bless you and strengthen you in your walk with Him.

My sister, Jaynie O'Flaherty, has been one of my best friends all my life. We've shared so many wonderful experiences together. It was her job promotion to Texas—and persistent urging about moving with her—that put me in the right place...in the right church...which allowed me to hear the truth of the Gospel that changed my life forever. I love you and thank you, Jaynie, for not only supporting me, but believing in me and the plan God has for me.

I would also like to give special thanks to my sister Gwen and family Larry and Jesse Bergman for their contribution in the technical areas. The timely success of the finished product is due to their knowledge and expertise. I love you and pray your generosity in helping me will also be greatly rewarded.

I also want to recognize four other close friends who have encouraged and supported me during this journey. Chris and David Clement, Jim Isaacson, and Linda Moore have been instrumental in this book reaching its audience. I love you all like family. Thank you, and I pray each one of you receives the harvest the Lord has for you.

And last, but by no means least, there have been so many of you who have continued to lift me up through your prayers. I felt them. They are the reason this book is in print today. I love you, and thank you!

From my family to my friends, I know your hearts are with me, and I know you will rejoice, as I will, every time you hear that someone's life has been changed, turned around, and freed to follow their divine path of destiny God established for them.

Most of all I want to thank You, God, for the opportunity to share what You have done for me with the hope it will encourage and bring others to the simplicity of Your great love and acceptance of them. To You be all the Glory, Honor, and Praise!

PREFACE

FEAR…What is it? Where does it come from? How do you get rid of it? Can you ever be free of it? These questions only reflect a few of the many concerning the most powerful, destructive, and paralyzing of all the emotions. Webster's Dictionary defines the word fear to mean, "to be afraid of: expect with alarm; to be afraid or apprehensive; an unpleasant often strong emotion caused by anticipation or awareness of danger." Fear can actually bring pain in the presence or anticipation of danger, and it most often is accompanied with anxiety and a loss of courage.

Fear is also associated with the word dread, which adds the idea of intense reluctance, as in facing or meeting a person or situation. Either of these circumstances suggests feelings of anxiety or aversion. Fright is another word that is associated with fear, and it implies sudden shock or a startling fear. Alarm works with fear, and it is a sudden or intense awareness of immediate danger. Panic is part of a reaction to fear. When fear is unreasoning or overmastering, it causes panic and hysterical activity. Terror is most definitely associated with fear because it deals with fear in the most extreme degree. Trepidation adds to fear and dread because it causes additional physical reactions such as trembling, timidity, and hesitation. The dictionary also lists words that are connected to fear like fearful, which implies a state of mind that is apprehensive, afraid of fear, creating a worrying temperament, and being suspicious of evil or danger.

In other words, fear is very real, and the effects of it are numerous and dangerous. The evidence of a "fear attack" can be seen and felt, both physically and emotionally.

Medical science has named over 525 different types of fear conditions. They're called phobias. They believe some phobias are treatable and some aren't. For example: Phobophobia is the fear or being afraid of fear itself. But the truth is fear debilitates. It paralyzes its victims, and even though it is diagnosed as an emotional or psychological disorder, it creates and then releases deadly poisons and toxins into the body. These toxins, if not dealt with, can and will surface in the form of physical illnesses. Simply put…fear is a killer.

However, God knew the effects of fear. He gave us the perfect antidote for a complete recovery to a perfectly peaceful and restful state of mind. What is this antidote? Where can you get it?

This brings us to the story at hand. "In the beginning" or "Once upon a time." Isn't this how many great novels or favorite stories begin? Good writers know in order to present an interesting, intriguing story there is one factor or event where you must start because everything else flows from it. For example, in a biography we already know the person has died, so the story tells us the end first. A book's story line could start at the very beginning of a person's life, and then give you all the details that lead up to who they are today in the present. It's these details that make a story believable or relatable. It helps every reader understand the plot or intentions of the writer, and it builds a relationship between themselves and the characters.

To this day, the number one selling book in the world is the Holy Bible. Over five billion copies have been sold in just the past two hundred years. The Bible, like other great literary works, also starts out with, "In the beginning." God, through the Holy Spirit and the many men who penned His Words in the Bible, also started from the beginning of time. It was purposefully written this way so we would understand His intentions, His plans for our lives or the "plot" if you will, and to get to know and have a close relationship with the main character, who is God Himself.

The Bible is a great work, but the real difference between it and all the other great literary successes is the Bible is truth that comes to life. The more you read it—the more you want to read it—and the more you read it—the more you learn. You'll gain a better understanding about who you were created to be, and what you were created to do. You'll learn about others, what to do in the highs and lows of life, and especially about God and His awesome plan for mankind.

Did you know you were in the Bible? Did you know the Bible is full of people just like you? They're also going through things just like you are! God gave us His Word in an almost "story book" form, so we would be able to relate to their daily struggles, fears, and emotions. Even though He may have shared the lives of other people, you'll find He has just told your story, too.

The Bible is relative, with timely information. It is wise counsel, wisdom and advice for business, marriage, raising a family, relationships, avoiding temptation, dealing with grief or suffering, and it will answer any and every question life may throw at you. It offers daily instruction. It will teach you how to live happy and successful lives. In truth…it is the best "self-help" book around. Every chapter and verse is packed with examples of men and women, including what they said or did, the outcomes of victory or defeat, and all of them teach us and empower us to be able to choose the right path.

Have you read it? Have you let God come alive and speak to you personally through His Word? Maybe you're thinking, "I've tried to read it, but I didn't get it." I can relate to that thought. "In the beginning" in my life's story with God and His Word, I felt the same way. I was afraid I couldn't understand it, and fear confirmed I was right. In fact, fear had me convinced the Bible was only for scholars, ministers or the highly educated. I thought it was a book written for people long ago, it was old fashioned, and it held no purpose for my busy life today. Maybe you have thought the same thing. Maybe you don't believe you can understand it, either. The bottom line is—I was so very wrong, and with the help of this book, I believe you'll find fear has lied to you, too.

The Bible says we perish for a lack of knowledge. Knowing God's plan for your life…your destiny…is available in the pages of His Word. Don't be afraid! He has shown me, changed me, and put me on the right road to my future. Isn't it time you let Him lead you down your "right" path to happiness, success, and victory?

INTRODUCTION

Several years ago, while sitting in a class at school, the instructor added a side note to the day's subject by briefly mentioning there were 365 "Fear Nots" in the Bible. This means there is one "Do Not Fear" for each day of the year. Then, without taking a breath or even pausing, he continued his lecture on the previous subject. It was at this moment the Lord spoke to me. He said, "I want you to write a book using these Scriptures to teach and encourage My people on a daily basis "how" to overcome fear."

The Lord went on to explain why it was so important to Him that His people get free of fear, to immediately recognize it, and never have to deal with it again! The devil's number one weapon is fear, which is really doubt and unbelief that the Lord God Jehovah isn't bigger than the problem or situation we're facing. Fear is the opposite of faith. Faith is what pleases God and brings Him onto any scene with our victory.

Now this "little chat" or conversation with God may seem strange to you if you haven't or you're not in the habit, "yet," of having regular conversations with the Lord. However, I've been speaking with Him for over 30 years. The Bible instructs us God has always talked to His people. He created us for just this reason…fellowship with Him. I thought I should mention this fact so you won't write me off as some kook who thinks they're hearing voices. With this being said, I'll continue with my story.

I finished that academic year. Then, one morning while watching TV, I heard another person speak the same thing. They asked, "Did you know God has given us 365 verses in the Bible to deal with our fears?" Instantly I was reminded of what the Lord had said to me that morning in class. I know there are no coincidences with God. The Bible says the footsteps of the righteous are ordered of God, so I knew this was my "wake up" call. It was time for me to pray about what the Lord wanted me to do.

Upon His direction I went to the computer. I was to look up, in five different Bible translations, all the verses that had "fear not" or "do not be afraid" in them. To my surprise and disappointment there were only about seventy verses, and some of those didn't apply to the message God wanted me to share in this book. I said, "Lord, what have these people been quoting? How and where did this information get started? I don't see 365 verses." Instead of waiting for His answer or further instructions, I did something very stupid. In my frustration and "fear" that I had already failed Him and thinking that I couldn't do what He asked me to do, I gave up on the project.

Even though I had been side-tracked from the right path, God's plan for me hadn't changed. Many weeks later, while in prayer with Him one evening, He asked me to turn to an inspirational book I had received as a graduation gift. I opened it to a page in the middle of the book and started to read. Here was a story about a woman whose husband had gone to the hospital for a serious operation. Her best friend had arrived at the hospital waiting room the morning of the surgery to stay with her. The man's wife expressed her fears to the friend about the outcome of the operation. The friend responded with "Did you know that today and everyday God has already prepared you to be able to overcome fear?" She went on to explain there are 365 verses in the Bible that help us deal with fear.

It didn't take long to see that God was still speaking to me about writing this daily devotional on overcoming fear. However, now I was even more frustrated than before. It was obvious how important this was to God, but I didn't have a clue how I was supposed to get started…let alone finish it. Finally I said, "Forgive me, Lord. Please show me the 365 verses you want your people to see. They must be in Your Word, and I don't know where they are."

A few nights later the Lord woke me in the middle of the night. He told me to turn on Christian TV. I watched a very good preacher give his message. He quoted several Scriptures to confirm what he was saying. At the end of the program I asked the Lord what it was He wanted me to see. He said, "Do you remember the first Scripture the pastor quoted? I said, "Yes." Actually, I remember it well because I speak it over myself each day. The Lord said, "When you use this verse or hear it, doesn't it remove fear and bring you comfort?" I said, "Yes, it does. This is the reason I speak it and usually out loud." He then said, "My Word is full of verses just like this one. Their very nature is to remove fear and all the destruction the devil brings because of it."

He then added, "Don't be afraid...you can do this. Ask the Holy Spirit. He will show you the verses." I said, "Thank you, Lord." It was then I became diligent in "being about the Father's business." It only seemed appropriate I would start the first day of this book with the first Scripture the Lord gave me as His example. This book, which was written by the Holy Spirit, too, will take God's Word, explain who wrote it, what they were going through, how God worked in their circumstances, and what God will do when we face the same issues today. It will give you a clear picture of God, His overwhelming love for you, and His superb plan for your future. This book will encourage you and make you absolutely certain, regardless of your circumstances...you don't have to be afraid.

God has already made a way for us to live fear-free and in complete victory. The truth is there are far more than 365 verses that encourage, lift us up, and confidently allow us to see that with God—who is always "more" than enough—we don't ever have to be afraid of anything or any one. But in order to know what these verses are and what they mean we have to overcome the <u>initial fear</u> most people have about the Bible. This fear is "<u>You</u> don't understand what it is saying." I know how frustrating and discouraging this is because I was there. However, God showed me a particular translation that with the Holy Spirit's help I understood perfectly. Now, because of it, the Word has transformed my life. There is a translation that will be the right one for you, too. God wrote the Bible so we could know Him, know ourselves, know the plans He has for us, and what is to come. He gave us this book to get rid of fear—not to add to it.

As I previously stated, in my studies of God's Word, I found more than 365 verses that deliver powerful, life changing truths about living free of fear. As I followed God's instructions in writing this book, I started each day of the first six months of the year by using Scriptures from the Old Testament. God wanted me to lay a solid foundation where you could get to know Him, personally, and you would get to know the great promises He had planned for you. He also wanted you to gain a better understanding of the original covenant He first developed with mankind. The last six months of the year will then cover the promises from the Scriptures in the New Testament. The New Testament offers us new and better covenant promises.

It is my prayer that while you read His Word on a daily basis, you will grow in your knowledge of it. However, don't grow just for the sake of knowledge. Instead, allow your internal heartfelt understanding of The Word to help you gain true spiritual wisdom and full acceptance of His great, unconditional, and magnificent love for you. This is the love we have all dreamed about, searched for, and desperately need. His perfect love is the love that casts out every fear.

God has a great plan just for you. You can fulfill your divine destiny. Follow His Word, and...DON'T BE AFRAID!

DON'T BE AFRAID

"HAVE I NOT COMMANDED YOU?
BE STRONG AND COURAGEOUS.
DO NOT BE TERRIFIED,
DO NOT BE DISCOURAGED,
FOR THE LORD YOUR GOD WILL BE WITH YOU WHEREVER YOU GO."

JOSHUA 1:9 (NIV)

JANUARY 1

"No weapon that is formed against
thee shall prosper;..."
Isaiah 54:17a (KJV)

One of the meanings of the word "no" is "not any." From the beginning of this verse, God makes it completely clear—not one thing could possibly hurt us. Why did He use the word "*weapon*?" Because the Scriptures tell us we are in a battle against good and evil. Now you might be thinking, "Well, I'm not a soldier. I don't fight against an enemy's weapons. How does this apply to me?" This may be true if you only think of weapons in terms of what's needed in combat for war, but there are weapons you face everyday. What kind of weapons? Has disease or illness attacked your body or a family member? Is there a threat of divorce in your marriage? How about addictions…drugs, alcohol, sex, shopping, over-eating? Have any of these seduced you or one of your children? Maybe words like "lay-off" or "unemployment" haunt your work place? What about the actual threat of war or some form of chemical disaster?

Are not all of these weapons—instruments that bring harm and destruction against us or the ones we love? All of these and more can be and are a big part of the world we live in today. They come to steal our peace, our health, our families, and most of all our sense of well being. And yet, God told us in simple terms that *no weapon formed against us would prosper*. In other words, even when we face problems that are so much bigger than we are, we don't have to be afraid. With God on our side—they won't have the final say—or prosper. The word prosper means to be favorable, successful, fulfilled or strong against us. There are no surprises with God, and the Word says He is not a man who lies. If He said to not be afraid of anything because ***nothing*** – "no thing" would be prosperous, fulfilled or strong against us, then we can trust His Word.

When any form of "weapon" tries to come against you, just quote this Scripture as a reminder that "all things" are already defeated. Why? Because God loves you. The Bible says He has already provided every defense you will ever need in Him and His Word. Don't be afraid. Trust God. Keep your focus on Him…not your circumstances. You'll soon realize He won't let you down.

JANUARY 2

> *"...and every tongue that shall rise against thee in judgment thou shalt condemn."*
> *Isaiah 54:17b (KJV)*

The first part of this verse instructs us that no weapon could harm us, but what does this second part have to do with weapons? Do you remember as a child hearing the phrase, "Sticks and stones might break my bones, but names can never hurt me?" Normally this was the final response in a verbal fight after every thinkable name, phrase, or derogatory statement had been exhausted. A harmless child's phrase, right? Not necessarily.

Words, especially negative words, spiteful words, degrading words can be weapons, and people use them as such. When spoken over us and often enough, they become believable. How does this occur? Fear enters. You begin to think, "What if they are true? Or this person is right?" Now these same words, whether true or false, carry enough power to change us and not for the better. Maybe you were raised in a verbally or emotionally abusive home? Do you have low self-esteem, lack confidence or suffer from other emotional issues? Maybe you were told you were never wanted or loved? If this describes you, don't be discouraged. God can and will restore you. His Word offers comfort and healing for past wounds and emotional hurts.

This Scripture tells us when we hear negative or critical words we can condemn or get rid of them. How do we do this? By renewing our minds to think and believe what God says about us in His Word. He says you are an overcomer, you are valuable, you have worth, and you have been created for a great purpose and plan. Will you choose to believe what Almighty God says about you or what man says? Don't be afraid! With His unconditional love and support, you will be able to forgive and forget all those who have hurt you. Cast down the words that don't agree with God's, and get on to a happy, peaceful, and productive life. This is the plan He has designed for you to live.

JANUARY 3

> *"So do not fear, for I am with you;*
> *do not be dismayed, for I am your God.*
> *I will strengthen you and help you; I will*
> *uphold you with my righteous right hand."*
> *Isaiah 41:10 (NIV)*

When we find ourselves afraid of something it can be for many reasons. Fear doesn't just attack in dramatic or unexpected ways. It can also hit us in our regular daily routine. For example: interviewing for a new job, speaking in front of a group or just driving on a busy freeway. Perhaps we experience feelings of fear because we are unsure of others and their feelings for us. Maybe we're afraid because of low self-esteem or we lack confidence in our own ability. We can be afraid of people we don't know and the intimidating or controlling person we do know. Fear can also be present in a "sudden" situation. Have you ever experienced car trouble while traveling?

Fear can be present in every arena of our lives. If you have ever found yourself in these situations, remembering the details can recreate similar feelings because of the strong emotion fear creates. There are inner feelings of anxiety, worry, stress, and dread. Fear can be the root of many physical illnesses, too. It can be overwhelming, depending on the individual circumstances you're facing.

However, God's Word demonstrates repeatedly how much He loves us and the divine plan of provision and protection we have in Him. The main reason we don't have to be afraid is God is with us…you are not in this by yourself. Have you ever felt afraid? Like you are all alone? This verse confirms you're not. Now when you start to feel fear rising up in you—stop it. You have the ability to take authority over your own emotions. How? By changing the way you think. How do you change your thinking? By replacing it with new thoughts of what God has promised you in His Word. Remind yourself…"He loves me," and you can also meditate on the above verse. Don't be afraid. You can put your mind to rest by renewing it to the promise God—your Heavenly Father—has given you. When He tells you to not fear because **He,** and He alone, *will help you and strengthen you*, you can believe Him.

JANUARY 4

> *"For I am the Lord, your God, who takes*
> *hold of your right hand and says to you,*
> *Do not fear; I will help you."*
> *Isaiah 41:13 (NIV)*

In this verse God repeats a second time what He said in verse 10. 1) He is our God; 2) He has a hold of our hand; 3) He is speaking to us; 4) DO NOT FEAR! 5) He will help us. Why did God think it was necessary to repeat this again? Because He knew fear would keep trying to come against us, and even though we had just read it a few verses earlier, our thoughts could have gone right back to what we had been previously thinking.

When I read Scriptures about God holding my hand, I am reminded of what a parent does when crossing the street with a small child. They get a tight hold on the child's hand. In fact, they hold it in such a way the child knows they aren't going anywhere, except where the parent leads. The parent doesn't risk letting the child be responsible to do the holding. Instead, the child's hand is positioned safely in the hand of the adult, and the result is both reach their final destination safely. The child never even senses this could be dangerous or has any fear because of the love and strength he feels from the hand that has a steady and secure grasp of his.

This is how it is for us with God our Father. He wants to take hold of our hand in the same way. All we have to do is let Him lead and guide us to that same place of safety. A child doesn't fear when their hand is in the palm of a parent who loves, guides, and protects them. Neither should we fear, knowing the Father has His hand extended to take hold of ours. God loves you. This verse is just one of many He has written as a daily reminder of that love. Don't be afraid. He is right there to be your friend and helper, to strengthen you through any and every trial you may be facing. Reach out your hand to Him, and let Him place it in His. He will keep you safe, and without being afraid, you'll reach your final destination, too.

JANUARY 5

> *"The Lord is my shepherd (to feed, guide and shield me); I shall not lack."*
> *Psalms 23:1 (AMP)*

The Bible was written by men as God inspired them with His Words. He made it understandable and practical to them by comparing the Word to current events, duties, and their daily experiences. The role of a shepherd is quite demanding. They are the only source of provision and protection for their sheep. They guide them by moving them each day to the place where the feeding is the best, and then they're brought home each night to a safe place that shields and protects them. Daily the shepherd examines each of the sheep as they come through the gate for injuries or pestilence. This is his guarantee they are not in pain or discomfort.

In other words, the shepherd's role today could be compared to a nurturing, loving, and caring employer. He is well equipped and knows his territory. He can lead every member of his company in the right direction, so they all will prosper. Everyone always has their needs met daily, and above all, he provides a safe haven from any outside attack. He is their constant companion, and because of it, he eliminates their fear. There is never any doubt about how much he loves them. They have no wants or lack of any kind.

This sounds like the kind of employer I want. How about you? The Bible refers to us as sheep, and it says we are the sheep of the Lord's pasture. When we allow Him to lead, guide and protect us, His provision includes no wants or lack, either. He becomes our "good shepherd." He demonstrates His goodness to us everyday by His unconditional and unfailing love. Wouldn't you like to have someone watching out for you? Someone who would daily check you and your family for trouble that could be a trap? This verse assures us we do have that someone…that loving, nurturing shepherd…the Lord.

This verse says, "*The Lord is MY shepherd*." Have you decided to make Him your shepherd? Don't be afraid. You can live a life full of peace and contentment without concern, worry, anxiety or fear of what today or tomorrow may bring. Just trust in Him, and He will be your good shepherd.

JANUARY 6

> *"He makes me to lie down in (fresh, tender) green pastures, He leads me beside the still and restful waters."*
> *Psalms 23:2 (AMP)*

One of the main responsibilities of a shepherd is to daily lead the sheep to the best pasture. It is also his responsibility to move the flock to a place where the waters would be quiet or still for easy drinking. This shouldn't be difficult for us to understand. Don't we want our food to be fresh and tender? Can you imagine trying to drink—especially something hot—from a cup that was constantly moving? What a mess that would be, right?

Life today has each of us so busy with all our plans, programs, and activities that sometimes we don't take the time for the proper diet, exercise, and rest we need. Have you ever skipped a meal because you were too busy to eat? We all have. There is a reason our "fast" food restaurants are so successful. However, these fast paced lifestyles keep us from eating and drinking balanced and nutritional foods, and our bodies tell the story. But this is not God's plan for us. After all, even He took a day to rest after working for six days to create the world. Think about this for a minute…Almighty God took a day for rest. When was the last time you took a day off—24 hours—for rest and relaxation? Stress, sickness and disease, fear and worries are not part of God's plan. God's ultimate plan is one of peace and balance. His love for us is so great that He is prepared to "*make us" lie down* in order for us to maintain healthy lives. When we let ourselves slow down we think more clearly, and we are capable of making much better decisions.

Is it time for you to slow down? Take a deep breath and prioritize the "happenings" in your life? God promised through Him we could have a care-free, worry-free, stress-free, fear-free life. If you've ever stood or sat beside a body of water that was barely moving, then you know how peaceful, restful, and relaxing it feels. This is God's plan for you. Peace—even in the midst of turmoil or chaos. Don't be afraid. Choose to let Him be your shepherd, and let Him lead you to a place of rest.

JANUARY 7

> *"He restores and refreshes my life—myself; He leads me in the paths of righteousness (uprightness, and right standing with Him—not for my earning it, but) for His name's sake."*
> *Psalms 23:3 (AMP)*

David, the writer of this verse, knew first hand what it was to need refreshing and restoring. The word restore means to be brought back to the original form. David had made a lot of mistakes, but he also knew what to do about it when he did. He would humble himself before God and ask for forgiveness. God forgave him, restored him, and continued to lead him unto the right path. A path filled with success and victory.

The King James translation says, "He restoreth my soul." The soul is made up of the mind, will, and emotions. These three can have a powerful impact on our peace and how we think about the past, present, and future…especially if we've had disappointments and failures. All of us have dealt with issues we would like to change. This verse encourages us, regardless of where we've been or what we've done, God will not only restore to us what was lost, but also refresh us for the future. His Word renews our soul to His ways—His path, which is the right way.

This verse also confirms that *He leads us* because of His love and desire to be in fellowship with us. He positions, leads, and guides us, "*for His name's sake*," to stay on a righteous path. Why is it important to know He does it? Because it reduces our feelings of fear, insecurities, worry, and anxieties that we couldn't do it on our own. We know it has nothing to do with our own abilities, skills, talents, education…or the lack of it…or anything else that has to do with us.

Maybe you can relate to David? Maybe you've made a lot of mistakes, too? The Bible says when we sin, we can ask God to forgive us, and He is faithful and just to do it. God wants you to be in a right standing position with Him. Plus, He wants you to be refreshed and restored. This is the only way we are equipped to attend to the matters we face everyday. Don't be afraid. His unfailing, never ending, unconditional love for you will always provide, protect, lead you and keep you on the right path.

JANUARY 8

> *"Yes, though I walk through the (deep, sunless) valley of the shadow of death, I will fear or dread no evil; for you are with me; your rod (to protect) and your staff (to guide), they comfort me."*
> *Psalms 23:4 (AMP)*

This is one of the most encouraging Scriptures in the Bible. Mankind's ultimate fear is death—because it is final. David ran for many years from a jealous king. He had been through times when death was all around him, and yet, he wasn't afraid. Why? The main reason is God was with him. The truth is God is still with us today. He isn't just watching from the sidelines. He is an active participant—comforting, protecting, guiding. This verse and many others assure us of where God is and what He is doing. However, the question is "What are you doing? Are you praying or calling on God for help?"

When we find ourselves in danger—as perhaps military personnel do, or people who risk their lives in rescue attempts, or people who are involved in tragic accidents, or acts of violence—we can call on God. He is there with us. We, YOU, are never alone. In this verse, He states once again, "He will *protect, guide, and comfort us*." This is how peace (no fear) comes to our soul, which is our mind, will, and emotions. This verse also makes it clear we're going "*through*" the valley. It doesn't say we camp out, build a house or have to dwell in this dark place forever. Trials will come, but we will not be destroyed. Why? Because God has a plan and His plan is for us to go on through to victory.

Maybe you're experiencing a rough time in your life? Maybe your valley or dark time includes being laid off? Losing your savings or retirement in the stock market? Losing a loved one? Your children, friend or loved one is on drugs? Or they're living an ungodly, rebellious life? Whatever the circumstances, God is there with you—all the while saying, "Don't be afraid." Even in what appears to be our darkest hour, we are encouraged to trust Him. He will protect, guide, and comfort you. He loves you, and HIS love is perfect. The Bible tells us that perfect love casts out <u>all</u> fear. Allow God's love to come into your life. In your darkest hour, His Word and love will bring you "through," and it will remove all your doubts and fears.

JANUARY 9

> *"You prepare a table before me in the presence of my enemies; you anoint my head with oil; my (brimming) cup runs over."*
> *Psalms 23:5 (AMP)*

When I think about sitting down at a table to dine, it's good friends, my family, great conversation or fellowship, and extremely good food that comes to mind. As strange as it may seem, when I'm meal planning, my enemies never seem to cross my mind. However, this Scripture states they will be there. "*In the presence of,*" could it possibly mean they could look upon the feast, actually having the ability to see what they are missing, but unable to join in?

God's love and covenant protection is extended to His children. When we follow His plan and obey His Word, we can and will be positioned in every circumstance to be blessed, rewarded, and fulfilled, regardless of what it may look like at the time. We have been given victory over our enemies, which means freedom. Freedom, with no more fear, of our past failures, relationships, family, co-workers or anything else that has tried to come against us. God's plan for us includes victory! Freedom! Doesn't this sound like a good plan?

This verse also says, "*He anoints my head with oil.*" The anointing is what breaks every yoke, weight, bondage or oppression. Are your problems weighing you down? Do you see a way out? Are you feeling hopeless? I want to encourage you because there is no circumstance too big for our God. "He fills our cup to overflowing, *our cup runs over.*" When something runs over it is because there is "too much." We serve a "<u>too much</u>" God. His promise is to provide us with more than we need.

With God we will always have a table to feast at and "too much" for whatever it is we need. Don't be afraid. There is never any reason for you to fear when you know how much God loves you and the good plan, His covenant plan, He has already prepared for you in advance.

JANUARY 10

"Surely or only goodness, mercy and unfailing love shall follow me all the days of my life; and through the length of days the house of the Lord (and His presence) shall be my dwelling place."
Psalms 23:6 (AMP)

The word *surely* is defined in Webster's Dictionary as, "without danger or risk of injury or loss: safely; confidently; certainly; indeed." God wants us to understand we can confidently, with certainty of no risk or danger, believe what He is about to say to us through His Word. *Mercy* is defined as, "compassion and forbearance to an offender or to one that is subject to another's power; to love and to show kindness to the distressed; pour blessings that is an act of divine favor or compassion, to be lenient of punishment due by showing compassion and kindness." Mercy, charity or love, clemency, grace and leniency imply compassion that forebears punishing, even when justice demands it. In other words, God's love for us is so great that He withholds punishment, even when we may deserve it.

Let's read this Scripture again, but this time we will insert the definitions of *surely* and *mercy* in place of the words. "Without danger, risk of injury or loss, safely, confidently, certainly, indeed only goodness, compassion, kindness, leniency, divine favor, no punishment when deserved, and unfailing love shall follow me all the days of my life." Wow! God's great benefits and promises to us can be summed up in this one verse. This promise alone is powerful enough to change a bad attitude into one of gratitude, and if you were ever afraid that God wouldn't forget what you've done or forgive you, this should kick fear right out of your mind—forever!

Maybe you have been rejected, abandoned or abused in your past "love" relationships? The Bible says God will never leave you. He gives you an opportunity to choose, and then stay with His "insurance policy of love." He also allows you to come into *His presence*, and not just as a visitor, but as His child to live there forever. Don't be afraid. Our Father's covenant plan provides anyone, who will accept it, a safe home—a *dwelling place* with Him that is free of worries, fears, and doubts.

JANUARY 11

"Do not be afraid; you will not suffer shame."
Isaiah 54:4a (NIV)

Shame is an emotion that some individuals carry with them forever. We all have done or said things we regret later. Guilt, shame, and regrets are the emotional by-products of those actions. However, these emotions can be tormenting, always at the forefront of our thoughts. They are hard to control, and for some they seem virtually impossible to make go away. However, it's dangerous when we allow these thoughts to continue for any length of time. Why? Because when we allow them to be all consuming, we literally start to feel a weight or the burden of them. The pain, heaviness, anger or hardness these burdens produce may start out in our emotions, but in the long run negative emotions will create physical illnesses, as well.

Why is shame or guilt such a powerful emotion that it can control our thought life, even to the point of causing physical illness? Because the foundation or root of these emotions is fear. After we have said or done something, especially if we aren't proud of it, don't we fear the result of our actions? What will people think? How will they now act? How will they act toward me? What if I really hurt them? How would I feel if they did something "stupid" based on what I said? The "What If" questions go on and on. Each one creating a need for an answer you may not have. The result is fear builds, and it does its most devastating work in our thoughts or mind through the unknown, the unsure or a new and different thing. But this verse says in times like this, if you don't allow yourself to become afraid, "*…you will not suffer shame.*"

God knew we would do things that would not be pleasing to Him or others. The Scriptures were written and this verse in particular, to comfort us in those times. God says, "*Do not be afraid.*" If you have found yourself in this kind of thought process, then you need to know the fear removing power that the love of God offers you. If you messed up, and we all have, ask the Father to forgive you. Then, ask the others involved to forgive you, too. God forgives when we ask. So let go of the heaviness. Release all those feelings of guilt and shame, forever. God's Word makes His plan for us clear, and His plan has no place for any kind of fear…past, present or future.

JANUARY 12

"Do not fear disgrace; you
will not be humiliated..."
Isaiah 54:4b (NIV)

Have you ever done something and later had to deal with being disgraced? Maybe the situation didn't involve you personally, but it included a close friend or family member, and you experienced disgrace or humiliation because of your association with them? Many years ago I was accused of something that was a blow to my character, and I was deeply hurt and humiliated. Humiliation tries to reduce you to a lower position, not only in your own eyes, but in the eyes of others, too. Most of us have experienced humiliation in some form or another.

Disgrace and humiliation are weapons of fear that are sent to steal our worth and value as a person. The result is we fear man (people) and what they will think and say about us. When these weapons attack, they don't care if you are innocent or guilty. They target your character because their purpose is to destroy your credibility or value as a person. Society teaches us our value is determined by what we do, who we know, and so on. Although it is important to live right, the truth is our worth is established in only one thing. What is that one thing? It is our relationship with God.

God said in His Word, He created us in HIS image. Think about this, "Would Almighty God be no good, have no worth or value?" We undoubtedly know the answer to this question is "NO." God says we are worthy, and we have much value in Him. When God created the world, He said this is good, but when He created man, you and me, He said this is "very good."

Don't be afraid. God loves you, and He doesn't make junk. Remember your heritage in the Lord. He created you to fellowship with Him and to be His child. If you're struggling with disgrace or humiliation from your past, then get rid of it. Replace it with God's Word for your life. Receive the love and forgiveness your Heavenly Father has for you!

> *"...You will forget the shame of your youth..."*
> *Isaiah 54:4c (NIV)*

The second part of this Scripture continues the teaching on disgrace and humiliation by addressing another area. All of us could confess to doing some pretty "dumb" things in our younger days. In fact, some of those decisions may still be affecting us today. The poor or bad choices, our "know it all attitudes," and uneducated actions of youth are different for each of us. For me, I married too young and was rejected by an unfaithful husband. Rejection, regardless of the source, is painful, but it especially hurts when it comes from those we love and trust the most. When my marriage ended in divorce, I was disgraced and felt like a failure. Looking back, I can see we both had other dysfunctions that contributed to the separation, but I believe they could have been worked out if we had known the Lord and known about the power of His Word. Unfortunately, at that time, we didn't know either.

Maybe you still feel the hurt or shame of something from your past? Maybe your past events were so devastating that you're afraid to embrace a new future? This verse tells us to *forget the shame of our youth*. In fact, God is giving us permission to forget those things that keep us tied to the past. Now, you might be thinking, "How can I do that? You just don't know what I've done!" This may be true. I don't, but God does, and He still wrote this in His Word, so we could be free.

Today, I don't feel like a failure about any of my past experiences, and neither should you. How did I do it? I used God's Word. It helped me to understand how much He loves me and the plan He has for my life. Yes, even when we make huge mistakes, God still loves us. Our relationship with others may change, but the key relationship that stabilizes us for the rest of our lives is the one we will always be able to have with our Heavenly Father. Don't be afraid. God's plan creates a way for us to have a great future, but we won't be able to receive it if we don't forget our past. This verse assures us we don't have to be afraid of what was behind. Be bold, and let God direct you to your new future.

JANUARY 14

"and remember no more the reproach of your widowhood."
Isaiah 54:4d (NIV)

The last part of this verse states again that we don't have to remember past mistakes or failures. Forget the shame, guilt, "*and remember no more the reproach.*" Webster's Dictionary defines reproach as, "to express disapproval, disappointment or displeasure; a rebuke; an occasion or cause to discredit, blame or disgrace." All of these words describe powerful emotions that can be devastating to an individual based on the extent of the trauma they have experienced.

Why does God keep repeating the same message to us about forgetting the things of the past? Because He knows the pain, heartache, and memories associated with each of these can be enormous, and if they keep us bound to the past, we can't get on with the plan God has for our future. The fear of past emotions can affect us in several ways. They can not only keep us from having healthy relationships with people now, but even more importantly, they can keep us from having a relationship with the only One who can help change us and make us whole…God our Father.

When God, in His Word, makes the above promise to us He is saying, "I love you," and even though things have happened, My plan for you has already made provision for them. His love gives us the ability to forgive those who have hurt us, and to also be able to forgive ourselves. Do you want to forget the things of your past? Ask God to forgive you. The Bible says He is faithful to forgive us when we ask Him. Then ask God to help you forgive your offenders. When you ask, He can change your heart and help you get rid of any and all of your negative emotions. This is how you will be set free from your past.

God loves you, values you, and created a plan just for you. Why should the fear of past failures keep us from receiving every good thing God has for us today? Don't be afraid. Let go of your past, and move into the present. Today, choose to receive all of His great promises.

JANUARY 15

> *"Hear me, you who know what is right, you people who have my law in your hearts: Do not fear the reproach of men or be terrified by their insults."*
> *Isaiah 51:7 (NIV)*

In Deuteronomy, chapter 6, God reveals His law to love Him with all your heart, soul, and strength, and to obey His commands, so it will go well with you. Part of the "going well with us" is we do not have to fear the reproach (disapproval, disappointment, displeasure, discredit, blame or disgrace) of any other human being.

We all want to be valued and respected by our family, friends, and peers. We value their ideas and opinions and hope they value or appreciate ours. However, there are times when we have made decisions and acted upon things based on what others thought, even though it contradicted our own thoughts or opinions. Why? Why do we risk not speaking or doing what we believe to be right because of what someone else might think? It's fear! When we are afraid of others, we let fear control, intimidate, and sometimes even belittle us.

God says we don't have to fear the differences of men, and furthermore, if or when they do insult us, *we don't have to be terrified.* The dictionary defines insults as, "offence; to affect one offensively and damagingly." The word terrified means, "to intimidate; to fill with anxiety or worry; to drive or impel a state of intense fear." In other words, we don't have to live in fear—be intimidated or worried—about what people say, think or may even threaten to do to us, especially when we are doing what God asks by keeping His commands.

God's plan covers every area of our life. Fear isn't an option in His "insurance policy of love." The Bible tells us God is for us, and then asks, who can be against you? Don't be afraid. God loves you, and nothing compares to the freedom and peace of His Word and thoughts toward you, if you'll receive them.

JANUARY 16

"Behold God is my salvation; I will trust and not be afraid: for the Lord JEHOVAH is my strength and my song; he also is become my salvation."
Isaiah 12:2 (KJV)

God uses the word *behold* to get our attention. In the original Hebrew language it means to get a view, a vision! From the first word of this verse, God wants our attention because He's revealing the most valuable plan, our future "vision," that we will ever need..."*God is our salvation*." The key is the meaning of the word salvation. According to Webster's Dictionary it means, "to save; preservation from destruction or failure; deliverance from danger or difficulties; liberation from ignorance or illusion; deliverance from the power and effects of sin." If God IS our salvation, then we can change the image or view of how we see ourselves to the "picture" He's created for us. He has saved us, preserved us, delivered us, and made a way for us to be free from sin, failures, dangers, and fear.

Would you like to be liberated or free of something? Smoking? Over eating? Feeling inadequate? Maybe you would like to be delivered from making the same mistakes over and over? Are you facing other difficulties in your marriage, with your children, at your job or overwhelming debt? What kind of trouble or danger are you in? Have you ever messed up and now face possible failure or defeat? The truth is we all have in some way or another. However, the good news is God has already provided deliverance and a way of escape for any and every situation or circumstance we may find ourselves in. It doesn't matter whether we caused the circumstance through our ignorance or we are the victims of some injustice. The Bible tells us He knew before the foundation of the world we were going to sin, which means to miss the mark or make mistakes. And yet, at the same time, He had already put a plan into place to restore us back to Him.

When the prophet Isaiah wrote this verse, he knew the key to a successful relationship with the Lord Jehovah would include letting go of old ways, habits, and thoughts. Once we do this, we can replace them with new "insight" or God's purpose and vision. Don't be afraid. The Word of God makes His vision for us clear. His loving plan from the very beginning was to save us, deliver us, heal us, restore us, and make us whole. Trust Him, and let Him become your *strength and song*.

"God is our refuge and strength, a very present help in trouble. Therefore will not we fear, though the earth be removed, and though the mountains be carried into the midst of the sea;..."
Psalms 46:1-2 (KJV)

The word *refuge* means shelter or protection from danger or distress. It can also be that place of shelter or protection or it can be your recourse in difficulty. The word recourse means to have an opportunity to turn to someone or something for help or protection, a source of help or strength.

God is that place and person who provides us with protection, shelter, and strength during our stormy trials. Even now, He is right there with you, a very *present help in trouble* or danger. You may feel like you are all alone in your "day to day" trials and circumstances, but the Bible tells us He never leaves us, nor forsakes us. Even if it feels like we are sinking or in our despair we wish the earth could swallow us up, the Word says God is our helper, protector, and defender.

Maybe you're thinking, "No one could possibly get me out of this mess, especially God. I've made huge mistakes, and now, the consequences are overwhelming." Or you're asking, "Why would God even want to help or protect me after all I've done wrong?" The truth is the Bible says man, meaning us, perishes or is destroyed for a lack of knowledge. What knowledge is God referring to in this verse? It's His Word. His Word offers us every bit of wisdom and direction we need for every circumstance. Plus, the Word confirms over and over that God loves you, wants to help you, and regardless of your past, He will <u>never</u> leave you.

Don't be afraid. God loves you, and He wants you to succeed. You are created in His image, His handiwork. This Scripture confirms to us His love and continued protection so we can live a fear-free life. Therefore, regardless of how bad things may look around you...look up instead. Let *God be your refuge.* Turn to Him. He's <u>always</u> there.

JANUARY 18

> *"For He has delivered me from all troubles; And my eye has looked with satisfaction upon my enemies."*
> *Psalms 54:7 (NASB)*

Delivered means to be set free. Have you ever found an animal or bird that was wounded and you nursed it back to health? Or maybe you have watched one of the animal rescue shows on TV? If you have, then you know it takes much time, care, and nurturing to bring these creatures to the point they can be returned safely to their natural habitat. From their pick-up to their release, all the workers involved share one goal, and they experience the same feeling of satisfaction when they can "set" the animal free.

When we find ourselves hurt, wounded, and unable to get on the right path, God does the same thing for us. He picks us up, and through His love and His Word, He restores us, so He can safely set us free. The word deliver also means to come through with or to produce. When God tells us He will do something in His Word, He produces. In other words, the Word produces. The Bible tells us the Word and truth are one and the same, and the truth/His Word will set or make us free. Once you have heard it, meditate on it, and then continue to apply it, the truth in it now becomes the truth in you.

This truth now gives you the inner strength and power to change. In fact, you'll have enough power to be delivered from any trouble, past hurts and trauma, bad habits, addictions, debt or any other enemy that has tried to rule over you. The Bible also says that he who is set free is free indeed. In other words, once you know God's Word, believe it and receive it, freedom comes. And when you begin to experience real truth and freedom, you won't want to go back to the old way ever again.

Don't be afraid. God's plan has always been to see us free of fears and the attacks of the enemy. With God as our deliverer, we will live a life that is filled with victory.

"Blessed be the Lord, who daily loadeth us with benefits, even the God of our salvation."
Psalms 68:19 (KJV)

Have you ever loved someone so much that you just wanted to do something for them or give them something all the time? Several times in my life I've adopted abandoned animals. In the beginning I was constantly giving to meet their daily needs. They needed much love, time, and attention. It is the same with a newborn child. The love you feel prompts you to make sure your baby has everything they could possibly want or ever need.

As God's child He wants to do the same thing for us. However, with God, love is not just an emotion or a feeling. It isn't something He does or gives if we are good or if we do what He wants. God doesn't always love our actions or decisions, but He never stops loving us. God is love. It is His nature, character, being. It is who He is, and He isn't capable of being anything else. When we understand the love of God is not just something He does, we come closer to understanding who God really is.

It is because of this great love that God, our Father, wants to *load us down with benefits,* or "the good life." Plus, He wants to give us these good benefits daily. What benefits? How about living free of sickness and disease? Enjoying peace by living free of worries and anxieties? What about favor on our jobs? No lack? No debt? Free of any and all fear? What about the promise of eternal life with Him?

This verse says *"even" the God of our salvation.* The same God that loads us up with benefits—the good things of life—is the same God that wants to save and deliver us. Don't be afraid. There is no room for fear when we learn to accept the love, plans, and benefits He makes available to all of us each day.

JANUARY 20

> *"My tongue will tell of your righteous acts all day long, for those who wanted to harm me have been put to shame and confusion."*
> *Psalms 71:24 (NIV)*

If you've ever known anyone that has had an active role in the military, they can share with you the "feeling of fear" that is present at all times. This fear stems from the pressure that someone may be waiting or watching to do them harm, even to their death. Most of us will never encounter this kind of intense fear, but we have, however, experienced what it feels like when harmful or "no good" intentions are shown toward us by another person.

On more than one occasion I've had people make up false accusations about me to destroy my reputation. In my work career I've dealt with employees who seemed to make it their business to harm me. They wanted either my position, wanted me out of the company or just for meanness wanted to cause me more work. At one company, my first month on the job, I was 540% over my monthly quota. I received the salesman of the month award. This upset things, and even though my performance made the branch manager happy, the clerk who was responsible for sending the sales orders to corporate wasn't pleased at all. She decided she could keep this from happening again by holding some of my orders. This would have been bad enough, but she also changed the amount of commissions due me on the sales invoices by crossing out the first number, changing a 25% to a 5% commission, and so on. With an average of 45 invoices to check and redo each month, you can see it required much effort on my part and the accounting department to make the corrections. Even though I always received the money owed to me, it came late and with much stress.

Maybe you can relate? Does someone come to mind? Someone that just seems to have it "out" for you? The above verse is just one of many that demonstrate the loving and protecting arm of our Father God. It encourages us to rest in God, because as His child, we know He will take care of those who mean us harm. I can tell you in every one of my situations the truth was revealed. *God put my accusers to shame.* The clerk was fired, and the others, even after years, are either going through life in the same place or worse than they were before. Their lives are filled with confusion, strife, and no definite direction or goal.

God's Word produces. What He has done for me, He'll do for you, too. Don't be afraid. Knowing His Word is comforting and encouraging. He loves you and provides for your every situation. Trust Him. You will find you won't ever need to be afraid of anyone or any circumstance ever again.

JANUARY 21

> *"After these things the word of the Lord came unto Abram in a vision, saying, Fear not, Abram. I am thy shield and thy exceeding great reward."*
> *Genesis 15:1 (KJV)*

The "*after these things*" this verse begins with refers to the battle Abram had just won. The King of Sodom and Melchizedek, the King of Salem, came out to meet Abram. Melchizedek was not only the king, but he was also the priest of the Most High God. He brought out bread and wine, and then blessed Abram and his God. He stated, "Abrams God, who is the creator of heaven and earth, is the God that delivers your enemies into your hands." Abram then gave the priest a tenth of everything. The King of Sodom tried to give Abram the goods or spoils from the victory, but he refused them. Abram didn't want anyone to say his wealth had come from a man. He wanted all to know his riches were the result of his covenant with God.

God made Abram rich in every way, and He promised he would have a son to carry on his seed, both naturally and spiritually for eternity. Abram and Sarai, whose names were later changed to Abraham and Sarah, were way past the age of having children. But they obeyed God, used their faith, and believed the Word of the Lord. God rewarded them greatly, and Isaac was born to carry on the covenant.

In His Word God uses average, everyday people as our example, so we can see He doesn't just pick the exceptional person to receive His covenant promises. The truth is He picks the available person. This means anyone who will use their faith and believe Him. God's covenant is still available to you, today. He told Abraham to not fear. He would be *his shield and exceeding great reward.* In battle, your shield goes in front of you. It takes the blows. It provides a defense. God's Word is our shield and defense. When we use it—speaking what it says and not what we think or see—God sees our faith. This moves Him to go before us to fight our battles. Don't be afraid. Today, God will be your shield, too. Believe His Word, and hold on to what He says. You can expect the exact same outcome Abraham did. Expect victory—the great reward—and absolutely no fear.

JANUARY 22

> *"And he said, I am God the God of thy father: fear not to go down into Egypt; for I will there make of thee a great nation: I will go down with thee..."*
> *Genesis 46:3-4 (KJV)*

God speaks to Jacob in this verse through a vision. However, it's important for us to know what has happened to him up to this point. Jacob's favorite son, Joseph, when he was very young had been sold into slavery by his older jealous brothers. They took the coat Jacob had given Joseph, covered it in blood, and told their father Joseph had been killed by a wild animal. Joseph is now sent to Egypt where he faces many persecutions and is unjustly sent to jail. But none of this changed God's divine plan for him. The day came when Joseph was summoned to interpret the dreams of Pharaoh. Because of the accuracy he was also allowed to implement the plan he interpreted. Joseph was then authorized to be second in command in all of Egypt.

During this same time his father's land was in famine, so his brothers went to Egypt to buy food and grain. Joseph revealed himself to them. They were afraid he would put them in jail because of the horrible thing they had done to him, but Joseph had forgiven them. Joseph also asked Pharaoh for provision for his entire family, so they could move to Egypt. In this verse God encourages Jacob to not be afraid to go to this new land, because as always...He would be with him.

Why did He tell Jacob, "*the God of thy father*?" Because God had already established a covenant with his grandfather, Abraham, and Abraham's firstborn, who was his father, Isaac. God wanted to make sure Jacob knew the covenant still stood, and He wasn't about to break it. This move to another land would restore Jacob's son back to him, it would abundantly provide for his entire family's daily living, and it reassured Jacob that God was going with him. He wouldn't be alone. So he needn't be afraid.

The Bible tells us if we choose to become one of God's children, we are a part of this same covenant. Could God be telling you the same thing He told Jacob regarding his circumstances? Is He telling you it's time to make a move in your life? Maybe a change is needed, and you don't need to be afraid because He will go with you, too? What or who has you so worried and stressed out? Let this Word encourage you. The Bible says God is the same yesterday, today, and tomorrow. His established covenant is still the same, too. Don't be afraid. Just trust Him and His Word. If He went with Jacob then...He will go with you now.

"Moses told the people, Fear not, stand still (firm, confident, undismayed) and see the salvation of the Lord, which He will work for you today. For the Egyptians you have seen today you shall never see again. The Lord will fight for you, and you shall hold your peace and remain at rest."
Exodus 14:13-14 (AMP)

God sent Moses into Egypt to deliver His people after 400 years of slavery. Pharaoh didn't want to let them go. Moses initiated many signs and wonders by the hand of God, but Pharaoh hardened his heart and refused. After the last curse, which brought death to every Egyptian's firstborn son, including Pharaoh's son, he then agreed to let God's people go.

Shortly after they left Egypt Pharaoh's heart was hardened again. He took his army and went after them. They caught up with the Israelites and pinned them between his army and the mighty Red Sea. God told Moses to lift up his staff over the water and *see the salvation* or saving hand of God. Moses raised his staff, God parted the mighty sea, and millions of Israelites walked across on dry ground. A huge fireball kept the army away until God's people reached safety. When God removed the pillar of fire, the army followed after them through the opened sea. God then released the water, and all of Pharaoh's army drowned.

Can you think of some things in your life you would like to have swallowed up or see disappear? Or maybe your troubles are so big, you feel like you're the one who is drowning? Be encouraged. God is in the trouble solving business. There is nothing too difficult for Him. He loves you and wants you free of fear and torment. Just as this verse says, "*the Lord will fight for you*," and "*you will be able to have peace and rest.*" How can you find peace and rest? Get rid of the fear, and believe God. Moses had a choice. He could do what God said or he could look at his present circumstances and react out of fear. He was in way over his head, and you may be, too. But faith doesn't look at what it sees. It trusts and believes what God says. Don't be afraid. Choose to follow God's plan. His saving hand in your time of trouble will bring you deliverance and peace, and the enemy that has tried to defeat you will no longer be seen, either.

JANUARY 24

> *"Be strong and courageous. Do not be afraid or terrified because of them, for the Lord your God goes with you; he will never leave you nor forsake you."*
> *Deuteronomy 31:6 (NIV)*

God had just informed Moses he was not to cross the Jordan River and go into the Promised Land with the others. Moses knew this would upset the people. So God told Moses to encourage them with the Words in the above verse. He told them *to not be afraid.* God Himself would go with them. God also instructed Moses to anoint Joshua as their new leader. Then He told Moses to remind the people of their prior victories…God had told them twice before to fight and take the land, and they were successful. Why did God remind them? Because they were still going to need to fight for their inheritance and God wanted them to be confident He would be with them. He would always go before them, every step of the way.

The Word tells us God is the same yesterday, today, and forever. It also tells us what God does for one, He will do for all, because He is no respecter of persons. Today, He wants His people, you and me, to understand it's still the same. Yes, there may be battles and conflicts in our own personal lives or our families and friends lives, just like it was for the children of Israel. The land was theirs, but they still had to fight for it. This verse confirms that *God goes with you, never forsaking you.* Once you know this, how could you be afraid? How could you be anything but victorious?

The word forsake means to renounce or turn away from entirely. God already promised us He would never leave us nor forsake us. He would always fulfill His part by never turning away from us or turning us away. He is faithful to do His part. Are you doing yours? Are you staying hooked up with God and His plan or are you still trying to do your own thing, even when you see it's not working? Don't be afraid. Make a decision to let Him be your guide. He loves you and has a better plan for you than you do. With God in charge, you won't have to be afraid or live in fear of your circumstances, regardless of what they may look like. With God, you are assured of the victory!

"And the Lord said to Joshua, fear not nor be dismayed, take all the men of war with you, and arise, go up to Ai; see I have given into your hand the king of Ai, his people, his city, and his land."
Joshua 8:1 (AMP)

In this verse God gave Joshua specific instructions to give to the people about taking the land that belonged to them. It was a part of their inheritance. God's war strategy was detailed, but when followed, it would bring victory. Joshua followed it exactly, and God did for them everything He said He would.

Taking down a king, his people, and the land was a major accomplishment. Joshua, even with the use of his mighty army, would not have achieved success if he had decided to undertake it by himself. Just thinking about this task would have appeared overwhelming. God understood this. That is why the first instruction he gave Joshua was to *fear not nor be dismayed.* To be dismayed means to be deprived of courage, resolution, and initiative through the pressure of sudden fear, anxiety or perplexity. It can also mean a sudden loss of courage because of a great alarm or fear. I could understand having feelings of fear, anxiety, and perplexity if I had orders to take a fortified city, especially if I didn't feel I was prepared or equipped. How about you?

However, many times in our daily lives, we face huge or "fortified" tasks. We're also put in difficult situations. Have you ever thought, "I'm in way over my head? I'll never be able to do this? How did I get into this mess anyway? How or why is this happening to me?" If you have ever been in this spot or maybe you're there right now, I would encourage you with the same words God said to Joshua. *Don't be afraid. Don't be dismayed.* God has a plan for you today, just like He had a plan for Joshua and His people then. Ask God for your specific, detailed plan. Then be true to follow it. God loves you and will provide for you in exactly the same way He did for Joshua. Fear not. Look to God. With Him you can expect victory.

JANUARY 26

> *"And the Lord said to Joshua, Do not be afraid of them; I have given them into your hand. Not one of them will be able to withstand you."*
> *Joshua 10:8 (NIV)*

After Joshua won the battle at Jericho and at Ai, the King of Gibeon realized he needed to make peace with him. A treaty was established. However, soon after this treaty was established another king, the King of Jerusalem, along with five other kings from the surrounding territories planned an attack on the King of Gibeon. The city of Gibeon was an important city. A royal city, large in size, and all of its men were great fighters. When the King of Gibeon heard about their plan to attack, he called on Joshua for help. Because of their peace treaty Joshua, with his best fighting men and entire army, marched toward Gibeon. On their way to battle the Lord told Joshua *to not be afraid*—not one of their enemies would be standing when it was over. Joshua continued to march all night. The next morning they took the enemy by surprise. Then the Lord supernaturally confused the opposing army. Joshua saw the Lord bring about a great victory.

Maybe you can relate to how the King of Gibeon felt when he found out all the other kings were planning to "gang up" on him? Have you ever felt at times like the whole world was against you? People, from all sides, plotting a surprise attack or so it seemed? Or maybe you're discouraged because nothing you do ever produces what you thought it would in the end? We all have felt like this. Disappointments of any kind, unreached goals or expectations, and shattered dreams are discouraging. Discouragement is a huge enemy. It steals our hope for tomorrow and our courage to want to keep trying. But God's Word tells us over and over to not be discouraged. You might be asking, "How can I not feel down, depressed or discouraged when it seems my life is falling apart?" The only way to overcome any battle, especially those negative feelings, is to know what God says about it in His Word. Then apply His life-changing Word to your situation.

When the circumstances seem too big and you don't have the answer, let God show you what to do. He has every answer you'll ever need in His Word, and His desire is to deliver you or save you from "your enemy." Don't be afraid. He loves you. He will fight for you. With God on your side, going before you, you will claim total victory, too.

JANUARY 27

> *"He said, Listen, King Jehoshaphat and all who live in Judah and Jerusalem! This is what the Lord says to you, Do not be afraid or discouraged because of this vast army. For the battle is not yours, but God's."*
> *2 Chronicles 20:15 (NIV)*

King Jehoshaphat received word that a huge, powerful army was preparing to advance against him. He knew this was too big for him. So he called all the people to a fast, and he asked the Lord for a plan of attack. During prayer, the Spirit of the Lord came upon the priest with the answer. God showed him the battle plan, which he then relayed to the king and the people. Their plan of attack was twofold. 1) Appoint singers to praise the Lord. 2) Send them out first; to go before the army. Now in the natural mind and that of a skilled, strategic war leader, how does this kind of attack make any sense? The truth is it doesn't, but King Jehoshaphat trusted God, and because of it He obeyed the Word of the Lord. Early the next morning they went out for battle. The singers went first, saying "Give thanks to the Lord, for His love endures forever." As they sang and praised God, the Lord set up ambushes against the enemy. This caused so much confusion in the enemy camp that they turned on each other. When King Jehoshaphat and his army got to the battlefield, all they saw were dead bodies. God had already fought the battle for them, just as He had promised.

You might be asking, "How does all this fighting relate to me? I'm not a soldier." The truth is whether you are in active duty or not, there are real battles you and your loved ones face everyday. Maybe the atmosphere in your home is like a "war zone" because of the arguing, anger, and abuse? Or maybe you live in a gang infested neighborhood? Is there violence all around your kids at school? What about fighting to save your marriage or getting out of debt? Any of these can feel like a "*vast army*" advancing. They are your enemies, and they come to destroy you and your loved ones. They come to torment you, to steal your peace and joy. But this is not God's plan.

God's Word helps us understand how much He loves us, and He protects His own. Just like the wise men of old, we can pray, fast, and seek God. When we do, we can have the same confidence we will receive God's plan and direction for our battles, too. A fail proof plan that God himself will help execute. Remember, *the battle is not yours, but God's*. Don't be afraid. God is so much bigger than your problem or enemy. Seek His path, offer Him praises, and watch Him deliver you to a place of peace and rest.

JANUARY 28

> *"You will not have to fight this battle. Take up your positions; stand firm and see the deliverance the Lord will give you, O Judah and Jerusalem. Do not be afraid, do not be discouraged. Go out to face them tomorrow, and the Lord will be with you."*
> *2 Chronicles 20:17 (NIV)*

This verse is almost identical to verse 15 of the same chapter. Why would God repeat what He had just told them? Because He knows when we are in the heat of the battle, it is hard to stay focused. The army that was advancing against King Jehoshaphat was vast in size and ability, and the plan God laid out for them to follow seemed ridiculous. Send out singers to praise God...and let them go before the warriors...when you're fighting the biggest battle yet? What kind of sense or logic is this? It isn't in our way of thinking, but God's ways and thoughts are much higher than ours.

This was going to take courage to go into battle with this kind of plan. But once again God makes His point by repeating what He had said to them earlier. "He would be fighting this battle for them. They didn't have to be afraid." All they would need to do was *take up their positions, and stand firm.* God was faithful to His Word. "HE" delivered them to victory.

God's Word never changes. This same truth works for us today. God is more than willing and capable of doing what His Word says He will do. The question is, "Do we even know what the Word says or what His plan is?" Then, are we willing to be obedient and follow it, regardless of how silly or unnatural it may seem to us or to those around us?

In God's Word, the Holy Bible, He has laid out a plan of divine health, prosperity for our spirit, soul, and body, peace, joy, and a life that is filled with abundance and victory. His plan wasn't for a select few. It was for all who would believe on Him and follow Him. Don't be afraid. Because of the immense love God has for you as His child, you can go out and face your trials. He will be with you, also. How can you be sure? His Word says so!

"The Lord is my light and my salvation—whom shall I fear?
Psalms 27:1a (NIV)

Have you ever walked into a dark room, felt for the light switch, and realized it was on another wall? Or maybe there isn't an overhead light, but a lamp, which is located on a table in another part of the room? Now, if you have ever stubbed your toe or bumped your shin while trying to navigate in the dark, you already understand how important it is to move slowly and carefully around the room. However, regardless of where the switch is, the moment you turn it on light floods the area…instantly! It doesn't start at one side and work its way to the other side. At once it repels the darkness, everywhere. It's all consuming. You feel safe, secure, and you can see your way around. Now there is absolutely no need to be unsure or afraid.

This is what the psalmist, David, speaks of in this verse when he talks about the Lord. In every instance in David's life, because of his relationship with the Lord, he had seen God's faithfulness to repel the darkness and change his circumstances from bad to good. David made many mistakes, and yet, every time he admitted he was wrong and asked God to forgive him, God offered him total forgiveness. God was truly his salvation. He saved and delivered David out of every circumstance and then changed the negative to be in David's favor. God was repelling the darkness, bringing forth the light, and canceling out any and all anxiety or fear.

Why would God be so willing to turn David's bad decisions into good? For the same reason He still does it for you and me today. God establishes a covenant with anyone who chooses to have a relationship with Him, and once this covenant is formed, He never goes back on His Word. David was an heir of God's covenant. When he admitted to his sin and shortcomings and asked God for help, he saw God's hand move on his behalf. Do you need some help? Maybe you've made some bad decisions, and now you need God to turn things around? Wouldn't it be nice to know that someone not only would, but could change things on your behalf? Don't be afraid. Choose to be a part of God's covenant, too. Let the Lord be *your light and your salvation.* When you do, fear won't have any place in your life, either!

"...The Lord is the stronghold of my life—of whom shall I be afraid?"
Psalms 27:1b (NIV)

In the first part of this Scripture, David said of the Lord, "He is my light and my salvation." In other words, the Lord had been there to bring him out of every dark and negative situation he experienced. God had also saved him from his enemies, which sometimes included himself. David didn't always make the right decisions. He allowed himself to be involved in an adulterous affair, and the woman became pregnant. He then had her husband killed, and took her for his wife. In these instances, David was his own worst enemy. Have you ever found yourself in circumstances that left you ashamed and even baffled as to how you ever got there in the first place? Well, David knew he had really messed up, but he also knew about his covenant relationship with God. David was quick to repent and get back to his right standing position with the Lord.

In the second part of this verse, David calls God his *stronghold*. The word stronghold is defined as a fortified place or a place of survival or security. Obviously David had reached a place in God and their relationship that he knew God would always be there for him. God would be there to love, forgive, guide, and protect. *No matter what*, David knew he couldn't lose with God on his side. It was not God's plan for him to be afraid—not afraid of God—not afraid of the circumstances.

Sometimes we have a hard time believing God will be there for us, especially when we have messed up and caused our own grief. It's true there are always consequences to our poor decisions. Consequences we may have to live with for awhile. David's first born, by the woman he got pregnant, died, but this didn't change the covenant David had with God. Even through the trials, David is a perfect example for us to see the continuous outpouring of love God offers His children. Don't be afraid. When we admit our failings and ask God to forgive us, He is faithful to forgive—regardless of who was at fault. This is what gives Him the liberty to turn every situation around. Trust the Lord. He will provide you with a safe place, a fortified place to come into, and a place where fear cannot stay.

"When evil men advance against me to devour my flesh, when my enemies and my foes attack me, they will stumble and fall."
Psalms 27:2 (NIV)

Before David became king there were many times he had to run for his life. David was a powerful warrior. After one of their victories, King Saul came home and the people cried out, "Great is King Saul. He killed a thousand men," but when David returned home, they cried out, "Great is David who killed ten thousand men." Saul was jealous. He thought the people loved David more. So he plotted to take David's life.

In the world today there are men who plot to take lives. For the first time many of us are feeling the pressure and torment of an evil enemy. War is upon us, and we face an enemy who thinks nothing about destroying foreign lands, our nation, and the freedoms of the people who live there. Surely we all remember the pain and devastation of what happened at the hands of evil men on September 11, 2001, and all the other ghastly attacks around the world since then. However, enemies are enemies, whether they are from around the world or live across the street. Anyone who opposes you with the intent to hurt you is your enemy. David, just like us, continually had the opportunity to deal with feelings and emotions of fear, apprehension, anxiety, disappointment, and grief. Yet, with confidence, he made the above statement about his enemies stumbling and falling. Where did he get this confidence, and how did he keep it?

These are good questions. Even though David had been anointed to be king, he still had to live in caves and run for his life for many years after. Where was the victory in this? How did he maintain peace—no fear—in an ever changing environment? The answer to David's on going victories can be summed up in one word…"relationship." David, even from a young boy, lived without fear of his enemies because of the relationship he had with God. He had seen God time after time change circumstances to his favor. Without fear, David knew he would have the victory with God. Without fear, we can also know we have the victory we need with God. Don't be afraid. Get to know God, your Father, and live with the confidence David had. The same "no fear" promises are available to you, too.

FEBRUARY 1

> *"Though an army besiege me, my heart will not fear; though war break out against me, even then will I be confident."*
> *Psalms 27:3 (NIV)*

David still expresses his confidence in God. He has been through many battles, both personally and as the king. His throne and his kingdom were always being challenged to war by someone or something. However, regardless of how intense the battle, David knew he had a faithful God, a God who loved him, and He knew God would stick to the covenant He had made with him through his forefathers. For this reason alone, David could say *my heart will not fear.*

Sometimes the pressures of life become so overwhelming we're afraid of what tomorrow may bring. Then, as if our own pressures aren't sufficient enough, we also hear the news of severe, extreme or negative world issues. Major concerns, fear based issues with newspaper headlines that read "War on Drugs, Gangs or Violence," the "War against Child Abductions, Sexual Predators or Abuse," or "War Breaks Out…The People Revolt." What about the "War on Terror?" It's obvious the world doesn't have all the answers or the problems would have been corrected by now. However, the fact still remains…the more you hear about the traumas, threats, death, and abuse…the greater the chances are for fear to come in and take over your thoughts and plans.

Will wars take place? Will trouble come? The Bible says they will, but God also tells us when we hear of wars or rumors of wars *to not be afraid.* You might be thinking, "How can God expect me to not be afraid when all of these dangerous events are going on all around me?" God doesn't expect you to not want to "feel" afraid, anymore than He expects you to stop the wars. However, He has "made a way" for us to not be moved by our feelings alone, but instead to trust Him and to be *confident* just like David. That "way" is through His unchanging Word. His Word offers us solutions for overcoming fears, worry, depression, and anxieties that accompany our tests and trials. There are no surprises to God. When evil appears in the world, even though God isn't the cause of it, He still has the answers. Don't be afraid. Regardless of what goes on around you, you can confidently choose His plan of love. When you do, you'll live your life as He created you to live it…totally free of fear and failure.

FEBRUARY 2

> *"I am still confident of this: I will see the goodness of the Lord in the land of the living."*
> *Psalms 27:13 (NIV)*

David clearly expresses what he believes God will do because of the eternal covenant and the promises it delivers to those who believe. To be confident means to be totally assured of something or full of conviction. Conviction is a strong persuasion or belief. How does one become so persuaded, assured or convicted? In David's case He knew what the promises of God were for him and for any other person who wants to be a member of the family of God. He was a witness that God kept His Word. If God said it, He would do it.

David grew up loving the Lord. While he watched the sheep, he talked and sang praises to God. He knew God personally. He felt God's power and presence with him. This is what gave him the courage to fight and kill a lion and a bear when they tried to come after the sheep. However, they could have eaten David just as easily. Yet, this young boy trusted God to be there with him in these battles, and God was there. Now we can see why David sang songs about God's goodness. His confidence continued to grow as his relationship with the Lord grew.

So how did a young shepherd boy become the king of such a great nation of people? God told Samuel the priest to go to the house of Jesse and anoint the next king. Jesse brought his sons out for Samuel to observe. Samuel was about to pick one of the older brothers because of their strong stature when God told him to ask the father if he had any more sons. When he asked, Jesse said, "Yes, my youngest, David, who is in the fields watching the sheep." Samuel told the brothers to go and bring David to him. When Samuel saw David, God told him this is the one. Samuel anointed David to be the king. Even though he was just a young boy, God already had great plans for David.

God knows the plans He has for you, as well. Good plans…great plans…fearless plans. Do you think David would have realized the great plans God had for him if he hadn't allowed himself to have a close, personal relationship with the Lord? Probably not. This is why the Word encourages us to get to know God for ourselves. So we can personally and intimately experience the goodness of God. Once this happens, we won't be afraid when the "lions" and "bears" of this century try to attack us. Don't be afraid. God loves you. He created you to fellowship with Him. When you do, your confidence will grow, and fear won't be a part of your life, either. We will sing a new song like David, and we'll be assured we, too, *will see the goodness of the Lord.*

FEBRUARY 3

> *"but whoever listens to me will live in safety and be at ease, without fear of harm."*
> *Proverbs 1:33 (NIV)*

David's son, Solomon, not only wrote this verse, but it is recorded he wrote 3,000 other proverbs. He also wrote over 1,000 songs. Kings from all over the world sent their men to listen to him. Solomon was appointed to be king at the age of thirteen. In 1 Kings 3:7-15 it states after Solomon became king, he asked God to give him wisdom and a discerning heart, so he could lead the masses of people. God was so pleased with his unselfish request that He not only granted him wisdom, but He also gave him riches and honor. It is recorded that Solomon became the wealthiest man who ever lived, and no other king would be his equal. The Word also says the wisdom, insight, and understanding God gave Solomon were each as measureless as the sand on the seashore.

Now you might be asking, "How did Solomon, at thirteen, know who or what to ask for in the first place?" For Solomon there was never any question about the "Who" being God because of the relationship he witnessed between God and his father. God had always helped his dad, and Solomon was certain if he asked, God would help him, too. How could he be so sure? The Bible states our covenant is everlasting, which means it never changes or ends. This is good news for us because we also know we can count on it, as well. The Bible says God remains the same...yesterday, today, and forever. If He wanted His people "in the know" then...He wants us "in the know" now. The Bible says God's people perish for a lack of knowledge, and God is not talking about worldly education. He is talking about His very own children not knowing Him, His Word, His ways, and His plan for their lives.

Solomon witnessed when his father asked God for wisdom and direction, and then obeyed Him, he never went wrong. Isn't it time you asked God for wisdom regarding your situation? Aren't you tired of doing it your way? How many times do you want to go around the same mountain anyway? Don't be afraid. God loved you enough to already have a plan in place long before you knew Him. All you have to do is ask! He has every answer you'll ever need, and He knows you better than you know yourself. Ask Him. Listen to His "no fear" plan. You *will live in safety, without fear of harm*, too.

FEBRUARY 4

> *"Cast your burden on the Lord (releasing the weight of it) and He will sustain you; he will never allow the (consistently) righteous to be moved—made to slip, fall or fail."*
> *Psalms 55:22 (AMP)*

To *cast* means to throw off, to get rid of, to discard without concern or caution of the landing point. Have you ever walked under a light at night and something unexpectedly landed on you or hit your face or head? If you have, you already know how quickly your reflexes react. You do whatever it takes—right then—to get it off of you. At that moment, are you interested in finding out what it is? Do you care where it lands? Absolutely not! The main focus is to just get rid of it... and fast. That's casting.

In this verse God makes it clear how quickly we can get rid of those things that *weigh* us down. Now, you may be thinking, "Well, that's easy for you to say. You don't have any idea what I'm facing or the hurt and pain I've been through in the past." This may be true, but there is One who does know about your burdens, both past and present, and He's the One who's telling you to give them to Him.

For most people the issue isn't that you don't want God to "fix" everything. The real issue is you're afraid to trust Him and His ways. When this takes place, a choice is made…a bad choice…to hang on to our problems. The result is we make it worse or we drag it out much longer than needed. His Word says *He will sustain us*…never allow us to *slip…fall…fail.* Sustain means to supply or to give support or relief. However, **He can't sustain until we cast.** If we don't do what He has commanded in this verse, in casting our cares or letting Him be our complete source of supply, could this mean we are setting ourselves up for failure? Could this be the reason you haven't been successful in solving your problems? Are you still trying to be the main support?

It's not necessary for you to continue to carry what the Lord has already taken care of for you. Don't be afraid to let go. There is no fear when you accept and understand that God planned for you to throw off heaviness, problems, grief, sickness, lack of finances, circumstances from your past, and any other thing the enemy tries to send your way. Remember, God loves you. Don't be afraid. Give your problems to the only One who can really do something about them. Accept His support, supply, and relief. You'll find you can trust Him. He won't let you fall. He won't let you fail.

> *"What time I am afraid, I will have confidence and put my trust and reliance on you."*
> *Psalms 56:3 (AMP)*

What David is saying is "when I am afraid, I will trust in you." He also claims he will *confidently* trust God. Confidence is defined in Webster's Dictionary as, "a belief or faith that one will act in a right, proper or effective way; the quality or state of being certain; a relation of trust or intimacy." What was it that brought about this absolute trust and confidence in God? It started when David was a young boy. He spent hours praying and praising God while he watched over his father's sheep. He developed a close and intimate relationship with God, which ultimately gave him the courage, strength, and confidence, to not only take on a bear and a lion, but also to fight and kill Goliath.

Who was Goliath? Goliath was a Philistine giant. He was not only big, but a powerful warrior. He had so intimidated the Israelites that their entire army was afraid to fight him, but not David. He said, "I will go up and fight him. God was with me when I killed the lion and the bear, and God will be with me now." When David arrived to fight Goliath, he found him covered in armor. There was also another soldier, standing directly in front of Goliath, holding up his shield. When Goliath saw they had sent a boy to fight him, he was furious. He cried out he was going to feed David's flesh to the birds. But with total peace and confidence David said, "You may come against me with sword and spear, but I come against you in the name of the Lord Almighty." As David ran toward Goliath, he reached into his pouch and took out a smooth stone. He positioned it in his slingshot, and then fired it. It struck Goliath's forehead causing him to fall facedown to the ground. David then took Goliath's own sword and killed him. God was with him. God brought the victory.

Maybe you're facing some "giants" in your life? Do you know God, your Father, intimately? Can you say, "I confidently trust Him?" God created you to be close to Him, so you would not doubt His ability to deliver you. He loves you and will fight your battles for you, just like he did for David. Don't be afraid. He will be with you. If you want to be free from fear, let God into your life. You'll learn you can trust and rely on Him, too.

> *"In God have I put my trust, and confident reliance; I will not be afraid; what can man do to me?"*
> *Psalms 56:11 (AMP)*

Have you ever known or worked with someone who tells you they will do something, only to discover they had no intention of keeping their word? We know in order for us to trust in something or someone there must be some kind of track record or proven history of dependability. We may trust them the first time, but not over and over again when they continue to follow the same unreliable pattern. In this verse David says he *trusts God with a confident reliance.* What he's really saying is he has found God to be reliable, dependable, which also makes one trustworthy. Once you understand his relationship with the Lord, you can see why he said, "*I will not be afraid.*" At this point, David had lived long enough to experience some of life's most difficult situations, but he had always found God to be reliable.

The Bible asks, "If God is for us, then who can be against us?" David knew he was valuable to God, and he feared no one because of it. Can we make the same statement today? Do you know how valuable you are to God? Maybe you find yourself worrying about what others think? Are other people's opinions "too" important to you? I've known individuals who are like chameleons. They change in an instant to become like whomever they're around. They have such an over powering need to feel accepted. Does this describe you? Do you find yourself willing to go along with others or needing their approval, even when it means not being true to your own feelings or plans? Trying to please others, at the risk of losing your own God given identity, is the fear of man. If you live your life this way, it becomes detrimental to your own emotional well being. In essence you're living a lie, wearing a mask. Eventually you will not only lose your own identity, but you will also lose the true, special person God created you to be.

God created us all uniquely. As much as we are alike, we are also going to be different in many areas. Learn to accept and appreciate those differences, not only in yourself, but in others, as well. In His Word God repeatedly tells us He loves us, we are valuable to Him, and we can trust Him. Don't be afraid. Throughout the ages, God has proven Himself to be faithful, trustworthy. You have no reason to doubt God or His Word. Receive His love for you, and then love yourself, too. When you come to know and accept the power of God's love, you'll soon discover you're no longer afraid of man or what he can do to you.

"By [the help of] God I will praise His Word; on God I lean, rely, and confidently put my trust; I will not fear. What can man, who is flesh, do to me?"
Psalms 56:4 (AMP)

In this Scripture David not only reminds himself of the faithfulness of God, but he teaches us how we can have the same kind of faith and trust. When we read the verses that follow this one, we discover that there were individuals who were twisting David's words, trying to bring trouble to his affairs. Their thoughts were always against him, they plotted evil for his hurt and destruction, and they would hide, wait, and watch his every step. David could have chosen to follow his feelings and allowed fear to enter his life, but instead he praised and thanked God for His goodness. He reminded himself of all the other times God had delivered him. David came to the conclusion that if God was faithful to him in the past, then why wouldn't He be faithful to him now? And if God is always faithful, then why should he be afraid?

Maybe you can relate to these circumstances? Have you ever been in such a difficult or confusing situation that you didn't know which way to go or what to do? Even now, maybe you feel like you're all alone, with no one to turn to. David knew these feelings very well, and yet, he said he didn't have to fear man. Why? How could he say this when men everywhere had it out for him? There is only one reason…his trust in God. He was so confident or assured of <u>his</u> God that even though the outward pressures were overwhelming, he still chose to believe what God said about him, instead of believing what man said.

Making the right choice is the first step to our victory, but David knew to go one step further. What did he do? He also chose to praise God for all the things He had already done. Everyday we all have to make choices. Some are simple. Others require much thought and preparation. David found a successful way of working out his problems and frustrations, not only with his fellowman, but with every other problem that presented itself, too. David chose to praise God, and when he did, he discovered fear vanished. He moved from a place of his own insecurity to a place of total rest and confidence in God's ability. Wouldn't you like to choose to rest in God's ability? You can. You can make the same choices David did. Don't be afraid. Believe God's Word. Just praise Him for what He has already done, and then, praise Him for what He is about to do. Your thanks and praise will produce courage, confidence, and faith in the Lord. Your faith will not only please God, but it will also remove your every fear.

FEBRUARY 8

> *"Then you will walk on your way securely in confident trust, and you shall not dash your foot or stumble."*
> *Proverbs 3:23 (AMP)*

Proverbs is considered the "Book of Wisdom" in the Bible. It is a collection of wise sayings and good advise for our daily living. Solomon, the son of David, wrote most of the proverbs. As a youth, when Solomon was made the King of Israel, God asked him what he wanted. Solomon said, "Lord, I need wisdom to rule such a vast number of your people." As the history is recorded in the books of Kings and Chronicles, God was so pleased that Solomon didn't ask for money or possessions, He not only granted him the wisdom, but He also gave him the wealth of the land. In fact, God gave him so much, it is recorded Solomon was the richest man who ever lived.

The Bible tells us Solomon's wisdom was founded on the 'fear' of the Lord. Fear in this instance refers to reverence or honor to the living God. In the preceding verses Solomon wrote, "My son, preserve sound judgment and discernment, do not let them out of your sight; they will be life for you." What was the sound judgment or discernment Solomon was referring to? It was doing things "God's Way." It was following "God's Plan." The same plan and ways he had witnessed through his father David. Solomon knew if he followed God's plan, he could expect the same results because God is faithful to fulfill His promises to all generations.

Maybe you didn't have a positive role model to follow when you were growing up? Maybe you are still struggling with circumstances that are the result of bad decisions or poor discernment? Take comfort, we've all made mistakes. The Scriptures tell us even Solomon disobeyed God at times and made mistakes. However, the good news is when we 'fear' the Lord, He will fulfill every promise He has made to us in His Word. Don't be afraid. If you've made mistakes, ask God to forgive you. Ask Him to show you His plan. He can give you a new plan for your future, and at the same time, show you how to correct your past mistakes. You, too, can have a relationship with your Heavenly Father. When you do, *you will walk securely, confidently*, fully aware that it is He who is making your path safe.

FEBRUARY 9

> *"When you lie down you shall not be afraid; yes, you shall lie down and your sleep will be sweet."*
> *Proverbs 3:24 (AMP)*

Solomon was a young boy with a huge responsibility to rule an entire nation of people. How could he not have been worried? Or what kept him from being afraid? Especially at night? Most kids are scared to be alone in the dark in the safest home. The truth is Solomon knew only one kind of fear...the fear of the Lord. In another proverb, Solomon states the 'fear' of the Lord is the beginning of wisdom. This is a reverential type of fear. Webster's Dictionary defines reverence as, "to honor or respect felt or shown; profound adoring; awed respect." In other words, Solomon discovered when he respected God, honored Him, followed His ways and His Word, everything progressed successfully. Because of his close relationship with God, he is able to experience the same confidence his father David knew. It is the same reverential fear that gives him the boldness to make the above statement.

Maybe you lay awake at night, not able to sleep? Your mind keeps rehearsing the same old thoughts? You feel helpless, out of control, not knowing which way to go or what to do? Has your income been affected by the economy? Or you have family turmoil? Maybe you have a run-away child? Or you're just lonely? If you have ever battled with sleepless nights because of an over active imagination, then you know how tormenting it can be. However, this verse proves this is not God's will for your life. Solomon learned there is a wonderful and positive solution to this problem and any others you may have. 'Fear' the Lord—reverence, honor, and respect His ways, and He will show you the way to go. He is the answer, your strength, and your comfort.

Now when you lie down and the enemy tries to stir up those tormenting thoughts, doubts, and all the "what ifs," you'll be able to say, "My God directs my path. My confidence is in Him. I will not be afraid." Don't be afraid. Trust Him like Solomon and his father did. Speak the Word over your situation, and you won't be afraid of the outcome, either. Then you will boldly and confidently say, "*Sweet sleep*, you belong to me!"

FEBRUARY 10

"Be not afraid of sudden terror and panic, nor of the stormy blast or the storm and ruin of the wicked when it comes [for you will be guiltless]."
Proverbs 3:25 (AMP)

Solomon was appointed to take over the throne from his father about 970 B.C. The proverbs he wrote took place sometime after. And yet, when you read this verse, it could be for us today. The tragedies of war in America and the rest of the world make this verse very relevant to our everyday living.

Neither Solomon nor his father David was a stranger to war and the other nation's hostile advances. With the rumors of war breaking out all round them, how were they able to make a statement like the one above? What would keep them from becoming afraid? Or what kept them from becoming weary with the repeated attempts of attack? Shouldn't fear be a natural reaction? When evil men plot destruction or devastation, is it even possible to stay at peace and not be afraid?

These are good questions. How are we able to keep our peace and joy when literally all "hell" breaks loose around us? The Bible clearly tells us that trials will come. However, it's important to know God isn't the creator of the evil that causes havoc. The Bible makes it clear the devil is the one who comes to kill, steal, and destroy. God is the giver of life, and this is a peaceful, abundant life we can enjoy, even during a raging storm.

The above verse, along with many others, confirms and assures us of God's unchanging love for us. His plan includes protection and deliverance for all those who 'fear' and honor Him. Understanding and knowing the Word of God for our lives is the way we keep our peace in the midst of any trial. Will you want to react in fear when troubles come? Probably, but this is when you remind yourself that God's Word is the final authority on any subject. Feelings change. His Word remains the same. The Bible says Heaven and earth will pass away, but the Word of the Lord will last forever. Don't be afraid. Accept Him, His love, and His great promises. When you do, you'll replace your fear with His wonderful peace.

> *"For the Lord shall be your confidence, firm and strong, and shall keep your foot from being caught [in a trap or hidden danger].*
> *Proverbs 3:26 (AMP)*

This Scripture is just one of the many throughout God's Word that clearly states the Lord's plan to provide protection for us, even in the midst of danger. When Solomon makes the statement, "*For the Lord shall be your confidence, firm and strong,"* it's obvious he had come to understand the reliable, delivering power of an Almighty God. How does this relate to us? We, too, live in a world that holds constant, sudden danger, whether it's fighting the enemy, battling nature's storms or just dodging the reckless driver on our local commute. We all need God's hand of divine protection and wisdom from such events. So, how is it possible to totally trust God?

Let's look at Solomon's life. We know Solomon had quite the example to follow through his own dad, David. The Bible states David had a heart after God. His father had been a living witness of the things of God. Was David perfect? No, he was far from it. But when he messed up, he was quick to admit it. He asked for forgiveness, and God was right there to pick up the pieces and help him begin again. Solomon witnessed this faithfulness. Plus, he came to believe and trust God through his own personal and intimate relationship with the Lord. As good as it might have been Solomon couldn't live off his dad's faith. Trust and confidence is developed through experience. Solomon had to learn through his own trials and mistakes that when you ask for forgiveness and help, God is still there. Without fail, this kind of love and support is what builds a *firm and strong confidence* in the Lord.

Today, God offers us the same opportunity, so our own trust, confidence, and foundation of peace will be built on Him. Now, this may seem difficult to you if you've never known anyone who followed God. Or maybe you've never received this kind of unconditional love and support? The truth is most of us haven't, but even if this seems strange, God's plan of protection, direction, and forgiveness is available to anyone who asks. Are you an any…one? Then His Word was written for you. Don't be afraid. His plan is for each of us to know Him in such an intimate way that we could actually feel His love for us, and through the power of His love, we would know that we are valued. You can trust God. The Bible says He never sleeps. His eyes go to and fro across the earth. He is the watchman, always on the lookout to protect you, to expose danger, and to keep your foot safely planted on the right path.

FEBRUARY 12

> *"Who forgiveth all thine iniquities;*
> *who healeth all thy diseases."*
> *Psalms 103:3 (KJV)*

What a comfort it is to know that when we ask God to forgive us of our mistakes and sins, He does. But did you know you could also ask God to forgive your ancestors for their iniquities, too? The Bible tells us Daniel prayed and asked God to forgive his forefathers up to the fourth generation. Why? So their sins would not become a weapon the enemy could still use against him. God takes sin seriously, but He never allows it to separate His perfect love from us as His children.

David, in verse 2 of this Psalm, reminds his soul (the mind, will, and emotions) to not forget all of the Lord's benefits. David was a powerful man, the king, anointed of God. Even from his youth, God had always been there for him. When David made bad decisions, He asked God to forgive him, and God was always there to forgive him. With this track record, why would he have to remind himself of the goodness of God? David found out, just like you and I, that we have an enemy, the devil, and he constantly looks for an open door, both spiritually and naturally, to come into our lives and destroy whatever he can. In reality, even though David was the king and he had all earthly power and authority, his life wasn't much different than yours or mine. He had major responsibilities and pressures with his job. How about you? He had health issues. How about you? He had rebellious kids who were in and out of trouble. How about you? He wanted to serve and love God, and yet, he repeatedly messed up. How about you?

Just as David reminded and encouraged himself of the goodness of God, we need to do the same thing. The word *all* in this verse means just that. Don't let the enemy tell you that you don't deserve it or what you did is unforgivable or you've had this sickness for too long or because everyone else in your family has dealt with this, now you'll have to, too. Webster's Dictionary tells us the meaning of the word all is all. There are no exceptions written in the Word. Don't be afraid. God has nothing but love and good things in store for you. Like David, get to know the Lord and His benefits. Daily remind your "soul" of the Lord's faithfulness to perform His Word and keep His promises. Then, be encouraged because <u>*All*</u> of God's benefits work…<u>all</u> of the time…for <u>all</u> of us!

"Who redeemeth thy life from destruction; who crowneth thee with lovingkindness and tender mercies."
Psalms 103:4 (KJV)

David wrote the 103rd Psalm while he reminded himself of God's benefits. What does he mean when he says, "*Who redeemeth thy life from destruction?*" The key word is *redeem.* Webster's Dictionary defines redeem as, "to buy back; to get or win back; to free from what distresses or harms; to free from captivity by payment of ransom; to help to overcome something detrimental; to release from blame or debt; to free from the consequences of sin; to change for the better; reform; restore; repair; to make good; fulfill; to atone for; to off-set the bad effects of; to make worthwhile." Now, we can see, just from this definition alone, that David covered a lot of territory when he made this statement. Yes, God had truly *redeemed his life from destruction.*

However, the truth is God not only did all of the above for David, but He will do it for each of us, as well. His plan covers our emotional, physical, financial, relational, and social areas of our life so peace is established along with that sense of well being. When we work within the guidelines of His plan, there are major benefits. It's like having an insurance policy. When you make the premiums or payments and do the other things they may request, then you know when you need it, you will have certain coverage or benefits. The only difference is our God doesn't expect a payment. His love for us is so strong that He loves doing acts of kindness for us and showing us mercy. We know the word mercy means to receive what we don't deserve.

Wouldn't you like this kind of plan? Aren't you tired of where you are? Why would you still choose a life filled with destruction, when you now know you could have His love, mercy, and compassion? A peaceful life without fear of what today or tomorrow may bring? God's plan or benefits package offers total coverage. Don't be afraid. Don't put off the decision to choose the Lord and His ways. There is no better policy, and no better time than right now to enroll in His long-life benefit plan.

FEBRUARY 14

> *"Who satisfies your desires with good things so that your youth is renewed like the eagles."*
> *Psalms 103:5 (NIV)*

If you are like most people, you have desires—inner dreams, plans or ideas—of the way you would like your life, your mate or your family to be. God understands these inner wants. In fact, it's quite possible God is the One who placed those desires within you. This verse states He will *satisfy*, which means to carry out the terms of something, as in a contract. It also means to make happy or gratify to the full or to make true by fulfilling a condition. This is what God does with our desires. He makes us happy and grateful because He fulfills our *desires with good things*.

According to this verse, God does this so *our youth is renewed.* Webster's Dictionary defines the word renew to mean, "to make like new; restore to freshness, vigor or perfection; to make new spiritually; to do again." What this really means for us is with God we have the opportunity to begin again.

Why would God compare us to eagles? Why or how is their youth renewed? When an eagle gets old, he must pluck out all of his feathers. While he waits for the new feathers to come in, which takes some time, he is in a very vulnerable position. However, this process is absolutely necessary. Once the feathers grow back and are fully restored, he has the same speed and agility he had when he was young. His youth has been restored. He now has new freshness and vigor. He's been renewed.

Isn't it great to know our God wants us to be able to begin again? You haven't made so many big or bad mistakes that He will not give you another chance? You may be thinking, "You don't know what I've done or this isn't the first time I've done it. God already gave me another chance, and I messed up again." My friend, we serve a God of the millionth chance…if need be. However, His mercy doesn't mean He's giving us permission to continually do whatever we want… just because we know we can ask for forgiveness later. But when your heart is right, you can ask God to forgive you, strengthen you, and to help you change from your old ways and bad habits. Don't be afraid. Ask Him to forgive you, and begin again. His Word says to call unto Him, and He will deliver you. He wants to fulfill your desires. He wants you to be on top…to be renewed…to be able to "soar" like the eagles.

"The Lord executeth righteousness and judgment for all that are oppressed."
Psalms 103:6 (KJV)

This verse confirms that our judge for justice will be none other than the Lord God Almighty. To execute something means to carry it out, to make or produce, to do what is provided, even required. Our God will always be able to carry it out or do what is required. Webster's Dictionary defines the word righteousness as, "acting in accord with divine or moral law; free from guilt or sin; arising from an outraged sense of justice or morality." In other words, God will carry out whatever is required to relieve His people from guilt and sin, especially if there has been an injustice or wrong done to them. This is good news to anyone who has ever been treated unfairly.

But who are the *oppressed*, and how does one get this way? God made it clear in His Word we have an enemy, the devil, who first became God's enemy while he was in Heaven. Satan actually thought he was powerful enough to overthrow God and had talked one third of the angels into going along with him. The plan didn't work, and all of them were instantly cast down to earth...defeated! The devil remains defeated today, but this doesn't stop his attempts to attack, to steal, kill, and destroy. One way he tries to do this is to use our circumstances or our relationships with our families, friends, work or other daily activities. Have you ever been in a situation that wasn't fair? Maybe you have even been falsely accused? These scenarios are part of his plan so we'll believe we are defeated, so we'll feel like victims. The real motive is to bring depression. Once we allow ourselves to become depressed, especially for any length of time, the weight of the problems can soon feel overwhelming. You lose all hope of anything ever being able to change. Now you're oppressed. The devil wants you to feel afraid and to believe it's hopeless, and you, as a result, are helpless.

But this verse causes fear to disappear when we know our Father—God Almighty—is the final authority. When you let God, who sees and knows everything, judge this or any other injustice that has been done to you, fear and oppression will leave. Why? Your position hasn't changed...God says you are victorious in all things. Now, you can make a decision to forgive your offenders, and turn it all over to the Supreme Judge. Don't be afraid. The Bible says God is a "just" God. With God, there is nothing to fear! With God, your *executer of righteousness and judgment*, you just can't lose the battle! With God, you'll be assured of having the victory!

FEBRUARY 16

> *"He made known his ways unto Moses,*
> *his acts unto the children of Israel."*
> *Psalms 103:7 (KJV)*

Many people have different theories or images of God. Some think He is this mystical, mysterious being that lives way up in the skies or out in the universe somewhere. Others find it hard to believe they could talk to Him on a regular basis. Then there are those who think He carries this great big stick, which He can't wait to use on them when they mess up. Maybe you can relate to one of these images? Most of us have accepted we will probably make mistakes during our life. So you can see why this "Big Stick" image of God could conjure up unhealthy feelings of fear toward the very One who created you and loves you the most, your Heavenly Father. As a parent, do you wait or look forward to your children making the wrong decisions, just so you can punish them? Of course not! You know they're going to make mistakes, just like you did, but your plan isn't to look for an opportunity to beat on them. Beating on us, when we make mistakes, isn't part of God's plan, either. God, our Father, is the greatest parent.

In Genesis it tells us God created man in His own image. His purpose was for us to be able to fellowship and have a relationship with Him. When Moses led the children of Israel out of 400 years of Egyptian bondage, and you think your trials have lasted a long time, the people were afraid to talk to God. They asked for Moses to be their spokesman. God honored their request, but this wasn't His original plan for His creation. Ultimately mankind cheated themselves out of having a wonderful relationship with their Heavenly Father.

Are you doing the same thing today? Are you afraid of God? Are your past failures or wrong thinking keeping you away from the very One who can direct you and lead you in the way you should go? The One who will lead you down the path of life that is filled with His blessings? This verse makes it clear. God was more than willing to show mankind His ways and to talk with them daily. Don't be afraid. God is still willing to talk with you today. In fact, He desires it. Regardless of the way your life is at the moment, don't cheat yourself out of a relationship with Him any longer. He loves you, and He is still wanting and waiting to show you His ways.

"The Lord is merciful and gracious, slow to anger and plenteous in mercy."
Psalms 103:8 (KJV)

David wrote the 103rd Psalm as a reminder of the covenant promises or benefits that God established for His people. Webster's Dictionary defines mercy as, "compassion or forbearance shown, especially to an offender or to one that is subject to one's power; also lenient or compassionate treatment; a blessing that is an act of divine favor or compassion; a fortunate circumstance; compassionate treatment of those in distress."

Are you in distress? Have the cares of this life become overwhelming? Maybe you are an offender of the law and have committed a crime? Or maybe you have become the most common offender? Maybe you're the person that offends others with your mouth by gossiping, lying or just telling someone off? We are all offenders, and we all need the mercy of God. The Bible says God's mercies are new every morning. Years ago I heard a man tell about going through an extremely trying day. When he arrived at home from work, about six o'clock, he went straight to bed. He said he felt like he had used up his quota or allotment of mercy for that day, and by going to bed early, he wouldn't have to face anything else until he had the "new" mercies God promised.

However, this isn't the way it works. Fortunately for us, God never runs out of mercy. There isn't a quota He sets for each of us, and this verse confirms God doesn't have a quick temper. *He is slow to get angry* or upset with us when we don't do what we're supposed to do. This blows away the "big stick" theory. God's plan is to show forth His goodness. This verse also confirms because of His great, unfailing love for us, He is more than ready, willing, and able to grant us mercy, compassion, forgiveness, leniency, divine favor with Him and our fellowman. Have you messed up? Do you need divine intervention in your situation? Maybe your problems need a lot of God's grace and mercy? Don't be afraid. *Gracious* is the Lord in His attitude toward us, and our covenant with God is *plenteous in mercy*...or far better than any "fortunate circumstance." The bottom line is with our loving Father, it just doesn't get any better.

FEBRUARY 18

> *"He does not treat us as our sins deserve or repay us according to our iniquities."*
> *Psalms 103:10 (NIV)*

God, once again, defines His great love for us. As our Father He tries to spare us from injury or harm from any source, which includes ourselves. God's rules for us to obey serve the same purposes as those established by our parents. They are there to protect us. Some may feel that God just doesn't want them to have any fun. Even the Bible says sin is pleasurable. This is true, but it also says it is only pleasant for a season. What exactly does that mean? It means, at first, internet pornography or cheating on your spouse may seem fulfilling; at first, drinking, smoking dope, crack or meth may seem to take the edge off for relaxation; at first, lying, gossiping or exaggerating the truth won't hurt anybody because they will never know.

The truth is, in any of these situations, both <u>God</u> and <u>you</u> will know, and it won't be long before others know, too. The Bible says what is done in the dark will be brought into the light. Besides, what's so fun about a spouse's love and trust being betrayed, a family broken apart, and children being raised in a one parent home? What's fun about you being addicted to drugs, alcohol or pornography? Why, if it's so fun, are you wanting and needing to quit, but can't? Can you relax now that you're afraid of getting caught? What could be fun about jail, a criminal record or losing your job from a random surprise drug test?

The Bible says we have all sinned and come short of the glory of God. When we sin, God isn't surprised, but it isn't the life He planned for us. He's holy, and sin separates us from Him. He created us so we could have a relationship. However, as much as He hates sin, it never affects His love for us. The unchangeable truth about God is He loves us…no matter what.

The Bible says the wages of sin are death. When we work at our jobs, don't we want and deserve the appropriate wages? Then, when we sin, why should this be any different? It shouldn't, and yet, God's Word assures us, *He will not repay us according to our iniquities,* which is our wrong doings. Sin brings fear, and God didn't create us to live afraid. Can you see why David reminded himself of God's benefits? We know he was far from always doing things right. Maybe you haven't done things right, either? Are you afraid of your past coming into the light? Don't be afraid. Ask God to forgive you. He will forgive and cleanse you, but you must forgive yourself, also. Then, follow David's example, and remind yourself of all the wonderful benefits God has to offer you on a daily basis.

"For as high as the heavens are above the earth, so great is his love for those who fear him;"
Psalms 103:11 (NIV)

Once, while flying in an airplane, I began to think about where the heavens would be. We were flying at an altitude of 33,000 feet, which is approximately 6 miles above the earth, and yet, I knew I was nowhere near Heaven. Scientists can measure the distance from earth to the furthest known planets or galaxies, and we know the heavens are far beyond them. My point is the heavens are beyond measure. God compares His love to us with the same equation, which makes God's love for us far beyond measure, too.

God's unconditional, unfailing love is available to us all. However, this verse states it is *for those who fear Him*. In this context the word fear doesn't mean to be afraid of God. This is the last thing He wants. The Bible tells us He created us to love and for us to love Him. This word *fear* means to show honor or reverence, to value or esteem highly, to show respect and to obey. When you combine the word *fear* with the word *healthy*, it seems like two contrasting thoughts, but when you honor, esteem, respect, and reverence God, the result is a "*healthy fear*" of Him and His awesome, mighty power.

So how do we reverence God? How do we get this healthy fear? First, we must recognize and acknowledge who He is, and what He has already done for us. Then, we give Him thanks for the plan He established for our lives. Thirdly, we learn to praise His name, and study His Word, the Bible. Last, but by no means the end, we set time aside to pray, which is just talking to God. We learn to wait on the Lord for direction, and just spend time together with Him on a daily basis.

God already knows you, but He wants you to get to know Him. How many of your friends would you really know today, if you hadn't spent time with them? It's the same way with God. Don't be afraid. Get to know Him for yourself. You, too, will feel the incredible, measureless love your Father has always had just for you.

FEBRUARY 20

> *"As a father has compassion on his children, so the Lord has compassion on those who fear him."*
> *Psalms 103:13 (NIV)*

The word compassion means to be sympathetic toward or to be conscious of others, especially if they are in distress. It isn't just having sympathy for someone and their situation, but it is also having a strong desire to help them alleviate it. This is the role of our Father through His covenant plan. He is always working on our behalf to help us with life's trials. Now you may struggle with accepting a loving, giving relationship with your Heavenly Father because of your relationship with your earthly parents. If you were disciplined with stiff punishment, no love or strong feelings of guilt, shame, fear and displeasure, then it's easy to see why you would expect the same type of treatment from your Father God.

Most earthly punishment is done while one is upset or angry. But it is vitally important to remember when administering discipline to keep the incident separate from the person or their value. Wrong decisions or actions don't necessarily make you a bad person. Separate the act from the person. This is how our Heavenly Father does it. He doesn't like the sin, but He loves us, and nothing changes this fact. His love is unconditional; it's perfect. The Bible says His love never fails.

However, just like He stated in verse 11, it is important to God that we fear Him. Remember, this word fear does not mean to be afraid of God. If the theory were true about God waiting with His 'Big Stick' in Heaven to get us when we make a mistake, we would have proven by now that none of us would be here. Right? I know I would have been gone a long time ago. In fact, the reason I am so confident this Word is true, the Word works, and God means what He says, is because I am still here to offer a praise report about His goodness and compassion. He has helped me get out of more of my own messes than I care to think about. He can and will do the same for you. Don't be afraid. He has great compassion for His children. Don't wait any longer. Only you can decide to let your past keep you from your future with the Father. Receive His compassion for you. Make the decision to fear and follow Him. It's the one decision you'll never regret!

"But the mercy and loving-kindness of the Lord are from everlasting to everlasting upon those who reverently and worshipfully fear Him, and his righteousness is to children's children."
Psalms 103:17 (AMP)

God's goodness, mercy, love and kindness to us, His children, is unlimited and it's everlasting. The word everlasting isn't common in our everyday talk, but it means enduring or lasting, as throughout all time or for eternity. A good way to think of it is "never ending" or forever. God and His benefits were here before you were born, and they will be here after you depart.

Maybe you've questioned if God really exists? Or wondered where you will go after you die? Maybe your life is such a mess you don't see where God fits in? The world's way of believing in something is you must first see it. Haven't you heard the old saying, "Seeing is believing?" But can you see gravity? Can you see the wind? You can't see either of these things, but you can feel the effects of both. Would you want to jump off a building without something to catch you? Probably not. And even though you see the trees blowing and hear the sound, you can't see the wind itself. We can't actually see the oxygen in the air or the water we drink, either, but it does exist. The same is true about God. We may not be able to physically see Him, but we can see His handiwork and His goodness all around us. Although God has given each one of us a free will to decide whether or not we believe, the truth still remains...God exists, too.

David believed. He knew God and His promises were the real deal. He started this Psalm by reminding himself of these benefits. Benefits he first believed, and then physically saw come to pass before his own eyes. This process is called faith. Faith calls those things that aren't seen as though they were already here. You can receive these same benefits if you do what David did. Fear God, by reverently and worshipfully acknowledging Him and using your faith. Don't be afraid. Only believe. He guarantees to love, heal, deliver, show acts of kindness, and eliminate earthly fear. Plus, these benefits aren't just for you. They're also available to your children. What or who else can offer you this fail proof guarantee—a fear-free promise for now and the future?

FEBRUARY 22

"For I know the plans I have for you, declares the Lord, plans to prosper you and not to harm you, plans to give you hope and a future."
Jeremiah 29:11 (NIV)

In this verse, through the priest and prophet Jeremiah, God declares the plans He established from the very beginning for His people. God sent His prophets to be a voice to all people. They were to bring direction, correction, and warning, even to the wicked. If God didn't care about all people, why would He bother to warn the wicked about changing? If you didn't truly accept, believe, and receive the truth about how loving and forgiving God really is, it could be very difficult to understand some of the events that took place in the Old Testament. However, the truth is God continually warned the people, and those who listened and obeyed God's voice were changed. As a result they lived and daily walked out the prosperous plan God had for them.

The same holds true for us today. God's plan is to prosper us, and He didn't just mean financially. God's description of prosperity may include finances, but what good would all the money in the world do you if your body was in horrible pain and you couldn't leave your house? The world would have us believe money is the answer to all our problems. It is an important part, but there is so much more to God's plan. *His plan was never to harm us, but to give us hope* for a new and better way. Why do we need hope? Because everything we desire, use faith for or believe for is centered on it. God knows exactly what it will take to keep us moving toward our future.

Maybe you're feeling like you have no future? Life has disappointed you, and you're feeling hopeless? Maybe you're even afraid of God because of your wicked ways? God's plan never included for us to be afraid of Him or anything else. Learn His Word. Listen. Then obey. He has given you His promise that He would bless you and never harm you. He loves you, and it's His desire that you will step into the plan He designed…just for you. Don't be afraid. You'll never go wrong when your hope and trust is in the Lord. This verse completely and thoroughly confirms His plans—prosperity, hope, and a fear-free future.

FEBRUARY 23

> *"The fear of man brings a snare, but whoever leans on, trusts and puts his confidence in the Lord is safe and set on high."*
> *Proverbs 29:25 (AMP)*

Solomon, the writer of this verse, had come to understand God was trustworthy. He had a father who taught him about having a relationship with God, and because of this, Solomon had come to trust in the Lord at a very young age. It was then he began his own relationship with God. God makes it clear in His Word He wants a relationship with us, but what exactly does this mean? The word relationship means the relation that connects or binds participants together, and the word relation means a form or quality that binds two or more parts or things, being of the same kind, that belong or work together. God created us, mankind, in His image. This is the very reason we can have a relationship with Him. We are of the same kind, and when we work with Him, this gives us the ability to accomplish His plan.

God has no fear in Him, and because we are of the same kind, we don't have to allow fear a place in our life, either. We don't need to be afraid of what life's experiences will bring. Our decisions will no longer be based upon circumstances, what man thinks or worse, "what you <u>think</u> man <u>may be</u> thinking." This is the point of this Scripture. God is appealing to us to *lean on and trust Him,* and Him alone. How do we do this? The only way is to get to know Him. Develop a friendship with Him just like you would with anyone else. Spend time with Him daily. How is it possible to spend time with Almighty God? Through prayer... and...reading the Word. Are you thinking, "I don't know how to pray? What exactly is prayer?" Prayer is nothing more than a two way conversation between you and God. You talk, and then, you listen.

The Bible, His Word, is God still speaking to us today. It isn't just a book that was written for or about people who lived long ago. It is our instruction manual, and it's as relevant today as it was then. Every answer you need regarding your life and the issues you face from day to day are in it. Don't be afraid. When you begin to study God's Word, you will be amazed how it comes to life. It does this because God is alive. You will see and feel His love and begin to understand His great plan. You won't need to be afraid of mankind or anything else because your hope, confidence, and trust will be in the Lord. When your confidence is in Him, you'll find that your future is not only bright and hopeful, but it's also going to be safe and secure.

FEBRUARY 24

> *"And he answered, Fear not: for they that be with us are more than they that be with them."*
> *2 Kings 6:16 (KJV)*

2 Kings tells us about Elisha who was God's prophet and adviser to the King of Israel. Israel was under attack by the King of Aram. However, every time Aram's army tried to attack them, Elisha had already warned Israel's king of their coming. The King of Aram met with his officers and demanded to know the name of the spy. His officers assured him there was no spy, but it was Elisha, the prophet, who was tipping off Israel's king. The officers said, "He hears every word you speak, even in the privacy of your own bedroom." The King of Aram demanded they find Elisha and capture him. The report came back Elisha was in Dothan. The king then commanded his strongest forces with their horses and chariots to go at night and surround the city.

Early the next morning when Elisha's servant went out, there was this massive army surrounding the city. He came with the report to Elisha and asked what should they do? Elisha said, "*Don't be afraid. Those with us are much greater than those that are with them.*" Elisha then asked the Lord to open his servant's eyes, so he could see what was happening in the spirit realm. It was then the servant saw the hills around Dothan were full of horses and chariots of fire. The enemy army from Aram was completely surrounded. Elisha wasn't afraid. Why? He knew God was a protecting God because of His covenant. We don't have to be afraid, either, because we know the same is true for us today. How do we know this? Because the Bible tells us that God is the same yesterday, today, and forever. He started the covenant, and it hasn't changed.

Maybe you feel like you're surrounded by your enemy? Or the pressures of every day living feel like the enemy? You're wondering how things could ever change? Maybe life has lost its joy, and now you feel discouraged, defeated? Disappointments and delays are accompanied by fear. The voice of fear that says—nothing will ever change. This is a lie. The Bible says there is only one thing that doesn't change…God and His Word. This means everything else is temporary, and if it is temporary, it is subject to change. Don't be afraid. If you feel this way, be encouraged. God is so much bigger than the enemy that has you surrounded. Ask God to open your eyes, and then you'll be able to look to a new and brighter day with Him.

> *"He that dwells in the secret place of the Most High shall remain stable and fixed under the shadow of the Almighty [Whose power no foe can withstand]."*
> *Psalms 91:1 (AMP)*

Whenever I hear the word secret I think about something that is personal, intimate, and it is shared with someone you love, trust or with whom you have a close relationship. In this verse God reveals to us there is a place where we can go to be that intimate with Him. He desires this kind of closeness with everyone. In fact, He encourages us to "*dwell*" in this secret, intimate place. This implies once we reach this state of closeness with Him, we can stay there.

The NIV translation states, "We will rest in the shadow of the Almighty." You might be thinking, "Rest…what's that?" With life's fast paced, hectic schedules, maybe you're finding less and less time for yourself, and as a result, you're feeling weary. Doesn't some peace and quiet sound good? God's "resting" place is an oasis in an anxious, dark, dry, and hopeless life, but this isn't the only good news. The truth is there is no travel expense because you won't need to take a boat, plane or car to get there. You don't have to schedule an appointment ahead of time. You can go anytime from anywhere. So where is this oasis, and how do you get there? Just stop what you're doing, sit down with the Word, and let yourself commune with the Lord. He's always been there with you. Maybe you were just too busy to notice. Even now, He's waiting for you to join Him.

God says we will have rest and stability in this place..."*under His shadow.*" When I was a youth I walked to and from school. I especially remember those warm walks home as I faced the western sun. However, I was offered a form of relief. On one side of the street the shops and buildings provided a shaded path. Needless to say, this was the route I took. I remember the relief I felt once I came in close to those sturdy structures. I was glad to receive the coolness, comfort, and protection that came from being under their shadows. The same holds true with our Father. How comforting it is to know He has provided us with a place that is so close to Him…a place that is stable, even in an unstable economy and environment. Don't be afraid. This verse is just one of the many that continually assures us we can find peace and rest in this fixed, secure place, and if or when we do, we'll also find it eliminates every fear.

> *"Surely He will save you from the fowler's snare and from the deadly pestilence."*
> *Psalms 91:3 (NIV)*

Why did God start this verse with the word *surely*? Webster's Dictionary defines the word surely as, "in a sure manner; without injury or risk of loss, safely; with assurance, confidently; without doubt, certainly." Right from the beginning of a verse that specifically relates to our current modern day issues, the Lord uses a word that guarantees us of what He's promising. Why? To eliminate any reason that would cause us to be afraid. Since September 11, 2001, have you been alarmed or afraid of the possible attacks of chemical warfare, anthrax, nerve gas or other acts of terror? We certainly know the results of all of these substances are meant to bring harm and death, and yet, God makes a statement of saving or protecting us like the one above, and He even goes so far as to start it with the word *surely.* The Lord never wanted us to have any occasion, regardless of the circumstances, to question or doubt His intentions toward us. He wants us to be totally and completely confident He will do what He says. This verse describes God's guaranteed protection and deliverance to us from what the entire world has faced and feared.

The *fowler's snare* is a trap that was used in putting a noose around a bird's neck or entangling them. The enemy, the devil, from the time he rebelled against God and was defeated has tried to trap us and cause us to fall, and he will use whatever and whomever he can. Terrorist's acts, suicide bombs, and weapons of mass destruction are from the devil, regardless of whose hands they are in. But we can still be encouraged, for the Bible clearly states satan was…is…and always will be defeated. As God's children, we *surely* do not have to fear this or any other form of terror.

This verse also refers to pestilence. Pestilence is another word for deadly diseases. Diseases that are contagious or infectious, and when they strike, they're usually in epidemic proportion. They're destructive, life threatening. Isn't it comforting to know, at a time when the world was afraid to go to their own mailbox, our God had already planned for our protection and safety? Don't be afraid. Call down the enemies of darkness in and around your life, and ask God to expose their plots beforehand. He is truly a God of provision. He "*surely*" guarantees it!

FEBRUARY 27

> *"He will cover you with his feathers, and under his wings you will find refuge; his faithfulness will be your shield and rampart."*
> *Psalms 91:4 (NIV)*

If you have ever visited a chicken farm or lived where chickens are raised, you may have had an opportunity to witness the action a mother hen takes with her chicks when she senses danger. The cliché, "Protective as a mother hen," stems from her overly protective nature. If she even senses there could be danger she lifts and spreads her wings wide as a sign to her chicks they need to come in close. Once they have gathered to her, she lowers her wings. Now, her little ones are totally covered, hidden, protected. If by natural instinct a mother hen knows how to protect and provide a safe place for her little chicks, how much more will our loving Heavenly Father provide a safe place for us?

The key here is running to Him and staying close to Him for the refuge He promises. A refuge is a place that provides shelter or protection from danger or distress. What God is saying is when we stay close to Him, we won't be afraid because He will provide all the protection we need. He also says His faithfulness will be our shield and rampart. Faithful means to be loyal, steadfast, and constant; it is the assurance, binding affection or allegiance we need; it is to be firm in the follow through of promises. In other words, if God says He will shelter or protect us from danger, we can count on it!

When David fought the giant Goliath, the Bible says another man stood in front of Goliath holding up a shield that totally covered him. Shields were a mighty piece of weaponry. They were used to defend, cover, and protect the soldier. However, shield isn't the only word used to describe God's covering. Rampart is also used. A rampart is a protective barrier, but it also means to fortify. So God clearly states that His faithfulness—constant assurance—will be our shield—or go before us—and He will fortify this covering to assure—or guarantee—our complete and total protection.

Are you afraid of today's news events? Or are there other areas in your life where fear has tried to come in? Don't be afraid. God declares "He" will be your constant affection, your fortified shield, cover or protective barrier. The key is you must stay close to Him. His faithful love to you will always be your refuge, your ever present help in time of trouble, your fortified shield. So take up your shield—*His faithfulness*—and receive His covering today.

FEBRUARY 28

> *"You shall not be afraid of the terror of the night, nor of the arrow [the evil plots and slanders of the wicked] that flies by day,"*
> *Psalms 91:5 (AMP)*

Nighttime can be intimidating for some, even frightening. Maybe it's due to the darkness itself; it offers no or limited vision which helps create an atmosphere that seems unsafe or uninviting. Policemen confirm that crime increases after dark, and your chances of being involved in a crime are greater, too. There is a fear—terror that is associated with nighttime. Webster's Dictionary defines terror as, "a state of intense fear; a cause of anxiety: worry; violence (as bombings) committed by groups in order to intimidate a population or government into granting their demands; one that inspires fear."

The enemy (devil) works "as one that inspires fear." The Bible tells us he is a thief and the father of lies. One of the ways he comes against us to create fear is to stir up negative situations that can turn our everyday routine into what seems to be a dark, reoccurring nightmare. Although he'll use whatever he can, his ultimate plan of destruction always includes feelings of hopelessness and despair. Have you ever or are you currently feeling like you have been fighting the same battle forever? A battle that looks like it will never change or you can never win? Now, because of it, your life is dark, depressing, even hopeless? This is the enemy's plan. Hopelessness and depression are just two of the emotional states that can occur from the terror he uses to discourage us and to deceive us into believing we are defeated.

When we witnessed the terror of evil men on September 11, 2001, we could literally see the *"arrow" that flies by day.* The enemy will do his best to make you feel afraid. The Word doesn't say we won't want to feel afraid, but it does tell us when these feelings of fear try to come, we can overcome them. How? By knowing what God's Word promises. When we know what God says, we already have the advantage. Why? The Bible says that nothing is impossible with God, so we know the outcome of our trials beforehand. If you feel like fear is trying to come on you about something…your job, kids or marriage, then you must get rid of it. The way to do this is to quote the Word. Speak what God says about your particular problem. The Word confirms the truth about these areas whether they are personal attacks or major attacks against our nation. God's Word is the final authority. Don't be afraid. His plan of love and protection already took into consideration the plans of the enemy to try to destroy. When God says, "*You will not be afraid,*" believe it. Speak the Word. It will encourage and strengthen you. Then remind yourself…He loves me, and He is my shield and safe place.

"Nor of the pestilence that stalks in darkness; nor of the destruction and sudden death that surprise and lay waste at noonday."
Psalms 91:6 (AMP)

This verse is a continuation of the previous verse which states we not only do not have to be afraid of the terror at night, but we don't have to be afraid of the evil plots of men or the arrow that flies during the day. In this verse God's Word extends our boundaries of protection to include not being afraid of *pestilence, any sudden danger or death.* Webster's Dictionary defines the word pestilence as, "a contagious or infectious epidemic disease that is virulent and devastating; something that is devastating or destructive to life; deadly; injuring or endangering society."

Doesn't this sound like the same threats evil men are working furiously to commit against our world today? What about nature's surprise attacks? They certainly brought injuries, destruction, and sudden death. All of these have become very real in our world today, and yet, God wants us to know that even when these things happen we don't have to be afraid. Regardless of how dark it may appear, God's plan still exists for us today, and this plan offers us His unchanging love and divine protection.

You might be asking, "How do I become a part of this divine plan? How can I be sure God will protect my family and me?" If you daily follow God's Word, which is our instruction manual for life, you'll discover He cannot lie. His Word is true, so you must trust and depend on Him. He wants all of us to accept Him and His plan. He wants us to humble ourselves, and call on Him. When you do, you'll find you really can trust and believe Him.

Have you struggled with inner peace because of the war or world threats? Or maybe all the current disasters have you worried? Do you find yourself afraid to leave your house? Do you even have a house to leave? Don't be afraid. The closer you get to Him the closer He is able to work in and through you. Once you get to know Him, you will never doubt His love for you, nor will you wonder if His Word works. With total peace and confidence you will be able to withstand the threat or result of any of our "modern day terrors" when they appear in this world, and you'll be completely delivered of anxiety and fear. If God said it… you can believe it!

MARCH 1

> *"A thousand may fall at your side, and ten thousand at your right hand, but it shall not come near you."*
> *Psalms 91:7 (AMP)*

In this verse God warns us of some of the tragedies that can and will happen. The Bible says in the "end times" there will be wars and rumors of wars. When you're in a battle, it's possible to see people dying all around you, and yet, God comforts the soldier and His child with the same words. He does it by starting verses with, "*Do not be afraid*," and He ends them with, "*It shall not come near you.*"

In an active combat mission things happen fast. When bullets are flying all around you, there isn't much time to think. You just do what you've been trained to do. In fact, the key to success and survival is found in the "trained to do." This is one of the main reasons the military requires every soldier, regardless of the specific branch, to go through basic training. This is exactly how it works for us. We, too, are to be pre-trained. Our training comes with learning the Word of God and being armed with His promises. However, the sad part is most people don't even realize they're in a battle. Oh, they know things are tough, but they just think it's all a part of life or their environment. The truth is we have a real enemy, the devil, and every day he looks for ways to sneak up on you and take you or your loved ones captive. This is why God wants us trained. The Word equips us with the knowledge and the power we need to overcome our enemy—every time.

This verse paints a picture that even when you're in the midst of the worst battle of your life and you are surrounded by the enemy…WITH GOD…you will make it through. We don't have to be afraid of the outcome because God is always with us, working things out on our behalf. Are you going through the toughest battle of your life? Have the ones you counted on for help or support disappeared? Does it seem like you're going it alone? God's Word clearly states—HE NEVER LEAVES US. God is right there with you, right now. However, unlike the devil who forces himself on you, God never pushes Himself on anyone. The Bible says if we draw nigh or close to God, He will draw close to us. It's our choice. Don't be afraid. God wants to fight our battles for us, but we have to let Him. Will you choose to accept His plan and ways for your life? He has your answers. Trust Him with your future, and you'll live in victory, too.

> *"If you make the Most High your dwelling—*
> *even the Lord, who is my refuge—then*
> *no harm will befall you, no disaster*
> *will come near your tent."*
> *Psalms 91:9-10 (NIV)*

The main theme of Psalm 91 is about our relationship with God, which is also the central point of the entire Bible. We need God. We, meaning mankind, cannot do it on our own. Our own strength, intelligence, and fortitude will never be enough to stand up against the weapons that have been unleashed in the world today. However, God already knew this, and He offers us a way out. This Scripture and many others assure us when we choose God and His way to be saved, there will always be divine protection. It's guaranteed to us because of the covenant God established with our forefathers.

David, the writer of this Psalm, had many adverse opportunities and battles during his lifetime, but he had learned the key to success was to *dwell* with the Lord. He came to dwell with the Lord in such an intimate way that he could make these statements from his heart with complete confidence. Without a doubt God was his refuge, shelter, and place of protection. Most Bible translations state this verse, "*No harm will befall you.*" Webster's Dictionary defines the word befall to mean, "to happen to especially as if by fate." God makes it clear through this verse that there is no "fate" or "coincidence" that would have more power over your life than God's Word or plan.

Have you been a victim? Do you feel powerless to change your situation or circumstances? Have you been deceived into believing you are doomed to this kind of life? This verse confirms we do not have to stay in a destructive lifestyle—just because it's all we know. It doesn't matter who or what has happened to you in your past. You don't have to continue with the same old patterns. God said "<u>no fate</u>." This means no race, economic status, education, sex, past injustice or any other disastrous situation will have the power to harm you. With God…you can be free. God promises when we stay close, dwell with Him, and believe His Word, *He will keep disaster from our tent*—or our houses and what's in them. Don't be afraid. Our loving Father has made every provision for us to live safely. We just need to dwell with Him, and believe His Word.

MARCH 3

> *"For he will command his angels concerning you to guard you in all your ways;"*
> *Psalms 91:11 (NIV)*

The Bible tells us we have many angels assigned to us, and they hearken—or respectfully give attention and listen—to direction from the voice of God. This means they take their orders from God. But did you know they also take orders from us? You ask, "How can they take orders from us? Aren't they over us?" The answer is "no," they aren't. When God created man, the Bible says the angels watched and wondered why God was making such a big deal over him. The truth is the big deal was because God had made us in HIS OWN IMAGE. What exactly does this mean? It means we have the ability to choose. We have free-will. We can choose between good and evil, life and death. This is why God tells us to choose life, so that we may live. This doesn't just apply to our life today, but it also means being able to live with Him forever.

The Bible makes it very clear the Scriptures are the inspired Word of God in written form. This means the Bible is God speaking directly to us. God's Word is His voice in the earth today. When we speak or use the Scriptures in and over our circumstances, it is as if the angels hear the voice of God. Then, they do what the Word says. Why? Because even though it's coming out of our mouth, it is still His Word, His voice. Remember, they hearken to His voice. This is why it is so important we not only know what God's Word promises us, but when situations arise, we speak out what the Father Himself would say about it. This is not always an easy task because we usually want to say what we see, what we're feeling or complain and ask, "Why is this happening to me?" There is a Scripture that says my people perish or fail because they lack knowledge. However, God is not referring to our educational system. He is talking about us, as believers, not knowing what He and His Word have already established for us to have authority over due to His covenant and the power in the spoken Word.

When the devil rebelled against God, he was thrown out of Heaven, and the Word says one third of the angels went with him. This means there are still two angels following and obeying God's missions and plans to every one demon. God will always be victorious, and so will we, if we maintain our relationship with Him and abide in His Word, love, and provision. His love for us is so great that He wasn't going to take any chances the enemy could hurt us. Don't be afraid. His plan is thorough, and it's complete. Who else would create a plan that included angels to be at your disposal to *guard you* or to watch over you *in all your ways* or your comings and goings? Who else, but your loving Father?

MARCH 4

> *"they will lift you up in their hands, so that you will not strike your foot against a stone."*
> *Psalms 91:12 (NIV)*

"*They*" means the angels, and this verse continues with the benefits we receive because the angels are at God's command to watch over us and to guard us from any and all forms of harm or disaster. This verse reminds me of the protection I received many years ago while driving my car in Dallas, Texas. I had just come to a stop at a busy intersection where it was permissible to turn left from two lanes. I was in the middle, center lane. The light turned green, I proceeded forward into the middle of the intersection, and started to turn left when I heard an audible voice say, "STOP…LOOK." Now keep in mind I was already in the middle of the street. I hit my brakes, and although I could have looked in many different directions, for some reason I knew to look to my left. The car next to me, which was in a designated lane that could only turn left, had decided to go straight. If I hadn't stopped when I did, I would have been hit. Because I received this warning and I obeyed it, I was able to get stopped in time. There was no accident; no injury to me or my car. I watched them drive right past me as I sat, stopped in the middle of the intersection. They never even saw me. But the good news is…God did!

Was it my guardian angel that spoke to me or the Lord Himself? I can't say I know for sure. But either way the Lord's hand of protection was with me, which is what He promises. In any case, I know if or when I need assistance, God is there to make sure I will not stumble or fall. It doesn't matter whether He sends out angels or He intervenes in the situation Himself. I know this may seem difficult to believe. Maybe you're even thinking, "That was just a fluke. How can you be so sure it was God?" That's a good question. However, after you read and study His Word—His promises—you will become as totally convinced as I am about these things. His Word says He is our source of protection and provision. What His Word doesn't say is that He will only be there sometimes or just once in a while. With Him there is no "maybe" to it. There are no coincidences, fate or flukes. He creates a place of security, a resting place, a place of no fear.

Wouldn't you like to know you have this same kind of security? Peace? Protection? You can. It's your Father's desire, and it is available to everyone. Don't be afraid. Make yourself available to the will of God in your life. You will soon see for yourself and even "hear" like I did that there is no better place on earth to dwell than being with Him.

MARCH 5

> *"Because he loves me says the Lord, I will rescue him; I will protect him, for he acknowledges my name."*
> *Psalms 91:14 (NIV)*

It may seem difficult to believe that it's important to our Heavenly Father that we love Him or that we choose to let Him direct our lives. However, this verse confirms that it is so. It also confirms God's plan to protect or rescue His own. Why is our love so important to God? Why would Almighty God need my love? He created us in His own image. Once you've had a child of your own this principle may be easier to understand. Children are a part of you. You not only look forward to the first time they speak a few syllables, like ma-ma or da-da, but also to the time when you will be able to have full communication with them.

However, one of the saddest things I've witnessed in my years of counseling is when children refuse to accept the help or wisdom their parents offer. The parent does everything within their power to help, and yet, the kids continue to choose a path of stubbornness and destruction. They refuse to accept there could be a different way, let alone a better way. God, as our Father, deals with hurt and pain in the same manner every time any of His children decide to go their own way or refuse to accept Him. Their stubbornness and refusal to follow a different path, a better path will ultimately lead them down a road of destruction, too. This isn't God's plan for His children.

The first and greatest commandment is to love the Lord our God with all our heart, our soul, and our mind. Our loving Him and then obeying Him out of our love is one of the keys that will release the power of God and His benefits into our lives. Have you acknowledged Him? Does He know you love Him? Are you committed to following His ways for your life? He has made every provision you will ever need for your safety and total deliverance. This promise of safety rejects fear and the negative effects it can have on us and our families. Make no mistake, God loves you whether you choose Him or not, but you loving Him releases a life of peace and guaranteed victory—a life without fear. Don't be afraid. Don't reject your Heavenly Father and the plan He has for you. He loves you. Become one of His little children, and reap all His benefits. They are far too numerous to count.

MARCH 6

> *"For I will restore health unto thee, and I will heal thee of thy wounds, saith the Lord..."*
> *Jeremiah 30:17 (KJV)*

In this passage Jeremiah delivered a Word of encouragement and healing from the Lord. He was anointed by God to be a prophet, and this message let God's people know the Lord was not only going to restore their health, but also heal their wounds. A wound is anything that penetrates the outer surface. Usually, when we think of wounds, we picture injuries to the flesh or skin. In this verse and others God promises to heal our every infirmity. He makes healing and restoring our health clear by saying, "*I will!*" However, life can bring more than physical wounds. There is another kind of wound that goes deeper and can even be more life threatening than a physical injury. What is this deadly wound? It's our words. When destructive, harsh or careless words are spoken to us or about us, they cause emotional hurts. These inner "wounds" cause our hearts to be hardened. We allow the fear of what others may think, say or do to bring offense. Once this happens we become bitter, angry, and resentful. However, other people aren't the only source of our injuries. We also wound ourselves when we allow past failures or shortcomings to cause us fear, feelings of guilt and shame, and a sense of unworthiness.

All of these powerful negative emotions, whether we were the cause of them or they were direct attacks from others, cause our bodies to produce "deadly" toxins. It has been medically proven when the body releases these toxins it literally poisons us and ultimately causes other major illnesses such as arthritis, high blood pressure, migraines, ulcers, even cancer. Are you dealing with health issues? Have you ever been hurt and took offense because of it? Are you still angry or bitter toward someone or some thing? Do you still carry feelings of guilt, shame or low self-esteem? Did you know your inner feelings or negative emotions could make you physically sick?

All of these are weapons the enemy uses to inflict pain and wound us, but God said in His Word that no weapon formed against you would be successful. He also said He would restore or bring total healing. Why let your emotions tell you how to feel? Or let them bring fear? God never created you to live in fear. The very fact that HE created you gives you value. HE loves you and has a plan just for you. This Scripture is proof He wants you to be restored to perfect wholeness...both physically and mentally. Don't be afraid. Trust God. Ask Him to forgive you. If you're offended, forgive your offenders. Then, release any fear, heaviness or negative emotions that can keep you bound. God will comfort you, and He will give you health—total restoration for your spirit, soul, and body.

MARCH 7

> *"The Lord hath appeared of old unto me, saying, Yea, I have loved thee with an everlasting love: therefore with lovingkindness have I drawn thee."*
> *Jeremiah 31:3 (KJV)*

This verse confirms God's unchanging love. Webster's Dictionary defines everlasting as, "lasting or enduring through all time: eternal; continuing long or indefinitely." God's love is like eternity…it goes forever…it's never ending.

Just recently while flying I met a man who had been diagnosed with a terminal illness. We talked for quite some time about his difficult treatment and the impact it had had on him and his family. Towards the end of our conversation I asked him if he was prepared for the outcome, regardless of how his life may end. A few moments passed. Then, without answering my question, he said he was humbled by so many that were praying for him and claimed it was the reason he was still alive. It was his next statement that surprised me and left me somewhat amazed. He said, "It's just that eternity is a heck-of-a-long time." Obviously he'd thought about dying and even understood it was forever, but I was saddened by the fear, sorrow, and emptiness I heard in his voice. He had a realization of how short his lifespan really was in comparison to eternity, but I knew he didn't "know" the life he could have after his physical body died. He didn't "know" the *everlasting love* of his Heavenly Father, either personally or intimately.

There is no greater feeling than to be free to express love and then to be fully loved in return or to be drawn to someone because of their kindness and goodness. When we experience this kind of love, we never want to leave their side. Well, God is so good to us, and His love is so fulfilling that leaving His presence can create the same feelings. The truth is most of us have never allowed ourselves to experience this kind of intimacy with the Father. Why? It's fear. We've been hurt by the "conditional" love of mankind, whether it was from our parents, another family member, friends or a lover. Now we are afraid to trust others...so how can I trust God? Why would He love me when others don't? God loves you because it's who He is…not what He does, and God loves you because He created you.

Don't be afraid. Let God into your life, your thoughts, your dreams. He wants you to be close to Him. He will draw you with His goodness, loving-kindness and compassion. Receive His love…His perfect, lasting, enduring—throughout all time—love for you. It will not only remove fear in this life, but it will prepare you for life with Him…forever.

MARCH 8

> *"I sought (inquired of) for the Lord, and required Him [of necessity, and on the authority of His Word], and He heard me, and delivered me from all my fears."*
> *Psalms 34:4 (AMP)*

David was confident God was a man of His Word. Maybe the reason he was so sure is because he'd given God many opportunities to show him. David *sought* or asked of the Lord, expected Him to show forth His mighty power, and God *heard and delivered* him. The NIV translation says God "answered him." If God answered him, it must mean they were having a conversation. Is this possible? Can you really talk to God? And will God actually talk back? The answer to all of these questions is YES. We can talk to God, and He not only hears us, but He will answer us and deliver us out of our tragedies, torments, doubts, and fears.

What are you afraid of today? What do you fear the most? What thoughts keep going over and over again in your mind? Statistics show one of the biggest fears we all deal with is rejection. It produces feelings of inadequacy, you have no value, you aren't good enough or you don't fit in, and if this is true, then why would anyone ever want you or be able to love you? Do you feel like no one will ever really love you for who you are? All of us have felt this way at some time or another. The root of these feelings is that our worth or value is based solely on what others think or their acceptance of us. The problem with this is people, good and bad, will come and go in your life, and when you base your self worth or identity on their opinions, you're on shaky ground. The truth is there's only one opinion about us that will ever count, and that opinion belongs to God.

His Word tells us who we are and who He created us to be. When we let Him, His love and His Word renew our minds. We have a new foundation that is no longer determined by others. We now follow a predetermined course with a new, stable, fulfilling identity that was uniquely designed for each one of us by God Almighty Himself. The Bible calls this a "firm" foundation. We are established on who God says we are which produces a no fear confidence like David's. David had called out to God many times, and God was faithful to deliver him each and every time. This verse confirms He will deliver us from all our fears, too. All is pretty inclusive. When you study the original meaning in the Greek and Hebrew languages, you discover the word all means ALL! Is there something you need delivered from—anger, rebellion, stubbornness, pride, drugs, alcohol, people pleasing or pornography? What about past offenses? Don't be afraid. Call on the Lord. Praise God. You'll see He does what His Word declares.

MARCH 9

> *"Those who look to Him are radiant, their faces are never covered with shame."*
> *Psalms 34:5 (NIV)*

David, the writer of this Psalm, knew how to praise and worship his God. He had been through difficult times, but had found the key to victory was to keep his eyes on the Lord. David states in this verse *those that look to Him are radiant. Radiant* not only means a bright light or glow, but it also means to be marked by or expressive of love, confidence, and happiness. The Bible gives the accounts of those individuals who had personal encounters with God, and afterwards, their faces reflected a bright light or had a glow to them. A person's face can reveal a lot about them. Have you ever witnessed someone being caught "in the act?" It's like asking a child if they did something. More times than not, you can tell by the expression on their face whether or not they're guilty. This is the look of shame. Shame is a powerful and painful emotion. It makes us aware of our shortcomings or imperfections in our character, and it cripples us with fear and regrets. We are not only a disappointment to ourselves, but to others, as well.

David understood those feelings of regret, guilt, and shame. He had made so many mistakes, embarrassing mistakes, mistakes that affected a lot of people. So, how did he overcome the guilt and shame that tried to plague him? What gave him the ability and confidence to state that one's face would not have to reflect the pain, but could actually appear radiant instead? Answers to these questions are found in understanding the relationship David had with God. He kept his eyes on the Lord, and when he messed up, he knew to ask God to forgive him. He ran <u>to</u> God in the time of trouble, instead of hiding from the Father. When he sought the Lord or *looked to Him* and asked for forgiveness, God forgave him and restored him in every way.

The Bible says when we ask God to forgive us, He is not only quick to forgive, but He also forgets the sin. The Word says He removes it from Him as far as the east is from the west. After all, what would God do with all the sins? He gets rid of them, and so should you! God loves you. Ask Him for forgiveness, and then, forgive yourself. If Almighty God can and will forgive you and forget the incident, then who are you to hang on to those past mistakes? Will you make a decision to let go of what you can't fix, and let God fix what only He can? Regardless of who was at fault, God can make things right, if you'll let it go. Don't be afraid. Let God fill your heart with songs of praise for His goodness, kindness, and His amazing mercy. Rejoice. *Look to Him.* Your face will also be *radiant*...marked by the reflection of His acceptance and complete love for you.

> *"This poor man called, and the Lord heard him, He saved him out of all his troubles."*
> *Psalms 34:6 (NIV)*

In this verse David refers to himself as a "*poor*" man. We've all used this word in reference to other things that have nothing to do with finances...for example, "Oh, the poor little animal." Some of the many meanings for this word include being small in worth, to be pitied, inferior in quality or value, humble, barren, unproductive, unfavorable, and less than adequate. Have you ever felt like you belonged in any of these categories? We all have, and so did David. However, the truth is even when David felt like he was at the bottom, he knew if he called or cried out to the Lord he would be heard and delivered once again.

You might be thinking, "What or how bad could it have been for David?" Well, in the beginning he spent many years of his life running from a jealous king who was trying to kill him. So even though David from a young boy had been anointed by the Priest to be the next king, he spent over 15 years hiding out in caves, living with the misfits and criminals. He had to believe God for deliverance. His life depended on it. He learned he needed to believe God for everything.

This kind of lifestyle is what provided the foundation for David to really know God and to be able to trust Him to sustain his very life. Hopefully, most of us haven't been in such a desperate situation. However, how each one of us handles our trials is unique. What may take one to the deep end emotionally may not bother you at all. But, we all have our threshold or breaking point. Where is yours? Are you stretched about as far as you can go? Are you sick and tired of being sick and tired? Are your circumstances managing you or are you managing them?

God said He would never leave us or forsake us. He is right there with you even now. He had all the answers David needed, and He has all the answers you'll ever need. Don't be afraid. If you feel like you're the "poor" man this verse refers to, then you can be encouraged like David. You don't have to carry your troubles alone. The truth is...you don't have to carry them at all. God said, "Call unto me and I will save you from all your troubles." Don't wait...make the call!

> *"The Angel of the Lord encamps around those who fear Him—who revere and worship Him with awe; and each of them He delivers."*
> *Psalms 34:7 (AMP)*

David knew what he was writing about here when he used the word encamp. It isn't a word we hear much today unless you are associated with the military. Encamp means to set up, occupy, establish or to make a place of camp. The word camp refers to being engaged in defending or promoting a position or a person. It can also mean a military service or life. David understood military terms. He was a strong leader in battle with many great victories to prove it. When David speaks of this *Angel*, what he is doing and where he is positioned, it is no surprise he uses military terms. The *Angel* is established, occupies, and is positioned to guard or defend those persons who fear God. This is what any soldier does if ordered to guard a post, group or commanding officer.

The Word says the *Angel* guards those who fear the Lord. What does it mean to fear God? Most people really are afraid of God, but for the wrong reasons. They feel they have messed up so badly that God could never want them or be able to use them for His divine plans and purposes. However, the Bible teaches this is not true, and this isn't the kind of fear David is referring to at all. God loves us and wants to have a friendship with us, but He is still a Holy God. Respect, reverence, and awe of His mighty power and majesty is expected and commanded of God's people. The Bible says the beginning of wisdom is to fear the Lord. This means we're to show Him honor and respect, not only for who He is, but for all of His magnificent ways, as well.

This verse confirms God's plan to position angels to occupy, establish, and defend us when we revere and worship the Lord. The added benefit is they are in position to deliver us, too. All of these benefits are because of our Father's love, mercy and goodness to us—even when we don't deserve it. When you develop a relationship with Him, you won't find it difficult to "fear" Him. Your love and admiration for Him grows daily. His magnificent love is a humbling thing. And when you know you belong to Him, and He has placed angels around you to protect and defend you, it totally removes any and all earthly fear. Don't be afraid. Worship Him and believe...you're really not alone!

MARCH 12

> *"O taste and see that the Lord [our God] is good! Blessed—happy, fortunate [to be envied] is the man who trusts and takes refuge in Him."*
> *Psalms 34:8 (AMP)*

What could David have meant when he wanted us to taste God? Is it possible to taste something without ever putting it in your mouth? Without it ever touching the taste buds on your tongue? Consider this: Have you ever been in such an unpleasant, unexpected, tragic or frightening situation that your stomach starts to ache or you get this burning sensation, and before it's all over you end up with this sour, awful, horrible taste in your mouth? You weren't physically trying to chew your problem then, were you? No, you weren't, but you could taste it, and it wasn't good, was it? David had gone through enough times to know and taste the difference between the sour opportunities life offered him and the sweet path that was available when he followed God.

The key to success, for anyone who will believe, is to do everything...WITH GOD. When we choose His way, we will experience His love...His plan...His power...His greatness...His kindness...His mercy...His grace...His provision... His protection...His benefits...His forgiveness...His wisdom...**HIS EVERY THING!!!** He alone is the reason our life starts to taste and even smell sweet.

Once you've "*tasted*" His goodness, you will no longer wrestle with following His ways, trusting Him, and surrendering your will to His will and plan for your life. When we move into this place of surrender, we can fully be positioned for the blessings He has for each of us. In fact, the Word says there are so many blessings that they make us the envy of anyone and everyone who sees what the Lord has done. These blessings also include being fortunate, which means to receive some unexpected good. I could go for that. How about you? When the phone rings late at night or there is an unexpected knock on your door, wouldn't you like to have some good fortune show up for a change, instead of bad news?

The Bible says all things are possible with God. This verse is just one of many that promise you a bright and happy future. A future that's filled with hope, not fear and doubt. A future that expects and trusts God. Don't be afraid. Take courage. You, too, will be able to *taste and see the goodness of the Lord.*

MARCH 13

> *"Fear the Lord, you his saints, for those who fear him lack nothing."*
> *Psalms 34:9 (NIV)*

This verse is really saying, "Worship, highly honor, and revere the Lord, you His saints or children, for those who worship, highly honor, esteem, and revere Him will lack nothing." What is worship? How do we revere the Lord? Let's look at David, the writer of this Psalm, as our example. When David was a young boy he was responsible for the care of his father's sheep. It was a huge job. While he was all alone in the fields at night, I'm sure he had occasions to be afraid, even if it was just hearing a "scary" sound or a wild animal cry. However, it was during these "alone" times that David came to depend on the Lord for his strength and courage. He learned to write songs, play his stringed lyre, and sing about the goodness of his God.

A psalm is a poem or song that is accompanied by a musical instrument. David used this time to sing and to worship the Lord for protecting, saving, and delivering him from every situation. The songs not only blessed God, but they stirred David's heart in such a way that faith and confidence in God became his firm foundation. Maybe you're thinking, "Well, I'm no song writer, I can't play an instrument, and you don't want to hear me sing. How can I worship the Lord?" There is a verse in the Bible that tells us to make a joyful <u>noise</u> unto the Lord. The good news is, even if the only sound you can make is noise, you're still following what God has asked you to do. God doesn't care if we have trained voices or not. What He hears is what comes from our heart. If the sounds are from a grateful heart, a heart that is joyful to praise Him whether the circumstances "look" good or not, He is moved to do what only He can do.

This verse declares when we worship, *fear the Lord…we will lack nothing*. Have you reached a place in your life where you lack nothing? If not, then follow David's lead. Open up your heart and your mouth. Offer up a praise and thanksgiving to the Lord. Now you may ask, "What if I don't feel like it?" When you're going through the heat of the battle, I can assure you, you won't "feel" like it. I'm sure there were many stressful, fearful times David didn't feel like it either, but he knew once he started to sing, the presence of the Lord was there to comfort him and to meet any need he had. Don't be afraid. The Bible says God inhabits the praises of His people. This means He shows up when we worship or *fear Him*. Imagine…a private visit with Almighty God! What could be better?

MARCH 14

> *"The young lions lack food and suffer hunger, but they who seek (inquire of and require) the Lord [by right of their need and on the authority of His Word] none of them shall lack any beneficial thing."*
> *Psalms 34:10 (AMP)*

David writes this verse to "bring home" the truth about the benefits of having a relationship with God and knowing His Word. David was a hunter, and he uses the example of a young lion to compare their needs being met to the way our needs are met. A young lion doesn't go out to find his own food, and he certainly doesn't go anywhere alone. His father is the head of the pride, and he is the one who searches for and kills the food for his family. He is their source, but only if or when he is able to find what they need. Without him the young lion will go hungry.

For us, with God as our Father, all we have to do is ask, and He will provide every beneficial thing. God doesn't have to look for our provision...HE IS the provision. We don't have to be afraid God can't find food or clothing or medical aid or finances, etc. The point is we don't have to be afraid of anything with God. Our part is to ask—or to *seek the Lord.* The Bible says when we seek, look for, try to discover, ask, request or inquire, and go to Him, He will be found. It also says He will answer, deliver, save us, guide us, and comfort us. He will make a way where there seems to be no way. Do you need a "way?" Have you finally exhausted your resources, and now you're tired and burned out from trying to do it yourself? Or have you figured it out—whether your life is just OK or it is in shambles—you need someone to help?

Even the young lion cub knows not to attempt life on his own. Why don't you follow his safe plan? God, your Father, has always been right there...waiting for you to come to Him. The Bible says we don't have because we haven't asked. Is this you? Why don't you ask? Are you afraid? This verse confirms as His child we have the right to ask—*seek the things we need, and we know this by the authority of God's Word.* Don't be afraid. Seek Him. You will find the answers to every question you've ever had, and more than that, those answers will also bring the right solutions, peace—nothing missing, lacking or broken—and God's richest blessings.

> *"The eyes of the Lord are upon the righteous,*
> *and his ears are open unto their cry."*
> *Psalms 34:15 (KJV)*

This verse comforts us with the knowledge that we are not living in this world by ourselves. It states that God watches and provides whatever we need, at the time we need it. However, there is one important requirement in having someone oversee our lives, and this is we must live a righteous life. What does it mean to be righteous? Webster's Dictionary defines it as, "acting in accord with divine or moral law: free from guilt or sin." This definition, whether it was originally planned this way or not, represents a condition, and then a benefit. The condition is—if we follow God's plan and live according to His ways—His divine or moral law—we will then reap the benefits, which include living free of guilt and shame.

When we accept the Lord into our lives and start to renew our minds to the Word of God, it isn't hard to turn your life around. I don't mean to imply you won't ever face trials or problems again because you will. But now you know you aren't alone. There will be someone who not only sees what you are dealing with, but also hears when you ask for the answer to change your situation. Plus, you will have past victories to reflect upon, instead of defeat. If God answered and helped you before—then you can be assured He will help you now.

David experienced this time after time in his relationship with God. Whether the battle was from an enemy or his own wrong doing, God was always there for him. Why? God's love was great toward David, and it's just as great toward you. Don't be afraid. The Bible says nothing can ever separate us from the love of God. Ask the Lord to come into your heart today, and yield yourself to His plan. When you do, the Bible says your sins are forgiven, totally washed away. You have been made righteous. If you have already asked the Lord to come in, but have gotten away from His plan, repent. Ask Him to forgive you, and let His love for you back into your heart. The Bible says His eyes continually go to and fro across the whole earth. Who is He looking for? Or listening to? It's you...His own, the accepted, the forgiven, the righteous...His beloved child.

MARCH 16

> *"When the righteous cry for help, the Lord hears, and delivers them out of all their distress and troubles."*
> *Psalms 34:17 (AMP)*

This verse begins with the word "*when*." It doesn't say "if" or "maybe." It says "*when*" we cry out, God rescues or delivers. This Word comforts us and assures us—it will happen—it's a sure thing. The moment we decide to ask God for help, He *hears and delivers*. Have you ever found yourself in a conversation, and after a short while, instead of hearing two voices, you only hear one...and it's yours? You discover that although the other party appears to be listening, they just aren't "hearing" you? This can be very frustrating. However, the truth is it's even more frustrating when you know that they've heard you, but they just can't do anything about it. This is why the word "*and*" in this verse is so important. God hears... AND...delivers. This means God does something. He demonstrates His love and compassion for us by taking action. *He hears our cries...and...delivers us out of all our trials, troubles, and distress.*

We've heard people say, "Back in the good old days" or "back then...when times were simpler." Obviously, they are reflecting upon a time in their past history when life didn't seem to have as many complications for them as they're facing now. The truth is life has always had trials. Haven't you always had trials of some kind or another? If things were so simple in the past, then how much simpler could it have been in Bible days? Yet, history still records they struggled with unbelievable events, traumas, and tragedies. They went through their share of problems, confusion, jealousies, enemies, wars, and trials. Life then, now, and in the future presents challenges. However, they learned what to do, and so can we. Just cry out; God saves.

The Bible says God is no respecter of persons, and He is the same yesterday, today, and forever. What this really means is if He has done it for one of His children, then He will do it for another, and what He did for the people in the Bible, He will do for us because He never changes. The Bible is full of people who went through trials and major distress, but God delivered them every time. Why? They were His children, the *righteous*. Don't be afraid! You can belong to Him and reap the same rewards. Isn't it about time? Open up your heart, and let the love of a saving God wash away your sin and guilt. Then call out to Him, and watch Him deliver you from your troubles.

MARCH 17

> *"The Lord is close to the brokenhearted and saves those who are crushed in spirit."*
> *Psalms 34:18 (NIV)*

Usually, when we think of a broken heart, we think about feelings of love intertwined with all the negative, hurtful emotions that come as a result of a break up or a parting of the ways. Whether it's a romantic relationship or an inner conflict that divides a family, when these separations occur, we are broken-hearted. However, being broken-hearted can also relate to so many other areas. I once heard an athlete tell about a state relay race he had run. His position on the team was to be the last runner because he was extremely fast. The race started; all was going well. The third runner came around the curve with the baton extended. It was a smooth transition, and now this athlete was off. He was about to cross the finish line when he realized he couldn't hear any of the other runners. He turned his head just slightly to see where they were. In that split second his opponent shot right past him…he had lost the race. If he hadn't taken his eyes off the goal and lost his focus, he would have kept his advantage and won. Naturally, he was disappointed, but even more than that…he was broken-hearted.

The unexpected loss of a loved one, a divorce, a job termination, overwhelming debt, a debilitating accident, any and all of these can leave a person stunned, crushed, disappointed, angry, and broken-hearted. All of us have experienced tragic events that have left us numb to people and our surroundings. There was a time in my life when it looked like my hopes and dreams…everything I had worked toward was going to fall apart. There was such a feeling of grief or loss. I was broken-hearted. I thought, "What am I going to do now? Do I even have the strength to begin again?" Maybe you've asked yourself the same questions? Has your world fallen apart, and you don't know which way to turn, either?

The above Scripture assures us God understands all these emotions, and He will do something about them. These types of circumstances are too big for us to manage by ourselves. We need help, and there isn't anyone more capable and willing than our Father. When the Word says He "saves" us, it means He delivers, restores, replenishes, removes, and replaces those broken feelings with His love, peace and joy. Do you need your heart fixed? Do you feel an emptiness or void? Is there still pain? Take a minute and think about the meaning of each of these words…deliver…restore…replenish…replace. Don't be afraid. Trust Him to do what only He can do. It's the only way to move forward. Let Him replace what you've lost with His overwhelming love, and then let go of the grief and heaviness. His love will lift you to a new place, and you'll find He still has a great plan and hope for your future.

> *"Many evils confront the [consistently] righteous, but the Lord delivers him out of them all."*
> *Psalms 34:19 (AMP)*

Today, more than ever, we are constantly being *confronted* or attacked by evil. With the continual threats of terror breaking out around the world and our troops in battle, it could cause even the strongest heart to be faint. All of us wonder if or when this will end. One of the definitions in Webster's Dictionary for the word evil is, "something that brings sorrow, distress or calamity." This can represent a variety of things...people, weapons and war, the weather, and so on. All of these are potential areas of evil we face daily. Some evils we see with our natural eye, and some we don't. This unseen evil is what takes place in the spiritual realm by the devil. Even though you can't see him, he is real, and his whole focus is to try to kill, steal, and destroy. However, he is no match for God or a child of God. That is if you know the Word, and use your authority God has already given you.

David, the writer of this Psalm, faced evil from every side. In the beginning King Saul wanted him dead and chased him for over fifteen years. After Saul was killed, David finally became king, but his troubles were far from being over. He lusted after another man's wife, slept with her, and she became pregnant. In an attempt to cover it up, David plotted and succeeded in killing her husband by stationing him in the most dangerous place of battle. Months later, when the baby was born, he was very sick and died a few days later. Were David's trials finally over? NO! In fact, years later David's son raped his daughter, another son killed his brother, and even one of his sons tried to remove him from the throne. Sounds like today's soap operas, doesn't it? When David states in this verse *the Lord delivers you out of all your troubles*, he knew what he was talking about.

You may be thinking, "Why would God help a man who brought all this pain and trouble on himself?" God helped David because he was in covenant with Him. David acknowledged God and repented when he messed up. He worshiped, thanked, and continually praised God for all He had done. God still offers us the same covenant plan. When we are afraid, tempted, and evil or the devil causes us to stumble, isn't it good to know that God already has a plan in place to deliver us? It should also encourage us that if God would forgive and continue to help David, then we know he will help us, too. Don't be afraid. The Bible says evil—temptations—will come, but you can choose the Lord and His ways. It's only through Him that we become righteous. When you do, you can be confident of this...*He will deliver "you" out of <u>all</u> your troubles.* Through it all, David still lived a victorious life, and God's plan for you is to see victory in your life, too.

MARCH 19

> *"The Lord redeems the life of His servants, and none of those who take refuge and trust in Him shall be condemned or held guilty."*
> *Psalms 34:22 (AMP)*

Today, in our judicial system, there is a program that offers a prisoner a "full pardon." The State Governor and the President of the United States are the only ones with the authority to grant this pardon. When it is offered, the pronounced sin or criminal sentence the individual was charged with is totally dropped; it never appears again. This Scripture promises us the same thing. Only this pardon is from "THE" Judge and Supreme Authority of all.

When we accept the Lord, we belong to God. This verse confirms *none of those who take refuge or trust in Him shall be condemned or held guilty.* What this really means is we will receive all His benefits like we had never sinned. You ask, "How can this be? Why would God be so willing to forgive? I thought He hated sin?" Oh, make no mistake, God does hate sin, but He still loves you and me. Because God is Holy, He can't be around sin. The Bible says sin separates us from the Father, but it also says "<u>nothing</u>" separates us from the Father's love. It is His unconditional love to us that offers us a second, third or how ever many chances we need to get our lives aligned with the plan He has for us.

God is the highest and ultimate authority in the universe, and He alone has every right to release us from the guilt and shame that comes from sin. He redeemed us, which means He bought us back from sin. He freed us from distress or harm. He freed us from captivity. The key to receiving our freedom from our past failures, guilt, and shame is to *take refuge in Him*. How do we do that? *We trust Him* to do what He promises in His Word. Do you know what He has already promised you? Are you aware that a "full" pardon for your sins, no matter what you've done, is yours for the asking? Did you know God had a purpose for your life before you were ever born? Everyone, regardless of where you are today or what you did yesterday, is still a candidate for their own unique plan designed by God the Father.

The truth is God is the original "God Father," and this is truly "an offer you can't refuse." Don't be afraid! You do not have to be a prisoner to sin any longer. Repent—turn from your wicked ways—and ask "The" Ultimate Authority to forgive you. Your pardon is here…right now. Just trust in His plan for your life. You'll find out how good freedom really feels.

MARCH 20

"I am the Lord, the God of all mankind.
Is anything too hard for me?"
Jeremiah 32:27 (NIV)

How many times in our journey through life do we face major situations that are out of our reach? A few years ago the Lord asked me to go back to school. When I found myself studying for tests, after 30 years, I thought, "What were you thinking?" The truth is, until that time, I hadn't given it much thought. You see, I submitted my life to His plan many years ago. So when He said go to school, out of obedience I applied, was accepted, moved to the new state, enrolled, and started classes.

"Pulling up stakes and moving" may seem strange or unusual to you. However, doing the "*unusual*" wasn't out of the ordinary for me. This wasn't the first time I had been obedient to what God was asking me to do and found I was "in over my head." However, I also found it was during these times I learned to trust Him even more and to not be afraid! I learned God is faithful, which means if He said it in His Word...He will do it! It is also at these times I saw God do the impossible, the miraculous, the "there is no way, but by the mighty hand of God," that this was accomplished. He proved to me, time and time again, there *isn't anything too hard for Him.*

You may be facing a difficult situation yourself; a crisis far more serious than a school test. Right now you're wondering, worrying, asking, "How or will I ever get out of this?" or "Will this ever end?" or "When will he, she or the circumstances ever change?" Each situation is different. I've heard it said, "The only thing in this world that is for sure is—nothing—is for sure." However, there is one thing that is for sure. In fact, it is the one and only constant in an ever-changing world. This one sure thing is God's Word.

What's the biggest trial you're facing? Are you ready to admit you can't do anything to change it...let alone fix it? Don't be afraid. Give it to Him. He is your answer, and *nothing is too hard for Him.* Speak the Word over your situation. Use your faith. Trust Him. Then, watch how He does the impossible in your situation, too.

MARCH 21

> *"Call to me and I will answer you and show you great and mighty things, fenced in and hidden, which you do not know—do not distinguish and recognize, have knowledge of and understand."*
> *Jeremiah 33:3 (AMP)*

Jeremiah, another great prophet of God, continues to repeat one of the key points God wants to make clear to us. The point is we can and should "*Call unto Him*!" God wants His people to know and understand that He not only wants to have a conversation or communicate with us, but He also wants us to be able to *recognize and distinguish things*—life's events or happenings—in advance. He encourages us to come to Him, and it's not just for a few things or the hard things or we can only come once in a while. He wants to have a regular, steady dialogue with us. This really shouldn't seem strange or unusual. Don't you want to talk with your children or the one you love every day? So does our Father, God.

Situations will continually arise that cause us to wonder which way we should go or what we should do next. God's Word is clear, "if" we will *call to Him, He will answer and show us great and mighty things.* In other words, God will direct our path. Why is this so important to God? Does He just have to be in charge all the time? The Bible says He knows the end from the beginning. His answers will keep us from making those painful and costly mistakes that not only can leave us devastated now, but sometimes for years to come. Just this past week I started to do something, when it occurred to me I hadn't asked God if this was what He wanted. I asked Him to forgive me, and instantly I knew I wasn't supposed to do what I had planned. Now this wasn't any huge, life-changing decision, and because it was so insignificant, I doubt anything tragic would have happened, even if I had done it. However, it felt good to know that I wasn't going to have to find out the hard way. God's ways are so much better than our ways. I've learned to ask Him, and then trust Him about everything. Our Father knows it all, so I can always rely on Him for my daily direction.

Is it hard for you to ask God about things? Sometimes, if we've been ridiculed or made to feel stupid for asking questions in the past, it becomes difficult or uncomfortable for us to ask now. I'm sorry if you've experienced this type of character assassination. However, the bottom line is God doesn't tell us to ask or to call on Him, and then sit back and poke fun or laugh at us for not knowing. He loves us, and He wants to *show* us things, *fenced in and hidden things*, so we can live a happier, healthier, more productive life. Don't you want to live a happier and healthier life? Don't be afraid. Ask Him or *call unto Him.* He is always ready to share with you His love and expertise on any and every situation.

> *"The blessing of the Lord, it maketh rich,*
> *and he addeth no sorrow with it."*
> *Proverbs 10:22 (KJV)*

The *blessing of the Lord* was highly cherished by the men of old. They knew the blessing was part of the original covenant God established with Abraham. God chose Abraham to receive this covenant of blessings because he had unwavering faith, and, as a result, Abraham is considered to be the father of our faith. One of the definitions of the word blessed is to be highly favored, but it also means to endow, preserve and protect, and to confer prosperity and happiness. The culture then and even in some parts of the world today, still practices the passing down of a blessing. Just before the father dies, he lays hands on the oldest son and imparts the blessing. The Bible tells of a young man who wanted the blessing so badly that he tricked his blind, elderly father into believing he was the oldest son, and in fact, received the blessing. Then and now it's important we have *the blessing of the Lord.*

Today, we talk about the goodness of God, which is certainly true. We say, "We are blessed." Most of the time when we make this statement, we are referring to the goodness of God because of what He has given to us or what He is doing for us. However, this isn't quite accurate. The big house, new car or the great job isn't the blessing. It is the result of or the effects of the blessing. For example: Take the wind. You can't see it. You can only see the effects of it when the leaves move or you may hear the sound of it, but you don't actually see the wind itself. This is the way it is with the blessing. God established His covenant with our forefathers years ago. When we stay with God's plan, the same blessing that was laid upon them still exists in our lives today. All the great things we have are just the benefits or the effects of this blessing or covenant with God, and with God's blessing, there is *no sorrow added to it,* either.

When we truly get an understanding of *His blessing* and that it belongs to us, we'll have no reason to fear the economy or any other worldly situation. The Bible tells us of men who were in covenant with God, and even during a famine, they prospered! Don't be afraid. When we believe and accept the plan of God, the same covenant is still available to us. Now we can expect the same results. The question is: "Do you know His covenant?" Has He made you rich in your relationships, employment, health, finances or emotional well being? Remember, God loves you. He wants to make you prosperous. He wants you to live an abundant, healthy, and favorable life…a life without sorrow.

MARCH 23

> *"You will show me the path of life; in Your presence is fullness of joy, at Your right hand there are pleasures for evermore."*
> *Psalms 16:11 (AMP)*

Before I decided to follow God's plan for my life there were times when I found myself at a crossroad. What I mean is there was more than one opportunity presenting itself at the same time. These opportunities would require a decision that could change or altar my future direction. Maybe you've been there, too? Maybe you've even been at this same crossroad before? How do you know which is the right way to go?

After God delivered the children of Israel out of horrible bondage and slavery in Egypt, He led them into the Promised Land. I wish I could say once they were delivered they "lived happily ever after," but the truth is it took them forty years to make a trip that should have only taken eleven days. What happened? They were at a crossroad in their lives, and instead of allowing God to show them His ways and plans, through His servant and leader Moses, they chose their own way—the old, comfortable, more familiar path. God wanted them to see they could trust Him for their every provision. He had a great <u>new</u> plan for them, but the biggest problem the Israelites faced was they wanted to continue in their old ways of thinking and doing. They were afraid of change.

However, just as God offered them a path filled with *His presence and fullness of joy*, He offers each of us the same. This verse confirms *He will show us the path* to take. Unfortunately, at times, we're just like the Israelites. We, too, want a familiar or more comfortable path. We want our own way. Why do we do this? It's fear. We not only struggle with the fear of making new changes, but we also have to deal with past fears that have come from wrong choices that escalated into bad experiences. The truth is we've all traveled down some pretty rocky, rough or bad roads that have left us with bent bumpers, broken windshields, flat tires, and now we're out of gas. Can you relate? Are you at the end of a long and dusty road? Weary from the journey?

Get ready to change your old thinking and doing. Nobody drives very far or very fast looking in the rear view mirror. It's time to change focus and move forward with God. This verse is our confidence *He will show us the path of life*. Don't be afraid. Pray, and ask Him. Worship the Lord, and move into His presence. In this place, "*His path of life,*" He will eliminate your past mistakes and move you into your Promised Land. There you'll find joy, peace, and every pleasurable thing His path holds for your future.

> *"The Lord is my rock, my fortress, and my deliverer; my God, my keen and firm strength in Whom I trust and take refuge, my shield, and the horn of my salvation, my high tower."*
> *Psalms 18:2 (AMP)*

The Bible tells us David faced nonstop battles. Even though he had to run for his life for over fifteen years from King Saul, he couldn't forget that he had been anointed to be king. It was God's plan for David, and He not only became their king, but he was victorious over his enemies. His numerous victories prompted him to write psalms or songs to God in gratitude. David is one of the greatest examples of God's faithfulness and His delivering power. Now, I admit, fifteen years may seem like a long time. It makes you wonder why God didn't do something sooner, especially when David had already been chosen and anointed to be their king. Maybe you're facing situations you've prayed and asked God about for many years, too? With David as our guide, we know not to focus on the when, but the Word of the Lord. If we continue to believe God's Word, use our faith, and not quit, we will reap the same results David did. We, too, will be victorious!

God is perfect, and everything He does is perfect. From this we would have to conclude that His timing is also perfect. God doesn't bring turmoil, tragedies, and torment into our lives. This is the work of the enemy, the devil. However, we know by the Word of God what to do when the attacks come. The Bible says we are not ignorant of the devil's devices. Our part is to use or speak the Word of God against the situation. The Word literally becomes our weapon against the problem. When we believe and use the Word we're releasing our faith. The Bible says it's faith that pleases God. Our released faith moves God to do His part!

David was also a great example of someone who continued to love, praise, and worship God. In the midst of his many problems the Word says he would encourage himself in the things of God and sing about all that God had done. Are you discouraged? Do you feel like you're running for your life? Hounding debt collectors? A violent or abusive relationship? Don't be afraid. Do what David did. Encourage yourself in the Lord, and don't be weary in your well doing! Do you need a new song? Praise God during your battle. He is always with you. *He is your keen and firm strength.* Trust Him. He loves you, and He will be your shield, refuge, strength, and deliverer.

MARCH 25

> *"I will call upon the Lord, who is worthy to be praised: so shall I be saved from mine enemies."*
> *Psalms 18:3 (KJV)*

Throughout both the Old and New Testaments there are many verses like this one. In fact, there are approximately 64 different verses in God's Word that command us to *call upon the Name of the Lord* or to cry out to God for help. Do you think God is trying to make a point about how reliable He is to not only hear us, but to also answer our calls? In the past, when I think back on some of the problems or unpleasant circumstances I dealt with, I'm amazed at how long I tried to work things out on my own. I did my best to fix things, but somehow I ended up right back where I started…or even worse. Then, in sheer frustration, I would ask myself, "Why?" Why would I want to continue to do things the hard way when God said, "Call or ask Me?" Why would I want to drag out this negative situation any longer than necessary when He's willing to do the hard part for me? The truth is it's pride. It is pride that makes any of us think we can do things independently of God.

Many times, as the last resort or in desperate situations, I've heard people say, "Let's pray." At that point it is evident they have exhausted all <u>their</u> resources and abilities. They have finally reached a place where they must admit, "I can't fix this!" Now they are willing to ask for God's help. However, the truth is God should be the first place we turn to for help…not the last. Are you still trying to work through situations using your own abilities? Why don't you ask God for His wisdom and plan? From my past experiences I can only encourage you with these two words…Don't Wait! Go to the expert. Knowing where to get the proper answer for every situation is the biggest part of any battle.

At times we've all watched people struggle with finding solutions to things that seemed obvious to us. You just want to jump in and help them or do it for them. Isn't this the way it is with children? Don't you want to help them, so they don't always have to learn things the hard way? God wants to help us in the same way…by giving us His wisdom. After all, He does have all the answers. Are <u>you</u>, in some way, still trying to get the victory? Or maybe you think you're bothering your Father if you ask for help? His desire is for you to turn everything over to Him. Don't be afraid. Humble yourself, and ask Him. Ask Him to help you with the "not asking" part, too. There may be specific reasons why you find it difficult or uncomfortable to seek His guidance, but He can fix these areas and restore you to a great relationship with Him. He loves you. His plan has always been to deliver you from *your enemies*. Just ask Him, and then praise His Name.

MARCH 26

> *"You give me your shield of victory,*
> *and your right hand sustains me;*
> *you stoop down to make me great."*
> *Psalms 18:35 (NIV)*

With the advanced warfare technology available today, fighting your enemy with a sword and shield in man-to-man combat seems strange. However, David, the writer of this Psalm, knew what it was to use these weapons. He was a mighty warrior and a great military leader. Many times, depending on the type of battle, another man carried the shield and marched in front of the warrior. David knew the added benefits this kind of shield provided. In this verse he makes the same reference to God by acknowledging Him as his shield. Not just a shield for those wartime battles, but also as a shield of protection for all those everyday battles he would encounter. The word *sustain* in this verse means to bring support or relief to something. David continually testifies that God has supported him, held him up, and brought relief.

The above verse is the kind of statement David makes over and over again. Why would God think it was necessary for him to keep repeating it? Do you think it could be that we still haven't gotten it? That somehow it just seems to be too easy or it's too good to be true. Or maybe you reject it because you have a hard time believing it could possibly be for you? It could maybe work for someone else—a "good person,"—but not for me!

God's covenant plan is too good to be true, but it is still the plan. He loves us, all of us, and He never wanted anyone to fail. The Bible says if you can believe it—you can receive it. Countless men and women throughout history believed the Word of God, used their faith, and then saw God do mighty miracles. David was just one of the many. Do you need a move of God in your situation? Do you need a miracle? Well, there is a God who still does miracles, and He just happens to be your Father. Don't be afraid. Trust Him to handle your every need. Turn it over to Him. He promises to shield you from those tormenting situations...*His right hand* will bring you relief and support you. How do you spell relief? Couldn't you use a break? Let God provide the victory you need. He will make a "way" where and when there is no other way. *He will stoop down. He will make you great!*

MARCH 27

> *"You broaden the path beneath me,*
> *so that my ankles do not turn."*
> *Psalms 18:36 (NIV)*

Have you ever tried to walk along a narrow retaining wall or a high curb? If you have, you know it takes much concentration and very good balance. Without these two it does not take much to lose your footing and find yourself on the ground below. Athletes can tell you about the importance and precision of each step, whether they're running a race, broad-jumping, walking the beam or throwing the disc. During high school my sisters and I ran track. During one of the races a competing athlete caught up with my sister. As she came from behind, she deliberately got too close to my sister's legs, causing her to fall. In the process the spike on the front of the competitor's shoe went straight through the back of my sister's heel. At that time track shoes had long metal spikes on the soles. Needless to say, they took my sister to the hospital where she received stitches for her injury. The other runner was immediately disqualified, but those few wrong steps set my sister's track activities on hold for awhile.

Life is like a race. We start it, but somehow find it can be very difficult to finish. How many times have you felt like you were running your race only to get knocked down? Maybe you, too, have been attacked from behind? Or maybe you have already discovered that some people and some events in your life just aren't fair? Life's traumas are tragic, not only for that time, but afterwards, too. If the pain or sense of loss keeps you from being able to move forward, the situation can even worsen. These kinds of tragedies cause us to be afraid to trust people. We feel like we have to walk a thin line. It's an emotional tight rope that makes life a very narrow path. But just like there was an overseer to disqualify the cruel and unfair runner in my sister's race, we have a God that oversees and brings justice to the events in our lives. Nothing escapes Him. He takes care of His own.

This verse is a visual of how God can take those tight spots we get ourselves into at times and open, loosen or *broaden our path* so we can find stable ground and have the room to move out, get into the open, and get free. The added benefit to a path that is wide and stable is you can travel on it at a much faster speed. Now it's no longer necessary to balance each and every step. Don't be afraid. God's ground is stable, and even though others have let you down, you'll find God won't. He is trustworthy. He will strengthen your frame to endure the race. Won't you allow Him to make the necessary adjustments in your life? Then, with a sure, steady foot you will be swiftly running your "life's race."

> *"For though the mountains should depart and the hills be shaken or removed, yet My love and kindness shall not depart from you..."*
> *Isaiah 54:10a (AMP)*

The Prophet Isaiah delivered God's messages of love and devotion to His people. The point he makes is still as valid today as it was then. What is the point? Just as God was always with them, He will always be with us. Sometimes, in the midst of our trials, we lose sight of whether anyone really loves us or cares for us. This includes God. When this happens it feels like the whole world starts to cave in. The weight and pressure of it all becomes a mountain that is too big for us to carry alone. However, when things around us seem shaky or unreliable, it's reassuring to know God's Word remains the same. It is reliable. It is dependable.

The Bible confirms God's magnificent *love and kindness will never leave us*. The concept of a loving Father who is always there—no matter what—is hard for some to grasp. It seems we go from one extreme to another. Either everything or everyone is constantly changing or nothing changes at all. It's been years, and you're going through the same battles. What makes us stay on the same track, making the same decisions or doing things the same old way when we see it's not working? The truth is we do it for two reasons. The first is it's a familiar routine, and habits have been formed. The second is we're afraid of change. We may hate where we are or what we're doing or even who we're with, but we hate the thought of changing even more.

Many times, because of our past circumstances, change seems impossible. One of the reasons is our past, whether good or bad, has taught us our way of thinking. And it's our way of thinking or how we process thoughts that develop habits or the behavioral patterns we live by. When our thoughts are negative or self-defeating, the choices we make will be, too. You want or need to change, but can't. Why? It's fear. You're not only afraid of the past, but you're also afraid the future won't be any different. Fear will keep you in the same destructive patterns. It is like a crippling disease that paralyzes you from doing the only thing that will make a difference, which is to change what you're doing. To continue to do things the same way and expect a change is the definition of insanity. The Bible says God did not give us a spirit of fear. It comes from the enemy, and God has already defeated him. It also says if we renew our minds to His Word, we will change our old ways. Don't be afraid. Regardless of life's changes, He loves you. *His love and kindness shall not depart from you.* Just receive it. Yield your past, your old ways and patterns to Him. He will change and direct your life to the plan you were created to fulfill, and when we follow His plan, we cannot fail.

MARCH 29

"...nor shall my covenant of peace and completeness be removed, says the Lord, who has compassion on you."
Isaiah 54:10b (AMP)

The first part of verse 10 assures us even though it may look like everything is falling apart, we do not have to be afraid. God loves us and offers us His kindness. In this verse He continues with the blessings of a covenant of peace and His great compassion. Webster's Dictionary defines covenant as, "a solemn, formal, and binding agreement; a written agreement or promise; a contract between two or more parties." The closest thing to a covenant we could relate to would be a written legal contract. However, we know in today's society it doesn't take much to break or even get out of a signed contract. We've all known individuals who don't think anything about breaking their word or promise to us...and...we do the same. "I'll call you tomorrow" or "Let's get together soon" are two examples of phrases we carelessly speak knowing we probably won't do either. Maybe not every time we say them, but our word or signature should mean something. It is hard to imagine less than a hundred years ago a handshake was a legally binding contract.

Nevertheless, God still established a solemn, binding promise to us that He would love us, never leave us, and continually provide for our needs in this life. Peace is certainly something we all want and need. In the original Hebrew language the word peace as it is used in this verse translates into our word prosperity. When the Lord used this word He wasn't referring to our state of mind. He was referring to our provision, our finances, and yet, you and I both know when there isn't enough money to go around at the end of the month, it can certainly disrupt our peace of mind, too.

God knows how to cover our every necessity for living, and He continually confirms it to us through His written Word. Don't be afraid. And you don't have to be afraid to trust God. He will be more than you will ever need for any situation or circumstance you're facing. This verse confirms He has given you His binding agreement to prosper and complete your every need. Why? Because He loves you and *He has great compassion on you.* Remember, you didn't make the covenant...He did! Accept it, and enjoy it.

MARCH 30

"For my thoughts are not your thoughts,
neither are your ways my ways, saith
the Lord. For as the heavens are
higher than the earth, so are my ways
higher than your ways, and my
thoughts than your thoughts.
Isaiah 55:8-9 (KJV)

When I first started to read and gain an understanding of God's Word, I was not encouraged by this verse. I thought it meant because of God's greatness I would never be able to understand His ways or how He wanted things done. And if this were the case, then how could I ever really get to know, please or follow Him? As I continued to learn more about Him and the Word, I soon discovered my interpretation of this verse was really wrong. What made the change? I received true revelation.

For almost thirty years I have let the Lord lead and direct my life as He desires. Many times I've gone through situations that I not only didn't know why they were happening, but I also couldn't understand why God would allow them to happen. However, it was during these critical times that I came to depend on what He promised me in His Word. I learned to take comfort in the fact that my God knew exactly what was happening. The Word says He never leaves me, so no matter what I thought or how difficult it seemed, I knew He was with me, and whatever purpose there was to be achieved, I would accomplish it. In every situation my character was strengthened, and I was better for it. I learned I could trust Him. I also learned I didn't have to be afraid, especially when I didn't know the answer because the great God Almighty did. I learned the key to moving forward with God is sticking with His plan, regardless of what I thought or how I felt. Since He knows the end from the beginning, I would remind myself He is not only God, but He is also my loving Father who has a super plan for my life.

The truth is He is your loving Father, too, and His plan hasn't changed for you, either. Maybe you're going through a hard time in your life? Or you're having a difficult time understanding what is happening? Don't be afraid. God sent His Word to encourage us and bring continued hope. He has all the answers, and they are always for our own good. The Bible says He is always working things out for us—to will and to do His good pleasure in our lives. Now, when those trying times arise, I thank the Lord He has the answers because His thoughts, ways, and plans for me are bigger and deeper than I could ever imagine. Just trust Him. He is bigger, greater, and higher than any circumstance you're going through, too. You'll have guaranteed success, if you stay hooked up with His plan and Word.

MARCH 31

> *"...so is my word that goes out from my mouth:*
> *It will not return to me empty, but will*
> *accomplish what I desire and achieve*
> *the purpose for which I sent it."*
> *Isaiah 55:11 (NIV)*

God makes it very clear in this verse that He doesn't just say and do things without a reason or purpose. He always has a plan, and this plan involves us. He created the world with words. Then He created us to enjoy the good thing He had done, to take dominion over it, and to have fellowship with Him. However, the Bible tells us God's people perish or fail their mission for a lack of knowledge. Education is important, but the Bible says knowledge by itself "puffs up." In other words, regardless of what you think you may know if it doesn't include knowledge of the Word of God and how to take action or literally apply it to your situation, it can cause both physical and spiritual death. When we begin to study who the Word of God says we are, what God planned for us, and how we can receive His promises, we are changed! No longer will you be willing to just sit back and accept what comes your way. You'll learn to not allow the circumstances to dictate your future.

How do you do this? By knowing, speaking, and following His Word. It is relevant and instructional for our day to day living. The Bible tells us how to handle every situation. For example: Are you worried about the economy? God's Word tells of men who continued to give and honor God with their finances during a famine. They received up to a hundred fold return within the same year. Where do you get 100% return on your money in today's investment market? Have you had a bad report from the doctor? Another Bible report tells of a terminally ill woman who had been to many doctors. She not only grew worse, but went bankrupt from their bills. However, she didn't go by what she saw, felt or heard. She believed God, released her faith by taking action, and then was miraculously healed.

Life's troubles don't discriminate. They attack us all. The only difference in reaching the right outcome is the strategy one uses in dealing with them. You need a plan, and the best defense is God's Word. If it worked when He used it, it will have the same force or power for us. Why? The Bible says we belong to God. It also says *His Words would not come back empty*. His Words are "life-giving." This means they have the power to bring change. Don't be afraid. Speak the Word. Whatever you're going through, the written Word deals with every issue, and it gives you the courage to fight without fear. Take action, and apply it. It is *His purpose,* and *it will accomplish what it has been sent to do.*

APRIL 1

> *"You shall establish yourself on righteousness—*
> *right, in conformity with God's will and*
> *order; you shall be far even from the*
> *thought of oppression or destruction,*
> *for you shall not fear; and from terror,*
> *for it shall not come near you."*
> *Isaiah 54:14 (AMP)*

How can one be free from the thought of terror and destruction when all you hear and see on the news today is a constant reminder of the occurring evil in the world? Is God aware that sons, daughters, husbands, and wives are fighting even now for their lives, our sacred freedoms, and world safety? The truth is God is very much aware, and He is with them. He is also aware of the ever increasing evil and the men who try to remove our precious freedoms by enforcing their man-made laws and doctrines upon us. Their goals are to keep individuals in fear and bondage to them. This is what makes this verse so relevant to the day and hour we are living in.

God is a righteous God, and He wants us to be in a right standing position with Him. This verse states we have the power to *establish ourselves on righteousness,* but how is this possible? It's possible if we choose to make the Lord the ruler of our life, and we choose to act in accord with divine or moral law. When we choose the Lord, righteousness is part of the package. You can't work hard enough or long enough or join the right church or organization to get it. The truth is you can't earn righteousness! It is a free gift, and with it comes all the other benefits...peace, joy, safety.

Have you ever purchased an item, maybe cosmetics or a fragrance, and when you bought the main product you got a "free gift" with your purchase? You didn't have to clean their counter, take the sales clerk to lunch or sign up to buy any other product. You just followed the rules, and the free gift was an added bonus. This is how it works with God. When we follow His rules, we get this incredible package—an added bonus—for free! This free gift includes a life without fear, worries and torment, sickness and disease, poverty, and not even a thought of depression or destruction. Why? Because the Word says when you accept His will or plan and become *established on righteousness*, these things will not come near you. Don't be afraid. Believe the Word of the Lord. Choose Him, and His plan. You'll find His free gifts, your benefit package, cannot be compared to anything you'll receive in this world.

> *"Behold, they shall surely gather together,*
> *but not by me: whosoever shall gather together*
> *against thee shall fall for thy sake."*
> *Isaiah 54:15 (KJV)*

This Scripture warns us there will be enemies. People, things or events *will gather together to come against us,* and when it states *"they gather"* it also gives the impression there could even be more than one thing come at you at the same time. Maybe you can relate? However, the focus here isn't that the gathering will come. God said we would have tribulation in this world. The real focus in this verse is God is not the source of the trouble, the divorce, the broken dreams, the guilt and shame, the thoughts of suicide, the addictions, the long term illness or terminal diagnosis. This verse clearly states the torments we experience are not from Him. He is not the author of evil. In fact, the Word says that every good and perfect gift comes from our Heavenly Father.

However, God has taken the rap for a lot of horrible things because we didn't know His plan and His Word. For instance, when any destructive force like a tornado, earthquake or flood destroys our lands, we call it an "act of God." This is not the truth. God said when you go through the fire…you won't be burned. When you go through the flood…you won't drown. Why would He put pain on you, and then offer you a way out? Don't these devastating events create fear? God continually repeats He didn't give us a spirit of fear, and He will deliver us out of all our trials.

Some people think God makes them sick to teach them something. If this was true and He was the author of disease, why would He heal at all? God doesn't put sickness or death on us one minute, and then, remember He loves us, so He heals us the next. He doesn't use evil to teach us anything, either. He uses His Word. If He didn't want us to know the truth, why would He have given us the Bible as our instruction manual for daily living?

The Word is clear about the goodness of God. So who does bring the evil? It's the devil—who lies, cheats, kills, steals, and destroys lives. The biggest lie is God's the blame. God's Word says my people perish for a lack of knowledge. If you knew the Word or had a close personal relationship with the Father, you'd never blame Him. Don't be afraid. If you've blamed God for your situations, ask Him to forgive you. He's the only One who can deliver you out of your troubles. This verse promises He will make your enemies fall and remove your every fear.

> *"Why should I fear when evil days come,*
> *when wicked deceivers surround me—"*
> *Psalms 49:5 (NIV)*

This verse could easily be the headlines of any newspaper today. "EVIL DAYS HAVE COME! WICKED DECEIVERS SURROUND US!" Who isn't afraid of what could happen to this world because of evil men—*wicked deceivers*—and their deeds? The September 11, 2001, tragedy affected the entire world. It was an attack from the devil working through men who don't know the truth and bought his lies of hatred and death. As devastating as these attacks were, the devil's ultimate attack is still in full force. This attack is to keep people in fear.

Fear is a powerful, paralyzing, confusing weapon the enemy uses in battle. In some cases it's obvious, but in others, the attack may come in the form of a lost job, illness, repossession of your car or home, bankruptcy, a failed relationship, and so on. All of these are major events that can change the course of one's life, and although these attacks are life altering, they aren't even the devil's real target. The real target is your faith. The devil's number one reason in launching an attack of fear that can cause you to feel utterly devastated, disappointed, and heartbroken is to steal your faith. Why? Because the devil knows God works with our faith. The Bible tells us it is faith that pleases God. You can't be in both fear and faith at the same time. It just doesn't work.

This means you have to choose. "Will I keep my same old thoughts? Will I be afraid when I read the headlines? Will I stay focused on my problems? Or will I make a decision to believe and release my faith according to what God says about the situation in His Word?" God knows the enemy works at our thought life. This is one of the reasons He doesn't start the above verse with bad news, and then try to encourage us at the end. He knows the moment we hear bad news our minds immediately go to the worst case scenario. Those thoughts, if not dealt with, have the potential to create fearful emotions. Because God is our strength, comforter, and deliverer He automatically deals with our thoughts first.

This should be our example of how to overcome fear, too. When you feel fear rising up on the inside of you, you must address it—immediately! Replace and renew your thoughts with God's Word. Don't let your imagination run wild. How can you do this? Stop thinking about how big the problem is, and concentrate on how much bigger God is. Don't be afraid. Read and speak the Word. Faith comes by hearing, and hearing by the Word of God. You'll see for yourself that fear must disappear in the presence of activated faith.

"PRAISE YE the Lord. O give thanks unto the Lord; for he is good: for his mercy endureth for ever."
Psalms 106:1 (KJV)

If you have ever found yourself in a compromising situation and chose the wrong path, you know you need the mercy of God. Mercy is the complete demonstration of God's love and goodness to us because it offers us compassion and forgiveness instead of punishment. David cried out many times for God's mercy and received it throughout his entire life. This is how he could make the above statement, "*His mercy endures or lasts for ever.*"

At times, like most of us, David fell back into doing things his own way. These old ways are habits, and good or bad, we all have them. However, they can be broken. But there is only way we can break our old familiar patterns. That way is we must replace our old thoughts with new ones. We must replace those old habits that keep us in bondage. How do we do this? We first have to change our "approach to be changed" in order to be changed. You might think you can just use positive motivational thinking or you can "will" yourself to change. These methods may seem to work for a season, but they cannot provide the long distance substance for a permanent, lasting change. How many times have you made New Year's resolutions? Don't you keep them for awhile? A very short while? Don't feel bad. We all fall into the same trap. God knew we would not be able to make the needed changes by ourselves. This is why He sent His Word. It frees us from old thoughts, familiar routines, and wrong decisions that continuously lead us down the same destructive path.

Maybe you are discovering, like I did, that the biggest problem you have to overcome is YOU? My problem was my self-talk wasn't good. What's self-talk? Self-talk is what we say to ourselves, and because we've repeated and rehearsed these thoughts for so long, now we actually believe them as truth. Where do these self-talk thoughts come from? Many of them were formed as a child. They come from past experiences or what we hear and see other people say or do. They are formed by our perceptions. Most of them are lies from the enemy. The Bible says he is the father of lies. We can believe him or we can believe our Father God. I learned to change my self-talk to agree with what God said about me…He loved me, He set a great plan in place for me before I was born, He is merciful to me, and if I follow Him, He guarantees me eternal life. He's your Father, too, and His Word is for you, also. Don't be afraid. Learn to change your self-talk by replacing it with His Words. Then without any fear your song will be like David's. "*PRAISE YE THE LORD! He is good, and His mercy will be there for ever.*"

> *"The fear of the Lord is the beginning of wisdom; all who follow his precepts have good understanding. To him belongs eternal praise."*
> *Psalms 111:10 (NIV)*

One of the things that makes the Bible so important and relevant today is it allows us an up-close and personal look into the lives of men and women who faced trials, slavery and bondages, overwhelming debt, death, sickness, terminal diseases, paralysis, war, famine, and other forms of destruction. Yet, they were delivered out of every situation by the hand of God. How did this happen? What did they do to get relief from their burdens? Is this burden removing power still available to us today?

God said in His Word He is the same yesterday, today, and forever. This is really good news. When we see what God has done for others, we know He will do the same for us, too. What made their outcomes successful every time? They found success depended on what this verse states, and that is "*the fear of the Lord is the beginning of wisdom.*" We have learned this *fear* is a holy reverence, an honoring, and worshipping the awesomeness and goodness of God. It is not to be afraid of Him, even when we don't do right. The men and women of old knew in the day of trouble not to run away from God, but to run to God.

Would you like some of your troubles to go away? How can you change your problems if you don't know what to do? Answers…wisdom…isn't this what you really need? These people got their answers because they worshipped and praised God, even in the middle of their crisis. They had relied on Him in their past situations and found He had always been reliable, dependable, trustworthy. In other words, God remained the same. He is faithful. He always does His part, but He also expects us to do ours.

This verse tells us what our part is. We are to *follow His precepts*, then, we'll *have good understanding*. What are His precepts? They are His ways and order of doing things. How can we know the ways of God? He has shown us His ways throughout His Word. It's our responsibility to study and learn them. Do you know His ways? Do you know His Word? Do you even know Him? Don't be afraid. Put away your previous beliefs, doubts, misunderstandings, and anger about God. Open up your heart. Learn the truth in His Word. Ask Him to give you His wisdom for your situation, and then praise Him for good understanding. He alone is every answer you'll ever need.

> *"The works of the Lord are great, sought out of all them that have pleasure therein. His work is honourable and glorious: and his righteousness endureth for ever."*
> *Psalms 111:2-3 (KJV)*

David, the writer of this Psalm, knew God. The Bible tells us he was a man after God's own heart. What exactly does that mean? It means David loved God with his entire being. It also means he loved, "*sought out*" or pondered the *great works of the Lord.* David took pleasure in thinking about all the great deeds the Lord had done for him. He had come to understand that the key to success in every area of his life depended solely on God and his relationship with Him. I emphasize God in this equation because most people, including those who already think they know the Lord, live their lives pretty much the way they want. That is until something happens. This something can be anything from a stubbed toe, broken arm or a life threatening disease. In other words, your problem or crisis could range from an insignificant, minor problem to the most urgent, extreme situation.

David chose to follow God. In verse one of this Psalm, David says he will worship God with his whole heart. Why? Because he had learned when he did things his own way, he usually found himself in a big mess. Ever been there? You suddenly find yourself wondering, "What happened? I mean we had our differences, but weren't we perfect together? Wasn't this supposed to be a sure investment? Where did I go wrong?" God can and does take the worst, most impossible situations and turn them around. He promises to help us, but just getting us out of our messes isn't His #1 plan. He has a better plan. A plan that allows us to see and experience "*how great are His works*, *how glorious are His deeds, and His forever, enduring righteousness*."

David held nothing back from God. Even if he learned it the hard way, he had learned God's plan was so much better than his own. The Bible says if we delight ourselves in the Lord, He gives us the desires of our heart. How do you "delight" yourself in the Lord? You do this by giving Him your whole heart which consists of all your affections and your attention. Are you holding a part of your heart back? Maybe your heart is broken, and you need God to make it whole again? Or maybe life's tragedies have you feeling numb with nothing to give at all? Don't be afraid. God loves you, and His love is forever. Don't reject the very source of love, fulfillment, wisdom, hope, and success for which you've been desperately searching. Be a person after God's own heart. Worship and praise Him for all His great works. You will enter into His presence. When you spend time with Him there, you will find there is healing and pleasure for you, too.

"He has made His wonderful works to be remembered; the Lord is gracious, merciful and full of loving compassion."
Psalms 111:4 (AMP)

Life's events are studied and documented by historians for several important reasons. One, they record life's events so we will remember them. Two, they hope to teach us from past historical occurrences, what not to repeat again. Three, they also hope we'll learn that if or when we're faced with a similar event, that we'll now have a different view, so we'll know what to do. History not only gives us knowledge, but insight. It helps us set up checks and balances for a better future. It teaches us how to recognize signs of caution or warning, so we will be prepared to slow down and take another look. Such preparation may include drawing an imaginary line of safety. This safety or boundary line can be paralleled to a builder's plumb line. He sets up his original starting point, draws the line tight, and then releases it. The straight line that is created is truth. Everything else must be lined up with it for the design to fit and work together properly.

God, through His Word, did the same thing. God's Word is our plumb line. It is truth. It is the standard we use to line up our affairs. It is the moral balance that offers us the ultimate living experience. The Bible, God's recorded Word, is our history and heritage. It clearly lets us know we don't have to be afraid. It offers us hope, even when we sin—which means we miss the mark—that God has already provided a way of escape for us. When historians write about an event, it's based on their own limited knowledge or the information available at the time. The Holy Spirit, on the other hand, wrote the Word of God. By divine order He gave men the words to write. This is the reason we can trust that we have all the facts. We can also trust that those facts are accurately recorded, as well.

When the recorded Word of God says demons are cast out, people are healed, the dead are raised, water is turned into wine, leprosy is reversed, you can walk across the bottom of the sea on dry ground, you can be in a fiery furnace and not get burned, you can sleep among wild lions and not be eaten, the meal barrel will not run dry, and a small bottle of oil can bring you out of debt…**you can believe it!** This verse confirms, for history's sake, *His wonderful works*. His miracles were recorded, "*remembered*," so we can see there is nothing too big or too hard for God. Don't be afraid. His mercy and His loving compassion are endless. Do you need a miracle in your life? Trust His Word. You won't be disappointed.

APRIL 8

"He has given food and provision to those who reverently and worshipfully fear Him; He will remember His covenant for ever and imprint it [on His mind]."
Psalms 111:5 (AMP)

This Scripture is one of many that focus on God being our total source. Because we're supposed to depend on God and His Word I've heard it said, "Christians are weak. They can't make it on their own. They need a crutch. That's why God isn't for everyone." However, nothing could be further from the truth. Today, as in the past, Christians from around the world are being imprisoned or losing their lives because of their public confession of the Gospel. Does this sound like the actions of a weakling or cowards? God loves us, and He wants to be actively involved in every part of our life, so He can share it with us. His promise or covenant includes making provision for all we need. Even though this verse covers our physical requirements like food, clothing, and shelter, God is so much bigger than the physical. He knows what we need from the inside out.

When I made the decision to let God lead and change my life, He introduced me to "ME." I thought I knew myself, but God knew me so much better. I thought I was in charge of my life. Instead, I learned my past was in charge. Past hurts and emotional scars that had not been dealt with and were now hidden deep in my heart were still dictating the way I thought, what I said, and what I did. The same old thinking will produce the same old response. Now, do you see how and why we can continue to make the same mistakes? The truth is I wasn't in charge at all. Maybe you feel the same way? Do you put on a front, acting like everything is under control, when emotionally you're falling apart? Are your decisions still based upon hurt feelings? Are you reacting or over-reacting due to unhealthy emotions that are the result of wounded relationships, disappointments or rejections? Why battle with the same issues when God provided you a new and better life? Only you can decide to depend on God's every provision, but you'll find He'll heal the issues of your heart and restore you to His original plan.

The real truth is without God we're all weak. It's those weaknesses that cause so many to turn to an outer substance as their coping crutch. However, because of His loving covenant we are made to be strong. He not only provides food and our most basic needs, but food for our inner wholeness, as well. Don't be afraid. You won't have to do this on your own. God will turn your dark nights into bright days. Every time you take a bite of food you can be reminded and thankful that *imprinted on HIS mind* is every provision you'll ever need for your spirit, soul, and body. With every part complete, you'll truly know how it feels to be full.

"Who is among you who [reverently] fears the Lord, who obeys the voice of His servant; yet who walks in darkness and deep trouble and has no shining splendor [in his heart]? Let him rely on, trust and be confident in the name of the Lord, and let him lean upon and be supported by His God."
Isaiah 50:10 (AMP)

Whether this Scripture was penned by David, Isaiah, Jeremiah, Moses, Daniel, Joshua or any of the others it repeats the same message. God will change any circumstance, make any provision, slay any enemy, and turn your darkest hour into the glorious light. Why? It's because of His covenant which promises He will never leave you. He is your loving Father. He is your God. In this verse Isaiah offers an answer to all who have believed or feared God, but seem to have no victory in their life. He asks if their troubles are over taking them or it seems dark or depressing. In other words, are they able to see the light at the end of their tunnel? We could ask ourselves the same question today. With all the pressures and stress in your daily living have you felt overwhelmed? Maybe you have even questioned if or where God has been during your trial?

Isaiah offers us a solution, and one that builds hope so we can make the needed changes. The Word of the Lord asks, "Are you *reverently* worshipping and honoring God?" If you are, then you're doing the right thing, and because you're doing the right thing or you're doing your part by relying and trusting in God, you don't need to feel discouraged or be afraid. If it still appears dark, it's only for a season. The Bible says, darkness may endure for a night, but joy comes in the morning. Isaiah confirms our final action for victory is to *completely lean upon, rely, and trust in the Name of the Lord*. God will *support* you. When I first read this, I didn't think the word *support* could adequately reflect the MIGHTY POWER of God. However, Webster's Dictionary defines support as, "to carry; to endure bravely; to uphold or defend; to pay the cost; to hold up or serve as a foundation; to keep from fainting, yielding or losing courage; to comfort." Now with this understanding, we can all be confident we can lean upon God's support.

Reverently fear God. Obey the Word of the Lord. You'll find you have the same confidence. Don't be afraid. God loves you, and this verse encourages us to be *confident in the Name of the Lord*. God, in His *supporting* you, will keep you from fainting or losing courage in your darkest hour. Just trust Him, regardless of the length of time involved. He will give you the victory, and bring you into the light of a new day. Remember, it's His covenant promise to you!

APRIL 10

> *"...to say to the captives, 'Come out,' and to those in darkness, 'Be free!'..."*
> *Isaiah 49:9 (NIV)*

The King James Version of this Scripture uses the word prisoner in place of captives, but both words create an image of someone behind bars. Although this verse could definitely comfort the prisoner, it also has the power to reach much further than a jail cell. The truth is, regardless of where we are in life, God uses His Word to not only bring revelation, but deliverance to our total being.

So many today live within the prison system. However, there is an even larger majority who live "imprisoned," but their jail cell doesn't have bars. How is this possible? How can you be in jail without bars? It means they may be free to walk around, but the fear of someone discovering who they really are or what they have done keeps them in bondage. It is like a heavy weight they drag around with them day after day, month after month, year after year. They are prisoners to their own thoughts and fears. They live in fear suffering from guilt and shame for a crime, whether it's real or imagined that was committed a long time ago. Worrying and afraid, "If anyone really knew what they were like, would they want anything to do with them?" Fear, guilt, and shame are great jailers. They will keep you "boxed in" to your cell for as long as you let them.

God's Word makes it clear that we all have sinned and come short of His Glory. The word sin means to miss the mark, and yet, in spite of our sin God's Word confirms He still loves us. He will forgive us when we ask, and He will never leave us. He wants us free...inside and out. However, sin does have natural consequences. When we break the laws of the land, there will be penalties, but God's truth still remains. Even if you are serving a sentence behind real bars, don't think that God has forgotten you or He doesn't love you. He loves you very much. He doesn't like the sin or the crimes, but He never quits loving you and guiding you to victory. His plan for your life has not changed. Nothing can stop you from having a loving relationship with your Father, not even those bars. You can *be free*, and live in peace from within. Remember, His promises are for everyone.

If you still pack around baggage from your past, make a decision to let God set you free. God's Word is filled with testimonies of individuals who made poor decisions and messed up, but God delivered and restored them back to the plan He had for them. Don't be afraid. Don't run from God...run to God. It's not too late for you. Ask for forgiveness, and turn from your darkness. His plan says you can "*Be free!*"

APRIL 11

> *"This is what the Lord says—he who made you, who formed you in the womb, and who will help you: Do not be afraid, O Jacob, my servant Jeshurun, whom I have chosen."*
> *Isaiah 44:2 (NIV)*

The Prophet Isaiah delivered this Word to God's chosen people, Israel. Jacob was the grandson of Abraham, the man God chose to receive His original covenant. Jacob came from a great lineage of godly men. However, he cheated, lied, and tricked people most of his life. In fact, Jacob means trickster or deceiver. When Jacob's father, Isaac, was about to die, Jacob even deceived him by dressing up as his older twin brother, so he would receive the blessing. After this happened Jacob feared his brother would kill him, so he left his father's house and started a journey that would change his life forever. While on the road one night, He met the Lord in a vision. It was a rough night, but by morning, God said, "I'm changing your name to Israel, I will bless you, and I will make your offspring great." When this verse says *O Jacob*, it is really referring to the nation of Israel.

One of the most revealing things about this Scripture is even though there was a period in Jacob's life where he went down the wrong path, God still knew him… *made him…formed him in the womb.* God knew Jacob before his inception, and regardless of what he'd done, *God would help him.* The Bible tells us what God does for one He'll do for us all. The Word also says He knew each one of us before the foundation of the world, and He called us by our name while we were still in the secret places of our mother's womb. This is life changing news if you were born in what the world considers unfavorable circumstances. Being born to an unwed mother or out of a crime like rape or incest doesn't make you any less valuable to God. Just because your parents or others called you an accident or said you were not wanted, doesn't make it so, either. The truth is there are no surprise births to God! There are no accidents or mistakes to God! There are no "just blobs of tissue until you are born" with God!

Verses like this one give you confidence and power to throw off any past hurt, rejection or shame, and lift up your head to the Father who always wanted you. He loved you then. He loves you now. You are His child. Are you ready to lay down sorrow, hate, blame of others and God for your situation, and accept Him? Can you ask God to forgive you…as you forgive others? Just as He told Jacob or His people Israel *do not be afraid*, He is saying the same thing to you…"Don't be afraid. My plan for you has not changed. If I could change and bless Jacob, I can change and bless you. I formed you, and I will help you." Trust the Lord. Let Him change you into your destiny. You'll receive the blessing of the Lord, too.

"Fear not, nor be afraid [in the coming violent upheavals]; have I not told it to you from of old and declared it? And you are my witnesses! Is there a God besides me? There is no other Rock; I know not any."
Isaiah 44:8 (AMP)

Isaiah served as God's prophet and mouthpiece under the authority of four different kings. During this time he foretold and witnessed many battles against the people of God. He warned and encouraged them of the Lord's plans. Verses like this one still ring true to us today. Not only because of the *violent upheaval* the world witnessed in America on September 11, 2001, but because of all the other tragic events that have continued to happen around the world since that time. However, God's Word is clear. He said there would be wars and rumors of war, but we do not have to be afraid.

In the Old Testament when God performed miracles or delivered His people out of impossible circumstances, the men of old always constructed an altar of rock or stone as a memorial. Each altar was named in honor of the blessing God had bestowed upon them. This memorial was a visual reminder of the "living" God, and His covenant of provision and protection to them. It would also serve as a future witness and reminder of God's faithfulness and power to all those who were yet to come. This verse confirms He is the One, true, and living God. If there were others, would He not know? Would He not tell us?

God says, "*I know not one other God.*" Today many are confused by the different religions. All of course believe each is the right one. However, Christianity was never designed to be a religion. God isn't about man-made doctrines, rituals or traditions. He is about relationship, and He can offer us a relationship with Him because He is alive. What other established religion or faith today has a living person who allows you to be in their presence? Or promises you a two way conversation? Most religions have had men who formed traditions or rules according to their opinions or what they believed, and they have since died. The only evidence they were ever a part of humanity is their grave.

God's Word says, "*In the beginning was God. He was, is, and always will be.*" God's Word is the final authority. Don't be afraid. God wants to reveal His plans to you, both present and future. We have a God who not only created the universe and everything in it, but you and me, too. Why settle for a substitute when you can have the real thing? When you can have a real relationship with a very real and living God? Choose God. *There is no other Rock*!

> *"I, even I, am he who blots out your transgressions, for my own sake, and remembers your sins no more."*
> *Isaiah 43:25 (NIV)*

I hear people ask God to, "Take my sin or my sickness or take away my smoking or drinking or take this abusive relationship or tormenting kids or just take whatever it is that keeps them from total peace." But I ask you, "What would God do with these things in Heaven?" We know in Heaven there is no sin, sickness, disease, poverty, stress, pressure, worries or torment. It's only on earth that these very problems try to plague us on a daily basis, and they are like plagues. In fact, Webster's Dictionary defines a plague as, "to smite, infest or afflict with or as a disease, calamity or natural evil; to cause worry or distress; to disturb or annoy persistently." Doesn't this describe your problems? Aren't they annoying, worrisome, distressful, sickening, and persistent? The Bible says trials will come, but we, through God, have the victory. So how do you get the victory?

The first thing is to check your relationship with the Father. Do you have one? If not, understand you can't win these battles on your own. Ask Him to forgive you for your sins. Right here is where most people fail. Their pride still has them believing they can fix it by themselves. Or if they are ready to accept Him and decide to make a change, the enemy brings guilt and shame upon them for their past mistakes. Guilt and shame want you to believe God won't forgive you. These are all lies. The Word says, "Pride comes before a fall," and the above verse confirms that God is the very One *who blots out*, wipes away, and totally removes our sin as though it never happened. God is the only One who can give you a fresh start. If He can forget your past, don't you think it might be a good time for you to do the same?

Through God's Word He has given us the authority and ability to be free of those things that keep us from walking in victory. God isn't a taker. He's the giver. The Bible says He's the giver of life and life more abundantly. He won't "take" your problems from you, but if you will surrender yourself to Him, His Word, His plan, and "give" your problems up, He fulfills His Word. Don't be afraid. You can trust Him. Your Father says it is "*I, even I*," who is quick to save, deliver, heal, forgive, and remember your sins no more!

APRIL 14

> *"Put me in remembrance—remind Me of your merits; let us plead and argue together. Set forth your case that you may be justified—proved in the right."*
> *Isaiah 43:26 (AMP)*

At first glance this seems like an unusual verse. Why would God want to hear anything we had to say? After all, isn't He God? Isn't He always right? Besides, what kind of an argument could I present before God that would change things? The truth is God wants us to have the kind of relationship with Him that allows us the freedom to speak what is in our hearts and minds. I mean, whom are we kidding? He knows what's in there anyway. However, the real purpose of this verse is twofold. It challenges us to not only really know God our Father, but to also know His Word. Then, in the midst of any trial or crisis, when we quote what His Word already says, we're actually *putting Him in remembrance* of what He has already promised to do. Does this mean God forgets what He has said? Not hardly, but He wants us to not forget it, either.

When an attorney prepares a case for court, he doesn't just look at his client's current facts. He also investigates or researches past closed files in order to find cases that might relate to or be similar in nature to the one he's trying. His goal is to find other cases in which the courts decided favorably for the same type of defense he's trying to present. If there is a past case, when he goes to court he will present case number XX, this person vs. this person, in the year XXXX for more evidence as his supporting arguments. Why would a past case have the potential to become a powerful tool for his client's victory today? Because the facts have already been presented, a decision was made, and now, it is written! Sometimes, this piece of evidence alone can provide the additional proof or information a judge or jury needs to reach the same verdict.

In this verse God tells us we can use the same process. For instance, depending on what we are up against, we might want to remind Him of the case of Daniel vs. the Lions; or Moses vs. Pharaoh; or David vs. Goliath; or Elijah vs. the Prophets of Baal. Without fear Moses and Abraham both argued with God, reminded Him of His Word, and won their cases. Their key defense was they knew what He had promised through His covenant, and they had a relationship with Him. Do you know the Word? Do you know what God has promised you? Don't be afraid. He loves it when we "know" the truth. Present your case. God gives us permission to remind Him of His own Words and deeds. With His established covenant promises you will achieve the same victory He planned for all His children. How can you be sure? "It, too, is written!"

> *"Behold, I am doing a new thing; now it springs forth; do you not perceive and know it, and will you not give heed to it? I will even make a way in the wilderness and rivers in the desert."*
> *Isaiah 43:19 (AMP)*

One of the most difficult things we go through in our lifetime is change. Even when change is a positive thing like getting married, having your first child, accepting a big promotion or moving into an exciting new career, change can still be a difficult transition. Why? It's fear. We fear the unknown. Personally, I enjoy change. My personality is one that likes new challenges, but what I really like is variety…doing new things, going new places, and meeting new people. However, there have been a few times when I experienced changes that were not real comfortable. That is in the beginning anyway. What made the difference? I didn't recognize or *perceive* God was "*doing a new thing.*" Consequently, I didn't give heed to the new thing, either. How did I miss it? I had become so involved in the day to day that I allowed myself to get distracted from the plan.

This is how the enemy works. Even on the battlefield, if you can divert the attention of your enemy, you can draw them into an ambush, split up their forces or weaken them in some way. But God is always our defense, so we can stay on the offense. This Scripture says God will "*even make a way in the wilderness.*" This means *even* if it seems like you are in the middle of nowhere, God has a plan. Or if you're weary from the "heat" of the battle, God has a plan. Or maybe you've messed up and can't figure out which way to go, God still has the plan. He knows the right path to get you from where you are to where you need to be.

Nobody crosses untamed or unknown territory without a guide. It should be the same for us. God will be our guide. He will lead us and walk with us through the unknown times and life's trials. The key is to stay close to Him. When we're in fellowship with Him, we'll know when we're getting ready to make a move. How will we know? God says He will tell us beforehand. Then He asks us if we *perceive* or recognize it? What's got your attention? Are you so focused on your turmoil that it has become bigger than God? Maybe it's the day to day blahs that keep you from pressing into the bigger plan? The truth is even when it seems like you're in the wilderness or the dark, backside of a desert, God says, "*I will make a way; I will make rivers.*" Don't be afraid. And don't be afraid of the changes. You'll see, just like I did, that the "new" plan is awesome. After all, aren't *rivers* (not just one) *in the desert* an amazing, refreshing, and welcomed sight?

APRIL 16

> *"...And call upon me in the day of trouble: I will deliver thee, and thou shalt glorify me."*
> *Psalms 50:15 (KJV)*

Throughout His Word God repeats this same message to call on Him for help. It must have been a problem for them, as well as for us today. The truth is all of us, at different stages during our life, could use some help. The world offers many different programs for self-help. There are 7 Basic Steps for this, 10 Positive ways to do that, the 12 Steps to Recovery, and so on. Do these programs help? Maybe, to some degree, but are you truly delivered from your situation after participating in them? It's true we may feel some relief or think we're better, but are we totally free? Probably not! God would not continue to tell us to *call upon Him* if all these other options worked.

God's rescuing plan involves two steps. I call...He delivers. Now you might be thinking, "Get real. It can't be that easy." I realize when we've been up against the same obstacles for any length of time, it doesn't seem easy. But nowhere in the Scriptures does it say, "I will deliver you," and then add a list of exceptions or reasons why it won't work for you. Reasons like you brought the trouble on yourself, you've had it for more than six months, you're from the wrong side of town, you're too old or too young or your whole family is this way. Then there is the biggest reason of all...you don't feel or think you deserve anything better. God's Word is clear. It's simple. It's for everyone who will believe it, and then do it!

You call...He delivers! So, why don't you call on the Lord? What's stopping you? And don't use the feeling guilty excuse about asking Him for help when there are so many starving children in the world or other major traumas. Do you think He can only deal with one thing at a time? Do you know how much He loves you? Do you know your problem doesn't have to be part of your destiny? Maybe you're afraid? God's Word tells us many times to call on Him, but even more times to not be afraid. Why? Because He knows there is no situation, trial, betrayal, crisis, broken heart or act of terror that is too big for Him. We just need to get Him in the picture. There is an old saying, "Don't put off until tomorrow what you can do today." I encourage you with the same words. Don't delay your freedom any longer. Don't be afraid. Throw out the words "What if" or "What about" from your vocabulary. Just trust God. Follow His program, and believe. No matter what...as long as you're with Him...the outcome is guaranteed success.

> *"Every valley shall be exalted, and every mountain and hill shall be made low: and the crooked shall be made straight, and the rough places plain."*
> *Isaiah 40:4 (KJV)*

If you have ever driven up the side of a mountain you know the roads can be fairly narrow, winding, and steep. It takes much concentration, not only on what you're doing, but on the other drivers, as well. Sometimes, you don't feel any safer on the inside going up than you do on the outside coming down. Your options, if not watchful, can be the same. You either damage the car on the rocks or you fall off the edge. However, mountainous driving isn't the only place that driving can be dangerous. Our city streets, when you suddenly hit a pothole that shakes you and your entire vehicle, can also be damaging. You think, "Where did that come from?" or "How did I not see it coming?"

Life's troubles hit us the same way. It seems everything is fine one day, and then BOOM! You hit a major pothole of life. The doctor's report is bad, the kids are kicked out of school, your company lays you off, your spouse or significant other leaves, the checking account is overdrawn, and so on. The trials are endless, and these are only a few that can and will shake your entire being. Fear grips your heart. You wonder, "How will I ever get out of this one?"

In this verse God states *He will raise up the low places like the valleys, and He will make the mountains and the hills flat.* If He's willing to make the road flat, do you think He would leave it rough and rocky? Or do you think He would only make the road available to certain travelers? No, He won't! He tells us He will make the roads smooth...*the rough places plain.* If you have ever driven for a long time on a difficult highway, one that has major construction, repairs or lane closings, then you know what a relief it is to come to a clear, straight stretch of road. You can take a deep breath, sit back, and relax. Now driving becomes easy and fun.

This is how God wanted our journey to be in life. Will obstacles appear out of nowhere or difficult times pop up on our highway? Yes, they will, but the key in safely and successfully reaching the goal is to let Him do the driving for us. He will make all the roads level and smooth. Why does He do this? He loves us, and He created us to live a glorious and abundant life. Don't be afraid. His plan allows us to enjoy the ride. His Word guarantees He will repair and level out even your roughest road, so you're assured of reaching your final destination.

APRIL 18

> *"He gives power to the faint; and to them that have no might he increaseth strength."*
> *Isaiah 40:29 (KJV)*

The Old Testament records the history of the Israelites and their struggles against good and evil. They had been persecuted for their faith in God, and yet, at times were so disobedient to God's plan that they put themselves in situations which caused them much pain and even danger. In this verse Isaiah encourages one and all to not become weary. Instead, they should ask or call on God who would strengthen even the weakest, most feeble one.

Making changes isn't something that comes easy to most people, and the longer you've done something the same way or the longer you've endured hardship the more difficult it is to even want to change. It doesn't matter whether the change is good for you or not. It takes work to change, and when you are already feeling like you are at the end of your rope, it seems easier to just go along with the program or give up. However, you and I both know that giving up never solves or changes anything. You need answers, and God's Word has the answers. With God you'll find that when you are at your weakest, He will not only give you *more power* to fight your enemy, but also *more strength* to be able to resist temptation. No matter how long or how great the need is He will be our strength. The NIV translation says, "He multiplies our strength and power and makes it abound."

Are you fighting a battle that seems to be getting the best of you? Have you had long term health issues? Or maybe you're discouraged because you've had to care for someone with long term health problems? Are you struggling to make ends meet…again? Maybe it's been bad for so long, you're just tired and weary of the battle? Sick, broke, devastated, tormented, alone, and afraid…"Does it ever end?" The Word says we will have trials, but it also assures us WITH GOD we will have the victory through them.

The Word also says what the devil intended for evil, God will turn to good for those who love Him and are called according to His purpose. This means you. Don't be afraid. You can turn everything over to the Lord. When you feel like, "I can't go one step further,"…**don't quit.** Ask Him to increase your power and strength. This verse confirms He will give us what we need. Trust Him. Accept His love. Remember, nothing is too difficult for Him.

APRIL 19

"But they that wait upon the Lord shall renew their strength; they shall mount up with wings as eagles; they shall run, and not be weary; and they shall walk, and not faint."
Isaiah 40:31 (KJV)

Once again Isaiah encourages the children of Israel with the promises of God. He instructs us to *wait on the Lord*, but what exactly does this mean? Webster's Dictionary defines the word wait as, "to watch; to stay in place in readiness or expectation; to look forward expectantly; a state or attitude of watchfulness and expectancy." In other words, God wants us to expect, look forward to, watch, and not be afraid to hope in Him for our every need in our future.

When we look to Him, all these other benefits belong to us. He says *He will renew our strength.* We will have renewed energy. Not only to walk without fainting, but to run. Today's exhausting pace requires one to do just that—run. From the stay at home mom to the top level executive everyone has a full schedule. Parents juggle their work schedules with all the extra-curricular activities of their children. Between the soccer, baseball, football, basketball, cheerleading, band, choir, chess club, dance lessons, and drama practices the kids need Day-Timers. Do you meet yourself coming and going? Wouldn't you like to have the energy of your youth? God says *He will renew your strength.*

In this verse God compares us to the eagle. Look at their flight patterns. They soar at heights and speeds like no other bird. Why? Because they have learned when you combine a specific altitude with a set speed, they no longer have all the responsibility of doing the work. Now with minimal effort the air currents help lift and carry them along their way. This is how it works for us with God's plan. When we follow His plan—His way, we find things move along smoothly because we aren't doing all the work, either. God's plan has always been for us to live victorious and abundant lives. This means we can run our race and not be weary or faint along the way. Sound too good to be true? Ask the eagle if the path selected for him to fly sounds too good to be true. He doesn't argue with how he reaches his destination. He just enjoys it! Don't be afraid. God loves you. He wants you to enjoy your designated journey, as well. Put your hope in Him. Wait…watch…then expect your strength and energy to be renewed.

APRIL 20

> *"I will cry to God most high, Who performs on my behalf and rewards me—Who brings to pass [His purposes] for me and surely completes them."*
> *Psalms 57:2 (AMP)*

If we took a survey today and asked the general public if they knew what they were called to do or what their specific purpose or destiny was, they wouldn't know what you were talking about. Or if they did know, most of them would confess they didn't have a clue what they were supposed to be doing with their lives. This is how most people feel. They really don't have any idea. The King James Version of this verse says, "…unto God that performeth all things for me." God wants us to know He has a plan—a purpose for each of us. We have been assigned a destiny to be fulfilled. Webster's Dictionary defines the word destiny to mean, "a predetermined course of events; to decree beforehand; to designate, assign or dedicate in advance; to direct, devise or set apart for a specific purpose or place." If you have ever been told you were an accident or a mistake or you would never amount to anything…this verse should change your entire life. God is the One who directs our course and leads us in the path we should go because He developed beforehand our predetermined course.

No one, not even your parents can keep you from the plan God has for you. However, there is someone who can. YOU! You can be your own worst enemy. Sometimes we don't need the devil lying to us about who we are because we think and talk negatively about ourselves without any outside help. Why do we sabotage ourselves? Fear is at the root of those lies. Fear you don't measure up or fear that you will never be successful. The only way to overcome low self-esteem is to read the Word and get a new vision of who God says you are. You are not a failure. With God all things are possible. You must change the mental picture you have of yourself, and replace it with what God says about you. If you have been in the habit of calling yourself names, bad-mouthing or putting yourself down…QUIT IT! You are made in His image. Are you telling God He's nothing or no good, too?

Read and apply the Word to every area of your life. Changes will occur, and God will unveil His exciting plans for your future. Don't be afraid. *He will bring to pass and surely complete his purposes for you.* Let Him reveal His plan…you'll love it. It might seem big at first, but He will break it down into bite size steps. There is nothing more thrilling and fulfilling than discovering and then being able to live out your own "predetermined" course.

"He will send from heaven and save me from the slanders and reproaches of him who would trample me down or swallow me up, and put him to shame. Selah [pause, and calmly think of that]! God will send forth His mercy and loving kindness and His truth and faithfulness."
Psalms 57:3 (AMP)

If you've ever questioned what God's intentions were toward you, this verse should help clear up any of your doubts. God's plan of protection is a better security plan than any bodyguard or today's super heroes could provide. Even if Clark Kent was in the exact location at the precise time you needed help—plus a phone booth was on site for him to jump into and then return as Superman—his services couldn't compare to an Almighty God. Besides, our phone booths are no longer what they used to be, so Mr. Superman might find himself hard up for a dressing room. Then what?

God says, "*He will send from heaven*" the assistance we need…anywhere…any time. God sees everything. In fact, the Word says His eyes go back and forth throughout the whole earth. He never sleeps or slumbers. Nothing escapes His watchful eye which includes the outcome for anyone who slanders or tries to bring a reproach against us. What is reproach? It is when someone tries to blame, disgrace or discredit another. It is false accusations or any plot or intent to destroy or tear someone down, whether it's personal or professional. But God, your defender and deliverer, promises to take care of anyone who slanders, disgraces, walks upon or tries to take you down.

Maybe you know how it feels to suffer reproach? If you can relate then this verse should encourage you. God actually turns the table. The shame they intended for you is now going to come upon them. God developed this protection for us to drive away fear, especially the fear of man's words. God never wanted us to be dependent on mankind, but to be solely dependent on Him. Don't be afraid. God loves you. He created you out of a heart of love. Why would He want to see you miserable, in despair or being mistreated? The truth is He wouldn't. Another thing this verse makes clear is God's character. He is compassionate, merciful, loving, kind, truthful, and faithful. In other words, God can be trusted for your over all well being. There is no reason for you to be afraid of your circumstances or what others may say or do. You not only have His Word on it, but you also have His help from Heaven to guarantee His promises.

"Be merciful and gracious to me, O God, merciful and gracious to me; for my soul takes refuge and finds shelter and confidence in You; yes, in the shadow of Your wings will I take refuge and be confident until calamities and destructive storms are passed."
Psalms 57:1 (AMP)

When the attacks and trials of life come, one of the hardest things to deal with is what goes on in our minds. Asking all those questions of "why" or "how" or "if." We mentally continue to rehearse each situation, past or present, which causes feelings of guilt, shame, and then regret to grow out of control. These "thought" dialogues are not only negative, but they're extremely self-destructive. If they're left unattended, they become a powerful, steady, underlying current of mental torment. These tormenting thoughts are caused by fear, and once fear gets a root, it's very difficult to see a way out. Quickly your emotions move from worry and anxiety to doubt and despair. Once you're here, your thoughts can turn from even trying to find a solution to "What's the point!" Maybe you've been there? I tell you on God's authority there is a way out. There is hope. *You can be confident until your calamities and destructive storms pass.*

How do you find this place of confidence? This verse says "*my soul*" *takes refuge, finds shelter or a safe place, and confidence in you.* David, the writer of this verse, learned that in order to find a safe place and regain confidence you must renew your soul—mind, will, and emotions—with the Word of God. The Bible says we are to renew our thinking with the Word of God. Why? Because His ways and thoughts are much higher than ours and He has all the answers. When David asks for mercy, he is asking God to be lenient with His treatment, to be compassionate, to show him favor, and to turn his distressful situation into a fortunate one.

Do you need God's mercy in your distress? Ask. God's offer is for you, too. When David was the closest to God, *in the shadow of His wings*, he laid down his fears and trusted in the delivering power of *a merciful and gracious* God. Maybe you've let your mind, will, and emotions get beat up during your storm? Maybe you're still rehearsing hurts and wounds from twenty years ago? Haven't you tried everything you know to do? Don't be afraid. Renew your thoughts. Let go of fear. Trust God to be your refuge and shelter. Cast down any thoughts that bring defeat because they're not from God. *In the shadow of His wings* you, too, will find the storms have passed, and you can confidently stand in the light and hope of a brand new day.

"For your mercy and loving kindness are great, reaching to the heavens, and your truth and faithfulness to the clouds."
Psalms 57:10 (AMP)

When we read these words in Scripture again and again, it is important to understand not only what God is saying to us, but also why He continues to repeat what He's saying. I have counseled for many years, and the biggest issue with individuals is they refuse to let go of their pasts. Why is this a big problem? Because it also meant they wouldn't allow themselves to receive help from God for a better and more productive future. I felt very sorry for them. Their lives could have been totally changed. I would ask God for the answers to help them, and I would also ask, "Why? Why won't they let themselves receive your goodness for a brand new start?" The Lord showed me there were two main reasons. One, they were afraid of Him because they didn't know Him. Two, they didn't feel they deserved *His mercy, loving kindness, faithfulness* or forgiveness because of their limited view or perception of themselves.

During these sessions I would try to share with them His goodness and all He's done in my life. The Bible says what God does for one He will do for everyone. However, what can you do when you offer someone a gift, and they won't reach out and take it? This is what God has done throughout time. He offers, and through unbelief, low self-worth, and an ignorance of His Word or truth, we reject it. What do you believe? Is your past keeping you from the best thing that could ever happen to you? God keeps repeating verses like this one to convince us He will have mercy on us, what He says in His Word is the truth, and He will be faithful to complete what He has said. In other words, without fail He will always love us, tell us the truth about our situations, and then help us get out of the trouble we are in.

I could give you an envelope with a million dollars in it, but if you won't open it or receive it, what good would it do? You might be thinking, "Well I'd take a million dollars." Let me ask you this, "Why would you settle for only a million, when your Father owns the universe?" Now we're back to the number one reason —you don't know your Dad. Only you can decide to receive all that God has for you. Don't be afraid. Lay down your past, your pride, your old beliefs, and receive this huge loving gift that *reaches all the way to the heavens—to the clouds*. His love, kindness, faithfulness, and provision are immeasurable. They have always been there for you. Just reach out, and receive it.

> *"He hath remembered his covenant for ever, the word which he commanded to a thousand generations."*
> *Psalms 105:8 (KJV)*

God, in His infinite wisdom, knew that when mankind was in the heat of the battle they would have doubts. Have you ever wondered if God really knew what you were going through? Does He know where you are? Does He truly care? God knew those nagging thoughts of doubt and unbelief would appear. He also knew we would even question if He was going to help us. Wasn't He right? Haven't you ever asked, "Where are you God?" Unfortunately we all have. However, this verse in His written Word confirms *He hath remembered* the promises He made to us through our forefathers, which means we don't have to be afraid.

In the Old Testament when two different tribes or groups of people made a covenant with one another, it meant you didn't deal with one group without taking on all those they were in covenant with, too. If your tribe was good at farming, but weak in battle, your goal would be to find a warrior tribe to agree with you in covenant. The two would compliment and benefit each other. An enemy tribe would have to think again about the risks before they would attack.

I've heard powerful testimonies of missionaries in Africa who received the chief's staff as a gift. This was his symbol of authority and covenant with them. As these men continued their missions work throughout the jungles, there were many different occasion when other tribes tried to attack them. However, they would raise up this staff…their symbol of covenant. Each time, at the sight of the staff, the enemy tribes realized they weren't just fighting the missionaries. Now they would have to fight all those who were in covenant with them, too. This sign of covenant, their staff, protected them time after time.

God's Word, His promise to us, is the covenant that protects us. When we are fighting a battle, we're taught to speak or lift up His Word. This is the ultimate "Chief's" staff. It's a shield against the enemy's blows, and it delivers us from the battle. Don't be afraid. God sees and knows the difficulty you're in, but do you know the covenant He has already put into place just for you? Do you use the Word as your shield and defender during your battles? If those missionaries hadn't understood the power that was in that staff and raised it up, what do you think would have happened to them? God has a plan in place for your victory, but you must get into covenant with Him. Lift up your provision, your power against the enemy, and your protection. Lift up His Word. The outcome of His covenant is always guaranteed victory…*forever...to a thousand generations*!

> *"Give us aid against the enemy, for the help of man is worthless, With God we will gain the victory, and he will trample down our enemies."*
> *Psalms 108:12-13 (NIV)*

This verse seems appropriate and relevant for today because of our nation's battles in foreign lands. It is also encouraging to know God will give us help or be on our side. This verse provides the soldier with comfort that there is an even "higher ranking" commanding officer who is with them to lead the way to victory. But what if you're not a soldier? What if you're just trying to make it against the battles of an enemy of lack, sickness, debt, rejection, abandonment, racial hatred, abuse, and the other evils that lurk across our land? What about the aid to fight the everyday crisis in our lives? God knew we were going to need help with the torments of everyday living. Nowhere in His Word did He promise that trials wouldn't come or that life would be a piece of cake. However, He did promise if we stayed focused on Him, we would go "through" the storm and win the war against the enemy's attack.

The plan for victory works the same way for us as it does for the soldier...we both must be trained. How do we receive combat training for life's battles? By learning and then applying the Word. God's Word is our weapon for battle, and it will defeat the enemy. How can we be sure? Because His Word—truth—is the base or foundation of all existence. His Word is the ultimate authority, and when it's used, it proves to be the ultimate power for change. The Bible says God will watch over His Word to bring it to pass. When we use it, we are as equipped for battle as any other trained military expert.

In this verse when the Lord talks about *the help of man being worthless*, He is referring to us looking to one another for the aid or help that only He can give. When we put all our trust in mankind's wisdom or our own natural understanding and strength, we aren't depending on Him. I've been in a few situations that no one could have helped me through except Almighty God Himself. How about you? Can you look back at a time in your life and think, "If it hadn't been for the Lord and the grace of God, I don't know if I'd even be here?"

This verse states again it is God's desire for us to *gain the victory*. It also encourages us with the knowledge that we have a "Commanding Officer" who has all wisdom. He is truly the only One who is able to give the exact orders that will strategically move us through life's trials. Don't be afraid. He goes before us. He provides aid, so that any and every foe that comes against us is trampled down. Let Him instruct you. Then watch your enemies fall beneath your feet.

> *"Surely he will never be shaken; a righteous man will be remembered forever. He will have no fear of bad news; his heart is steadfast, trusting in the Lord."*
> *Psalms 112:6-7 (NIV)*

God promises we will overcome the fear that accompanies bad news and the dark and negative affairs of this life, and He tells us how to do it. The key is to be in a right-standing place with Him. That's what being righteous means. This verse also tells us another benefit the righteous man experiences is *his heart is steadfast.* This means the heart is not subject to change, it is immoveable or in a fixed position. Why is the condition of a man's heart so important? Because in the battle if we allow ourselves to become tired and weary, we know what usually happens. We become afraid. Fear comes in, and as a result we can become heart broken, lose heart, put up walls to guard our heart, become faint at heart, harden our heart or even have a heart attack due to the stress or pressure. Maybe you have already experienced pain due to any or all of the above?

However, when we know the truth and promises of God's Word, we don't have to let the events of the storm scare us. In the worst tornado or hurricane there is a place, right in the center, that is peaceful and calm. God provides us His peace, right in the middle of our storm, no matter what kind of damage it appears to be doing on the outside. In our heart there is now peace instead of fear because we know we can trust God to do what He said. No longer are we shaken or even tossed around when destructive words or bad news comes swirling around our door. Maybe you've heard a negative report? Was your heart strong, steadfast or did it melt when you heard it? Our heart's reaction is a true gage of whether we trust God or we are afraid when we hear things.

Isn't it time you removed all the fears and doubts from your heart? That you let your guard down, and believe God's Word? This verse says "*surely*" *he will never be shaken.* Surely means to be confident, positive, without doubt, certain, assured, reliable, trustworthy, indisputable, guaranteed, bound to happen, destined, definite, steadfast—not subject to change. Do you get the picture? God wants us to be free from the force of fear. It's destructive, and it always takes us down a shaky road. If your heart is sick or filled with fear…Don't be afraid. Let God's Word be your daily medicine. It has the power to strengthen and repair the damages so you, too, will be unshakable, steadfast, and without a doubt you'll be able to trust in the Lord.

> *"His heart is secure, he will have no fear; in the end he will look in triumph on his foes."*
> *Psalms 112:8 (NIV)*

"*In the end*." Are you wondering if your situation will ever end? Constantly asking why the same things keep happening to you? Why every relationship goes sour, you're the one who gets laid off, a cold always turns into bronchitis or pneumonia? Or maybe your train of thought is, "If it was going to happen to anyone, it would be me?" Life, at times, does have some rough spots to overcome, but being afraid of the end or future never brings victory. So what can you do to change these reoccurring events? This verse tells us one way is to prepare our heart, so it will remain secure without fear of the "what ever." How do you prepare your heart? You keep it open and ready with the Word of God. When a crisis shows up, you know and use the Word as a weapon against your circumstances.

For example, what if you've been prone to seasonal infections? Once you get a cold it usually goes into something much worse. The next time you start to "feel" the symptoms coming on...change your thinking. DON'T say, "I'm catching a cold or I'm going to be sick." Instead, use the Word against it. Quote verses like, "Forget not all His benefits, God heals all my diseases; by His stripes I am healed; sickness and disease are under the curse of the law, and I've been redeemed from the curse," etc. When your heart is secure and steadfast, you're new reaction will be to speak healing Scriptures over your body. When you do, you won't get every bug that comes around.

Most importantly, in any and every situation, DON'T speak the problem. Speak what God says about it. When people say it's flu season, thank God you are no longer subject to every kind of disease or virus because of His divine covenant of health He's already provided for your body. Then don't hang out with people who are always sick, afraid, negative, down in the dumps, guilt-ridden, and so on. Don't accept that you have to live the way you have in the past. Change your environment. Spend time with people who know and understand the Word of God. They can help teach and agree with you for the power of God to work in your life, too. These are all ways you can prepare your heart to fight against fear that keeps you insecure. Don't be afraid. There is an end to your repeating problems. Say out loud, "Today is the end of past failures in __________. With God's plan, I am secure in my heart. I am not afraid. His Word promises and I believe I will be triumphant over my enemies." Now, let this be your daily or hourly (if needed) confession. Believe it, thank Him for it, and then, receive it!

APRIL 28

> *"He settles the barren women in her home as a happy mother of children. Praise the Lord."*
> *Psalms 113:9 (NIV)*

There are many stories in the Bible of women who were not able to conceive a child. As they cried out to God or as they served the man of God they were granted their heart's desires. They all had a child. God's original covenant was established with Abraham who is considered to be the father of our faith. He was getting older and asked God about a child for his inheritance. God told him his descendants would be more numerous than the sand on the seashore and the stars in the sky. But nothing happened. That is nothing happened until both his and his wife's bodies were too old to perform naturally what it would take to have a child. God wanted everyone to see that He is not only the God of the impossible, but when He says something you can count on it. When Abraham was 100 and Sarah was 90 years of age, Isaac was born. The lineage continued; God was faithful.

The Bible tells us the Shunamite woman prepared a place in her home for the Prophet Elisha and his servant. Because she had been faithful to provide for them Elisha called to her and asked what he could do for her. He offered to speak on her behalf to the king or the army commander, but she replied she already had a home among her people. It was Gehazi, Elisha's servant, who reported she was without a child, and her husband was old. Elisha then told her by this same time next year she would have a child. It came to pass just as he said it would.

I share these testimonies in the event you've had struggles in this area, too. Now you're afraid it will never happen. I encourage you to relax, and trust in the creator. This verse is God's Word to you, so you can be encouraged through the waiting period. He knows your desires, and it pleases Him to give them to you. Don't be afraid. Worship Him, and enjoy your time in His presence. Praise and thank Him for His goodness and His love for you. He isn't withholding a child from you for any reason, and this includes a past abortion. Don't let the enemy lie to you about this being God's punishment. Shame is of the devil. If this has been a part of your past, just repent. Ask God to forgive you. Then forgive yourself. Let God do in His perfect timing what only God can do. In the meantime...hold on to His Word. Remember, nothing is too hard for Him!

> *"For great is His love toward us, and the faithfulness of the Lord endures forever..."*
> *Psalms 117:2 (NIV)*

It is very important to God that we know and understand how much He loves us. Most of us have never known unconditional love. We always had to prove or work or earn the love of someone else. It is a rare and wonderful thing to find someone you can have a relationship with that accepts you. Not only for who you are, but just the way you are!

However, there isn't one of us that wouldn't like to change a few things about ourselves, especially if we thought it would make us more appealing, fun or more of what our loved ones desired. We think if we lose weight, change the color of our hair or if we could just get more hair that we might be more pleasing. So it is only natural we would want to try to "fix" ourselves up before coming to God, too. "I'll just clean up this area or I can quit this or that, and then I can give my life to God." However, God isn't asking us to straighten ourselves up in order to receive His love and plan. The Bible says He loved us when we were still sinners. The truth is, without His help, we'll never be able to clean ourselves up enough or lay down those areas that keep us in bondage. So, why keep yourself from the very One who can make the changes you need to live happily?

AND with His unconditional love comes His faithfulness. His never ending program of doing for us what we cannot do for ourselves. He loves you, and He loves doing for you. I have found God to be a showoff. When my circumstances are way too big for me to handle, He says, "Doesn't My Word say this...or... watch Me make a way where there is no way." He is called the "Way Maker." Do you need someone to make a way for you? Are you tired of trying to change or fix yourself up, only to be rejected? Have you found in your trying to please others that you don't know who you are anymore? Maybe you're feeling desperate for love and acceptance?

The Bible says nothing separates us from the love of God—not height, nor depth, nor length, nor breadth—and *His faithfulness endures forever*. That's an extremely long time. Don't be afraid. His kind of love is "positively" fulfilling. Believe His promises to you. Accept and receive His great and never ending love. It will truly transform your life!

"This is the day which the Lord hath made; we will rejoice and be glad in it."
Psalms 118:24 (KJV)

When God created the earth, it is recorded He worked for six days and rested on the seventh. At the end of each day's work He looked at what had been done and said, "It is good." The day He created man He looked and said, "It is very good." God knew each day held great and wonderful things for His creation. This hasn't changed for us today. When you get a revelation of the plan of God for your life, it is easy to get up and be grateful for each day. You know He loves you. He only gives good gifts, and when the trials come, you already know what the Word says about it. How can we lose when God promises to turn to good all that the devil intended for evil? All God asks is that we love Him. Who wouldn't love someone who always watches over them and keeps their best interest at heart? What can man do to you, if God is for you? If God is for you, then who can be against you?

If you don't feel this way or you dread getting up in the morning, then I don't need to tell you there is a problem. Have you let your circumstances over take your thoughts, and now fear lives in your heart? It doesn't have to be this way. This isn't God's plan. You may be thinking, "You just don't know what I'm going through. If you had my job…life…family…you would hate getting up each day, too." OK, let's look at your job situation. The Bible says all promotions come from the Lord. Are you doing the right things on your job? Or are you doing sloppy work, talking to co-workers or making personal phone calls instead of working? Do you take an extra five minutes or more for breaks or lunches, come in late, slip out early, steal pens, paper, stamps, kitchen supplies, and so on? And what if everyone else is doing it? It still doesn't make it right. Work or your job is only one example. What about honesty or integrity in your marriage? Do you make time for or even have a relationship with your children? What about your finances? Are you accountable in all these areas, too?

God sees it all. If you want to make a change from the things you dislike, then the first change has to come from you and your attitude. Many times a bad or disagreeable attitude is formed because we're afraid things are going to stay the way they are. However, everything in life is subject to change, including you. Don't be afraid. Most of the time, our biggest problem is how we "look" at our problem. If you've had a bad attitude, ask God to forgive you. Ask God to help you stay focused on His goodness. Use God's Word, and believe what He says about you and your future. Do the right thing, and watch the Lord work on your behalf. You will soon be able to relax, rejoice, and be glad for each new day the Lord makes for you, too.

MAY 1

> *"Every word of God is tried and purified;*
> *He is a shield to those who trust and*
> *take refuge in him."*
> *Proverbs 30:5 (AMP)*

For most people when you buy a product with "Installation Required" printed on the box, feelings of anxiety and fear soon follow. You see the bag with fifty bolts or screws, their own matching washers, and this odd looking tool that allows you to fit them all together. However, as unsettling as this seems, there is comfort in knowing that you aren't the first person nor will you be the only person that's had to put this together. How do you know this? Because in each box, along with the parts, is something that becomes the key for one and all to successfully reach the desired end. What is this something? It is the instructions, and "if" they're read and followed exactly, you are guaranteed to receive a finished product. The instructions make all the difference, and one of the most comforting things is you already know the manufacturer has tested, tried, and proved the process. You know the instructions don't just work once in awhile or for a select few. You know that every time they're followed you're guaranteed the same outcome.

God's instruction manual to us, the Word, works exactly the same way. Why? Because *God's Word has been tried and purified.* In fact, this verse confirms *EVERY Word* is proven. By this we are totally assured that when we follow it, we'll have all the right tools we'll need for success, and we won't end up with the wrong parts or going down the wrong roads. This is why God gave us His Word, to instruct and guide us and to eliminate fear. When Almighty God is the manufacturer or creator, why would we look for or turn to anyone else for help?

The NIV says, "Every word of God is flawless." This means it's perfect; it has no defects or weaknesses, especially ones that detract or hinder effectiveness. Why is this so critical to us? Because in a world that is constantly changing, it's hard to know what's true, and who you can trust. Knowing and believing His Word allows us to not only trust in God, but to also trust every Word from God. The Word alone provides us a base line for truth. The Bible says the truth will set us free. Wouldn't you like to feel released from your turmoil? Wouldn't you also like to know how to change your direction in life and get on the winning side? God's Word can do both. Don't be afraid. Renew your mind by reading and studying the Word. When we come into agreement with His Word and follow His plan, we find *He is our shield and refuge* against life's battles. God's plan for your life has always come with instructions. Just believe. Trust Him. Follow His Word, and you'll receive the truth—His answers and directions—for the installation that's required to move you toward a new and victorious life.

MAY 2

"Your word is a lamp to my feet
and a light for my path."
Psalms 119:105 (NIV)

Years ago I had the opportunity to go fishing. It was just about dark when we arrived at the riverbank. The parking was some distance away, so we quickly gathered our gear and began the journey. Shortly we came to a field that was thick with weeds…chest high weeds. Now I am following behind the person with the light. However, without parting the weeds and looking down, it was impossible to see if there were snakes, other unwanted pests or rocky ground. It wasn't until I looked up that I realized they were way ahead of me. It was now so dark I couldn't even see them. All I saw was the light. Quickly I moved toward it; but I was scared and intimidated. I wished I would have had my own lantern, my own light. It would have shown me the way and eliminated my anxiety and fear.

Anytime we can't see the way or we don't know which way to go, there is the opportunity to have feelings of fear. This is why God gave each of us our own light…a light that will never get too far ahead of us or grow dim. That light is His Word. When we put His Word in front of us and follow it, it offers us a safe, fear free place to step. It not only tells us where, but how and when to do what it takes for us to reach our destinations safely and successfully. It becomes a way for us to go through our trials, and it helps us get on the right path. Do you feel like you're going down the wrong road? Maybe you feel like you're stuck in a ditch? Or you're not even on the road? Do you know the Word? And if you do, are you using it? When David wrote this verse, he was showing us how to get insight and answers to our current, most pressing problems. God's Word is what changes us and our circumstances. It not only provides us with the wisdom we need, but the power we need to align ourselves with the original plan God established for us.

The Bible is God's inspired Word, and it is our daily instruction manual. Every topic is covered from training for marriage, raising children or how to manage finances. It covers issues that keep people bound like addictions, sexual improprieties, dysfunctions, and abusive emotional disorders. It addresses generational curses, demon spirits, and it provides us with the "how to" information so we can get free of it all. Don't be afraid. God's Word is *"the" light,* and it will show you the way to go, regardless of how dark or hopeless it looks now. Your circumstances may be bad, but God's Word is tried, proven, and flawless. It always works. When you enter a dark room and turn on the light switch, doesn't the dark go away? You can do the same thing with those dark, fearful, unproductive areas of your life. You can make them disappear, too. Turn on God's light for your situation. Turn on the Word, and you'll discover how bright your path really is.

"Thou art my hiding place and my shield: I hope in thy word."
Psalms 119:114 (KJV)

Many years ago I was required to attend my company's annual meeting. Right in the middle of the President's presentation he changed the subject and brought up an area we all knew needed attention. Then, he paused for a few moments and asked, "What would you do?" To my surprise, out of the hundreds of management personnel in attendance, he pointed to me for an answer. The room became very still. Every eye was on me. Needless to say, everyone was now paying very close attention. They were afraid if I didn't have the answer, he might call on someone else or what if he asked another question? I gave my answer. He smiled, nodded approvingly, and went on with his speech. In the seconds that followed the reality of what had just happened set in. I was first embarrassed, but then came the fear of man—"what if" I hadn't been listening, "what if" I didn't have the answer or "what if" what I thought would work was wrong? What would people think? Have you ever been in an embarrassing or uncomfortable situation? If you have, did you ever want to hide, run away or just disappear?

At times we've all found ourselves in situations that caused us embarrassment or fear. Afterwards, we're positively sure, we don't ever want to experience anything like that again, nor would we want our blunders to be written about for the whole world to see. And yet, this is exactly what God did in His Word. He reflected the lives of individuals, so we could see first hand their good days, as well as their bad. Why would God focus on the bad, too? Because we are no different than they were. We face major issues just like they did. Sometimes they didn't make the right choices, and neither do we. They couldn't go away, hide their heads in the sand or disappear any more than we can. However, through their mistakes, trials, and the enemy's attack they discovered there was a place of safe retreat, a place of hiding or refuge…even during the midst of the battle.

The good news is the safe place they found is still available for us today. Where is this safe place? How do you get there? You get there by knowing God's Word. They had *hope in His Word*, and we can, too. The Bible is God speaking to you, and He will talk to you about everything. In fact, the Word says we should ask when we don't know. He will not only give us the answer, but He won't think we're dumb for asking. Don't be afraid. When you know what God has to say about something, it removes fear. His Word brings hope that causes confidence to rise up in you. This confidence allows you to follow His plan, stand behind His shield, and believe for His ultimate, victorious outcome. It is a safe, peaceful hiding place, and once you've experienced it, you will be glad you're there.

MAY 4

> *"The entrance and unfolding of Your words gives light; it gives understanding—discernment and comprehension—to the simple."*
> *Psalms 119:130 (AMP)*

One of the biggest myths or lies concerning the Bible is you have to be a scholar, minister, theologian or seminary graduate to understand it. However, God did not write life's instruction manual for all mankind, young and old, and then make it too difficult to understand. This verse clearly confirms the Bible is written so that every Word from God will bring light to every situation for everyone.

At one time in my life I ran from God's plan. I didn't know Him, yet, and I bought the enemy's lie that I could never be good enough to please God. Haven't you believed the same lie? Even though I had achieved what some would call success, it wasn't ever enough to fulfill me or bring me lasting joy or victory. I needed help—direction—instruction. I knew the Lord was the answer, but I didn't know how He could help me. It wasn't until I made a decision to fully accept God's plan and then started to read His Word that I saw it. God could help me, but I had to change and retrain my thinking patterns. How do you do this? You read and study the Word. All those thoughts of failure, unworthiness, and fear left after I began to read God's Word. This verse clearly states the reading or *entrance of His Word opens up light, wisdom, and understanding.*

You might be thinking, "Well, I tried to read the Bible, but I didn't understand it." I can relate. At first, I thought the same thing. Then I bought another lie of the devil—fear that I was too dumb to understand it. However, I had heard the Word says, "You have not because you ask not," so I asked God to help me understand, and He did. A short time later, He answered my prayer by showing me another translation of the Bible. My eyes were truly opened to be able to read and understand all God had for me.

I encourage you—if you have tried and didn't understand it the first time around, maybe you need to look at a different translation, too. God's Word gives light, direction. It brings light to a dark and seemingly hopeless situation. He wants you to know what it says. It is vital we know what it says. The Word or the Bible is called the "Sword of the Spirit." It is your weapon, a lethal weapon against the enemy. Once I saw what was in it, I could also see why the devil tried to keep me ignorant of it. Don't be afraid. Read it. <u>You can understand it</u>. Use it as your weapon. There is no defense that can stand against it. Once you use it, you'll see your victory unfold.

MAY 5

> *"Out of my distress I called upon the Lord; the Lord answered me, and set me free and in a large place."*
> *Psalms 118:5 (AMP)*

Even though we may be distressed when we find ourselves in trouble, God is not shaken, surprised or afraid for us. He knows we have an enemy who tries to make life miserable with his lying and deceitful ways. The Word says the devil came to kill, steal, and destroy everyone, but he really hates the child of God. Why? Because until satan rebelled—tried to exalt himself above God—and was cast out of heaven he was one of God's highest angels. At that time the devil not only worshiped and praised the Lord, but everyday he was allowed to experience the awesomeness and glory of being in God's presence. The devil hates the child of God because we will have…for all eternity…what he'll never have again.

The devil was and always will be defeated, but that doesn't keep him from trying to defeat us. Fortunately, God's plan for us does not include defeat. He says repeatedly in His Word that He will deliver us out of all our troubles. This verse is one of many that confirm troubles or distress may try to overtake us, but we serve a God who is bigger than any problem. The part I especially like about this verse is *He sets me free, and He will set me in a large place.* You may be thinking, "What does set me in a large place mean?" When you are really in a difficult situation and the pressure is on, have you ever felt like you've been backed into a corner or a tight spot? Now you have no other place to go? You feel trapped? You aren't sure of your next move or the exact thing to do? Your vision is narrowed, fear takes over, and you feel helpless, almost paralyzed? This is the plan of the enemy—to confuse us, to keep us afraid and focused on the problems, so we can no longer see our way out.

This verse teaches us God will not only free us from those pressures, but He will move us from the tight spot we're in to His bigger picture. The view is always clearer from a broader, wider angle. God's plan sets us free of our pains. We have all been through sorrowful times. Maybe you're still going through a hard place right now? Has your situation turned out to be much greater than you ever expected it to be? Don't be afraid. The Word of God is true. It offers freedom for your specific need. If your crisis is that much greater, then how much more do you need to be free? Just trust God. He will heal you of your infirmities and deliver you from past pain and hurt. *He will answer your cry of distress. He will set you free.* Let Him relocate you to a larger place, and let His Word work for your every need.

MAY 6

> *"The Lord is on my side; I will not fear: what can man do unto me?"*
> *Psalms 118:6 (KJV)*

When I was in elementary school, we played a game called Red Rover. It involved two teams. One of the hardest parts of the game was choosing the team. You wanted to pick the biggest, meanest, toughest individuals to be on your side. The goal of the game was to get all the players on your team. This was accomplished by picking the weakest player from the opposing team to run toward your team's united line. When you said the words, "Red rover, red rover, send ______ over," you needed to know that your line would be impenetrable. If they couldn't break through, they joined your team. However, if the runner broke through your line, they would pick your strongest team member to join their team. The team with the most players won.

I realize this was only a game, but as you progress through life you find there are still teams with a winning and losing side. If you have ever been assigned a major project at your job, you know you want the best employees to work with you. Why? Because deep on the inside of us there is a desire to be on top—to be successful at whatever we do. If you don't believe me, just watch a game of professional sports in a room full of fans. Neither side wants to be associated with the losers…only the winners. However, not everything in life brings victory. We all have suffered major losses, from the stock market to our love life, and losing hurts. But the good news, according to this verse, is whether mankind is for us or against us, we don't have to be afraid. Mankind will never be able to guarantee our outcome.

The truth is there is only One who can offer us a fearless, fail proof plan. He is God our Father. His love and direction in our "game plan" for life will always tell us when to throw the ball, kick the ball, run the ball or call a needed time out for special instructions from Him. Regardless of the play, you want and need the Lord on your side. It never works when you're trying to call the plays. Why? Our view of the entire field is too limited, and most of us aren't prepared for that three hundred pound lineman's tackle. Maybe you're feeling like it's too late? Maybe you've already been tackled by life? The weight of your problems has crash landed on you? If this is the case, then aren't you ready for help from a "personal" trainer…an experienced coach who can call the shots? Don't be afraid. Nothing is too big for God, and *He's always on your side, so what can man do to you?* Plus, you'll have the "home" field advantage because His game plan is unbeatable. Learn the key to becoming fear-free and staying undefeated…let Him call the plays.

MAY 7

> *"In peace I will both lie down and sleep, for you, Lord, alone make me dwell in safety and confident trust."*
> *Psalms 4:8 (AMP)*

Many times during counseling sessions I've heard people talk about not being able to sleep. It doesn't matter how sleepy they were when they started to the bedroom. The moment their head touched the pillow they were wide awake. However, not being able to sleep at night, which causes mental and physical exhaustion the next day, is not the plan of God. This verse tells us we can lie down and sleep, and we can expect peace and safety when we do.

So what keeps people in torment? They haven't learned to take God at His Word. When nighttime comes their biggest problem is they're "thinking"—trying to work out how "they" are going to fix or come up with all the details they need. They not only worry about their problems outcomes, but they also rehearse the situation over and over. The bottom line is they are afraid. I don't mean they are afraid of the dark or not sleeping, although this may be the case for some. But the majority of non-sleepers are afraid because they have already tried to take care of the problems by their own means and have found they can't fix them. This keeps them rehearsing the problem, hoping to come up with some new angle or idea.

Unfortunately, when you reach this point, the real problem is no longer the crisis. Now, it's fear…fear that keeps you from being able to totally let go and trust God to do what only He can do anyway. Fear keeps us from the peace of God. It also keeps us from having a close relationship with the Father. When we are close to Him it's easier to believe "He is all the while working things out on our behalf." This is what the Word says God is doing, even when we don't think He's moving fast enough for our liking. If you really stop and analyze every single concern you have and the outcome you desire, you would realize you don't want anything for your loved ones that God doesn't want, also. Doesn't He love them? Doesn't He have a plan for them, too? Is God not bigger than their problems?

So what's the cure for sleep disorders? Move into a closer relationship with the Lord. Let Him be in charge of you and all those you are so worried about. You aren't the one who made Him aware of the problem in the first place. He saw it all…and long before you realized it. Don't be afraid. Fear doesn't move the hand of God, but believing His Word and trusting in it does. Want to see your trials and situations change? Then, whether the "thinking" process starts during the day or attacks you at night, speak God's promises. You don't have to give up another night's sleep. Delegate Him to take the night watch. I'll bet you He can handle it.

> *"In my distress I called upon the Lord,*
> *and cried unto my God: he heard my*
> *voice out of his temple, and my cry*
> *came before him, even into his ears."*
> *Psalms 18:6 (KJV)*

If there is one thing David makes plain in the Word it's he knew to call on God. In the two previous verses he states the cords of death were entangling him and destruction seemed overwhelming. Most of us may get into serious situations, but rarely does it bring the threat of death. The pain is sometimes so great we might wish it could all be over, but the reality of us dying is pretty unlikely. However, for many years, each day for David included hiding out in caves, running for his life. During those troubling, "cave dwelling" times, David must have had days he felt deserted and alone. When we're in the midst of trouble, loneliness can be one of the most difficult emotions to overcome. We question if anyone cares, and if or when you pray, you aren't real sure if God hears you or cares, either. It's verses like this one that assure us God hears and responds to our prayers.

Are you in a place where your circumstances have you feeling alone, desperate, and overwhelmed, too? Maybe you are close to losing your freedom or possibly your life? Maybe you've been involved with the wrong people, a gang, and now you live in terror because of what they might do to you? Listen, God knows your situation. If your problems are this severe, you can't wait. Call on the Lord in your distress. Who else do you think can turn this around? You may be thinking, "But you don't know all that I've done. God couldn't possibly want to help me." The truth is, regardless of what we do, sin is sin. The Bible tells us if we will turn from our ways and ask God to forgive us, He is quick to forgive. I encourage you to ASK! He loves you, and just like He promised, He still has a plan for your life.

God's Word makes it clear He never leaves us nor forsakes us. He is a friend who sticks right by us. He is closer than a brother, and He hears us when we call upon His Name. Plus, this verse confirms, regardless of the seriousness of our distress, God hears and knows each of our voices. *He not only hears the voice, but our words go into His ear.* In other words, there is no way He doesn't hear us, and once He hears, He takes action. Don't be afraid. God loves you. He is right where He has always been, and He knows right where you are, too. God knew David was in those caves. Didn't He save him? Protect him? Provide for him? And in God's perfect timing, didn't He promote him to be Israel's King? In your distress, why don't you follow God's Word and call unto Him? When you do, you can expect the same delivering results.

MAY 9

"He reached down from on high and took hold of me; he drew me out of deep waters."
Psalms 18:16 (NIV)

Many years ago, while on vacation in Mexico, I was body surfing the ocean waves and found myself in deep waters. I hadn't been paying attention and suddenly realized I'd gotten out too far from the shore. When I turned toward my friend, who was even further out than I was to let them know I was going back to the beach, I saw this huge wave about to crash down on me. Instantly I tried to position myself, hoping I could get on top of it. Didn't happen! Instead, it forced me to the bottom of the ocean. I mean it pushed me to the ocean floor with such force it not only knocked the air out of my lungs, but my head and body were partially buried in the sand. Now, I have no breath, I'm partially buried with my head face down in the sand, and I'm under approximately twenty feet of water. This is when something very unusual happened. Before I could even begin to think fearful thoughts or worry, I heard this calm voice coming from the inside of me saying, "Don't panic." I focused on those words and kept repeating to myself "Don't panic." Within a few short seconds, I felt my body being propelled to the surface. I swam to shore in amazement of what had just taken place.

I don't know much about scientific calculations like a person's body weight to water ratio, the buoyancy factor, etc., to know if I would have floated to the top anyway. But I believe there was more than science happening that day. I believe there was another hand involved, a hand that lifted me to safety. He literally *reached down from on high, took hold of me, and drew me out of deep waters*. Was I afraid during my "deep water" challenge? Yes, at first. When I saw that huge wave about to overtake me, I knew this could be the end. But at the same time I also felt peace, an inner knowing. I knew I had to let go, not panic or fear.

Today, many times our problems are so complicated and confusing we feel like we're drowning, and we aren't even in water. However, God is a rescuer. This verse confirms He always offers us hope and help for any and every situation. Just like that wave came from behind to overtake me, the devil tries to hit you the same way. You turn around and…BOOM…there is a crisis so overwhelming that you feel like the air is knocked out of you, too. Your first instinct is to panic and to be afraid. Maybe you can relate? Has life's trials about knocked you down? Don't be afraid. I can assure you God's CPR plan works. Take a deep breath. It doesn't matter how big, deep or dark the problems are or if they keep crashing against you like the waves. He's there for you. God promises to *reach down from on high, take hold, and lift you up.* You will reach a place of safety, too.

> *"He delivered me from my strong enemy, and from those who hated and abhorred me; for they were too strong for me."*
> *Psalms 18:17 (AMP)*

If you were asked to identify your "*strong enemy*," would someone or some thing come to mind? Most of us, at some time or another, have dealt with individuals who made it clear they didn't want anything to do with you, regardless of your attempts. It might be on your job, it could be one of your children's teachers, it could be a neighbor or it could even be a member of your church. It seems they enjoy making life miserable for themselves and others, and now for some unknown reason, you are their newest target.

Years ago I worked with someone who was jealous of me and wanted the position I held within the corporation. Several times, during our executive meetings, they would lie or falsify reports against my department to make me and my staff look inefficient. However, the night before each of the attacks the Lord would tell me what they were up to and what reports I needed to prepare. Sure enough, the next day at the meeting they would fire off their accusations. Because of God's faithful warning I was able to say, "I just happen to have that report with me." I would then hand the proper documentation to the president who would briefly look it over. Each time his comment was the same, "It looks OK to me. I'm sure things are in order. Don't worry about it." After several of these embarrassing and fruitless attempts, they quit harassing me. God warned me, prepared me, and delivered me from my strong enemy.

There isn't anything the enemy loves to do more than to use someone who is close to us or at least comes in contact with us to hurt us. When someone deliberately lies about us, gossips or judges us it hurts. We are offended, and rightfully so. However, harmful words or actions are the plans the enemy uses to bring offense because it stirs up anger, hatred, and bitterness in us. Its effect is twofold. It initially hurts us, and then, from our hurts or offense, we do the same thing to others. Even though we hate what they are doing to us, we usually end up joining them. How? We talk about them, their faults or the situation to our listeners, too. Don't we want a sympathetic ear? The sad part is when we let their words and actions dictate our response, we've all fulfilled the devil's plan. The truth is we need a defender, a deliverer, and this verse confirms God is the One. Don't be afraid. His plan includes rescuing us, and there is no enemy too strong or too powerful for Him. Let God be your defender. When you do, you won't fall into the enemy's backbiting trap or any other trap he might have set for you. You'll rise to the top of your battle and see victory in every direction you look!

MAY 11

"You, O Lord, keep my lamp burning;
my God turns my darkness into light."
Psalms 18:28 (NIV)

Have you ever walked along a country road or highway late at night? There is dark, and then there is really dark. You know, so dark you can't see your hand in front of your face? It's at times like this you appreciate a battery operated light. Even if the batteries are weak, in a dark place the dimmest light can make a way. You might not be able to see way down the road, but if you directly point the light in front of your feet, you can see to take one more step. David claims in this verse God is his light. How is this possible? It happens in two ways. First, God allows us to have a close relationship with Him. It's in this closeness that we can hear His voice and receive the right direction. He illuminates our path. Secondly, He gives us His Word, which is our written guide. The Word is also God talking to us. However, they are both designed to do the same thing. They show us the way by bringing wisdom or specific information to any area.

Life has a way of draining us. The enemy waits until we let ourselves get run-down or too tired. Then he launches the attack. Right in the middle of your busiest schedule ever…isn't this when things seem to have a way of finding your last nerve? This is when it is vital to take the time to get recharged. It's true, even a weak battery provides some light, but when the devil launches "war" against you or your family, do you want to go into battle with a little power or a whole lot of power? Do you want to take him on in your own strength or would you like to know the Almighty is your Commander in Chief?

God's Word is designed to bring light to any and every situation we may encounter. The light of God's Word becomes our battery charger. If we keep our minds renewed daily to the Word, then the enemy is powerless. We can take the Word and use it like a scud missile. This type of missile finds and takes down the enemy's weapons when fired. We have the power to do the same thing. When we see the attack coming, we launch the Word as our counter attack. The enemy never has been nor will he ever be a match for the Word of God, and he knows it! God is the only One who can keep your lamp burning, and it's by His Word that we have the right light in order to see things more clearly. He will give you new direction if and when you need it. Just ask! You can believe and trust Him to remove the darkness in your life. If it's dark in your life right now…Don't be afraid. Look to God. He will renew and restore you. Let Him be your battery charger. Just plug yourself into Him, and let His Word and ways build you back up. You will see the light, and light always causes the darkness to flee.

MAY 12

> *"With your help I can advance against a troop; with my God I can scale a wall."*
> *Psalms 18:29 (NIV)*

Most of us today would not be familiar with this kind of terminology unless we had military training. In the current war situation our soldiers have come up against both, and they relied on their training to successfully carry them through. So how does this verse apply to the rest of us? How does it apply to me, if I've never had to fight the enemy? The truth is all of us have our own types of "troops, enemy or foe" to face in our everyday living. Haven't you ever felt like you've hit a brick wall? A wall you couldn't move? A wall there was no way around—except to go over the top?

Life's challenges can be great. When we come up against them, our survival depends upon the training we've received. We wouldn't send our soldiers out to fight a war without the proper training, and God doesn't expect us to fight our circumstances without being skilled in battle, as well. How or what training do we have? 1) He gave us all authority to command the angels to go to battle for us. 2) He gave us the best fighting manual ever written…the Bible. The Supreme General of all time wrote its commands. When it's followed, it guarantees our victory. God makes it clear we have an enemy, and there will be trials, but He also makes it very clear how we can and will defeat our enemies every time.

I've witnessed God's power and delivering force in my life. No matter how great the adversity…my God was greater! Now when I read this verse, I'm encouraged because I know nothing can hold me down or hold me back from the things of God. There is confidence and a boldness which creates an unstoppable atmosphere. *WITH GOD, I can run through any troop and leap over any wall*, and so can you. What huge obstacle stands in your way? Have you tried to beat it down in your own strength, only to find you're bloody from the battle and no further down the road? Aren't you tired of dealing with it…even looking at it? The enemy's battle strategy is to scare you into thinking it's too big, it can't be changed. However, the Word says "Nothing is impossible with God!" If you're staring at what seems to be an unsurmountable situation in your life, then you already know there is no other way except WITH GOD! This verse confirms He will give you the ability to do it. Don't be afraid. Quit looking at your circumstances. Focus on God. You will see, *with His help*, your enemy is truly powerless, and there is nothing so big that you can't get over it!

"As for my God, His way is perfect! The Word of the Lord is tested and tried; He is a shield to all those who take refuge and put their trust in Him."
Psalms 18:30 (AMP)

The word perfect, according to Webster's Dictionary, means to be, "entirely without fault or defect, to be flawless; an expert, proficient; lacking in no essential detail, complete, whole, entire, intact." It goes on to say that "perfect implies the soundness and excellence of every part, element or quality of a thing." In this verse God wants us to understand His way is the right way, and this way is *perfectly* designed for each one of us.

The Word of the Lord is tested and tried. If I had not been doing what the Word said all these years, I might still have some doubts if it were really true. However, I chose to believe it, and just like millions of others, I applied it to my daily living. Now we all know first hand, if He said it in His Word, then it's a sure thing. Why or how are we so sure? We know it by His past faithfulness to us and our faith. When we continually hear the Word, it builds our faith. The Bible says faith without works is dead. By this we know faith requires action. When we use our faith and speak the Word, it acts the same as a boxer's two-fold jab. He punches with one hand, makes a few strategic moves, and before you can see it coming, there's the hit again. When we follow the perfect plan of God, we not only know when to throw the punch—speak the Word, but we also know when to get our gloves up and make a "faith" shield to cover ourselves.

At some point all of us have felt the blows of the enemy, and when it happens you feel as if you were the one that just got slapped upside the head. You're dazed…you see stars…your ears ring…you wonder, "What happened? How did I get here?" Maybe it has been months, and you're still feeling the effects of that last blow. The devil doesn't play fair, and hitting below the belt is his favorite shot. It takes courage to stay in the ring and keep fighting, especially if you've ever been knocked down, but God said we can trust Him. When we do, *He becomes our shield, our refuge.* Don't be afraid. No matter how many punches the enemy tries to pull, God's plan for you is perfect, flawless. His Word is tried and true. Use it! It won't take you long to see the Word is an effective weapon. You, too, will have proof it works, and when God does the final count, you will be the one still standing…you will be the champion He's created you to be.

MAY 14

> *"It is God who arms me with strength*
> *and makes my way perfect."*
> *Psalms 18:32 (NIV)*

The word perfect means the soundness and excellence of every part, element or quality of a thing. It means to be without fault or defect, to be flawless. In today's world of broken dreams, unfortunate circumstances, and everyone out for themselves, it is hard to imagine anything being perfect. In fact, if I asked you what would make up your "perfect" day, the answer might sound like this, "No yelling kids, my car didn't break down, everybody showed up for dinner on time, my co-worker actually smiled at me, the bills were paid, I found time for a round of golf or I treated myself to a manicure and a pedicure." For each of us it's different, but this isn't what God was referring to when He said He would *make our way perfect.* The above events, at the time, might lessen our stress level, but the *perfect* plan of God is to keep us on the right path.

If you've ever had to drive to a new location, isn't it easier to find when you have the exact directions along with the physical address? And if you have signs along the way, like at this corner there is a gas station, and the next place you turn there is a mini-mart, etc. Doesn't this add to your ease? Every piece of information makes your journey that much easier, right? God has all the pieces just like a road map. The right pieces you'll need to make life's journey, and His plan says it will be perfect. We can follow His directions and avoid the major potholes, road closed for repairs, and the dead ends in our lives. Doesn't this sound like the kind of journey you want to be on? Why keep backing up and driving around the same block forty times? We're told in His Word to ask for directions. Why? Because when we don't, the same old "fruitless path" wears us down, weakens us, and ultimately brings fear.

God said in this verse He would *arm us with strength.* This actually means He is giving us strength as a weapon. He's empowering us to be able to stand or endure our trials. The perfect life doesn't mean you won't have problems. Remember, the devil is still trying his best to destroy you. However, God's *perfect* plan—a sound and excellent plan without fault or defect—includes clear and precise directions. With His plan you won't be defeated, and you'll have joy and strength during the process. Don't be afraid. It's not too late. God's plan for you has not changed. We're all God's masterpieces with a plan that is undergoing His "perfect" construction.

"The Lord is good, a strength and stronghold in the day of trouble; He knows—recognizes, has knowledge of and understands—those who take refuge and trust in him."
Nahum 1:7 (AMP)

The Prophet Nahum, along with the other prophets, witnessed the goodness of God. He knew God was a delivering God, and in this verse he encourages the people of Judah about their release from the wicked people of Nineveh. He stated for them and now for us that God will be our strength in the time of trouble. He will fight our battles for us...He's on our side. It's important when you come up against the enemy to know who is for you and who is against you. We've all heard and read about certain individuals, both men and women, who during war times gave the appearance of fighting for one side, but in the end were actually spies. A spy's mission is to secretly watch a person or thing to obtain information that could be used against them, usually for hostile purposes. This process of "finding out" may work in the world, but it is totally unnecessary with God. This isn't how God becomes familiar with us. He never sends someone out to "get the goods" on us. Why? It's because, as this verse confirms, *God already knows—recognizes, has knowledge of and understands*—who we are, especially when we're trusting Him to be our strength and stronghold. When we do this, He makes it His business to bring us out of trouble.

The Bible says God never sleeps or slumbers. His eyes go back and forth across the whole earth. The good news is He doesn't just know who we are, but He knows who our "spies" are, too. In other words He protects us from the ambushes of life. Spies aren't just used in military wars. The enemy will use people in our daily routine to be negative, misinterpret what we say, gossip about us, speak lies against us or secretly obtain information to betray a confidence. Even now, can't you think of someone who has betrayed you, hurt you, used you or has tried to create trouble or fear in your life? God sees these individuals, too, so you don't need to be afraid. He said you could take refuge or find a safe place in Him.

Nahum was not the only prophet who witnessed God's power when His people were being mistreated or under the threat of battle. God sees it all, both then and now. *He will be your strength, your stronghold.* Why? Because nothing the enemy does moves or shakes Him. Once you grab hold of Him and His perfect ways, it's like a life preserver in deep water. Don't be afraid. He loves you. He's faithful. Choose to have the Lord watch out for you and fight your battles. Aren't you ready for a strong arm for support and help? You'll see *the Lord is good.* He's already on your side. All you need to do is trust Him for your victory!

> *"What do ye imagine against the Lord?*
> *he will make an utter end: affliction*
> *shall not rise up the second time."*
> *Nahum 1:9 (KJV)*

In this verse God told His prophet Nahum to let Judah, His chosen people, know that He was going to deliver them. It is with absolute authority and all power the Lord says, *"Who could imagine coming against me?"* The NIV says, "Whatever they plot against the Lord he will bring to an end." Another translation asks how mad is your attempt that you actually think you could plot against the Lord? In other words, who would be crazy enough or insane enough to disregard God or not believe God or His Word? God is God. Whether you accept it or not, doesn't make Him or His Word any less real or true. When the God of the universe wants to have a personal relationship with mankind, it's a very unfortunate event for any individual to refuse to believe He exists. God is real, and if you've decided to truly accept Him into your heart, then you already know He's true and have felt His sweet, life-changing presence.

However, it's the last part of this verse that is extremely encouraging. The word affliction, according to Webster's Dictionary, means "the cause of persistent pain or distress; great suffering; to cause anguish, trouble or to injure." Have you ever felt pain, nagging torment or fear from a persistent problem? How many treatments have you received because of a negative doctor's report? How many months has it been since you were laid off? How much longer will you stay in an abusive relationship? How many more times will you resort to something—sex, food, drugs, alcohol, work, shopping—other than the Lord to relieve your deep, past emotional wounds, scars, anguish, and pain?

This verse says "affliction…trouble or injury" will not rise up again. This means affliction may come, but when we use the Word and trust what God says…WE can keep it from returning a second time…or a third…or a fourth, and so on. How many times have you dealt with the same situation already? This isn't God's Word to you. If you thought your crisis would never end, now you know it is God's plan for you to be free of it…once and for all. If you've had a bad report in any area…Don't be afraid! Use the Word. What does God say about it? Start speaking what God says about any "persistent cause of pain." When we use the Word as the weapon God intended it to be, we will confidently be assured we will not see persistent troubles and suffering rise up again.

MAY 17

> *"Do not gloat over me, my enemy! Though I have fallen, I will rise. Though I sit in darkness, the Lord will be my light."*
> *Micah 7:8 (NIV)*

God used the Prophet Micah to warn the rulers, prophets, and priests about their sinfulness and oppression of the people. He also spoke of God's promise to restore and bring a kingdom of peace to all who trusted in Him. In this verse Micah encourages anyone whose surroundings or circumstances look dark or defeated to not lose their hope or trust in the Lord for He is their way out.

At times, we've all gone through crisis situations where it felt like we'd hit bottom—a real low point. You knew the only way out was up, but it hurt your neck to try and look up that high. Maybe you can relate? This is when it feels like your enemy has gotten the best of you, and the devil, your real enemy, gloats in two ways. The first way is when we knowingly do wrong, get caught, and then endure suffering while paying for the consequences. Anytime we find ourselves in an embarrassing position guilt and shame set in. Then we feel we deserve whatever comes our way, even if it's the enemy's gloating. However, the Bible is full of people who made mistakes, and yet, God worked with them and restored them to victory. The Bible says, "All have sinned and come short of the glory of God." No one is perfect, but God still chose to love us, and He wants us to get back to His plan.

The second type of gloating is the hardest to endure. What about when you have done the right thing and it looks like you are still in the hot seat? What about when you have been falsely accused or lied upon? What about an unfair evaluation or mistreatment by another? What about when it looks like you're all alone and now left in the dark? Obviously God knew there would be times we'd experience a feeling of falling, of failing. Either way, this verse makes it clear He will still be the light that shows us the way out of any dark circumstance. Our enemy will not be able to rejoice for long. In other words…Don't be afraid! AND…Don't count God or yourself out of the picture too soon! God promises restoration and peace to His people if they stay confident in His Word and promises. If you were at fault, then do what it takes to make it right. God will be with you. If you have been a victim, then continue to do what is right, and God will be with you, also. With Almighty God on your side, you will rise up. With God, there is no way you can lose.

"And rend your heart, and not your garments, and turn unto the Lord your God: for he is gracious and merciful, slow to anger, and of great kindness, and repenteth him of evil."
Joel 2:13 (KJV)

Joel was a prophet of God. A prophet is someone who is gifted with more than ordinary spiritual or moral insight. They have the ability to "see" and "speak" by divine inspiration. When a severe locust plague hit Palestine, Joel "saw" it as a sign and warned the people that it was not too late for them to repent for their sins. He assured them of God's love for them, and that God also wanted to be merciful to them. This verse, along with many others, completely blows away the theory that God sits in Heaven, waiting with a big stick to beat us every time we do wrong. If this were the case, then why did He bother to send prophet after prophet to warn the people? Or why would He be so willing to show them the way back to a relationship with Him?

This type of Scripture points to the obvious fact that God loves us, and He isn't the one who destroys us. It is sin that brings our destruction. Most people get sucked into a sin lifestyle because they don't know God, His Word or plan. Nor do they take the enemy seriously. The devil watches to see how you react to certain things. For example: If you don't handle stress very well and feel like you need a drink, snort, smoke or hit of drugs to help you calm down, you better believe the devil will continue to bring problems at home, your job, in your relationships, and any where else that will cause you additional torment. The enemy never wants you to feel like you can deal with the situation. The whole time he is lying in your ear…"Look, you just need a little of this or some of that to take care of your problem. You know, just to take the edge off or help you unwind." Or "Your spouse will never understand you like they do." Or "Why not? Everybody else does it!" Maybe you've heard him make these statements or say similar things to you?

The truth is it may only start out with one drink or hit or just an occasional lunch with a "friend," but it never ends up with just one of anything. Now, you really do have a situation you can't deal with…that is by yourself anyway! God is not the one who destroys lives. However, even when we make wrong choices, if we will return to Him, He revokes and resends His judgment. He always offers you a way out. Don't be afraid! Repent and turn to God. Ask Him to forgive you and help you change. He is *loving, compassionate, merciful, and slow to anger.* Don't wait any longer. Even now His arms are reaching out to you, and they are always filled with LOVE and FORGIVENESS!

"For this God is our God for ever and ever:
he will be our guide even unto death."
Psalms 48:14 (KJV)

The greatest fear man faces is dying. We all know we are going to die sometime, but the fear is "what then?" Many false prophets have tried to offer explanations or comfort by implying there is life after death through reincarnation. However, the Bible clearly states it is appointed for man to die once. The thought of coming back as an animal, insect or worse—as someone who has to try to pay for or redo the errors they made in a former life—is not comforting, especially when you know the truth of God's Word. The Bible says we can receive His forgiveness for our sins right now.

Originally, God never created mankind to die. So how did death come about? In Genesis, the Bible's first book, God created man and woman in His image and they had fellowship with Him. God gave them everything in the garden for their pleasure except the fruit from the tree of good and evil. After many years the devil appeared, lied to the woman, and convinced her that if she ate from this forbidden tree she would be like God. The Bible says God created man in "HIS" image. This means she was already like God. However, being deceived, she ate the fruit. She then gave it to the man who also ate it. The real truth is when God told them if they ate of the tree they would surely die, He wasn't just talking about a natural death. He was talking about a spiritual death. Their disobedience was a sin, and sin separated them from God. This sin or act of rebellion and disobedience opened the door to the curse. The curse of the law of sin and death ultimately brought natural death upon the earth from that time until now.

However, the men of old weren't afraid of dying. Why? They had a firm understanding of the covenant God established with their forefathers. They believed and received just like their fathers before them. There was never any question about whether God existed or was real. They had witnessed too much not to believe. From generation to generation the truths were handed down, and each day they saw the hand of the Lord go before them. If you were crossing a desert with millions of other people and there was a cloud by day and a pillar of fire by night to guide you…for forty years…would you ask if God was real? They never had to ask because they knew it to be true for themselves. They never debated whether God would be with them because His Word says "*For this God is our God for ever and ever.*" Can you make the same claim? Don't be afraid. His covenant promise is still the same to His people today. *He will be our guide... even unto death.* With God's plan your future can only go "Up" from here!

> *"Do you not know? Have you not heard? The Lord is the everlasting God, the creator of the ends of the earth. He will not grow tired or weary, and his understanding no one can fathom."*
> *Isaiah 40:28 (NIV)*

These are still relevant questions for us today. Do you know the Lord? Have you heard of His love, goodness, mercy, and His plan for your life? In this verse Isaiah confirms, just in case you haven't heard, God is the creator of everything. He is the beginning and the end, and He will be our God forever. The next few lines try to help us understand more of the characteristics of God, but the truth is most people don't really know God. They may know about Him, but having a personal relationship with Him is another thing altogether. We try to fit God into our box with our own plan, desires, and goals. For the most part it makes us feel like we are still in control, and in some respects, if we won't let Him do all He has planned for each one of us, we are the ones in control. This is unfortunate because when we're under this kind of daily pressure, we're the ones who grow tired and weary. The question is: Why don't we want to release our lives into the very capable hands of the One who created us in the first place? It should be obvious He would know us better than we could know ourselves. Does the potter not know the clay? Does he also not know what the clay is to become?

Fear is what keeps us from trusting the One and only trustworthy God of all creation. Why are we afraid of Him? We don't know Him. If you were the architectural designer of a major building, would anyone understand the plans as well as you? Probably not in the beginning, but as one looked at it more closely, studied it, asked questions, and got to know the designer better, they could gain the understanding needed to follow the plan. Then it could be built exactly the way it was designed.

God is our architectural designer. When we study His Word, which declares the plans He designed for us, we will not only get to know Him and the power of His great unconditional love, but we will also see who it is God created us to be, too. We can then go about building our lives with a firm foundation on the Word of God. We'll learn to trust His ways and methods over and above what we might think or feel. Don't be afraid! God doesn't build junk. His children, you and I, are to be masterpieces. Maybe you've found cracks in your foundation? Or rotten boards that need replaced? Or a few leaks that need sealed? Whether it's a new work or restoring the old, trust Him to do the job. Give Him, as your designer, full control. His Word promises *He will not grow tired or weary.*

"So shall you find favor, good understanding and high esteem in the sight [or judgment] of God and man."
Proverbs 3:4 (AMP)

Solomon, the writer of this verse, knew what it was to have the favor of God. He was appointed to be king at a very young age, and because of this he asked God for wisdom so he would know how to manage the people. God was so pleased that Solomon didn't ask for money or possessions that He not only granted his desire for wisdom, but He blessed him with wealth, too. It is recorded Solomon was the wisest man and the wealthiest man who ever lived. It is a great thing to know you have the favor of God, but it is an added benefit when you know God will have mankind show you favor, as well. Webster's Dictionary defines favor as, "approving consideration or attention; friendly regard shown toward another especially by a superior; to prefer; to afford advantages for success." Wouldn't you like to receive preferential treatment from a superior? How about a few advantages for success? Most of us would find any of the above appealing and be extremely grateful.

This verse assures us God offers us favor—not fear. With God we can and will have success in whatever we do because both He and man will show favor—approving attention—toward us. Are you in a legal battle you must win? Do you need help with a promotion? Are you negotiating a business transaction and need some pull for your side? Then take God at His Word. Speak what He says about you. I know people who use this verse to get a close parking spot when they go to the store or shopping mall, and it works every time. You might think this seems like a pretty small or selfish request when God is so busy, but if you think this way, you don't know the Father. He loves for us to ask, and then believe. This is how we use our faith. The Bible says it's faith that pleases Him. When we use it, He responds. Besides, what request isn't "small" to a MIGHTY GOD?

Remind yourself of the promise in this verse. Also, use the other Scriptures that relate to whatever area it is you need to see changed. Don't be afraid. God won't think you're being silly, and nowhere does the Word give a list, offer suggestions or questions that fall under the "worthy of asking God for" category. This means every request is important to God. The Bible says God cares about the things we care about. Apply the Word, use your faith, and speak what God says about your situation. Expect favor, expect special consideration. God said it's yours. Once favor begins, you'll wonder how you ever got along without it!

MAY 22

"Trust in the Lord with all thine heart; and lean not unto thy own understanding. In all thy ways acknowledge him, and he shall direct thy paths."
Proverbs 3:5-6 (KJV)

Years ago I heard a woman testify the only way she finally learned to trust God and let Him be in charge was she pretended her life was like a car. God was the driver behind the wheel, and she sat on the opposite side as the passenger. She had removed herself from behind the wheel of life. At the time I thought this sounded like a good idea, but I have since discovered, for myself and maybe most people, this still isn't far enough away. Even as the passenger, it's too easy to reach over and try to take control of the situation again, especially if we don't think we're going fast enough or making all the right turns when we want. For me the safest and most prosperous place was in the back seat. I admit it was uncomfortable letting God drive me around at first, but now I wouldn't want it any other way. He not only knows me, but He knows every road, hill, ditch, turnpike, and so on. I certainly don't care to drive the same old path day after day, year after year, especially if the weather or road conditions could be hazardous to my health. How about you? Even if the scenery is beautiful, let's just get on down the road.

Before traveling have you ever called a service that prepares your entire road map from your starting location to your final destination? Their plan makes it simple to follow the already selected highways, restaurant guide, and hotel/motel information. Well, God is our ultimate travel guide or trip planning specialist. He loves being the tour guide of life, planning and mapping out the sweetest most pleasant course for His children. He knows our starting point, but even more importantly, He also knows our final destination. He alone can assure us we will arrive there safely.

The key to us reaching our final destination with joy and success is up to us. We have to let Him—trust Him—to make all the arrangements. Don't be afraid! He loves you. Every trip, whether it's business or pleasure, will be enjoyable and fulfilling. Even when you hit some rough spots along the road or have repairs, you already know He designed the map and has made the proper provisions. When we let Him direct our paths, we can end the going around in circles. We can get on to better and higher ground. Aren't you ready? Let Him be your chauffeur. Oh, what an adventurous ride it will be!

> *"My son, do not despise the Lord's discipline and do not resent his rebuke, because the Lord disciplines those he loves, as a father the son he delights in."*
> *Proverbs 3:11-12 (NIV)*

Discipline has become a very controversial issue in today's circles. Even the strongest in heart don't like to hear this word. For most it conjures up unpleasant emotions of past wrongs. However, the word discipline means to train, instruct or develop for the benefit of one's own self-control or mental and moral character. So, in order to be fully trained, learn self-control or become mature, discipline is the essential component. It's better when we can discipline ourselves, but in those situations if we feel we can't or just choose not to, discipline will still come. Only now it may feel like punishment. Either way, it is necessary. Why? It brings about the same developed end in one's moral or physical character.

If you have ever worked out you know it takes discipline, especially in the beginning, to get to the gym everyday. Then, when your body starts to talk back with sore muscles, it gets even harder. Although you might feel like this is a form of punishment, it is really building and developing self-control and a healthier body. God, as our Father, loves us. It is His responsibility to discipline us. His ways are higher than ours are, and when He teaches, instructs or disciplines us it isn't to be negative or to punish. When you teach a baby how to stand and walk, what and what not to touch, what they can and can't put in their mouth, you're training...disciplining them. In effect, you are helping them develop self-control. You train them to stay away from those things that could be harmful. Why do you bother to train or instruct them? Isn't it because you love them and want to protect them? When you discipline a child for running into the street without looking, are you punishing them or teaching them a better and safer way? As you can see, discipline is a necessary part of training for productive living.

Discipline from the Father is a good thing. It is training that is done out of love not only to keep us from hurting ourselves, but others, as well. If you have made mistakes and now feel like God just wants to punish you or you are afraid of God's discipline, then you don't know how great the love of the Father is for you. Don't be afraid! And you definitely don't have to be afraid of God. Ask for forgiveness. Turn from your ways to His ways, so your character and morals will be developed and matured. This verse makes it clear, *He disciplines or chastens those He loves, so don't despise, resent* or look down upon His teaching and guiding hand. He wants you to return to a close relationship with Him. Remember, you are His child...*the very one He loves and loves to take delight in.*

"Be still, and know that I am God; I
will be exalted among the nations,
I will be exalted in the earth."
Psalms 46:10 (NIV)

The New American Standard translation says it like this, "Cease striving and know that I am God." This is probably one of the most difficult commands for us to follow. It's hard to *be still* when we live in a fast paced—no time to wait—drive through life, which includes everything from eating to banking. "Really Lord, you see the kind of day I have scheduled. Who has time to *be still*?" However, when God created the universe, He gave us 24 hours in each day, 7 days in each week, and one of those days was a day to rest. Since He knows everything, has it occurred to you that when you don't have enough time to do everything on your list or in your daily planner that some things just don't belong there? Now, you may be thinking, "Well fine, if you can show me what and how to eliminate it, I'll do it." God has wanted to show you how to manage every area in your life for some time, but the problem is you must get still to hear Him.

Have you ever observed a second or third grade classroom that's out of control? The teacher could have the greatest, most applicable information, but if the students won't be quiet when their instructor tries to talk or they continue to get up and down to run around the room, how effective do you think the information would be? Would they even hear it to receive it? Probably not. It's really the same principle between us and the Father. If we continue to keep the pace we've set for ourselves, we won't be able to hear what the greatest teacher of all has to say to us, either.

God's ways and plans are so much higher and better than ours. Why would we run from the very One who can change, fix or make every area of our lives new? The very things we strive so hard to make right? Fear! It's fear of not knowing Him, it's fear of asking Him, it's fear that when we ask, we might not get what we ask for, it's fear we might not like what we hear, it's fear we can't hear His voice, it's fear of what other's think, it's fear of stepping out of the old comfortable routine, even though we aren't happy with the current situation. Listen…fear is not and never has come from God! God loves you! He has great and mighty plans for you, regardless of who you are, what you've done or where you've been. Nobody knows and loves you like God your Father. Don't be afraid! You know you need help. Turn to the only One who has the answers for your every need. *Be still*…get quiet…wait on the Lord. From now on make Him the first thing on your "to do" list. Your new schedule may pleasantly surprise you.

> *"For the Lord giveth wisdom: out of his mouth cometh knowledge and understanding."*
> *Proverbs 2:6 (KJV)*

This verse is like so many others that demonstrate the goodness of God to us. It's understandable that God, the creator of the universe, has wisdom and knowledge about everything, but the fact that He is open and willing to give it to help us is astounding. If you were asked to reflect upon a time that wasn't so successful in your life, would you agree the main reason was a lack of information or wisdom? Maybe it involved a business decision? Or you were starting a new relationship? Whatever the occasion, would you make the same decision with the knowledge you have today? Or would you choose a different path? Most of us have areas we would definitely change or do differently because of what we have discovered in the course of our experiences.

Life, regardless of how old you are, is still a school, and we need to keep learning. Even though trial and error can be one of the methods we use to learn, it's not always the easiest or the best. However, trials and errors are two words that can be managed, especially the error part. We know the Word says we will have trials, but we also know with the Word we cannot be defeated. The trials or tests become part of our testimony, which allows us to share the power and love of God with others. It's the errors our Father is trying to keep us from making. Granted, not all negative experiences are bad, but if there are too many and they come in succession, it makes it hard to want to keep trying. The fear of failure will eventually beat you down, and quitting may seem like the only option. Many individuals, who live on the streets today, fall into this category. Fear and failure have caused them to give up, to accept a defeated path.

Have your disappointments made you feel like quitting? Are you tired of getting "dead end" results? Everyone has felt this way at some point, but it's fear that tries to make us believe things will never get any better. However, this is just not true. When you feel like life is hopeless, beyond change, this should be your first clue this is not from God. God is the giver of life. This verse confirms He gives to us every time He speaks—*out of His mouth comes knowledge and understanding*—not fear. Are you making time to talk with God? Talk…as in a regular dialogue? Do you wait to hear what He has to say? He loves you. He wants you to know who, what, where, when, and how for every situation. Don't be afraid. The Bible says, "Ask and you will receive." Go ahead. You'll soon learn it's just that simple, and now learning really can be a fun experience.

MAY 26

> *"But thou shalt remember the Lord thy God: for it is he that giveth thee power to get wealth, that he may establish his covenant which he sware unto thy fathers, as it is this day."*
> *Deuteronomy 8:18 (KJV)*

God's original covenant of health, wealth, and prosperity was established with Abraham because of his faith. It has been passed down to us through the lineage of Abraham's son Isaac, then his son Jacob, and so on. The Bible states these men were so favored of God that they were envied by all. People knew not to mess with them because it was obvious whoever was in covenant with God received the blessing. Outsiders were afraid to take on God's people because they knew they were taking on their God, too. God still offers us the same covenant agreement He established years ago with our forefathers. He does it now for the same reason He did it then. He wants His people to prosper. When we do, it not only brings glory and honor to Him, but it continues to make the same statement to others about the goodness of God.

However, the verse prior to this one warns us to not think our blessings or "good fortune" have come by the strength of our own hands. I've heard it said, "God may pass up an opportunity to come early, but He's never late." This statement is not found in the Bible. This is man trying to explain why it may seem like God doesn't show up until the final hour of our need. I believe, upon occasion, God may wait because somewhere, deep down on the inside of us, we still think we can pull it off or we can get ourselves out of our own troubles. There is not a total trust or reliance on God alone. Sometimes, it is only in the final hour when we become desperate, that we cry out to Him. Now we have to admit there is no other way without God. When this happens we discover how faithful He is, and we know He does it because of the covenant that has already been established for us.

This verse says, *"Remember the Lord…it is **HE** that gives you the <u>power or ability</u> to get wealth."* The truth is God gives us the power and the ability to do everything—think, move, speak. Why? He wanted all to know His plan of covenant. In His Word He said, "He knew the plans He had for us, plans to prosper us and not harm us, plans to give us a hope and a future." Don't be afraid. He loves you so much. Even if you don't know the entire plan right now, make a decision to just trust and believe Him. His covenant has been tried and tested by too many for too long. It worked for our forefathers…it will also work for you. The key is to *remember the Lord your God!*

> *"It is the Lord that goes before you; He will [march] with you; He will not fail you or let you go, or forsake you [let there be no cowardice or flinching, but] fear not, neither become broken [in spirit] (depressed, dismayed, and unnerved with alarm)."*
> *Deuteronomy 31:8 (AMP)*

God gave Joshua and the children of Israel orders to march around the city of Jericho. He told Joshua He was giving them the city. Then God laid out their plan of attack. Now you wouldn't think your "war strategy" would be to march around the outside walls of a city for seven days—six of those days not saying a word. Then on the seventh day, at the appointed signal, everyone was to shout with the voice of triumphant. This was supposed to bring the walls down. Did it work? God's plans always do. Let me remind you, these were no ordinary walls. These walls were so high and wide that Jericho used to hold chariot races on the top of them, and yet, these mighty walls fell straight down into the ground. The children of Israel captured the city. God was with them. His plan did not fail them. They were not afraid.

It all sounds great now, but how could they have believed such a silly plan would work? They believed and never doubted it because they had seen God deliver them time and time again. They had seen His faithfulness. They knew He loved them and would protect them? Do you know the same thing? Can you have the same confidence for your mighty obstacle? Are there some walls that need to come down in your life? God has a plan for you just like He did for them. Are you prepared that it may seem ridiculous? Maybe He has already told you to do something, and you have let the enemy convince you it isn't right or it couldn't be God? What if the children of Israel had thought this was a stupid idea or had let fear keep them from being obedient? I think we know the outcome would have been different.

The same is true for us. If we want and need a victorious outcome regarding our circumstances, we need to follow exactly what the Lord says. This Scripture confirms God is not only very much aware of your situation, but He intends to go through it right along with you. Why? So regardless of your trial, you'll never fear, lack courage, be depressed or alarmed. Don't be afraid. Don't lose heart. Trust Him. *He will go before you and be with you.* He will never leave your side. He loves you. Obey Him, and you will see the victory in your life, too.

"Have I not commanded you? Be strong and courageous. Do not be terrified, do not be discouraged, for the Lord your God will be with you wherever you go."
Joshua 1:9 (NIV)

God spoke this reassuring Word to Joshua shortly after Moses died. Joshua was anointed to be the new leader of the millions of Israelites who had been wandering in the desert for forty years. Now it was time for them to cross the Jordan River and take possession of the land God was giving them. God told them everywhere you place your feet will be yours, and it was a vast amount of land. God assured Joshua He would be with him, just like He was with Moses.

Scriptures like this one are so relevant to us today because of our current war situation. You or I may not literally be fighting to take the land, but there is a spiritual and physical battle going on in the lives of people who have been held in bondage by terrorist leaders and their followers. God's plan for His children never included this type of mistreatment, abuse or fear. We must use courage and stay strong during these trying times, and it is vitally important that we continue to pray for safety and God's wisdom through it all.

However, we can't forget that we're engaged in a war of our own. The truth is it's the same enemy. We might not be using aircraft carriers or missiles in our battle, but we still need weapons. We also need the same assurance God gave Joshua and Moses. We don't have to be terrified or discouraged, either, because God will be with us no matter where we go. God wants you to know He didn't create you to be defeated. He doesn't bring you out of one battle, so you can be wiped out in the next. The plan is for you to be an overcomer every time the enemy strikes at you, your family, your work, your pets, your property or land, and everything that's on it.

How do we stay on top and not let the enemy defeat us? We follow God's command…Don't be afraid. God asks in this verse, *"Have I not commanded you? Be strong and courageous. Do not be terrified; do not be discouraged."* This was a command from God. Why? Because He knows the enemy's number one weapon is FEAR. Remember, the devil came to deceive. All fear stands for is F̲alse...E̲vidence...A̲ppearing...R̲eal. Fear is a lie, a bluff, a smoke screen. How will you know? When you see it, hear it or feel it, does it agree with the Word? This is your answer. Don't be afraid. If you're afraid of your outcome, get rid of the fear! Trust God. He's right there with you…your strength and your protector.

"May He give you the desire of your heart and make all your plans succeed."
Psalms 20:4 (NIV)

In this verse God gives us permission to have desires or dreams in our heart. We all have things we've longed for or hoped for, and God promises to fulfill those dreams. Part of that promise is to make us prosperous, but we have to remember we serve a God of balance. If our motives or the intent of our heart is wrong or if it could hurt us or others, God loves us so much that He may not grant us those desires. That is at that time anyway.

I learned this for myself when I decided to buy another car. I found the car I wanted. A few days later, when I went to trade in my car for the new one, a salesman pointed out another car. I was surprised to hear it was priced lower than the one I had originally selected. It was a beautiful car, so I took it for a very short test drive. I really liked it, and I asked God if I could have it. I didn't hear an answer. A few days later I asked again. I still didn't hear anything, but my desire for this car hadn't left. Several days had passed when I heard the Lord say, "OK." It never occurred to me to ask Him why the delay. I bought the car. It looked great. It felt great to be in it...BUT...I quickly learned my test drive hadn't been a true test. Even with power steering, the steering suspension was so tight that it took both hands to turn the wheel. Now I'm in my car a lot, and this may seem silly to some, but I had been used to one finger driving. This car's steering was so tight that it actually caused me to have neck and shoulder pain. Driving it was work, and I didn't like it. What was I going to do now?

I learned a valuable lesson about asking God for the things in my heart. I don't buy anything today without His approval, and when I don't hear right away...I don't ask again. The Bible says God's will for us is good, acceptable, and perfect. It wasn't that God didn't want me to have this car. It was that He knew my body and how uncomfortable it would be for me to drive it. He said OK, but I've learned to accept "His will" or intentions and purposes for me because they are perfect! I found when I put God first and followed His plans and will for my life, that my desires changed. The things that once seemed so important to me had little or no value anymore. When I choose to receive only the things He desires for me, it's always for the best. Both He and I are pleased, and I wouldn't have been in the market for another car only four months later. The Bible repeatedly tells us God wants to give good gifts which will fulfill our heart's deepest desires. Don't be afraid. Ask the Lord for His perfect will for you, too. Believe, and trust Him. *He'll make all your plans succeed.*

MAY 30

> *"I will instruct you and teach you in the way you should go; I will counsel you and watch over you."*
> *Psalms 32:8 (NIV)*

Many times we find ourselves going in one direction, and then something happens that causes things to come to a sudden halt. Reality hits. You're wondering, "How did I get here?" Or you wake up thirty, forty, fifty, sixty years old and you have no idea what you were placed on planet earth to do. In early history, usually at the age of thirteen, young men were taken aside by their fathers or another older family member to be mentored to learn a business or trade. An experienced mentor is priceless. You not only have the opportunity to learn from their vast knowledge, but you also can see what experience has taught them along the way. You have the unique advantage of being able to apply their successes without having to experience the pain of their failures.

This is the same kind of program God wants to set up with His children. After all, there is no greater mentor. He designed everything—including you—so He knows how perfectly each component must work together in order for us to achieve success. His Word is filled with verses just like this one. He wants us to ask Him for direction and wisdom, so *He can instruct us and teach us* about what is right for each one of us. Why would you mentor with someone about nursing if you wanted to be an auto mechanic? Why do we continually ask our friends, family members, and others for counsel when only God really knows us and what's best for us? The Bible is very clear that God wants to help us, teach us, counsel us, and deliver us. All He requires is that we ask.

The Lord's desire is for you to be prosperous, healthy, and to be able to enjoy the fullness of life that He planned. He has a plan that's just right for you. Don't be afraid. You are not too young or too old. Ask Him. He will not only tell you what the plan is, but He will also mentor you to keep you from making those costly mistakes. Wouldn't you like to know where you've gone wrong or missed it? Wouldn't you like to know in advance from now on, so you won't miss it again? Ask Him. He loves you. *He will watch over you and teach you His ways.* Remember, the Bible says, "His ways are perfect."

"The Lord will preserve him, and keep him alive; and he shall be blessed upon the earth: and thou wilt not deliver him unto the will of his enemies."
Psalms 41:2 (KJV)

God is faithful to provide comfort in His Word regarding life's situations. None of us like to think about being in a place where the danger is so great we could lose our life. However, there are such situations going on all around us everyday. No place is exempt. Look at the violence in our schools—drugs, suicides, gun and knife injuries—it's staggering. What about our highways? Who would have thought somebody would pull out a gun and shoot you for accidentally pulling in front of them? Anger, rage, fear…they're at an all time high, and they don't discriminate. Most of us would have to admit if it had not been for the delivering hand of God, we would not be here today. I know this is certainly true for me.

In His Word, God is faithful to cover every area the enemy will use to bring fear and destruction. Today one of the biggest war zones the enemy is using to attack us is right here on our inner city streets. It is more violent and we are literally losing more lives there each day than in the war. In Los Angeles alone there are over 250,000 kids in street gangs, warring against each other over nothing of any worth or value. The facts are most gang members don't live past their early twenties. So you can see why their thinking would be, if they die at 16 or at 22, what difference would it make. They are lost with no hope for their future and no revelation of what God has planned for them.

Do you have loved ones that are in any of life's war zones? Are they overseas? Or maybe they're in gangs, on the streets, in school or in prison? Be encouraged. God knows where they are, and He loves them, too. Regardless of your specific details, if the enemy is trying to steal lives, speak the words in this verse over you and your loved ones. Make it personal by inserting your name or your loved ones name in the verse. Then, believe God to change their hearts and to protect them until they can come home.

The Scriptures are full of men and women who were up against huge odds, but God delivered them out of them all. He is a "way making" God. Turn it over to the Lord. If you don't, the enemy through fear, worries, and anxieties will try to destroy you, as well as them. Don't be afraid. God is still God, and He's so much bigger than your circumstances. Hold on to the truth of God's Word. It's your weapon of protection for you and your family. Just keep using it!

JUNE 1

> *"The Lord will sustain him on his sickbed and restore him from his bed of illness."*
> *Psalms 41:3 (NIV)*

This is one of many verses in God's Word that confirms it is the will and plan of God for His people to be well. The Word makes it clear we have an enemy that comes to steal, kill, and destroy. It also makes it clear we have a God who loves us, created a great plan for our lives, blesses us, and not only gives us life, but gives it to us more abundantly.

Now that we have established the foundational truths in God's Word, let's take a closer look at sickness and the consequences of it. When we are sick, especially if we have to stay in bed, are we living life to the fullest? Are we able to spend time with our loved ones and friends? Or is the enemy destroying our lives and our relationships? If we have major medical bills and those costly prescriptions, aren't our finances being stolen? If you had a choice, wouldn't you rather spend it in other ways? What about the deterioration of the body? So the question still remains, "What good comes out of illness?" The truth is…Nothing! There is not one good thing about sickness or disease. The Bible says, "Every good and perfect gift comes from our Father." So, if there isn't anything good about sickness or disease, wouldn't you agree we can totally and finally rule out the possibility of it coming from God?

So where does sickness and disease come from? The devil—the very one whose only intentions are to kill, steal, and destroy. Some say that God uses sickness to teach us. This is nowhere in the Word. The Word clearly states, according to John 14:26, that God uses His Word and the Holy Spirit to teach us and guide us into all truth. Why would Almighty God commission the devil to teach us anything? If being flat on your back or in constant pain humbled you enough to call on the Lord, read the Word, pray or praise God more, you may feel like you got closer to the Lord because of it. But the reality of it all is God loves you enough to do what the Bible says, "He will surely turn what the enemy intended for evil to good to those who love Him." Why? So we can't lose!

Don't accept for one second any affliction against your body is from God. GET RID OF IT! Take God's Word, His promises of healing, and put them in your mouth just like you would your medicine. Then speak them out so your body can hear what God's plan is for it. Remember, no weapon formed against you shall prosper, but you must use your weapons. Don't be afraid. God loves you. Use His Holy and powerful Words like medicine. The Word truly is health to your whole body.

> *"My son, pay attention to what I say; listen closely to my words. Do not let them out of your sight, keep them within your heart; for they are life to those who find them and health to a man's whole body."*
> *Proverbs 4:20-22 (NIV)*

Solomon, the writer of this verse, had asked God for wisdom, and God granted it to him. At that time, he was known throughout the world for his wealth and his wisdom. In fact, kings and queens came to see and hear how Solomon managed his kingdom. If Solomon was valued to be that wise, maybe we should do as he wrote and *pay attention*, also! The Scriptures continually tell us, from one writer to another, about the power and authority in God's Word. For some, this may not be difficult to understand or even agree with…after all, the true author of the Bible is none other than God Himself through the Holy Spirit and men.

So why don't we pay attention or listen or keep His Words within our sight and within our heart or find them to be health to our whole being…spirit, soul, and body? The reasons are the same for all. It's not that we don't always believe what He says. The part that becomes the most challenging for us is accepting that when we use His Word, it will achieve the exact same effect as it does when He speaks it. I mean, He is God, the Almighty, the Creator, the Lord of all. Naturally things would change when He speaks, but who am I? Why would things change just because I said so? These are valid questions, but understanding the chain of command or authority is the key. When a general gives an order and it is repeated through the ranks of command until it reaches those who will carry it out, does each commander say, "I can't say that. No one will obey my order. I'm not the general." No, they don't. Why? Because they know when they hear an order, they better pay attention, listen, and respond accordingly or it could mean serious consequences. If they're disobedient, it could actually affect their health.

God, as "The General," and Highest in Command not only gave us His Word, but the authority to use it. This is why it is so important we know what the Word promises us. The Bible tells us there is power in the tongue. We will speak life or we will speak death. It also says we will eat the fruit of the words we speak. In other words, our speech is like a seed, and it will produce a harvest. So what kind of fruit or outcome do you want to see? Don't be afraid. Get to know what God is saying to you from His Word. Keep it in your heart and mind so at the first sign of trouble, it's HIS Word that comes out of your mouth. You'll see the difference it makes when you speak what HE says and not how you think or feel at the time. *You'll find His Words will be the "Life" and "Health"* you've been missing!

JUNE 3

"The reverent, worshipful fear of the Lord leads to life, and he who has it shall rest satisfied; he cannot be visited with [actual] evil."
Proverbs 19:23 (AMP)

The NIV states it like this, "The fear of the Lord leads to life: Then one rests content, untouched by trouble." It is easy to see if we believe we're truly protected by God and His covenant, even to the point where trouble has no way of reaching or touching us, we would be in a place of peace…contented and satisfied. How many today can truthfully say they live in a peaceful atmosphere? They're contented? Or even satisfied? And yet, this verse confirms it is possible. There is a way, and there is a place where we can live fear-free of evil.

However, the key in finding this place of peace and rest is contingent on our relationship with the Lord. This verse, which was written by one of the wisest men who ever lived, Solomon, explains there is only one thing that leads to this kind of *life*. This one thing is "*the fear of the Lord*." Now we know we don't have to be afraid of God. That isn't what fear means in this verse. In this context fear refers to our attitude or the condition of our heart in reference to God. It helps us see it's the reverent, respectful, full of awe and wonder, worshipful attitude or expression that *leads us to life*…that is a real life with God.

God doesn't look at us like the world does. God sees our hearts. That's why our attitudes are so important. They are a direct reflection of what we really think and feel. The Bible says that every issue of life flows out of the heart. It also says out of the abundance of the heart the mouth speaks. In other words, we can't hide how we really feel about something because sooner or later our true feelings will come out. We may think we're successfully hiding them from others, but there is no hiding the things in our heart from the God who created it. The truth is we don't hide it very well from others, either. However, if we don't address issues in a timely manner or we try to bury them in the inner recesses of our being, most times when they finally do surface, it erupts in anger, followed by abusive words or actions. Can you relate? Is this how you deal with emotional issues? This reaction is not only unhealthy for you, but it is not the restful, peaceful, contented or satisfied life God planned for you. The Bible says you can cast every care, worry, and fear on the Lord because He cares for you. Don't be afraid. God can change your heart, if you'll give Him permission. With a clean heart you'll reverently worship and fear Him, too. This *fear will lead you to life*. Then, just as He promised, you'll find a place of total rest, a safe place, untouched by trouble.

> *"You hear, O Lord, the desire of the afflicted; you encourage them, and you listen to their cry, defending the fatherless and the oppressed, in order that man, who is of the earth, may terrify no more."*
> *Psalms 10:17-18 (NIV)*

Affliction, according to Webster's Dictionary, is "to be so severely stressed, tormented or troubled to the point of persistent suffering or anguish." And yet, in this verse it is comforting to know that we have a God who not only sees our every situation, but hears us when we cry out to Him. Once we call unto Him, He defends and brings us peace by casting down fear or terror. Webster defines terror as, "intense fear." Terror brings violence, and its purpose is to intimidate the masses into meeting its demands. But terror's target isn't just the masses. It can strike anyone, from the child who is afraid of the dark at bedtime, to the businessman whose deal has turned sour or the single mom who doesn't know where or when her child's next meal is coming. All of these situations have the ability to create "intense fear."

Why is terror and fear so dangerous to us? Because they stir up powerful, negative emotions that cause us stress, uncertainty, worry, and anxieties. When they're not identified or treated, they can quickly become something far more harmful....depression, even oppression. Webster defines the word oppression to mean, "a sense of being weighed down in body and mind; unreasonably burdensome or severe; overwhelming or depressing to the spirit or senses; to crush or burden by the abuse of power or authority." It is obvious there isn't anything good or positive that comes from working or living under these conditions.

However, God confirms in this verse it is not His desire for anyone to experience these emotions. *He defends and encourages the fatherless*—all those who are alone or unprotected—*and the oppressed.* How does He do this? By being our Heavenly Father, and by offering us His plan of love and destiny. Maybe you've experienced a time of affliction? Or you've grown up without a father or a real relationship with your dad? Have you become depressed by your circumstances? Are you suffering from feelings of oppression? Don't be afraid. You aren't alone. Turn your problems over to the greatest Father of all. Once you decide to trust Him, and let go of the emotions that have weighed you down, you'll be able to feel His love for you. You'll also discover what a great plan He has for your future.

"Bless—affectionately, gratefully praise—
the Lord, you his angels, you mighty
ones who do His commandments,
hearkening to the voice of His Word."
Psalms 103:20 (AMP)

In this verse we get a revelation of who the angels are and what they are supposed to be doing. There is a lot of focus today on angels in the media with TV shows and movies. All of them try to depict the role of *God's mighty ones*. Although the Bible is very clear about God's heavenly host, there are few verses about them. In fact, the Bible warns us of placing more emphasis on them than on God Himself. When this happens, we have made them idols, and we become idol worshipers. The Bible teaches we are not to pray to angels or have a personal relationship with them. The truth is when God created man, the Bible says the angels watched, baffled and in much awe over who we were. The Bible also says they wondered why God would give us so much attention.

God assigned angels to come along side us to help. So how do we activate our angel's assistance? This verse let's us know that *they hearken to the voice of God*. However, this doesn't mean God is Heaven's military general, and He gives them orders. The truth is when God created mankind, you and me, in His image, He said, "Let **them** have dominion on earth." This means the authority belongs to us. This is why it is so important we watch what we say. Remember, the Bible is God speaking to you. When we speak His Word or quote verses that are pertinent to our specific needs, the angels in effect are hearing God. His Word, coming out of our mouths, is God's voice in the earth. Once they hear it, they hearken to it by going into action to see that it comes to pass.

Daniel prayed and asked God to help him. The Bible records God sent an angel immediately, but because of the spiritual warfare—fighting demonic spirits in the heavenlies—it took the angel twenty-one days to get there to complete God's mission and answer the prayer. If we don't speak the Word or ask God for help, our angels just stand around, waiting for orders. Maybe you can now understand why God puts so much emphasis on us knowing what He says in His Word…and …why the enemy does everything he can to keep us from reading, hearing, and speaking it. Are you speaking God's Word over your situation? Don't be afraid. Put your heavenly host to work. They are powerful agents working on your behalf, and they will respond to your command—God's Word—God's Voice in the earth!

JUNE 6

> *"When anxiety was great within me, your consolation brought joy to my soul."*
> *Psalms 94:19 (NIV)*

Anxiety is another powerful and destructive emotion. It torments the soul, which is our mind, will, and emotions into believing the worst, and it quickly turns any situation from a mole hill into a mountain size crisis. Anxiety comes from fear. Fear steals and destroys our peace, which steals and destroys our joy, which steals and destroys our strength, which steals and destroys our faith. Doesn't this sound like the work of the devil? Didn't he come to kill, steal, and destroy? The Bible says we are to be anxious for nothing. You may be thinking, "But you just don't know or couldn't possibly understand how bad it is. I can't help but worry. I care too much. I'm afraid of what might happen." God knew you would be going through your battle, and yet, His Word commands us to not be anxious. The Bible says be anxious for nothing. "No-thing." In today's traumas this seems almost impossible. So how does God expect us to walk through life worry free?

In this verse David says it was *God's consolation that brought joy to his soul*—which is his mind, will, and emotions. It was God's consolation that replaced great, even tormenting anxiety. What was this consolation? How did David receive it? Webster's Dictionary defines consolation as, "to alleviate the grief, sense of loss or trouble; to comfort; something that consoles." David made a decision to think about the things of God. He reminded Himself that God was bigger than any lion, bear or giant he was going to have to kill. He didn't waiver or doubt. He put His hope and faith in the Faithful One. For most of us when trouble comes, we seem to forget that although it is a surprise to us, it isn't a surprise to God. He already has our answer. Plus, there is "no-thing" too big for God.

It is possible to go through life worry free, but it's our choice. We can focus on the problem or we can exchange those thoughts with what God says in His Word. We can remind ourselves we don't have to be afraid because our God is bigger than the attack of the enemy. The Word says, "If God be for me then who can be against me?" Who is trying to come against you, anyway? Isn't it the devil with the same old lies, the same old health issues, the same old problems at school, the same old boss, the same old________. You fill in the blank. But the truth is the devil was already defeated! So what do you think the outcome of this crisis will be, too? Don't be afraid. Get in the Word. Follow David's lead and think on the goodness of God. Remind yourself of God's faithfulness to you in the past. He loves you. He loves your family. Let God alleviate the grief or loss. Receive His consolation and comfort. He will completely restore joy to your soul, too.

JUNE 7

> *"Your Word, O Lord, is eternal; it stands firm in the heavens."*
> *Psalms 119:89 (NIV)*

The Bible says, "Heaven and earth will pass away, but the Word of the Lord will remain forever." The Word is God speaking to us today, and this verse confirms that the Word is the one constant, continual, forever weapon we can use to defeat fear and the enemy, regardless of our problems. Why is there such value put on God's Word? It's not just because it comes from God. The Bible says, "God magnifies the Word above Himself." God is stating for the record…HIS WORD NEVER CHANGES. Once He says it…it becomes law. If He ever changed it, even one time, then the devil would be able to defeat us.

The word eternal means everlasting or an infinite duration. Webster's Dictionary defines it as, "valid or existing at all times." The Bible says, "In the beginning was the Word, and the Word was with God, and the Word was God." In other words, it has always been, and it always will be. God gave us His Word. Not only to be our constant companion, but to be our force or weapon against any attack of the devil. Most people, even Christians, don't understand how powerful it is. This is why they don't read it or speak it when they are in trouble.

However, the enemy knows its power, and he takes it seriously. The Bible also says the enemy comes to steal the Word from us…for the Word's sake. What does this mean? It means he knows the Word will defeat him. So, if he can keep us distracted or too busy to read it or study it, if he can stir up confusion in doctrine or bring division within the church, if he can keep theologians arguing about interpretations, if he can cause an argument after the Sunday morning service between a husband and wife or their children, then he knows the chances of anyone remembering the Word, and using it against him, is pretty slim. This is his plan…distraction, chaos, confusion, division, turmoil. All of these things are designed to keep the Word from sinking into our hearts and renewing our minds, so we can be transformed.

When we become distracted or so focused on our own problems, there isn't much time to share the good news. This is partly how the enemy keeps people in bondage. However, God said the knowledge of the truth would make us free. Don't be afraid. His *eternal Word stands firm in the heavens.* It is the truth…the ultimate authority. Do you have knowledge of it? Maybe you still need to be free in some areas? God has done all He can do. Now, it's really up to you. Learn the truth. Learn the Word. Then, speak it! Let the enemy know who will be having the last, final, forever, eternal Word on the subject…your Father, GOD!

JUNE 8

> *"In my distress I cried unto the Lord, and he heard me."*
> *Psalms 120:1 (KJV)*

This verse is repeated in a variety of ways and numerous times throughout the Scriptures. They all have the same theme. 1) If you have distress, trouble or problems. 2) Call on the Name of the Lord or cry out to God. 3) He will hear, He will answer, and He will deliver you out of them all. The problem is most people don't believe God hears them. Nor do they believe they hear from God. It doesn't matter whether they've known the Lord for six months, ten years or even longer. They still feel like they don't hear God's voice. However, the Bible says, "The shepherd knows the sheep's voice and the sheep know His voice." So how can you know for sure it's His voice?

If a few days after we first met I called you on the phone and said, "Hi, how's it going?" do you think you would recognize my voice? Probably not. We might have to talk for a few minutes or you may even have to ask, "Who is this?" But if we talked daily or several times a day, I could call and just say "Hi," and you would know who it was. Why? Now my voice sounds familiar to you. It works the same way with God. When you pray to God, which is a two way conversation, and you talk with Him often enough you will learn to recognize His voice, too. Plus, the Word is God speaking to you. Are you reading it or are you spending any time with Him? When you pray, do you expect to hear by waiting for conversation? Or do you hurriedly speak out your requests then dash off to your busy schedule? Prayer is nothing more than a dialogue with God, and dialogue is a two way event. God wants a relationship with you.

Maybe you have waited and you do hear a voice, but you aren't sure if it's God, the devil or yourself. Can you know? Is there a sure way to tell? Here is a good rule to follow. If your answer or what you hear isn't what you were expecting or what you would think about or even what you would want to do...it's not from you. And if the answer will bring Glory to God and serve His purposes on earth ...then it's not from the enemy, either. In both cases what you're hearing is coming from the Lord. Remember, the more you talk with Him and read the Word the better acquainted you'll become with His voice and His ways. Don't be afraid. The enemy tries to trick us into thinking we don't hear the Lord. So, out of fear, we don't do anything. Get rid of the fear. God loves you. Even now He's waiting to talk with you. Trust Him. He knows your voice, and His Word promises you'll recognize His voice, too.

"Know therefore that the Lord our God is God; he is the faithful God, keeping his covenant of love to a thousand generations of those who love him and keep his commands."
Deuteronomy 7:9 (NIV)

Once again Moses, God's chosen leader, is instructing the people of the things of God. The Israelites had been delivered out of 400 years of slavery. They had witnessed God's powerful hand when He parted the Red Sea, which allowed them to cross over to safety on dry ground. Then, after they reached the other side, they watched Him close up the same mighty waters and drown their enemies. They had seen God provide a cloud by day and a fire by night to guide them. They daily ate the fresh food which He alone provided for them. After God told Moses to strike a rock, they had drinking water. Clean water for over two million people. Can you imagine a rock, from the desert, offering water for that many people?

It is for this reason Moses confidently says, "***Our God is God,***" and *He is faithful* to deliver and *keep His love* toward them just as He promised *for a thousand generations.* Now medical statistics show that a generation is approximately 51.7 years. Since we know God doesn't lie, this would mean His covenant would be established for 51,700 years. No one can argue that His original covenant is still available to us today. God's covenant made a way for them, and it is still making a way for us.

The greatest part of this covenant God created for us is it is a covenant of love, and He makes it available to *those who love Him and will obey His commands.* I ask you, "How could you not love someone who loved you first? And because of this love, has already made from before your birth, special provision for you in His plans and purposes?" He wants us to follow His commands, but when you are so loved by someone, it isn't hard to do what they ask. In fact, most of the time, they don't have to ask because you are already trying to please them, right? Genuine love is a great motivator, and God's love is real. It's unconditional, and the Bible says nothing—not one thing—can ever separate us from God's love.

If you don't have this kind of relationship with your Father God, then you are missing out. Don't be afraid. Lay down any former views and opinions of Him, and get to know Him. He loves you, remember? And just as He promised Moses and the children of Israel that He would be with them forever, we still have the same covenant promise today.

> *"Strengthen the weak hands, and make firm the feeble and tottering knees. Say to those who are of a fearful and hasty heart, Be strong, fear not! Behold, your God will come with a vengeance, with the recompense of God; He will come and save you."*
> *Isaiah 35:3-4 (AMP)*

Have you ever witnessed a child being bullied by someone, and at just the right moment their big brother shows up to save them? Regardless of the fighting that may go on between these two at home, when he sees someone trying to take advantage of his younger sibling…it's all over! The bigger, older brother is coming with a vengeance. You better believe recompense will be with him. Recompense means to return in kind or to compensate. Now, if our natural instincts are to fight and protect our loved ones, how much more do you think God will fight and protect us…His loved ones?

Once I got caught in the middle of a situation that caused me so much fear I couldn't stop my knees from knocking together—and I was sitting down. The details aren't worth telling, but I found myself in serious danger. Have you ever come face to face with life-changing fear? If so, then you know how overwhelming it can be. I didn't know this verse at the time. Actually, my biggest problem was I didn't know the Lord at that time either. If I had, I wouldn't have been in the mess I was in. It was only the goodness of God and His great love that offered me the complete protection I needed that day. God is love, and His love to us is immeasurable. He knew the plans He had for my life, and that day He came and saved me…He made firm my feeble and tottering knees.

God also knows the plans He has for you. You may feel like it's too late, but it is never too late with God. In retelling this event, it's like I'm talking about someone else. Now, because of my relationship with the Lord, I'm not the same. God has helped me overcome my past. He can help you overcome yours, too. Maybe you have done things you regret? We're all guilty of doing things we are now sorry for, but whether we brought fear upon ourselves or another inflicts it upon us, God protects, strengthens, saves, and encourages us. His Word to us is, "*Be strong and fear not!*" He is the "big brother" many of us never had, and His plan of love and guidance doesn't change. Don't be afraid. Don't let the mistakes of your past keep you from God or your future. You'll find God will come to save and strengthen you, too, and this verse confirms that when He comes *He always has recompense* or compensation in His hand.

"BUT NOW, this is what the Lord says—he who created you, O Jacob, he who formed you, O Israel: Fear not, for I have redeemed you; I have summoned you by name; you are mine."
Isaiah 43:1 (NIV)

Verses like this one should put the skeptic's doubts or questions about where mankind came from to rest. Once you study the Word of God and its thorough explanation of how God created every living thing—including man—it takes more "faith" to believe the other theories than it does to just accept God's supernatural power, wisdom, and design. Why was it important to God for His chosen people to understand that He was the One who created and formed them? Because He wants us all to know there isn't anything He doesn't already know about us. The truth is He knows us better than we know ourselves. This is vitally important because it allows us to be able to trust His ways and decisions for our lives. Even if it makes no sense to us at the time, due to our own limited thinking, we can still be obedient to what He said in His Word or directly to us through prayer. We then just follow His plan. This trust or faith is what produces the confidence to continue to follow Him, regardless of what is going on around us.

The events in our lives are no surprise to God. This doesn't mean everything comes from Him because we know the Word clearly states that only good and perfect things come from our Father. It also warns us about the tricks, pitfalls, and devises the devil uses, too. When we find ourselves in a hard or devastating time of life, our Father has made a way for us to go through it and come out on top. The truth is when we come through, we are stronger in character, and our faith has always been increased. Do you need help? Are you tired of "going it alone?" God never intended for any of us to do this "life thing" by ourselves. Do you know when He created you He also created a great plan for your life?

God says to, *"Fear not, for I have redeemed you."* In other words, God has changed things for the better, freed us from distresses or harm, helped us overcome negative opposition, and freed us from the consequences of sin. Why? Because we are His and He redeems His own. Don't be afraid. If you haven't made the decision to come into the family of God, don't wait. Do it now. He is calling you...*summoning you by name.*

> *"When thou passest through the waters, I will be with thee; and through the rivers, they shall not overflow thee: when thou walkest through the fire, thou shalt not be burned; neither shall the flame kindle upon thee."*
> *Isaiah 43:2 (KJV)*

One of the encouraging parts of this verse is the word "*passest*" because it tells us we don't have to stay in our situations. We won't be camping out, nor will we have to stay in our troubles or distresses. We are going to go through. The Word describes how the children of Israel literally went through many rivers and deep waters in order to reach their Promised Land, and God was with them each time.

The Word also tells of three young Hebrew men who would not bow to a false god. They were bound and thrown into a furnace that was made to be seven times hotter. When the guards opened the door to throw the young men in, they were killed instantly, so other guards came and threw them in. Minutes later the king said, "Weren't those men bound, and weren't there just three men? Why do I see four men, loosed, and the fourth man looks like the Son of God?" That day the wicked king bowed his knee to the real and living God. The Word also says when these boys came out of the fire…they didn't even smell like smoke. How can this be? The Bible says all things are possible with God and to those who believe.

Years ago in a worship service I saw a very young girl come and kneel at the altar. She was sobbing desperately. I remember wondering at the time what could have caused her to be in such grief or agony. Instantly the Lord spoke to me that the enemy doesn't care how old you are. In fact, if he can inflict his pain and injustice on you as a child, it can be harder to let your guard down, move past the trauma, and trust people. This ability to trust also includes being able to trust their Heavenly Father. Maybe you're still carrying wounds and hurts from your childhood? God will not only deliver you from them, but you won't smell like the "smoke" of your fire, either.

Life isn't fair, and nowhere in God's Word did He say it would be. However, it continually says that God is "just." This means He sees everything, and because He is "just," He will make it right. Isaiah 35:4 says, "He comes with vengeance and recompense." It wasn't fair these Hebrew men had to endure the fire for their beliefs, but God showed up, the king's heart was changed, and these men were promoted to be leaders. Is what you're facing unfair, too? Don't be afraid. God is with you, and the good news is…you aren't stopping here…*when thou passest through.* With God, you will pass on through to your intended victory, too!

"The Lord will keep you from all harm—
he will watch over your life; the Lord
will watch over your coming and going
both now and forevermore."
Psalms 121:7-8 (NIV)

Webster's Dictionary defines the word watch to mean, "the act of keeping awake to guard, protect, or attend; the state of alert and continuous attention; close observation." One way we find ourselves appreciative of these attentive actions is how it relates to us and the weather. Today meteorologists use highly sensitive and advanced weather equipment to pinpoint the most devastating storms. This sophisticated equipment usually gives people in the area enough warning so they can secure their possessions and still have time to get themselves to safety. If your community has ever needed this information, you're extremely grateful to those individuals that stay on "watch" in your area.

This verse comforts us with the knowledge that we each have a "watchman" in our life, and the benefits affect more than the weather. With God watching over us, we can be assured nothing will escape His vision, including the present storm you're trying to come through right now. He also wants us to know from this verse that His shift never ends. He doesn't put in His forty hours, and then we're on our own. He also doesn't take off holidays or weekends. Nor does He look for a substitute, so He can take a vacation. This is a forever, full-time job. One He takes very seriously.

The Bible says, "God knows the end from the beginning." Wouldn't you like to know how everything you're going through is going to end? Wouldn't you also like to know in advance what's coming? Most people do. This is why psychics, astrology, and other so-called spiritual mediums are so popular today. However, they are extremely dangerous. They can open the door to demonic activity which gives evil spirits the right to come into every area of your life. You think you have problems now? You won't believe how bad it can get! Remember, one of the ways the devil works is through deception. But the good news is the Bible tells us God defeated the devil…he has no future. So, why would you want to consult with someone that has no future about yours? God has all the information we will ever need to know about the present and upcoming attractions in our lives. Wisdom says we'd be further ahead asking the creator of life. This Word confirms He <u>*watches*</u> everything, *our coming and going*, and He will keep us from harm's way. He will warn us in advance…if we ask. Don't be afraid! Ask Him. He'll answer every question you have, not only for today, but forever more. Plus, you will never have to wonder if His answer is the right one for you.

> *"The Lord has done great things for us, and we are filled with joy."*
> *Psalms 126:3 (NIV)*

If you think back over your life, I'm sure you can remember a time that brings back happy or fond memories. It may be a special birthday, an anniversary celebration, your wedding day, college graduation, the birth of a child or a career promotion that brought you joy and a sense of fulfillment. These are some of life's sweetest treasures, but they're only the special highlights in a person's life. This verse, however, creates a picture of a lifetime of *great things* from God—not just moments, a particular event or even a season. When you know all His blessings and goodness will abound to you as part of a life-long covenant package—joy overcomes you. This new life is the greatest joy and fulfillment.

You might be thinking, "I don't know what that's like. How can someone way up there be good to someone way down here?" Well, the first revelation is God isn't "way up" anywhere. The Bible says when we ask the Lord to come into our heart, to cleanse us of our sin, and to lead us in His ways—He does just that. As strange as it may sound, He truly comes and takes up residence in our heart. How is this possible? We are a three part being. We're a spirit, with a soul—our mind, will, and emotions, and we live in a body. When we ask God to come into our heart, our spirit is reborn. This is where the term "born again" originated. God is now able to communicate with us because He is a Spirit. His Spirit, living on the inside of us, is what gives us the confidence and ability to understand His Word and His ways.

God loves you, and He desires to have a relationship with you. Have you asked Him into your heart? Or maybe you did at one time, but the trials of this life have forced you to turn your back on Him? Maybe you prayed, but you don't feel like God gave you the outcome you wanted? The enemy would love to trick you into blaming God for your situation. However, the truth is no one loves you more, has already done, and wants to do more for you than your Father. Why wait? Don't be afraid! Ask the Lord now to come and live on the inside of you and to forgive you. If you have been angry or left His path for your life, return to Him, and ask Him to forgive you. He'll never turn you away. He promises to bless <u>you</u>, protect <u>you</u> from harm, never leave <u>you</u>, always love <u>you</u>, and so very much more. His *"great things"* will truly make <u>you</u> glad!

> *"In the day when I cried thou answeredst me, and strengthenedst me with strength in my soul."*
> *Psalms 138:3 (KJV)*

The NIV translation says when God answers our cry He makes us bold and stouthearted. The important thing this verse says to us is when troubles come, if we will cry out to God, He will not just answer, but He will provide the strength of heart to sustain us, too. For example, if you received a bad report from the doctor, you may have cried out to God to heal you. His Word is "He heals all your diseases." But how do you continue to walk out your faith, keep yourself free of fear, and stay strong and encouraged during the battle? The answer is… your focus—you don't look at your problem.

In any battle the first adjustment you make is to take your eyes off your problems, and put them on the problem solver. You focus on God. You focus on His goodness to you from your past troubles, and you stay focused on what the Word says about your situation. Yes, your soul will try to talk to you. Your mind, will, and emotions will want to rehearse every word the doctor, lawyer, banker, boss, ex-spouse, etc., has ever had to say about the matter. It's at this point you have to decide, "Who ya gonna call?" I'd suggest calling on the biggest problem buster around—the Lord God Almighty! His Word tells us to call on Him. He will be our every provision, encouragement, strength. He will make us bold and stouthearted.

Stouthearted isn't a word you hear often. It means to not be faint at heart. Why would this be important? When we're at our darkest hour, weak or faint at heart, fear manipulates us and takes root. The truth is without a strengthened heart, you'll never even make it to the hard part. You will have already settled for what you've heard others say. Then you will start to question where God was in your ordeal. A stout heart is crucial to you getting the victory. If you have ever dealt with a long-term problem you already know what I'm talking about. The enemy continually fills your mind with horrible thoughts about your outcome. If you don't keep your mind renewed to what God says and stay in the Word, you will become weak and lose heart to push onward. God's plan of deliverance is thorough. He doesn't just give us the answer. He gives us all we need to keep the faith until we see the victory. Don't be afraid. If you feel you have lost heart or you're close to caving in, be strengthened by God's Word. Re"mind" yourself of this verse, and draw from the strengthening power of Almighty God.

> *"The Lord is gracious; and full of compassion; slow to anger, and of great mercy. The Lord is good to all: and his tender mercies are over all his works."*
> *Psalms 145:8-9 (KJV)*

The Bible never strays from reminding us of how good, loving, and merciful God is. Why is it so important to God we get a revelation of His love? Because He knows the underlying root of every dysfunction is a love deficit. When we need an outside source to fix an inner emotional need, it's because somewhere deep within us fear exists, and we don't feel loved. Most people would admit they don't even love themselves. They have very little to no self-worth. So they aren't surprised when others don't love them or a spouse or significant other wants to break off their relationship. The truth is people are so needy to have their "love cup" filled that when it doesn't happen they become desperate. Then they feel the need to resort to drugs, alcohol, sports, sex, pornography, work, TV, shopping, eating, ______. You can fill in the blank. Anything in excess is a replacement for an inner emotional need.

However, people are not able to fill this inner hole by themselves. It can't be filled by another individual or with outside sources, either. This hole or void can only be filled with the love of God. His love is whole and satisfying. It is the only love that ever completes us. This verse also states God is slow to anger. Anger and love don't mix. Why would God slip this phrase in with all the love talk? It's because most anger or discipline we've experienced has certainly not been done out of love. Most earthly anger is abusive. It is a direct response of a heart that is filled with disappointment, hurt, and its own lack of self-worth. It is not gentle or kind. It is conditional. The truth is, just like anger, most of the earthly love we receive is conditional, too. God wants us know this is not His way. He is "*slow to anger, full of compassion, good to all, gracious, and of great mercy.*"

God is gracious and merciful. He doesn't blow you off, and there's no fear He will walk out or abandon you, either. If someone you love has rejected you or spoken harsh, negative words of defeat over you, let God fill those hurts and deep holes with His great compassion. Don't be afraid. Let go of those past words or phrases that were spoken over you. Don't allow them to fill your thoughts, and <u>QUIT</u> repeating them. It's not what God says about you. Remind yourself of this verse instead…"*The Lord is good to all.*" The Bible says <u>we</u> <u>are</u> <u>all</u> God's handi-"work." This verse confirms *His tender mercies are over all His "works."* So, you can rest assured and be confident this includes you!

"Your kingdom is an everlasting kingdom, and Your dominion endures throughout all generations."
Psalms 145:13 (AMP)

In an ever-changing world, is it important for us to be able to rely on basic truths that are not always changing with the times? God must think so because the truths found in the Bible are as right for us today as they were when He gave them to each individual person to record. Think about it. How could you believe and take action for your life if you thought He would change His mind? Or next year none of it would be relevant anyway? His Word is a life saver…like CPR. Let's look at CPR training. What if one year you're trained to open their mouth and breathe in, but two years later the training is changed to only pumping their heart because mouth to mouth is too personal for people? What kind of help would this be? And how effective would the former training be, either? What if you forgot what year it was and didn't do anything? If we change the foundational truths of CPR from using both procedures when needed, then we might as well throw it out.

The same holds true for the Word of God. This is really what a lot of individuals have tried to do with the Bible. They have manipulated the foundation by trying to discredit parts or take a few verses out of context to make it say what they want. However, the Bible warns to not add to or subtract from the Word. Do you really think God would put a plan into place for our lives and then not realize it's a "new millennium?" Could this be why the Bible states He is the same yesterday, today, and tomorrow? How could He be the same, and yet, the foundational truths He established be constantly changing? They aren't! And when we come into agreement with the great plan He has for us, it becomes totally clear He knows exactly what He's doing with our lives. He is the one stable, permanent piece all mankind desires.

In this verse God clarifies He was here from the beginning, and He isn't going anywhere until He says it's the end. The Bible says He is the Alpha…AND…the Omega. This means He is the beginning, and He is the end, too. This verse also states *His dominion endures forever, throughout all generations.* The word dominion means supreme authority; absolute ownership. In today's words, "He's the Man." Don't be afraid. You can trust Him. He loves you, and His Word is your firm foundation because it holds life's absolute truths. Let His Kingdom be your kingdom…forever.

"He upholds the cause of the oppressed and gives food to the hungry. The Lord sets prisoners free..."
Psalms 146:7 (NIV)

Oppression is a weight that burdens the mind and the body. Most times it is overwhelming, all consuming, totally debilitating. How is oppression able to get that kind of a grip on someone's life? Its root is fear. Fear forces us to be a prisoner, whether we're in jail behind bars or not. You might ask, "How can I be a prisoner if there aren't any bars?" Have you ever witnessed the big elephant at the circus with his leg connected by a chain to a small little ball? Isn't this the same animal that moves the tents, poles, and is capable of packing hundreds of pounds? How can this one tiny ball and chain be strong enough to hold him? The truth is...it isn't! So why doesn't the animal run away? It's due to its former training. When an elephant is still a baby and it hasn't developed its strength, the owners chain it to a very heavy ball. If the elephant tries to get away, it can't. Over the years, even though it has grown in size and strength, it is still under the same mindset that it can't move that heavy ball. So now it doesn't even attempt an escape.

Many of us are just like the elephant. We have been in our situations for so long that we don't try to flex our muscles, either. We have a fixed mindset about where we're at, too. We have chosen to believe the lies of the enemy, instead of the Word of God. What kind of lies? "You'll have this sickness until you die. Disease is hereditary. If your parents were poor, then you'll be poor. You're not loveable, and no man/woman will stay with you. You'll never be promoted or amount to anything. Your father was a failure and you are, too. You're an accident, not wanted, pretty or smart." Do I need to go on? After you listen to these kinds of lies long enough, you'll convict and sentence yourself to a life behind the bars of a preformed mindset. Now, just like the elephant, you not only won't try to move, but your own self-sentencing has made you afraid to believe God for a change.

Have you been struggling with the same problem? Has the devil told you it can't be beat? After trying and failing on your own, are you afraid he's right? I want to encourage you. Don't be afraid. It's not too late. Even if you're literally serving time in prison—it's still not too late. God's love and plan does not change. It doesn't matter where we are. We need to use our time to seek out the Father's will and purposes. This verse assures us, regardless of our overwhelming past afflictions, His Word brings truth and liberty. His Word alone will bind fear... every kind of fear...and it will set every captive free.

JUNE 19

> *"...the Lord gives sight to the blind, the Lord lifts up those who are bowed down, the Lord loves the righteous."*
> *Psalms 146:8 (NIV)*

If there was ever a question about God wanting to heal His people, this verse should help prove the point. His Word assures us that His will and desire is to see us healed and free of bondages. His compassion and mercy is extended to us in every situation, and at all times. However, when the pressures of life intensify, it feels as if we're the ones carrying the weight of it. Although we know our problems aren't literally sitting on our shoulders, there is a real physical weight our body experiences from life's cares. These trials and burdens cause stress which medical science has proven can be fatal. They can and have caused heart attacks, strokes, organ failure, nerve and muscle disorders, severe headaches, high cholesterol, mental and emotional fatigue, and all types of break downs.

So what is really at the root of our stress? It's fear. Oh, it will disguise itself in the form of your children, finances, job security, and so on. But fear's job is to convince us life's troubles can't be conquered. Then they become so heavy…it's as if we do physically feel bowed down from the weight. Be honest. Do you feel the difference in your body when your problems appear to stay the same? Or what if you can't complete something in the time frame allotted? Now you might be thinking, "Well, that's not why I'm stressed. My schedule is just too full. I'm trying to do more than what's humanly possible in a 24 hour day." If this is true, then why don't you cut things out? Aren't you in charge of your own schedule? The truth is when others are involved, many times we don't change the plan because of fear they won't like it. What will they say? What will they think if you or your children don't participate in this anymore? Any excuse to not make the needed changes can still be fear based.

God didn't design us to operate under the weight of fear. If you've been praying and asking Him to help you manage stress or fear, He won't. Why? Because He doesn't want you to just manage it…He wants you to get rid of it, and His Word gives you the ability to do so. I challenge you to examine your situation honestly. Aren't you really afraid that you don't see how you can win in some area? Or maybe your trial has now become bigger than life, and fear is controlling you? If you are trying to cram more than is humanly possible into a day, then you already know you need the supernatural ability of God to help you. Don't be afraid. The key to living stress-free is to learn to give it all to Him. Release any fear and heaviness. *God will lift you up* and provide the cure for any and every one of your challenges.

> *"Because of the Lord's great love we are not consumed, for his compassions never fail. They are new every morning; great is your faithfulness."*
> *Lamentations 3:22-23 (NIV)*

This verse, like a song's chorus, repeats the theme of God's great love for us and His never ending compassion. The word compassion in this verse refers to the mercy of God. Webster's Dictionary defines the word mercy to mean, "a blessing that is an act of divine favor or compassion; compassionate treatment of those in distress; lenient or compassionate treatment." In other words, God's divine favor and compassion is a blessing that is shown to us at all times; when we are in distress and even when we don't deserve it. This verse confirms it is *because of His love* that He is lenient with His treatment to us, and *because of His love* we *are not consumed.* It all comes down to *the Lord's great love*, which never fails us.

Consume is a powerful word. Webster defines it as, "to destroy or to do away with completely; to use up; to fully engage or engross; to waste or burn away or perish." Many times in life we experience devastating traumas, deaths, bankruptcies—emotional and financial—long term illnesses, and so on. They leave us feeling like we've been eaten up, used up, and maybe even completely destroyed. Have you ever felt like you were about to be consumed by your circumstances? It's at times like these we must turn to and trust in the living God. This verse is only one of many we can use to encourage ourselves. We can count on His love, provision, and His tender mercies.

The good news is God said His mercies would be new every morning. We don't have to be afraid He won't be there for us or we have to share our mercies. We'll never have to be concerned we have already used up our portion for the day, week, or even the month when it's just the fifth day. We aren't on a quota of how many times we can draw from the mercies of God. This verse confirms one more time, *God is faithful.* The Amplified translation says, "Great and abundant is your stability and faithfulness." If you have ever made a mistake, then you know what a relief and comfort this is. The truth is all of us have made bad decisions; some of the consequences may still be evident in our lives today. However, God's plan is big enough, lenient enough, and compassionate enough for you to work with your current circumstances. Don't be afraid. *His love and compassions never fail.* This means He will be there for you...every time! Just remember, *GREAT is His love and faithfulness* to you.

> *"Turn you to the stronghold [of security and prosperity], you prisoners of hope; even today do I declare that I will restore double your former prosperity to you."*
> *Zechariah 9:12 (AMP)*

Zechariah was also one of God's prophets. His prophecies to the people began about 520 B.C., and it was during a time when they had just started to rebuild the temple. God wanted them to understand several key issues. First and foremost they were to listen to Him. Then they were to stay encouraged and comforted by the long range plan God had for them. They were to obey God by acting fairly and mercifully to one another, and they were to be obedient to God in their relationship with Him.

We still have prophets today who speak the Word of God into our lives, but they couldn't speak any truer or more relevant words than Zechariah. Why? Because God is still saying the same thing to His people today. They may have been rebuilding the temple because of its destruction, but God is rebuilding His church because He still has a plan for His own. He continues to encourage and comfort us through His Word. We need a relationship with Him so we can hear His voice, understand His Word, and continue to hear our future instructions. The Bible says, "Faith works by love," so if we want our faith to work and we want to please God, we must love others as God loves us, and we must continue to work toward helping our fellowman.

Expecting double and then God granting it, isn't new. Many prophets called forth God's promise of a double return for their losses, grief, sins or troubles, and they received it. In the book of Job we see Job went through extreme troubles that weren't "fair," but he held on to his faith in God, and everything was restored back to him…double. This verse states God will do the same thing for us. How can this be? Where does it all come from? God Himself makes the way. The Bible says all things are possible with God. Wouldn't you like to have everything the devil stole from you paid back? Double? We all would, and we can count on God to keep His Word in this verse just like we can when He says He will heal or protect or give guidance for our daily living in the other verses. Maybe you're thinking, "Well, that's a lot to expect?" God wouldn't have said it, if it were not part of His plan. However, if you don't believe you'll be paid back, you won't, but you need to realize it's fear that keeps us from believing God's Word. Don't be afraid. God is a big God. He loves to make the devil "pay up." Believe God… take Him at His Word…expect double!

"For you created my inmost being; you knit me together in my mother's womb. I praise you because I am fearfully and wonderfully made; your works are wonderful, I know that full well. My frame was not hidden from you when I was made in the secret place. When I was woven together in the depths of the earth, your eyes saw my unformed body. All the days ordained for me were written in your book before one of them came to be."
Psalms 139:13-16 (NIV)

The greatest fear man struggles with is his identity and how that relates to his destiny. We all have a purpose in being here, and we go through life searching for meaning and fulfillment. I know if your birth circumstances were not the most favorable, it may be difficult for you to believe these verses. But what you have to remember is there are no surprises to God. If your mother conceived you out of wedlock or you were the result of rape or abuse, do you think it caught God off guard? I don't mean to minimize the pain and offense that accompany these situations, but this doesn't mean God's Word isn't true for you. God still saw you, formed you, and created you. You are as fearfully and wonderfully made as the child who was born in the most ideal settings.

You might be thinking, "Well if God knew about my past, then why would He allow such a negative situation to happen?" God gives all of us a free will to make our own decisions. When we don't follow His ways and plan, we end up with "not so great" consequences. However, God has never left your side, and these verses prove He has always had a plan for you, too. It's not too late for you to get into His plan and fulfill your destiny.

Do you battle with feeling unworthy? Do you wonder about your purpose or if you even have one? Are you convinced God could never use or want someone like you? God wants to show you His plan for your life. He loved you before you were formed, and He still loves you now. The Word says nothing separates us from God's love, but you can separate yourself from Him. How? By rejecting Him—His love and plan. Don't be afraid. God doesn't make mistakes, nor does He change His mind about our outcome half way into the program. This verse proves He has always had a plan for you. You belong to God. Follow Him. You'll walk out your destiny, too.

*"Even there shall thy hand lead me,
and thy right hand shall hold me."
Psalms 139:10 (KJV)*

In the verses prior to this one David is asking God, "Where could he go that God's Spirit and Presence would not be there, as well?" He suggests if he went to the heavens, God would be there or if he went to the depths of the earth, God would be there, too. He states if he took the wings of the morning or went to the uttermost parts of the sea, God would be there, also. In other words, David had come to recognize that God went with him everywhere. In this verse he summarizes it is *God's hand that leads him*, and it's *God's right hand* that offers David every support he will ever need.

David realized "with God" he was never alone. This eliminated any fear his circumstances tried to produce. This should be a comforting thought to us, as well. We don't have to be alone or afraid, either. We have a Father who loves us and wants to be with us, regardless of who we are or where we go. The fear of being alone is a huge problem, especially today. The extreme success of the cell phone confirms that people don't want to be by themselves. In the beginning they were mainly used for convenience, business or emergencies, but not anymore. For most it has become a steady, constant, reliable companion…that is…as long as they can stay in range and the reception is good.

In this verse David confesses that God's "reception" and "roaming power" reaches everywhere. His Spirit and awesome Presence will be with us, as it was with him. Plus, God leads, guides, and can simplify even the busiest of schedules. How would you like to know in advance about an accident or road construction, so you don't have to sit in bumper-to-bumper traffic? Or how would you like to know which business deals would be a sure thing? Do you need wisdom or would you like someone to be with you when you meet with the banker, doctor or your boss? God is willing to be your constant companion. He never intended for you to make this journey through life by yourself. Don't be afraid. He loves you and wants to be with you. Regardless of your situation, you don't have to feel lonely ever again. The next time you start to pick up the phone to call a friend, why not make the decision to talk to your "best" friend…a "true" friend… instead. A friend, the Word says, "Who stays closer than a brother." He's right there—"*even there*"—as David writes. You'll quickly discover your conversations and time spent with Him will be so much more enlightening!

> *"Behold, the Lord thy God doth set the land before thee: go up and possess it, as the Lord God of thy fathers hath said unto thee; fear not, neither be discouraged."*
> *Deuteronomy 1:21 (KJV)*

God spoke this verse to Moses as it was time for them to enter the Promised Land. Moses then sent one man from each tribe, twelve in all, to spy out the land. When they returned, only two of the spies were willing to "*go up and possess the land.*" What happened? The others were afraid of what they saw. The land was exactly how the Lord said it would be, but the people who were living there were giants. Ten of the spies said they couldn't do it "because we are grasshoppers in their sight." Now God had just told them to *fear not and to not be discouraged.* Do you think He might have known the giants were living there? Is it possible His "fear not" speech was not only trying to warn them, but also encourage them because of it? However, because of fear they chose to disobey God. As a result that generation never received God's full provision. That is, all but the two spies who believed they could do it. Forty years later, with strong faith, they led the new generation of God's people into what He had promised for them all along.

For the most part when feelings of fear try to rise up in us, what we think is going to happen rarely happens. The enemy uses fear as his biggest weapon because he knows it keeps us from believing God. If we don't believe, then we probably won't obey His plan, either. We set ourselves up to fail. How? Because one of the consequences of disobedience is we aren't positioned in the right place to receive the fullness and goodness of what God had originally planned. This is clearly demonstrated to us by the spies' actions. They never talked to the giants, and yet, they said the giants saw them as grasshoppers. The truth is this is how they saw themselves.

Aren't we the same way today? Be honest. What kind of value or opinion do you have of yourself? Based on past experiences or relationships do you believe you don't have much significance, either? Do you see yourself the way God sees you? If our view of ourselves is incorrect, it will keep us from becoming who God created us to be, which also keeps us from doing and receiving all He has planned. God's Word spells out who we are, and He makes it clear we don't ever have to be afraid. His Word, which is the truth about any situation, is available to assure and strengthen us to keep moving forward. Don't be afraid. Let us learn from the mistakes of our ancestors. Let us trust God—no matter "how big or how small" the trial. When we believe and obey His Word, we, too, will successfully go through life with a "*fear not, neither be discouraged*" attitude.

"Roll your works upon the Lord—commit and trust them wholly to Him; [He will cause your thoughts to become agreeable to His will, and] so shall your plans be established and succeed."
Proverbs 16:3 (AMP)

Most of the Proverbs were written by Solomon who is considered to be the wisest man who ever lived. What had Solomon come to know about the ways or works of God that he was sharing in this verse? He wanted us to understand the only way to accomplish true success is to trust God and to get into His plan. Solomon uses the word commit which means to deliberately put into action or to entrust. In other words, Solomon deliberately or purposefully made a decision, and then, took action to entrust himself into God's capable hands. Solomon learned when he put his faith, trust or confidence in God's plans that somehow his personal thoughts regarding a subject were soon changed to agree with God's plans and thoughts. Why would this be important? God cannot fail, so when Solomon's thoughts, which produced actions, came into agreement with God's plan, it automatically assured him that he would achieve success, as well.

God wants us to be assured of the same success. The problems arise when we don't ask God for direction. Or even if we do ask, we don't follow them after we receive them. Why would we choose to not follow God Almighty's advice? It could be that most of the time, when we hear God's directions, they don't make much sense to us; we don't like or even agree with what we've heard. However, not following His instructions will bring automatic failure. When we commit to or trust God, we need to do what He says. It's in the walking it out process that our thoughts and wisdom are enlightened. Only then are we able to see what God is truly doing, not only in our life, but in all those around us, too. His plan has now become our plan. *So shall your plans be established and succeed.*

I was in my late twenties when I decided to follow God's plan for my life. Although I had reached a level of success on my own, I had also made enough mistakes to realize I didn't have all the answers. Have you discovered the same thing for yourself? Maybe this period of "trials and mainly errors" is what made it easier for me to commit my ways to the Lord's ways. Even when my answer from God made no sense to me or others...I knew Him well enough to know not to leave the plan. The Bible says God's ways and thoughts are higher than ours. I have learned—like Solomon and millions of others—I can't go wrong if I follow God's plan. If you decide to follow His plan, you won't go wrong, either. Don't be afraid. You can trust His plan for you. He loves you. "Deliberately" decide or commit all that you do to the Lord, and watch "your—His" plans succeed.

> *"When a man's ways please the Lord, he maketh even his enemies to be at peace with him."*
> *Proverbs 16:7 (KJV)*

When you're going through a period of war or any adverse situation, it seems impossible that God could change the heart of your enemy. However, this verse confirms He *makes* it so you and your enemy can live in peace with one another. I have seen God do this very thing in my own life. I had a co-worker, who for some unknown reason to me, continually tried to cause trouble for my staff and department. The accusations were unfounded, but to research it and prepare the reports or proper documentation to prove it would have cost me much time and extra work. After numerous attacks I finally went to the Lord and asked, "What is the problem?" And "What do You want me to do about it?"

The Lord explained this person was very insecure. They were also going through a difficult time at home. He told me to pray for them and to believe their heart would be changed. He told me to bind fear in their life so they could trust God for what they needed. I obeyed and immediately started to pray for them. Just two days after I started praying and the last attack, my boss notified me that "my accuser" had contacted them to say they had made a mistake. It was no longer necessary for me to investigate the problem. I never had any other problems from this person again. Through my obedience and prayer, God *made* my enemy live at peace with me.

Are you at war with someone in your life? Is the devil using someone to attack you? God is able to change your situation, too. This verse reminds us the key is to *please the Lord*. What if my response to God's request would have been, "Pray for them? Are you kidding? They're the problem…not me! Besides, they're treating me unfairly. They don't deserve prayer. Just get them out of my life." Do you think God's response to my situation would have been different? Do you think the change would have occurred in just days, after months of persecution? I believe God responded to me because I responded to His Word and direction. My ways were pleasing to the Lord, so He brought peace. God can change the hearts of your enemies, too. Will you do what He says? Will you follow His plan, walk in love, and pray for those who willfully and spitefully persecute you? This is what the Bible says we are to do. Don't be afraid. Greater is "HE" that lives in you, than "he" that lives in the world. Bind fear, and receive His love. Receive His plan for you. A plan that includes a life of peace…with everyone.

"Pride only breeds quarrels, but wisdom is found in those who take advice."
Proverbs 13:10 (NIV)

The Bible says there are seven things that are detestable to the Lord. One of them is a haughty or proud look. Did you know "pride" has a look? You might be thinking, "I thought we were supposed to take pride in things like our job, our families or ourselves? Why does God hate pride?" The main reason is it puts the focus on the wrong source. Many of the things we are proud of are external and they give us a false sense of self-worth. If we are in bondage to things for our worth, then what happens if we lose those things? History has shown us what happens to people whose worth is tied up in money or possessions, regardless of how hard they worked or sacrificed to achieve them. The fear of living without "their" things drove them to take drastic measures.

A proud look is the reflection of an attitude that holds you in a higher regard than others. How do you view others? Are you only attracted to those whose dress, car, house or outer exterior says, "I've arrived?" God's plan includes the best, but when the best is necessary in order for you to draw identity or self-worth…you are asking for trouble. Fear of man and putting on an image for others is bondage. After awhile, the biggest problem is the devil convinces you this is really who you are. Then you get on life's treadmill cycle of needing even more. Fear and pride are both relentless driving forces that can create unquenchable desires.

This verse says *pride only breeds quarrels*. In other words, it is an instigator of arguments. Does this sound like your life? Is it hard for you to discuss things with friends, family or co-workers without disagreeing or a quarrel breaking out? Do you always have to make your opinions, comments or ideas known? If so, pride is at work. However, the root of pride is fear. Fear and pride will always tell you…it has to be your way…you have to be right. Unfortunately, the truth is either of these results are just cover-ups for deep insecurities which make you feel like you have no value, unless you're the one calling the shots. The Bible says, "Pride goes before a fall," and it's any or all of the above that puts you into this category. Approval from others doesn't add worth to your life. People and things come and go, but God will be with you forever. This verse also points out the importance of receiving advice. In fact, it states it is a wise man who receives advice…even if it's in the form of correction. Fear can close both your ears and heart to hear from God and man. Don't be afraid. God loves "you," and He made "you" in His image. Let the advice found in God's Word bring you encouragement and direction. When you do, you'll find it reveals your true identity, gives you legitimate value, and fulfills your ultimate purpose.

"Thus saith the Lord, thy Redeemer, the Holy One of Israel; I am the Lord thy God which teacheth thee to profit, which leadeth thee by the way that thou shouldest go."
Isaiah 48:17 (KJV)

There should be no dispute...**God is God,** and He has always had a plan for us. This plan offers us a life that is fulfilling. The NIV translation says, "...I am the Lord your God, who teaches you what is best for you, who directs you in the way you should go." God wants us to have success, but there is only one way of achieving true success. This way is to follow Him and the plan He established for each one of us.

God promises to lead and teach, but this means we have to position ourselves to become like a student to hear and learn. Are you willing to let Him direct and lead your every decision? We all have areas that need to be changed, but the most difficult part sometimes is knowing what to do and when to do it. The best move you can make is to get the Lord involved. Don't you think it's time to turn it over to Him? God has the answer that will change your problem. Why don't you want to ask Him what to do? Or why do you wait until the last minute to surrender to His ways? True wisdom is...the sooner you give it over to God, the sooner it will get fixed.

Once, while I was stuck in eight lanes of bumper to bumper traffic, I thought about my next move. How far would I have to go before I could get off? Should I get off or would it be faster to stay on the freeway and wait it out? I then saw a helicopter fly over me toward the cause of the delay. I thought I'd sure like to know their number. I'd call and find out what happened and where the problem was located. Then I'd know for sure which move would be the right move. It was then the Lord spoke to me. He said, "I have the same, even better view of the situation. Why don't you ask me?" It was true. I could ask Him. I could ask the God of the Universe for the answer. No doubt, He could tell me the way to go.

I learned a valuable lesson that day, and I knew He wasn't just talking about the traffic jam. He was referring to every situation in my life. Think about it! He does have a bird's eye view, and not just of our outward affairs. God also sees the hearts of all those involved. Don't be afraid. There is no getting around the fact that God has the answers. The good news is He wants us to have them, too. Don't wait. Ask Him to *teach and lead you.* You won't go wrong. This verse confirms He promises to make all your ways profitable.

"Create in me a clean heart, O God; and renew a right, persevering and steadfast spirit within me. Cast me not away from Your presence, and take not Your Holy Spirit from me. Restore to me the joy of Your salvation, and uphold me with a willing spirit."
Psalms 51:10-12 (AMP)

The Bible tells us that David, the writer of this Psalm, was a man after God's own heart. We also know he sinned many times before and during his reign as King of Israel, but it didn't keep him from having a close relationship with God. He revered or feared Him, which really means he honored, admired, respected, and worshipped Him. David also offered many sacrifices for the goodness God had shown to His people. David learned that God is loving, merciful, forgiving, and more than faithful.

Scriptures like these can be or even should be a part of our daily prayer. Why? Because they cover a lot, whether we have just committed a sin or we simply have a deep desire for a closer walk with our Lord. God sees our heart, so it is important we keep it pure, clean, and holy. The Bible says it is out of our heart that every issue of life will flow. In other words, if we are heartbroken, heart-sick, discouraged or depressed, our whole outlook is affected by how we really feel. Allowing ourselves to receive God's Word and His love is the only cure for a broken or distressed heart. David discovered there was joy for his broken heart in the saving grace of God's hand. He just had to keep his spirit willing or agreeable to God's ways and His perfect timing in order to receive it.

It is the same for us today. If you have accepted the Lord, you know the joy you experience. You also know you are dependent upon His wisdom and power to show you what to do. Verse 12 in the NIV states, "…and grant me a willing spirit to sustain me." This was a vital part of David's continual success. He had come to understand his own will could be the biggest obstacle he'd have to overcome. In fact, his will could actually be an enemy to God. What about you? Do you feel like it's a form of weakness to ask for help? What is it that has you so afraid? God sees the mess we're in and loves us anyway. And He doesn't require us to try to clean ourselves up before we come to Him, either. Don't be afraid. He will create the new heart you need. These verses are just confirmation that He wants to restore and renew you. Are you willing? He is willing to grant you everything you'll ever need—just ask Him!

"Then the Lord said: "I am making a covenant with you. Before all your people I will do wonders never before done in any nation in all the world. The people you live among will see how awesome is the work that I, the Lord, will do for you."
Exodus 34:10 (NIV)

The Bible has much to say about God's covenant. We know it is the agreement He established between Himself and mankind. This verse tells us His agreement includes doing marvels, wonders, and great miracles. God states these signs and wonders will be awesome, and the amazing part is they have yet to be seen by anyone from any nation. His Word is true. Each new generation has seen God move in more powerful ways—greater miracles than their forefathers witnessed.

The Bible, from book to book, chapter to chapter, verse after verse, is written documentation and proven testimony of God keeping His Word...His covenant. This covenant is extremely important to God, and rightfully so. It is His Word—His contract with us. Today, you wouldn't think about going into business or forming a partnership with someone without a written contract. This contract becomes the necessary, legally binding terms between two or more parties. Webster's Dictionary defines covenant as, "a formal, solemn, binding agreement; written agreement or promise under seal between two or more parties for the performance of some action; to promise by pledge or contract." All of God's Word is a written promise, His contract of what He will do in the form of action for us, His people.

The above verse demonstrates the overwhelming goodness of God. It is and always has been His desire to bless us and grant us every good and perfect thing. Do you need a "miracle" in some area of your life? Do you believe God not only can do what you need, but He wants to do what you need? Do you see that He must perform what His Word says as part of the covenant? Have you accepted your part of the contract? Remember, a covenant is between two or more parties. This means God can't do it by Himself. Don't be afraid. There is nothing too big for God. Give Him the opportunity to prove His goodness, loving-kindness, mercy, faithfulness and power to you. His works are still awesome, and He is ready to do even more than this world has seen. Are you ready for a miracle? Get ready for your miracle!

NEW TESTAMENT INTRODUCTION

In the days and months to follow we will continue to read God's inspired Word, but now it will be from the New Testament. The Bible tells us the Old Testament is a "type and shadow" of the things that were to come in the New Testament. One example of this is the Old Testament introduces over 330 different prophecies or predictions about the coming Messiah. Each and every one of them was fulfilled within the Scriptures of the New Testament. Why is this important? Because every detail of each prophecy came to pass *exactly* as it was foretold, hundreds, even thousands of years earlier.

It is important to both our faith and our future that we recognize and understand the complete accuracy of God's Prophets and the written Word. Why is this still so important? How does it affect our future? The written Word still affects us because there are twice as many prophecies of the Messiah's second coming in the New Testament as there were prophecies of His first coming in the Old. Wouldn't it stand to reason as the Old Testament prophecies about the coming Messiah, His life, and His death came to pass, were all documented to be true, and are now fulfilled, that we should study more closely, receive, and believe the prophecies of His return in the New Testament? Wouldn't it only seem logical and probable that these events will take place, too? If this is the case, then according to the New Testament prophecies, we need to be prepared—soon—to see the Lord, our Messiah, and King coming again.

The Old Testament encouraged the family of God to be on the lookout for their King. The prophets proclaimed the Messiah's coming. The problem was that many were not looking for Him to come in the form of a baby. They also weren't expecting Him to be willing to give up His life to be the world's sacrifice for sin.

Why did God send a baby? Why did God's Son have to die? The Old Testament tells us when God created the first man, Adam, and then his wife, they were given dominion over every living thing on the earth. In the garden there was only one tree from which God had forbidden them to eat. When the devil came to Adam's wife and deceived her about eating this beautiful fruit, rather than obeying God, Adam went along with the lie. They both ate of the fruit from the forbidden tree.

This disobedience became sin against God and brought death into the world as we know it today. Sickness, poverty, crime or evil was not in the original kingdom. Their sin not only brought spiritual separation from a personal relationship with God the Father, but physical death to man's mortal body.

However, God wasn't surprised by this action. The Bible says, "Even before the foundation of the world," God already had a plan in place. Jesus, the second part of the Triune Godhead, agreed to come to earth to be the living sacrifice to pay for our sins. How could this happen? There was only one way this could have taken place. The family line on earth is carried through the male seed. Because Adam, who was the original male seed, was disobedient and sinned there was no one on earth who would be able to pay for the sin. The sacrifice must be pure and sinless. Jesus was qualified because He was sinless. But how does God become man?

God's plan was to impregnate a virgin, a young woman whose name was Mary. This conception would be made possible by the power of the Holy Spirit who is the third part of the Godhead. Because the child she conceived had no earthly father, the seed wouldn't carry the sin bloodline. Being born of God gave Jesus the same heritage the original man Adam had when he was first created. The Word says, "Unto us a child is born and unto us a son is given." This is how Jesus Christ became the child, being born of Mary, but He was also the Son that was given because God was His Father.

In the beginning God created Adam in Their image…he was a spirit. Jesus was created the same way by the Holy Spirit, but He was born of a woman so He could belong to the human race. The Bible calls Jesus the second Adam... God's gift to man for our redemption. The Scripture says in Romans 5:15, "But the gift is not like the trespass. For if the many died by the trespass of the one man, how much more did God's grace and the gift that came by the grace of the one man, Jesus Christ, overflow to the many!"

Why would God be willing to sacrifice His only begotten Son for mankind? Because He created us to have a relationship with Him and sin had come between us. The only way we could be reconciled back to the Father and to the first state of man was to have a sinless, holy sacrifice pay the debt of our sin. This holy sacrifice would release us from the penalty and curse of the law of sin and death. This sacrifice would pay the way for us to be free. Jesus, God's Son, became our sacrifice. God loves you and me. He wasn't going to lose us to the scheming tricks and deception of the devil.

Through this great plan of God, Jesus was born, grew to maturity, and taught all those with ears to hear about the Kingdom of God. He lived a sinless life. He was not a victim. Nor was He murdered. He willingly surrendered His life. He laid it down as a sacrifice for our sins by being crucified on a cross. He died and went to Hell. After three days and nights God the Father, by the power of the Holy Spirit, raised Him from the dead. After His resurrection from the grave, He stayed on earth for another forty days. Over five hundred people personally interacted with Him during this time. They witnessed the open wounds in His hands, feet, and side. On the fortieth day He ascended into Heaven. Now, He sits at the right hand of God the Father, and He makes intercession for you and me.

After Christ ascended into Heaven, He sent the third part of the Godhead to live and dwell in us. He sent the precious Holy Spirit. The Holy Spirit is also a free gift. He's available to each one when they accept God's plan of salvation. Jesus said the Holy Spirit would comfort, lead, and guide us into all truth. He is also called the "Spirit of Truth."

As great as the covenant was in the Old Testament we know that through Christ we have an even greater covenant in the New Testament. The shed blood of an animal only covered the people's sins for one year, but it was the shed blood of His one and only begotten Son that bought back our rights as a child of God. Through the shed blood of Jesus, our sin is removed. We are reconciled back to God, and now as heirs of His Kingdom, we have the same authority as Christ. According to the Bible this means we can boldly enter the throne room of God, our Father, and speak with Him about what is in our hearts.

God **is** love. It isn't what He does if He feels like doing something nice. He loves us, and He still has great plans for us to be free of the works of the devil. Through His Word and the power of the Holy Spirit, we are able to live above a life of sin and destruction. God's Word says we all have sinned and come short of the Glory of God, but it also says His plan is that all would come to the saving knowledge of His Son Jesus Christ. It is God's desire that none would perish. There is a Heaven, and there is a Hell. Only you can choose where you will spend eternity.

After the past six months of reading about the goodness of God and how much He loves you, it is my prayer you have already made the decision to accept the Lord. You have come to understand we all have sinned, and we are not able to save ourselves. We need a Savior. Jesus is waiting, even now, for you to say "yes." If you want to accept the plan of God for your life, you can make Jesus Christ your Savior and Lord. There is a simple prayer you can pray for this to happen. It is found in the back of this book. Once you pray this prayer you will never need to look back at your old life again. The Bible says that all things are made new, so you can now look forward to the great future your Father has for you.

However, if you haven't been able to make the decision yet, it is still my prayer that once you continue to read about His goodness through His Son, Jesus, you will decide to accept His plan of salvation. You will become God's child and a member of the family of God. We're all waiting for you to join us.

Now, let us continue our journey in the New Testament as we look at what God promised us in His Word. Through His Word and the power of the Holy Spirit, we can continue to walk totally free of fear and every type of bondage.

JULY 1

"For God hath not given us the spirit of fear; but of power, and love, and of a sound mind."
2 Timothy 1:7 (KJV)

The Apostle Paul wrote this verse to a fellow worker in the Lord to encourage him during troubled times. Who was Paul? Why would this mean so much coming from him? Paul, whose real name was Saul, was one of the highly educated, elite leaders of the early church. He chose to reject Jesus as the Son of God. After Christ's death, Paul was aggressive in his pursuit to track down Jesus' followers and kill them. On one such killing expedition, while he was on the road to Damascus, the Lord knocked him off his animal and blinded him. At that moment Saul cried out, "Lord." The Lord asked Saul why he was persecuting Him, and then instructed Saul to go into the city and wait. Meanwhile, the Lord told another man to go and lay hands on Saul for his sight to be returned. The man was obedient and Saul was able to see. God then changed his name to Paul and eventually released him into ministry.

Here is the account of a man who not only sinned, but was also killing the very ones God had called to teach His Word. Do you think he had reason to feel afraid? If not from God Himself, what about having to go back to the cities and work with some of the relatives and friends of the very ones he was responsible for putting to death? He had every reason to fear both God and man. Yet, Paul learned about and accepted how much God loved him in spite of his actions. He totally received the saving and forgiving power of Jesus Christ.

This verse is clear. Fear does not come from God. When those feelings try to come, don't receive them. Instead, rely on the tools God has equipped us with… power, love, and a sound mind. The Amplified Version refers to a sound mind as "a calm and well balanced mind of discipline and control." If confusion comes, you don't have to be afraid of losing it because you already know you have a sound mind. We all have opportunities to feel afraid. Maybe you can relate to Saul? Maybe you've said or done horrible things to others? Maybe you've even committed murder or other serious crimes? Don't be afraid. You can either believe the lies of the devil or God's Word. This verse confirms fear is not God's plan. Change your heart, and look to God. You, too, can be forgiven and walk free of fear from your past. Ask and believe. His plan is still available to you.

JULY 2

> *"Casting the whole of your care—all your anxieties, all your worries, all your concerns, once and for all—on Him; for He cares for you affectionately, and cares about you watchfully."*
> *1 Peter 5:7 (AMP)*

Peter, the writer of this verse, knew about worries. He knew how it felt to allow concerns or fears to force you into doing what you really didn't want to do. You see, Peter was the one who told Jesus on the night He was betrayed that he would never deny Him. But he did deny Him, and not only once, but three times before the cock crowed, just as Jesus had said he would. Now you may be thinking, "If he denied Jesus, how did he end up in ministry?"

The Word reports that early one morning, three days and three nights after Jesus had been crucified, two women went to the tomb where He was buried. When they arrived, the stone that was blocking the tomb entrance had been rolled away. The body of their Lord was gone. Instead, there was an angel inside who said Jesus isn't here...He has risen. JESUS IS ALIVE! As they turned to leave they saw a man. When He spoke they knew it was their Lord. He told them to go, tell the others, <u>and</u> Peter what had happened. Later, Jesus appeared to the disciples and stayed with them for forty days before He ascended to be with the Father in Heaven.

What if Jesus had not specifically asked for Peter? Do you think Peter would have thought God could or would even want to use him after what he'd done? If you were in his spot, would you? What about today? Are we quick to forgive those who lie or mistreat us? Jesus was quick to forgive Peter. He knew the enemy was already trying to fill Peter's mind with fear and doubt, which brings guilt and shame. These are also tools the enemy uses to keep us in fear. That day Peter learned how to *cast or throw off all his cares, worries, anxieties, and fears*. He chose to let God's love and forgiveness replace the thoughts that would have not only kept him bound to the past, but defeated, as well.

This is exactly the plan the devil has for your life. Doesn't he continue to remind you of all the mistakes or nasty things you've done? Doesn't he tell you that you don't deserve God's help, love, forgiveness or blessings? These are lies. When you ask...God forgives. Peter also learned to forgive himself. Have you? Don't be afraid. Let go of your cares, concerns, and worries. Let God go to work. He loves you, and <u>He</u> will *affectionately and watchfully* handle your cares.

JULY 3

> *"So that we may boldly say, The Lord is my helper, and I will not fear what man shall do unto me."*
> *Hebrews 13:6 (KJV)*

This verse continues to confirm God's position in being there to help us in every situation. Everyday we face opportunities that can create feelings of fear. Most of these occur when the "what if, what about or what will they think, say or do" questions start to bombard our thoughts. Can you relate? Are you one of those people who rehearse conversations over and over again, trying to figure out what you should have said or done? Or maybe you "fly off the handle," and speak whatever pops into your mind? Then, days later, you beat yourself up when remorse, guilt, and shame try to take over? Either way, our own thoughts will create some of our biggest problems and fears.

The devil knows this. That's why he works at reminding us of our pasts—the mistakes, failures, and imperfections. The Bible says he came to kill, steal, and destroy. Have you ever considered…if he keeps you in the past, you never get to enjoy today? And without a today, you won't have a tomorrow? If our thoughts keep us tied to the past, it's hard to get into the present. No present…No future! This is how the enemy steals our future. Maybe things have not been the best for you? Maybe the enemy has already tried to make you "think" you have no future because it seems nothing can change your situation? However, God's unconditional love will fill your hurting places and the void that even the best life can't fulfill without Him.

The truth is when we renew our minds to God's Word and accept what He has said about us, we learn to depend on His thoughts…not our own and certainly not on others. The Bible says His ways and thoughts are higher than ours are, so it only makes sense when we do things His way, fear is not able to rule over us or our circumstances. The Word also asks, "If God is for you, then who…or what man…could harm you?" This verse states again the *Lord is my helper*. One of the ways God plans on being that help to us is through the knowledge of His Word. When adversity comes we will be encouraged and strengthened by what God has already said in preparation of our troubles. We have confidence it works, so we boldly speak the Word, and use our faith. Don't be afraid. Nowhere in the Word does God ever tell His children, "You're on your own." Instead, you'll see He loves you, and He continually reminds us by saying, "You're not alone…I'm right here…I'm with you…I'll help you."

> *"For God so loved the world, that he gave his only begotten Son, that whosoever believeth in him should not perish, but have everlasting life."*
> *John 3:16 (KJV)*

This verse alone sums up the Gospel and the will of our Father in Heaven. He loves us. He isn't going to let anyone or anything stand in the way of us being able to reclaim our rights and having our relationship with Him restored. He sacrificed the most valuable thing He had...His Son. Could you give up one of your children? Or your only child? This one act alone demonstrates the over-whelming love the Father has toward us.

The second part of this verse also reveals God's love when He uses the word "*whosoever.*" God wanted to make it plain to all that He isn't prejudiced. Nor would He play favorites. Being able to receive eternal life with Him wasn't just for the educated or the rich or the smart or the gifted. It wasn't only for males, it wasn't only for females, it wasn't for just one race, and it wasn't for just one nation. God's saving plan IS FOR EVERYONE!

However, there is one condition. God did not have His only begotten Son pay the price for our sin, and then not keep His Word to Him. The Bible states that no one comes unto the Father, without going through His Son. Because of what Jesus was willing to do for us in becoming our sacrifice, His name would be exalted above every thing that is named and unnamed. This means, if we want the blessings of God and want to be adopted into His family, there is only one way this can happen. We must believe on His Son, Jesus!

The last part of this verse shares more of God's plan. When we believe in Him, we will not die, but have everlasting life. I'm not saying our outward man, our bodies, won't die. They will. But when this happens, our spirit will instantly be in Heaven with the Lord and our Father. Our last natural breath on earth will be our first spiritual breath in Heaven. Why would we need to be afraid of death when we know we will be with the Lord? The truth is we don't. God never wanted us to live or die afraid. His plan included living with the hope and confidence of His love, and through His Son, Jesus, our every fear would be defeated. Don't be afraid. You are loved. Decide today to accept Jesus. Lay down your worries, cares, and fears. Receive God's plan and love, and receive the comfort He offers in knowing that you not only can spend time with Them now, but you'll have eternity with Them, too.

JULY 5

> *"But God shows and clearly proves His [own] love for us by the fact that while we were still sinners Christ, the Messiah; the Anointed One, died for us."*
> *Romans 5:8 (AMP)*

This powerful verse leaves no doubt about God's unconditional, unfailing love for us, and it proves this in several ways. The key phrase here is "*while we were still sinners.*" This lets us know we did absolutely nothing to gain His love. It also means we don't have to be good enough or try to earn His love through hard works or service now. The verses prior to this one point out how rare it is for anyone to be willing to die—even for a good man. The truth is we could never have done enough to pay for our sinful condition. And yet, God had a plan to restore us back to our original status because of His great love.

Two of the most common fears mankind has is God not only doesn't love them, but unless they straighten up their lives—"We get our act together," we can't ask or expect anything from God. Many who are enticed by drugs, alcohol, sexual addictions or other worldly lusts believe they must first give these up before God will accept them. The sad truth is without the help of the Lord and the Holy Spirit working in your life, you won't be able to get rid of these types of problems. Remember...***while you were yet a sinner***...means God has already done all the work through Jesus for your deliverance. If we could have done it on our own... if it had truly been possible for man to restore himself...why would God have let His only Son die to do the same job? Doesn't that seem redundant? Even a waste? Jesus' death would have been the tragedy of the ages, and all He suffered in order for our freedoms to be restored would have been in vain. God loves us, but not enough to make a mockery of His own Son.

Why do we choose to struggle through life on our own? It's fear. It's also a false sense of pride, and it's not feeling worthy enough to ask for help that prevents us from turning to the only One who can make a difference. Aren't you tired of the same old battle? Nowhere in the Word does it say we have to do anything to receive His benefits...except to receive His Son. Don't be afraid. Don't let fear of not being worthy keep you from receiving the Father's blessings—including becoming His child. God loves you and wants you. In all your mess and sin...HE STILL WANTS YOU...and He always has. Jesus' actions proved the Father's love. Accept the Lord. Receive Their love. It's truly life-changing!

JULY 6

> *"Ye are of God, little children, and have overcome them: Because greater is he that is in you, than he that is in the world."*
> *1 John 4:4 (KJV)*

John, the writer of this verse, was referred to as "the disciple Jesus loved." Now we know Jesus didn't love John any more than He did the others, but what we do know is John received Jesus' love and felt it in such a way that he couldn't keep quiet about it. The same is true for us. When you accept the Lord, He fills you with such an overwhelming sense of love and acceptance that you want to share it with everyone.

The moment you accept Jesus, you become a child of God. "*You are of God... little children"* is what we must first <u>become</u> in order to be able to <u>overcome</u>. So how does this happen? It happens when we say "yes" to the plan of God, and ask Jesus into our heart. Then, He truly comes and lives there. We have this assurance. Now you and I both know a grown man doesn't show up and try to jump into our organ called the heart. It is a spiritual transformation that takes place. By the Spirit He dwells on the inside of us. So when this verse states, "*Greater is He that is in us than he that is in the world,"* it is referring to the overcoming power of Christ that is now dwelling on the inside of us. The "he" on the outside is the work of the devil as he tries to bring sin, sickness, poverty, and destruction in any way he can to steal our peace and joy, which are promised to us by our Father.

As His children, God is our Father, and we belong to the creator of the Universe. This alone creates an inner peace and confidence, which produces strength when a battle arises. Are you battling with keeping your joy? Has the enemy convinced you—you can't win? Do you think the devil is bigger than your God? The devil's trick is to make the problems appear so big we will be afraid it can't be fixed. Remember FEAR means: <u>F</u>alse <u>E</u>vidence <u>A</u>ppearing <u>R</u>eal. The devil is no match for the King who now lives on the inside of you. This verse declares when we look to the greater One within us—"<u>we will *overcome them*</u>." "Them what?" "Them" refers to problems…like runaway kids, addictions, no job, an unfaithful spouse, and anything else that lies to you about being bigger than "HE" who lives in you. Don't be afraid. You are His child. He loves you. There is absolutely nothing too big for God, and now because of His power living and abiding in you, there is nothing too big for you, either.

"I can do all things through Christ which strengtheneth me."
Philippians 4:13 (KJV)

While in a Roman prison for preaching the Gospel, the Apostle Paul wrote this in a letter to the church in the city of Philippi. Regardless of his circumstances, Paul had joy and peace. In fact the words "joy" and "rejoice" actually appear 14 times in this letter. How could a man who was imprisoned, an innocent man at that, still have joy and believe he could do all things?

Years before, when God knocked Saul/Paul off his animal and blinded him, he must have felt like his life was over. Actually, the life Saul had lived did die that day, and the new life of Paul was birthed. Paul saw the light, both literally and spiritually, and he accepted Jesus as his Lord and Savior. God had huge plans for Paul, but from the time he started teaching about the Gospel, he was beaten and spent much of his time in jail. What if Paul had decided to give up? What if he had "copped" an attitude? Or how much of the New Testament would have been written if he'd spent his thoughts and time complaining to God about where he was or how hard it was, instead of writing letters of instruction and encouragement to the believers? Do you think he would have successfully completed his mission or the destiny God had called him to?

The Bible says, "The joy of the Lord is our strength." Paul had learned this. He also learned God turned every situation to His Glory. Was it God who put Paul in prison? Absolutely not. However, because Paul chose to remain focused on God he was not only strengthened, but he was able to use the time to write and record what God had taught him. I'm not convinced Paul himself really knew—in the midst of his darkest hour—how much his letters to the different churches would not only encourage and teach them the Word of God and the things of the Spirit, but, in fact, would become a major portion of the New Testament in which we study and learn from today.

Maybe you're at your darkest hour? Feeling like you've taken a beating you don't deserve, either? Maybe you are disappointed with how things have turned out in your life…a lost promotion, an illness or accident, a divorce? Now you're afraid nothing you do will ever be worthwhile? Paul could have felt the same way. However, God said *we can do all things through Christ*, and His overcoming *power would strengthen us*. Don't be afraid. Joy is a decision, and the enemy can't steal it if you don't let him. Keep your joy, regardless of how it looks. Trust and believe God's Word. His plans for you are great, and with His strength, you will accomplish every one of them.

JULY 8

"As the Father hath loved me, so have I loved you: continue ye in my love."
John 15:9 (KJV)

This is a command Jesus gave His disciples. Most would not argue that God the Father loved Jesus. After all, Jesus was perfect. He was God's Son. Yet, in the same breath, they would also admit they don't believe God really loves them. Why? Because they still want to base the foundation of God's love for them on the type of love they've experienced…"earthly love" is always conditional. Or they want to compare or examine their own life with the messes they've been in and think, "There's no way God can love me after all of this!" The truth is God doesn't look at our failures. Throughout the Bible, God's greatest men missed Him at times and made major mistakes. Did it cost them? Sure it did. There are always consequences to our decisions, both good and bad. But the good news is God was always there with them. He picked them up, cleaned them up, and they went on about His business. The Bible says, "God never changes," and one of the things that never changes is His unconditional, never ending love toward us.

Jesus loves us just like God loved Him. This verse should finally clear up any doubt about Their love for us. And if there were conditions to Their love, don't you think this would have been a good place to put them? God doesn't insert stuff in fine print, hoping we won't see it until it's too late. His Word is clear. Then this verse says, "*…continue or remain in my love.*" However, if you don't believe the love in the first place, how can you continue or remain in it? God keeps repeating it. Why don't we want to believe it?

It's fear. We're afraid we won't measure up to what God expects. We've made too many mistakes to go back. Fear attacks our worth and value as a person. This is what keeps us from accepting love from a perfect God. Maybe your parents or friends rejected you? Maybe at a time when you needed someone the most, they turned their back on you? Maybe when you didn't do the right thing, those you counted on to help you walked away? When we suffer emotional injuries, it's hard to let our guard down and trust or believe in others again. We are afraid of being hurt or abandoned. However, the Word says, "Jesus will never leave us, nor forsake us." It also says, "He is a friend who sticks closer than a brother." Don't be afraid. Give those hurts and past failures to the Lord. Receive the very thing that can heal your memories and give you a new start…His love. Then you, too, will be able to continue in His love.

> *"Peace I leave with you, my peace I give unto you: not as the world giveth, I unto you. Let not your heart be troubled, neither let it be afraid."*
> *John 14:27 (KJV)*

Jesus spoke this to His disciples just days before He was crucified. When Jesus used the word *peace* here He wasn't saying there would be no more wars or battles. In the Hebrew language peace means to uproot the authority of chaos. It means nothing is missing, nothing is broken, and nothing is lacking. It means to be totally whole. The peace Jesus had to give us was all of the above, and by giving us His peace, He also gave us permission to use the same power and authority He did. Jesus used His authority to uproot chaos, fear, destruction, and the devil everywhere He went by healing **all** who were oppressed, casting out demons, and healing **every** form of sickness and disease. He gave us peace—His peace. Why? So when troubles in the world come, we wouldn't be afraid.

Are you operating in that peace? Do you have peace of mind? Is everything in your life whole or complete? You may be thinking, "Have you looked at our economy? Or the war situation? And you ask if I have total peace?" I realize there is major chaos in the world today, but Jesus also realized these things would come. Do you think the Lord is surprised by our current events? The Bible says trials will come, there will always be wars and rumors of wars, but it also says He knew the end from the beginning. Regardless of our outside chaos, His intentions are for us to lack no good thing and to have total authority over the devil. So how do we do this?

You make sure you're in the family of God, and you know what God's Word says about your situation. God's Word is the final authority regarding any subject. While Jesus was ascending to the Father, He said all authority had been given to Him, and now, He was giving us the same authority. When we accept God's Word, think it, and then speak it, our confession not only changes our behavior, but it changes things and others around us, too. Are you using the authority or peace Jesus gave you? Do you know your rights as a child of God? Don't be afraid. The devil wants you to think you're nothing, so you won't come against him. The truth is Jesus, God's Son, gave you all authority, His peace—nothing missing, broken or lacking—total wholeness. Use it. Then watch "*peace*" drive away fear and bring an end to those seemingly endless troubles from within your heart.

"So have no fear of them; for nothing is concealed that will not be revealed, or kept secret that will not become known."
Matthew 10:26 (AMP)

In the preceding verses Jesus told His disciples of the times they were about to come into. He cautioned them to be on their guard. In this verse, when He said to *have no fear of "them,"* He is referring to the evil plots or deeds that would try to stop them in the future. He's still saying the same thing to us today. This verse explains why we don't need to be afraid. God sees everything, and He promises that whatever is done in secret will be revealed.

Many World War II stories reveal how the different battles would never have been won without the divine intervention of God. There was no rational explanation why Hitler stopped his troops or pulled out of an area when they, with very little more effort, would have had the victory. How did we decipher their code anyway? Because God said He would bring what is concealed, done in the dark, to light. The same holds true for us today in our battle against terrorism. We also discover secret hiding places, codes, supporting documents, and planned attacks from men with evil intentions. God still places or speaks to people in ways that lead them to the very spot where the information or evidence is located.

Now you may be thinking, "Well, I'm not fighting in a war? How does this "secret revelation" affect me?" We all have battles we face daily. Haven't you ever done something, even a "little" thing, and were amazed you got caught? Or what about when someone does something dirty to you, and it "looks" like they got away with it? Nobody likes being in either situation. Maybe you're afraid something in your past will be exposed? You're even tormented by it? Has the fear of being discovered stolen your peace and joy?

The Bible says to confess your sins. The punishment, if necessary, may be easier than going through the agony of being found out. If you haven't done the right thing, go to those involved and ask for forgiveness. Even if they refuse, you've done what God asks. If you've been wronged, then forgive your offenders. You may be feeling, "They don't deserve to be forgiven." Maybe not, but how do you deserve God's forgiveness? The Bible teaches forgiveness isn't for others. It's for us. It releases you, and now this area can no longer be a weapon the enemy uses against you. Don't be afraid. Ask God to forgive you. Then receive His forgiveness. Forgive others. Forgive yourself. When you do, fear will leave, and peace will come and dwell in your heart and mind.

"Are not two little sparrows sold for a penny? And yet not one of them will fall to the ground without your Father's leave and notice. But even the very hairs of your head are numbered. Fear not, then; you are of more value than many sparrows."
Matthew 10:29-31 (AMP)

Another huge lie and fear the enemy brings against us is we are worthless. One of his standard accusations or tormenting phrases is, "No one really cares about you, especially God." Against an already fragile, low self-esteem, it can make you feel hopeless. However, God created all things and gave them life. Everything has a purpose...even the sparrows. Although the world may place little value upon them, God sees things differently. In these verses we see God takes notice of every bird's funeral. If He cares for, pays attention to, and takes notice of them, how much more will He care for and watch over you? He knows the number of hairs on your head. Think about it...the hairs on each head...over seven billion heads. I don't know the number of hairs on my own head. Do you? But God knows. Plus, He knows every other intimate detail about us, too.

In my earliest school years, almost daily someone told me they hated me because I looked nice or I always had something new to wear. After years of this I thought, this isn't the real reason they don't like me. There must be something wrong with me, and if "nobody else" likes me, why should I like myself? This thinking put me on a self-destructive path for quite a few years of my life. Now I can see the truth—it wasn't "everyone"—it was only two girls. Have you let the devil exaggerate your situation? Or has he used someone close to you to tell you you're not important, stupid, you can't do anything right...you're worthless? It doesn't take long to believe it. Even the voice tone or body language someone uses can be devastating. When I received Jesus' love and accepted that God wanted to be "my" Father, the fear was broken. I've never been the same.

The truth is, in and of ourselves, we aren't worthy. BUT the Bible says when we accept the Lord we become joint heirs with Him. God adopts us as His own child. Our worth is through Christ and His shed blood. Has the enemy been lying to you? Do you feel unloved, unwanted, unaccepted? Maybe, like in my case, he's tried to convince you there is something wrong with you? Don't believe what he says. The Bible says he is the father of lies. Talk back with the Word, and boldly declare who God says you are. Don't be afraid. This verse confirms for us again that God Almighty the "Highest Father" values us, so we don't have to live afraid. What more could we ask?

JULY 12

> *"But thanks be to God, which giveth us*
> *the victory through our Lord Jesus Christ."*
> *1 Corinthians 15:57 (KJV)*

Are there days when you just don't feel like you have the victory? The circumstances at your home are unpleasant or your workload just keeps piling up? Maybe you've overslept…now you're late…the kids are fast and furiously eating breakfast so they can catch the school bus? Like most of us, when these things happen you wonder, "Where is the victory in this?" Some days do present more challenges than others, but the truth is, on these days in particular, we need to *thank God for the victory* that already belongs to us.

I am not a morning person, so I have to talk to myself in order to get going. I used to speak how I felt, but the reality was it never changed anything. However, once I learned about the power of my words and began to speak "The Word," everything changed. Now I thank God for His goodness and faithfulness to me. I thank Him for giving me another day to fulfill what He has called me to do—I rejoice and I'm glad in it. I thank the Holy Spirit for being with me and for His wisdom and counsel in all truth. I thank God for His Son, Jesus, and His promise of eternal life. I thank God I have favor with Him and with man. After I make these confessions, I "feel" like I have the victory! However, God doesn't want us to operate solely on our natural feelings. Why? Our feelings are fickle. One minute we like something, and the next minute we don't. This is why God gave us His Word to speak and stand upon. God doesn't change. The Bible says Heaven and earth will pass away, but God's Word will never pass away. This is a powerful statement. The Bible also says there is power in the Word. When we use it we come into agreement with God's will and plans for our lives.

This reminds me of a conversation I heard between a mother and her younger son. She told him to go and tell the older son to come to the kitchen—right now! The younger boy obeyed. He yelled to the older brother, "You need to come to the kitchen…right now." However, it was the next part that got my attention. He quickly added, "MOM SAYS!" At that moment the Lord said to me, "The boy's statement packed no punch until he added "Mom said." This is what gave it the power and the authority to stimulate action." God went on to explain it is the same principle when we use His Word and the Name of Jesus. Why? His Word and Name pack all the authority and the power we will ever need. Are you feeling powerless in your circumstances? Fearful? Defeated? Don't be afraid. Use God's Word. Give thanks. You will not only change your feelings, but the problem, too. With the Lord Jesus Christ…victory is always yours.

JULY 13

> *"All whom My father has given (entrusted) to Me will come to Me; and him who comes to Me I will most certainly not cast out—I will never, no never reject one of them who comes to Me."*
> *John 6:37 (AMP)*

Jesus makes it very clear that when we ask Him to come into our hearts to be our Lord and Savior, He doesn't reject our invitation. Once and for all He dispels the fear that His plan is only for a select few. In this verse, Jesus states, "*ALL who come, I will accept.*" There is no disclaimer or small print to disqualify you at a later time. The Lord wants everyone to come to Him.

However, the devil doesn't want you to accept Jesus or to be restored to the Father, so he lies to keep you from making the decision. Maybe he's told you... you aren't good enough? You'll never amount to anything? You're an accident... failure...mistake? Or maybe he's tried to convince you God won't accept you until you change or clean yourself up. Haven't you already tried to quit? Were you totally successful? No? Then you already know you can't change your harmful habits or sinful ways without the Lord. However, the good news is...this is why He came.

Another lie the devil wants you to believe is you can work or earn your way to Heaven. The Bible says salvation doesn't come through works, so that no one could boast that they had done it for themselves. The devil will also lie to you about being a "good" person. After all, why would a good person need the Lord? Whether our behavior or our deeds are good or not, the Word says we have all sinned and fallen short of God's Glory. Nevertheless, God had no intention of letting our sins keep us defeated or separated from Him. Instead, He offered us His Son, Jesus, so we could be free of sin and its penalty.

But the most effective lie the devil tries to use is you don't need to do it today. Regardless of what you have or haven't done, he wants to convince you there will be time. Just do what you want now, especially if you're young, and when you get older and are ready to settle down...then you can do it. The problem with this is in the meantime the enemy is doing his best to tempt you and set traps to kill, steal, and destroy you. Remember, that's what he came to do. But Jesus came to give you life, a fulfilled, more abundant life. We all know we're sinners. Sin requires a sacrifice. We cannot save ourselves. If we could have, God would not have shed His Son's blood. Don't be afraid. Don't listen to the lies of the enemy. Jesus said *He would never, for any reason, turn away or reject anyone who comes to Him.* Ask Him now, so you can receive His best life now.

JULY 14

> *"But seek ye first the kingdom of God, and his righteousness; and all these things shall be added unto you."*
> *Matthew 6:33 (KJV)*

In this verse Jesus states our number one priority is to seek after the things of God. According to Webster's Dictionary the word seek means, "to go in search of; look for; to try to discover; to ask for or to request; to try to acquire or gain; to aim at; to make an attempt." Jesus tells us if we go in search of the Kingdom of God, the Father will see that everything else we need is added or supplied. In other words, put God first and live fear-free of your needs and your desires.

In the previous verses Jesus discussed with the disciples the worries and fears that would try to come when their focus was on the basics like food or clothing which God knew they needed. Today we find ourselves worrying about the same basic needs—food, clothing, houses, cars, employment, and so on. If we're single, we think about a mate. If we're married, we think about our spouses and families, and we all have parents or other relatives that can cause concerns. Jesus isn't telling us to not think about these things, but when the thoughts turn into concerns, worries, doubts, and fears, we've let them become more of our focus than the things of God. God is a big God. He not only handles our daily events, but He can handle Uncle Joe's and Grandma's needs, too. The key is to stay focused on His love, power, goodness, and faithfulness, instead of the problems that bring fear.

You may be thinking, "But I'm so busy with everything that goes on in my life, family, and work that some days I don't have much time for God." The truth is if you put God first, you'll find the other areas will run so much better. You'll see where changes should be made for greater efficiency. Are your daily tasks insurmountable? Are you managing your schedule or is it managing you? Busyness can be an enemy to the things of God. Webster defines the word busy as, "engaged in action, occupied, full of activity." But it also means to be, "foolishly and intrusively active, full of distracting detail." In other words, the very thing that keeps you occupied or full of action may also be a distraction or foolishness. Take a moment to think about this. Does the devil have you going nowhere? Chasing rabbit trails? Running…with no goal line in sight? Don't be afraid. It's not too late for a change. Seek after—look for His ways and plans—His righteousness. He will ADD all you need and even much more.

"So do not worry or be anxious about tomorrow, for tomorrow will have worries and anxieties of its own. Sufficient for each day is its own trouble."
Matthew 6:34 (AMP)

Jesus speaks to us again about not being afraid or troubled by the things we may encounter in our daily living. What things could He have been referring to in that day? What worries could they have had? After all, weren't they with the Son of God? It's true, they were. However, Jesus knew He wouldn't be with them in the flesh forever. He was teaching them, just like His Word and the Holy Spirit continue to teach us about the ways of God today.

Have you noticed how fear always seems to have a way of showing up? Fear constantly looks for an open door, so it can be at the root of everything that happens to us. If you have ever battled with fear, then you know how powerful an emotion it is. As a child I had a horrible fear of being alone in the dark. Since I was usually with my family and my sister and I lived together after I got older, I really didn't have to deal with it. All was well, until my sister had to travel with her company. Her first trip was a real eye opener for me. As bedtime approached, I couldn't go into my bedroom. I was too afraid. Because I had received the Lord into my heart a few months prior to this, I decided to stay up all night and read the Bible. The second night, the same thing occurred. The third night came. I'm exhausted from no sleep. I sat there looking at the Bible—the indestructible, ever-living, Word of God. Right then, looking at His Word, I made a decision that brought me freedom to this day. I said, "God, either your Word works or it doesn't." I released my faith, believed what the Word said about fear not being from God, closed my Bible, and went to bed. I immediately fell asleep, and I slept in peace throughout the night. From that time until now, I've never looked back. That night I was totally delivered from fear forever.

God's Word works against fear, anxieties, and every tormenting thought the devil sends our way. Are you anxious? Has worry, fear, and doubt got you wringing your hands during the day or tossing in your sleep at night? These emotions are not from God. It may be natural to want to develop these feelings based on your circumstances, but this is where the Word comes in. We don't go by our feelings. We stick to the Word. When tormenting thoughts come…STOP…ask yourself, "Is this what the Word says?" Don't be afraid. When you use God's Word with your faith, whether it's today, tomorrow or next year, you'll find the results are always the same…you can be free of your worries, too.

> *"THERE IS therefore now no condemnation to them which are in Christ Jesus, who walk not after the flesh, but after the Spirit."*
> *Romans 8:1 (KJV)*

The Apostle Paul, the writer of this verse, certainly could have been an authority on condemnation. No one could have had more feelings of guilt and unworthiness than Paul because of his past crusades against the Christians. And yet, from the time he accepted the Lord and His plan, Paul used the same fervor he had previously used to kill believers in now joining their efforts in bringing people to Christ. How does God use a killer? God uses all of us in the same way. We must first repent of our sins, and accept the Lord Jesus.

The Bible says God is quick to forgive. However, our biggest problem isn't always with believing or accepting that God will forgive us…it's with us doing the forgetting. Many times we don't need the devil to remind us of our past. We can be our own worst enemies, especially if we were fully aware at the time we were messing up. But the life of Paul is one of the greatest examples of how God uses anyone who is willing. Paul was quick to repent. Repent means to turn around, make a 180 degree turn, and go in the opposite direction. Paul, when he was Saul, had been zealous in finding those who believed in Christ as the Messiah to destroy them. However, when Paul learned the truth, he made the turn. Then and now, he brings life—not death—to all those who believe on the Lord Jesus Christ. Paul had truly repented.

Paul also says he doesn't pretend to have all the answers, but one thing he did know was to stay focused on pressing toward the high calling of Christ Jesus. How did Paul stay focused on the things to come and not let his past interfere? He couldn't have done it without receiving in his heart the transforming and forgiving power of God's love. It was the power of God's love that delivered him from the guilt and sin in his past. Now he is able to walk by the Spirit—God's ways, and not his flesh, which are his own thoughts, feelings, and emotions. Through Christ, we have the same power to walk by the Spirit. Do you still have negative feelings, emotions, hurts, disputes, and disappointments from yesterday? Guilt and fears are heavy. Aren't you tired of carrying the weight of it all? When we stay in the past, it always holds us back from the "new" thing God has for us today. Don't be afraid. Isn't it time you let go of all those condemning thoughts? Aren't you ready to receive the loving, healing, forgiving power of God? Have you accepted His Son? Asked for forgiveness? Then you have nothing to fear. Through Christ, your past is wiped clean, too. All is forgiven and forgotten.

"We are hedged in (pressed) on every side—troubled and oppressed in every way; but not cramped or crushed; we suffer embarrassments and are perplexed and unable to find a way out, but not driven to despair; We are (persecuted and hard driven,) pursued, but not deserted—to stand alone; we are struck down to the ground, but never struck out and destroyed."
2 Corinthians 4:8-9 (AMP)

These verses could summarize life and the challenges it presents at times for each one of us, and yet, regardless of how dark or despairing it may appear, it still guarantees us the victory. It has never been God's plan or will for us to be destroyed or defeated. Yes, opposition will come, and at times it might seem unbearable, but we can and will overcome every obstacle with God. When Paul wrote this verse he had…worked harder, been imprisoned more often, been flogged more severely, exposed to death countless times, received a flogging of 39 lashes—one less than death—five different times, was beaten with rods three times, was stoned and left for dead, was shipwrecked three times, and spent time on the open sea. He faced danger from the Gentiles, Jews, bandits, and false brothers. He was in constant danger in the city, in the country, on the sea, and in rivers. He knew what it was to go naked and to survive without sleep and food.

Now, you'd have to admit, even though you've had some rough seasons in your life, none of them would compare or compete with this man's life. Right? And yet, he is telling us we will not be destroyed and can have the victory. How is this possible? Was he super human? Didn't he feel the pain and pressures against him? Undoubtedly Paul felt what every one of us feels when we have to face the perils of this world, but he was able to overcome them. How? He learned to not lean on his own thoughts or feelings, but to trust and to lean on his relationship with the Holy Spirit and God's grace. No one God used in the Bible lived a pain free life. Each one had their own trials and heartaches, but they all experienced the Lord was greater than their problems, and when they trusted in Him, He always delivered them.

Do you need delivering? Have your problems got you buried? Or maybe you feel like you've just taken the beating of your life? Don't be afraid. Let this verse comfort you, and know that you are not alone. Just keep trusting in the Lord. Keep your faith. You will overcome the struggle you're in. How can you be sure? God always guarantees a sure way to victory when we follow Him!

> *"Ask, and it shall be given you; seek, and ye shall find; knock, and it shall be opened unto you: For every one that asketh receiveth; and he that seeketh findeth; and to him that knocketh it shall be opened."*
> *Matthew 7:7-8 (KJV)*

In these verses Jesus encourages us to not be timid or fearful about the things we want or need. He gives us three different ways to achieve this...ask, seek, and knock. He annihilates the enemy's lie and blocks all fear that God couldn't be speaking to you by following it all up with *"every one."* God is no respecter of persons. What He does for one, He will gladly do for all.

This verse can be viewed in several ways. First, it could relate to God's salvation message. It could mean we ask Christ into our hearts, and He comes. It could mean when we seek out the ways of God, we will discover or find them, and it could mean when Jesus stands and knocks at the door of our heart, we will open it and let Him in. All of these would be true. However, as I have walked with the Lord these many years, I have found God's Word to be multipurposed. The truth is we can ask the Father for anything. The key is having a right relationship with Him, and releasing our faith so we can receive His blessings. This might sound simple enough, but many are afraid to even ask God. Religion has taught it is selfish to ask just for you. After all, what about the starving children and all the other needy people that live around the world? Well, what about them? Do you think God isn't aware of them? Do you think His arm is too short to take care of your requests and theirs, too? The Bible says God's arm is not too short, so when you pray, ask for you and then, ask for others, as well.

Besides, the blessings from God aren't just for us. We are blessed to BE a blessing! This means we continuously give out of our bounty from the Lord. The enemy has lied to us that "true humility" is to only ask God for just what we need. But I ask you..."How or what would you have to give, if you only have just enough for you?" God created us in His likeness. From the beginning God proved to be a giver. Didn't He give us the ultimate gift in His Son? Why would He hold back anything else? Don't be afraid. If you've been afraid to ask, seek, or knock at God's door for the things you need or desire, then get rid of it. Fear is not from God. Believe the Words of Jesus. He said *all who ask **will** have the door opened...they **will** find...and they **will** receive.*

> *"If ye then, being evil, know how to give good gifts unto your children, how much more shall your Father which is in heaven give good things to them that ask him?"*
> *Matthew 7:11 (KJV)*

Once again Jesus reiterates the importance of our asking the Father. He also eliminates any fear associated with our asking by assuring us that the Father will give to all those who do ask. The verses prior to this one asks the reader if they were a parent and their child asked for bread, would they give them a stone? Or if they asked for a fish, would they give them a snake? The Father used simple illustrations so we would be sure to get it. You may be thinking, "What if you didn't have good or kind parents?" Maybe you were put up for adoption or you spent most of your life in and out of foster homes? Maybe you were mistreated or even abused while you were growing up? When our earthly situation is far from ideal, it is hard to make the connection to a Heavenly One. If the very one you can see and touch wanted nothing to do with you, then why would God, whom you can't see or touch, want you? These are valid questions.

It is very difficult for a child to adjust and remain emotionally stable when the home environment isn't stable either, but what adds to the emotional disruption is when the dad is also absent. Absentee fathers aren't just the divorced or the ones who die. They are also those who travel and are out of the home for days or weeks at a time. They are those who are at home every evening, but offer no emotional support. Instead, they sit in the easy chair, flipping through the TV channels or their head is buried in the newspaper or computer until they fall asleep. Does your dad fit into one of these categories? If he does, this could explain why you struggle with being able to trust the Father above.

My dad died when I was young, and my mother didn't remarry until I was in my mid-twenties. I am one of the many who grew up without a father. Several years after I accepted Christ, I heard a voice during prayer say to me, "You know my Son very well, but you don't know Me at all." I realized I was talking to God the Father. The conversation that followed totally changed my life. When I found out, that with God, I could have had a dad all those years I was amazed, and yet, I was also very grieved because of what I'd missed. Regardless of the relationship you may or may not have with your natural father, don't cheat yourself any longer out of the "ultimate Father" relationship. Don't be afraid. Your Heavenly Father won't treat you like your past relationships. He loves you. He's always been there for you. There is no way He will leave you now, and when you ask, this verse confirms He has only good gifts to give you.

"Come to Me, all you who labor and are heavy-laden and over burdened, and I will cause you to rest—I will ease and relieve and refresh your souls."
Matthew 11:28 (AMP)

When Jesus spoke these words, He was speaking to all of us. If you work and have to juggle your family's schedule, too, then you know how it feels to be over burdened. However, Jesus offers us the ultimate escape. When we come to Him, we gain rest and a refreshing that would put "Take me away Calgon" out of business. Obviously, the Lord knew we would have times and even seasons when everything would happen all at once. He also knows when we are tired, stressed, and being pulled in too many directions, we are weakened, more apt to be fearful, and we become a target for the enemy.

Jesus says, *"He will ease and refresh our souls."* The soul is our mind, will, and emotions. Now you may be thinking, "If I can't get things under control, how is He going to do it?" Well, you'll be surprised at what He not only can do, but will do to straighten things out. The key is...will we let Him? This is why He says, "*Come to Me.*" He never knocks us down or pushes His way into our affairs. I hear people say, "Why doesn't God do something?" Or "Why won't God help me?" Have you asked Him? If you have asked Him, did you let go of it so He could do it His way? I've also known people who didn't think He was doing things "right," which would have been to their way of thinking. Or they didn't think He was doing things quickly enough, and soon they were back into it again with both hands and feet.

God wants us to ask Him. Then we must believe what He says in His Word, and release our faith. It's faith that moves the hand of God…not need. If it were need, the whole world would already be fixed. God wants us to use His Word. The truth is if we speak the Word all the time, we're less likely to get into those tight spots. But when we do get overwhelmed, we must stop and decide to do the above. The next time you're at your wits end, feeling like you have one nerve left and everyone is on it, what are you going to do? I pray you will follow His orders, and go to Him. You'll lay it all down, and ask Him to show you what to do. Don't be afraid. Just give Him your troubles. Then do exactly what He says. Trust Him, and you'll find rest, ease, and relief. Plus, your soul will become totally refreshed in the process.

"Take My yoke upon you, and learn of me; for I am gentle (meek) and humble (lowly) in heart, and you will find rest—relief, ease and refreshment and recreation and blessed quiet—for your souls."
Matthew 11:29 (AMP)

Jesus continues His message to us about coming to Him and finding the relief we need for a weary soul. There are several reasons He speaks of this again. 1) He is fully aware of the turmoil our day-to-day living brings. 2) He also knows how we procrastinate and hesitate to come to Him for help or guidance. Why is this? Many individuals, because of a lack of relationship with the Lord, feel He is too busy to help them with their concerns. Others live their lives in such a manner that they don't even factor God into the equation. Some actually believe because the problem is so big to them, they think it's too big for God, too. Regardless of the individual or the excuse, when the Lord, throughout His Word, tells us we can…Ask of Him…Cry out to Him…Use His Word…Believe…Release our faith…He will answer…we need to obey Him, and do it!

In this verse Jesus is appealing to all those who are tired, weary, abused, and overly burdened with the cares of this world. Maybe you can relate? Aren't there some days when *relief, ease, refreshment, and recreation* are just what you need, but trying to figure out how to get them just adds one more thing to your already packed to do list? This is why He says to, "*Take My yoke upon you, and learn of me.*" The Bible tells us His yoke is light, useful, easy, and when we *learn about Him* as this verse instructs us to do, we will quit focusing on the problem and actually be learning about the answer. The Lord is the answer to every question or concern we may have. Now this may seem like an overly simplified way to look at things, but the truth is if you have truly made Him the Lord of your life, to lead you and guide you, then whose responsibility is it to take care of things?

The Bible calls Him the Great Shepherd. If a shepherd took his herd out to pasture and something happened, would one of the sheep be to blame? No, they wouldn't. It's the same scenario with us. So in reality, the biggest problem we all face is allowing ourselves to be led by the Spirit and not by our flesh. The sheep submit, and when we do likewise, we find our needs and wants are more than provided for, too. Remember, He makes me to lie down in green pastures…He leads me besides still waters…He restores my soul. Don't be afraid. The plan God established for mankind from the very beginning included a life of peace and rest. Have you truly turned it all over to Him? He promises, when you do, your new yoke—His light and easy yoke—will bring *blessed quiet to your soul.*

JULY 22

> *"For My yoke is wholesome (useful, good)—*
> *not harsh, hard, sharp or pressing, but*
> *comfortable, gracious and pleasant; and*
> *My burden is light and easy to be borne."*
> *Matthew 11:30 (AMP)*

Jesus explains in this verse what His yoke is and why we don't have to be afraid to take it on. He also explains what it isn't. If His yoke had been hard or harsh, sharp or pressing, who would have wanted it? Jesus didn't die for us because of His great love, and then not want anything to do with us now. He died for us because He wanted to restore the original relationship mankind had with the Father. His pure sacrifice was the only way it could have been done.

If I believed in "luck," I would say this makes us pretty lucky. However, as a believer, we know God orders our footsteps. This takes the "coincidences" and "luck" out of the equation. The Bible says when we are obedient…we are blessed. It also assures us we not only have a sure future with the Lord, but a firm foundation, too. It's so much better than trying to guess what's going to happen, and this is only a part of the benefits of a relationship with the Almighty. When you need answers, He says in His Word to ask, and He will tell us. He also says He won't think we're dumb for asking. He does this so we won't be afraid to ask. This is good news if you've ever been made to feel stupid for asking.

In my life today, I can't imagine trying to do business without the Lord. When I don't have the answer…I always know who does. I have to admit, I didn't always understand why He wanted me to do things a certain way, and I can't say I always agreed with what He was telling me to do. But what I can say is…HE WAS ALWAYS RIGHT! It is such a comfort to know and feel all the pressure is no longer on you. In fact, I have learned that if I start to feel the weight, then it's my first clue I have taken on my own yoke and not His. He says, *"His burden is light and easy."* When my path feels heavy, I know He is no longer in control. Somehow, I have tried to get back behind the wheel so I can be in the driver's seat. I learned a long time ago the best place for me was in the back seat of God's car. When I sit in the front with Him, it's still too easy for me to reach over and try to take control of the wheel. How about you? Have you turned over "your yoke" for His? Don't be afraid. Get in the back seat, and let God handle your affairs. You can trust Him. *His useful, gracious, pleasant, and comfortable yoke* is exactly what you've been looking and longing for in life.

"Immediately he spoke to them and said,
Take courage! It is I. Don't be afraid."
Mark 6:50b (NIV)

Jesus was teaching and ministering to a crowd of people along the seashore. He had just demonstrated a miracle by feeding about 5,000 men, plus the wives and children with five small loaves of bread and two fish. Afterward, Jesus needed some time alone to pray. He told the disciples to take the boat, and go to the other side of the shore. He then left them. Evening came, but because of high and rough winds the boat was still a considerable distance from the other shore. Jesus walked across the water to get to the boat. When the disciples saw Him they were terrified. They thought they were seeing a ghost. Jesus spoke the above Words and encouraged them to not be afraid.

Jesus is still saying the same thing to us today. *Take courage! It is I.* I'm here. *Don't be afraid!* Didn't He show up in the middle of their storm to rescue them from destruction? Why wouldn't He do the same for you? One of the first things we have to deal with when fear shows up is the loss of courage. We lose heart. There is an overwhelming sense of defeat that accompanies fear. You feel paralyzed and trapped. At that moment, if we can make any move at all, we tend to just jump out. These decisions are usually not the best. I've learned when it feels like my back is up against the wall, that's not where God put me, so it's got to be the devil. Now I know not to make a move. I don't care how great the pressure is. There is peace of mind when God is directing you. If His peace isn't present, then don't let the devil force you into a decision. These are the decisions you'll regret, and it doesn't take very long for you to find out why.

As soon as Jesus saw they were afraid He *immediately* spoke to them. He wanted them to be comforted. He wants us to be comforted with the same thought. Jesus is here—and if He is here, then why am I afraid? What are you worried about? A medical problem? An unpaid debt? A divorce? A rebellious, uncontrollable teen? Whatever it is...if Jesus is right there with you, then you have nothing to fear. The Word says He is an "ever present" help in the time of trouble. Don't be afraid. If you have asked Him into your heart, then He lives there with you. He has the answer to your need, and He has given you His peace for every situation. Let yourself receive all that He has for you. Just take His hand, and you'll also be able to take courage!

"And I will give unto thee the keys of the kingdom of heaven: and whatsoever thou shalt bind on earth shall be bound in heaven: and whatsoever thou shalt loose on earth shall be loosed in heaven."
Matthew 16:19 (KJV)

Jesus spoke these Words to His disciples. He knew His time with them was short, and He needed them to understand their authority in the earth. This verse says *He has given us the keys of the kingdom.* What were they? There are many different keys, but in this verse He makes it clear it is the power to control earthly things in order to achieve the same results as in Heaven. How do we do this? By first accepting the authority He's given us, and then, "we" must take action to bind or loose our problems. God expects us to do it, and it first takes place on earth.

This is probably one of the weakest areas for us today. We try to argue with God about our position of authority because we don't feel like we have the "right" to it or, even worse, that we don't "deserve" it. However, the Bible says we are joint heirs with Jesus. This means whatever the Father has for His Son…He has for us, too. This is hard to comprehend because Jesus was perfect, and we're not. The truth is it had nothing to do with us. It was only made possible for us through Jesus' shed blood. Now comes our part…to believe and accept the Lord. When we do, we are adopted into the family of God. If you are adopted by natural parents and they should die, all the siblings are entitled to receive the same. God has adopted us, so we, too, are entitled to receive the same inheritance. We receive every right and privilege Jesus has because we are also God's children.

It is also through Christ that we've been given all authority. According to this Scripture, when we speak to things here on earth, we have the power to bind them or loose them. Webster's Dictionary defines bind as to, "restrain with legal authority," and loose means, "lacking in restraint or power of restraint." Would sickness, disease, poverty or abuse exist in Heaven? The Word says no. By this truth alone we know we can use our authority and bind or restrain from us or our families any area that doesn't line up with God's promises. How do we do this? We "command" them to "go" in Jesus' Name. His Name is why we have the authority to command the devil and demons to go. The Word says when we submit to God, the devil must flee. Jesus wanted His disciples to understand the power and authority they had before He left them, but this power wasn't just for them. Becoming a son of God and being adopted is available to whoever asks. Don't be afraid. Accept your authority. Speak His Word to your situation. Bind and loose as Jesus directed. You'll see you can create Heaven on earth, too.

JULY 25

> *"But my God shall supply all your need according to his riches in glory by Christ Jesus."*
> *Philippians 4:19 (KJV)*

The Apostle Paul wrote this in a letter to the church at Philippi. Once again, you hear his confidence and trust in the Lord for his needs. This is quite a statement coming from an innocent man, in a Roman prison, awaiting trial for his beliefs in the Lord Jesus. A man who could have felt like God deserted him or certainly didn't care what happened to him. A man God had called to preach the Gospel. But the dilemma Paul faced was, "How was he supposed to accomplish this important mission when he was confined to a jail cell?"

Have you ever found yourself in a situation and wondered how you were ever going to accomplish what you needed to do? It's frustrating, isn't it? And if your obstacles persist for any length of time, you start to feel like, "What's the use?" These times or seasons in our life are perfect set-ups for the devil. When it "looks" like it's the end, he hits us with the fear of failure. The truth is this...the only way we ever fail is if we quit. Paul was one man who took more than his share of persecution for the Gospel's sake, but he never complained, nor was it his intention to quit. In fact, it is recorded he spoke and wrote with more joy in this letter than in some of the others. His letters were filled with praises and thanksgiving for the goodness of God.

How did he do it? What kept him on the right track, against all odds, when he should have given in? It was his faith in the Lord, and what he knew he could do in any situation through Christ who strengthened him. This verse states our *God will supply all.* This means everything, nothing missing, nothing broken, nothing lacking, total wholeness. Isn't this the peace Jesus said He was giving to us? And according to this verse, He is supplying "*all your needs*" according to *HIS riches.* It's not about our deserving them, working or earning them or our qualifying for them. It is simply by the grace and goodness of God. How's your supply? Are you just barely making ends meet? Has the sickness that attacked your body been there for so long it now feels like an old friend? This is not the way of the Lord. Even from prison, Paul never feared. He knew his God was much bigger than anything he would ever have to face. Have you made the same discovery? Or do you still believe your problems are bigger than God? Don't be afraid. Decide to trust Him. Follow His ways. He will, by *His glorious riches*, supply all you need and more. Speak it...Believe it...Receive it!

JULY 26

> *"...You do not have because you do not ask."*
> *James 4:2b (AMP)*

James, the writer of this verse, was the half brother of Jesus. Even though he grew up watching his older brother, he didn't fully understand who the Lord was any more than the other disciples did. However, unlike the others, James should have understood the power and authority Jesus walked in. He had witnessed the very first miracle Jesus ever did. They were at a friend's wedding celebration, the wine ran out, and this was not acceptable. Jesus' mother said to Him, "They are out of wine." Jesus replied, "Why do you involve Me? My time has not yet come." His mother turned to the servants and said, "Do whatever He tells you." Jesus saw six huge stone water jars. He told them to fill them with water. Then He told them to draw some out, and take it to the master of the banquet for a taste. When the servants did this, the master was so pleased he stated, "While others serve the best first, you have saved the best wine until last."

James learned that day if His brother Jesus said it…it would come to pass. But he also learned if his mother had not asked the Lord, it would have been a humiliating event for their friends. In the Bible, God's Word to us, we are repeatedly instructed to ask. Now, James is taking it a step further by telling us we lack because we haven't asked. What is your current situation? Could you use some help? Are you still depending on your boss for your raise or promotion or have you learned that every good and perfect gift comes from your Father. Maybe you've been playing up to the wrong guy?

The truth is we are taught from children to not ask. We visit friends, see a candy bowl, and the first thing a child does is ask if they can have a piece. Their parents reprimand them for asking. When you get older the teacher asks if there are any questions. Peer pressure will keep you from asking. Now you're out on your own. No way do you want to ask for help. After all, you're finally "independent," and it's humiliating, even humbling to ask. Asking puts pressure on our friends or loved ones. Fear rises. What if they can't, won't or don't want to help? For most people, asking is awkward and uncomfortable. This may be how the world processes asking, BUT NOT GOD. He's a giver, and He's more than able to provide not only what you need, but what you want, too. Making and giving wine to "save face" at a wedding should more than prove this point. The truth is He can and wants to give to you because He loves you. Don't be afraid. "Ask" your Father. Then let the riches of Heaven bless you!

> *"Again I say unto you, That if two of you shall agree on earth as touching any thing that they shall ask, it shall be done for them of my Father in heaven."*
> *Matthew 18:19 (KJV)*

Jesus tells us in this verse if we agree with someone concerning the things we want or need and release our faith together, that His Father in Heaven, who is also our Father, will grant to us the things we ask and agree upon. How could you doubt the willingness of the Father to give to you after a statement like this one? However, asking must be a huge issue with our Father because He talks about it too many times. There must still be a problem with it, and most assuredly the problem isn't with Him. This leaves the responsibility with US. This verse is clear—"if"—we will ask and agree—our Father in Heaven will do it. He also made it simple. We don't have to find a whole room full of people to agree with us. We only need one other person. If you believe, then half the equation is already done.

Now you might be thinking, "How do I agree? What does this mean? What do I do?" Agreeing means to come into harmony or to be in one accord with someone as it relates to a particular thing. When we're asked to agree with someone, we need to know the details, and the Word they are standing on in order to believe the same way they do. Then, once we release our faith together, we expect God to do what only He can do. One thing you don't do is say "OK" to someone's request, and then not really stand in faith with them. Not too long ago, I asked someone to be in agreement with me about an issue. Their response was "OK," but they didn't pray with me, we didn't touch or hold hands, the Word wasn't spoken over it, and as a result, I felt absolutely no power. The truth is I knew they didn't have a full revelation of the power of agreement, and it wasn't possible for this verse to be fulfilled. Well, not with them, anyway.

The Bible also makes it clear when we ask according to His Word, He hears and answers. Don't let fear or any other excuse keep you from asking the Father. If you don't ask—then you won't receive—it's that simple. It doesn't matter what anyone else has tried to teach you about asking. The Word is clear and precise about what the Father will do when we ask. Don't be afraid. Lay down any false teaching or pride you may have and receive His blessings. He loves you. Ask, and agree in faith with someone who will stand and believe with you. Faith says you receive when you pray. So all you need to do now is thank Him in advance for your victory!

JULY 28

> *"For where two or three are gathered together in my name, there am I in the midst of them."*
> *Matthew 18:20 (KJV)*

When Jesus speaks in this verse He encourages us with the realization that He is with us—in our midst. This is especially comforting when we are going through those life situations that cause us so much conflict. And if He is here with us, then why should we be afraid? There is no other religion today that allows you to have a loving, intimate relationship with a "living" God. One of the benefits of this is being able to feel His love, comfort, and support in the midst of pain and trials. But the best benefit is we can also feel, by the power of the Holy Spirit, His Presence when we gather together in His Name. It is an awesome realization when you know that The Living God "IS" right there, too.

In the Old Testament when God told Moses to go to Pharaoh, Moses asked, "Who shall I say sent me?" God's answer was, "I AM that I AM." This verse says, *"I AM" in the midst of them.* It's still the same God doing and offering His same power to us as believers. Are you feeling alone or lost? There are many strong faith believers who will pray with you about the areas you want changed, but it's important to come together. The enemy loves to get us off by ourselves. We are easy prey if he can isolate us from other believers. The Bible says he goes about "like" a roaring lion. Isn't this how lions catch their prey? Don't they try to separate them from the main herd? The Bible also says, "To not forsake the assembling of ourselves together." This means it can be dangerous if you stay isolated from other believers, and one of the church's responsibilities is to help strengthen and carry our fellowman through their hard times or adversity.

Maybe you're thinking, "I've tried church, and I can't say I liked it. I thought it would be different. They sang too long, preached too long, the nursery workers didn't act right, and so on." The problem is "your" expectations of what you "think" church should be like. The church won't be perfect because it's made up of people just like you and me, and we aren't perfect either. The devil uses any excuse as an attack to keep you isolated and out of fellowship with others. Fear produces isolation, which produces more fear, which isn't God's plan. Yes, it's true, the church still needs work, and some Christians should improve their love-walk with others. As each one of us works on our own areas of weakness, we can also learn to use imperfections as an opportunity to practice praying for others. Besides, how can you discredit God's Word, reject His Presence or blame Him because others have misbehaved? Don't be afraid. Why don't you give it another try? This time, ask Him where He wants you to go. Then remember, you'll be in "good" company because now you know the Lord will be there, too.

"But Jesus beheld them, and said unto them, With men this is impossible; but with God all things are possible."
Matthew 19:26 (KJV)

Jesus speaks to His disciples about the overcoming ability of God. All of us have faced situations that were too big for us. That's why it is so important to have a relationship with a God who loves you and watches out for you. He gave us the Bible, His Word, a hands-on instruction manual with the "How To" for successful living. If your circumstances have started to get the best of you, take a look at what you've been doing? Or better yet, look at what you haven't been doing. Most times our problem is we talk about our troubles, instead of speaking what the Word says. You might be wondering, "Do I have to keep speaking certain verses over and over?" The Bible says it's faith that pleases God, and faith comes by hearing the Word. When we continually speak His promises, it builds our faith, and it gives Him access to do the impossible. This is how you use the Word to change things. Do you confess what God says about your situation? Speak the Word, use your faith, and you'll be amazed how quickly fear goes.

I learned the hard way about not using the Word. Years ago I was involved in three major car accidents. For years I had to work at rebuilding my body. After the last accident, even with much physical therapy, I was in constant pain in my neck and back. Then one night in prayer, God did what was impossible with man and only possible with Him. He healed and totally restored my body. I had no more pain! God also showed me that accidents were attacks of the devil from a past generational curse, but the Word says Jesus took the curse on the cross to set me free. I took communion and reminded myself of all that Christ had paid for on the cross for me. Then I took authority over the devil, repented for the sins of my forefathers up to the fourth generation, and thanked God I was delivered! From that time until now, when I get into my car I say, "No weapon formed against me shall prosper in Jesus' Name. That means no near misses and no accidents to my body or this car." I say the same thing every time, regardless of who is driving. I'm not going to open the door to the devil's attacks again. Since I started making this confession, almost 20 years ago, I have been accident free.

Does the Word work? Did it remove any fear or apprehension I might have had about future accidents or injuries? Yes, to both questions. Is the enemy trying to use your life as a battering ram? Do you see an area that causes you continual problems? Finances? Relationships? Employment? Don't be afraid. Jesus assures us that when we or anyone else can't seem to fix it, Almighty God can. Believe His Word. Trust God. Then, watch Him do the impossible thing in your life, too.

"And Jesus answering saith unto them, Have faith in God."
Mark 11:22 (KJV)

Jesus and His disciples had been journeying all day. Jesus was hungry. He saw a fig tree in leaf in the distance. As they approached it, He went to see if it had any fruit, but He found it had nothing but leaves. Jesus then spoke to the tree, declaring that no man would eat its fruit again. The next morning as they all traveled back into the city, they went by the same fig tree. The disciples noticed it was now dried up from the roots. What Jesus spoke had come to pass. The example Jesus wanted His disciples to see was the power of our words when we use them with faith.

When Jesus said, *"Have faith in God,"* he was laying the foundation for our faith. For many today their "faith" starts and ends with this one belief. They think that believing in God is enough. However, just believing God exists isn't the complete answer, for the Bible says even the devil and his demons believe in God. And, if it were as simple as that, then why would the rest of the Bible tell us what to do or what to <u>say</u> for all the other situations we come up against? We must believe in God, but that's only the beginning.

The actual meaning of this verse, according to the original text, is we are to have the "God" kind of faith. In other words, we are to believe the way God believes. Obviously God believes in Himself, but didn't He still speak to the earth and command light to come forth? In the book of Genesis it is recorded He spoke to everything that was formed. Now if God, who obviously knows His own power, still had to speak and use words, then why wouldn't we have to do the same? We're made in His image. This is where so many fail in receiving the full blessings of God. And the enemy is right there to tell you His Word doesn't work or it doesn't take all that. This is the devil's biggest scam. If you don't think faith works or is even necessary…then you won't use any. But the truth is the Word says it's "faith" that pleases God. I want to please the Father. Don't you? It's my faith with His Word that turns my impossible into possible with God!

The Bible says we perish for a lack of knowledge. This knowledge is found in God's Word. It is the truth that can and will deliver us from every form of evil and fear the enemy has planned. Do you know how God feels about you or what He really thinks about your circumstances? He wants you to know. Don't be afraid. Jesus would not have told us we could have the same kind of faith God has if it were not possible. Just step out. Use your "Godly" faith. God's Word changed the world. With His "kind of faith" you can change yours, too.

"For verily I say unto you, That whosoever shall say unto this mountain, Be thou removed, and be thou cast into the sea; and shall not doubt in his heart, but shall believe that those things which he saith shall come to pass; he shall have whatsoever he saith."
Mark 11:23 (KJV)

In this verse Jesus clearly states the way to gain victory over our "mountain" of circumstances is to speak to it. However, the biggest problem most of us have is we want to talk "about" our mountain or problems, instead of talking "to" them. If we ever doubted the importance of our words and how they can change our circumstances, for better or for worse, the Words of Jesus should set the record straight. This verse uses the word "believe" only one time, but it uses the word "say" three times. Does it take three times the talk to have the belief? Good question. But the truth is, if Jesus said it…it is the way it works.

Sometimes I've found myself thinking about something or dealing with a problem for days when it occurs to me, I haven't spoken the Word and used it as my weapon against the problem. When I realize it, I feel like the person in the commercial who slaps their head and says, "I could have had a V-8!" I want to slap myself and say, "I could have used the Word, and this would all be over!" It is only natural, when problems surface, that our first instinct is to react or to wonder what "I" should do. But if we could do it, why would we need God or His Word? And the bottom line is "if" we could have already done something about our situation, then why aren't things changed?

So why don't we talk to our mountain? We don't speak to it because fear keeps us from believing the Word. The enemy comes at us with doubt and unbelief… "What if it doesn't work? What if you don't get healed? What if your spouse doesn't come back? What if you can't pay the rent?" Or he'll try to remind you of someone else…it didn't "seem" to work for them. Of course, you don't really know where their faith was or what they were confessing during the crisis. However, the Voice of God would ask you, "What if it does work? What if I will do everything you have asked me? What if I am faithful to keep My promises?" Truthfully, will anything change the way it is now? Are you willing to take the chance? The moment you start to feel afraid should be your first clue the devil is nearby and lying to you about your situation. Just believe the opposite of what you're hearing and the fear you're feeling. Don't be afraid. Trust God, and take Him at His Word. It was Jesus who said, *"You can have whatever You say."* Just believe, and keep speaking God's Word to your mountain. You'll see the victory!

AUGUST 1

"Therefore I say unto you, What things soever ye desire, when ye pray, believe that ye receive them, and ye shall have them."
Mark 11:24(KJV)

In the verse prior to this one Jesus speaks to us about the importance of our words and using our authority to speak directly to our problems. If we speak the Word of God over our circumstances and believe, we can have what we say. However, there is another required action which propels the Word to come into play. This action is to believe or to use our faith. You must believe in your heart and not doubt you have received what you say. The question is when do you believe you receive? Is it when you physically see it? Or is it right at the moment you pray for it? The Word says we believe we receive it the very moment we say or pray it. Faith is now…so if you believe you've received what you asked for… right then…how would you respond? Wouldn't you be happy? Glad? Wouldn't you want to rejoice and thank God?

Now you may be thinking, "What if I don't see a change or have it right then, wouldn't that be a lie to act like I did?" Not according to faith. The Bible says that faith is the substance of things hoped for, the very evidence of things not seen. Your faith is real…it's substance…and that substance becomes evidence. Faith itself **IS** the evidence that produces what you need, whether you see or feel it right then or at another time. Faith is now, current, active, present. We continue to speak the Word, which builds our faith, and thank God in advance the work is already done. The results will appear, if we stay in faith.

God is a faithful God. When Jesus went to the cross, the Bible says He became the curse for us. He paid for our every freedom. His body was broken so we could be whole, He became poor so we could be rich, the chastisement of our peace was upon Him, and by His stripes we "were" healed. He has already paid for sickness, poverty, mental and emotional well being. His shed blood paid for your sin and iniquity. When we accept the work of the cross we are made whole, and we are forgiven. This forgiveness allows us the privilege of entering the throne room to be with God the Father. Now, if someone already paid for you to have a gift and delivered it to you, would you have to do anything except reach out and accept it? Don't be afraid. Forgiveness, healing, prosperity, and total wholeness in every area of your life are gifts from God. Jesus paid the bill over 2000 years ago. Receive what He has already given you. *Believe…receive…*and *you shall have what so ever you desire.*

> *"The thief comes only in order that he may steal and may kill and may destroy. I came that they may have and enjoy life, and have it in abundance—to the full, till it overflows."*
> *John 10:10 (AMP)*

In this verse Jesus clarifies that He isn't the one who takes away. He is the One who gives. He gives us true life, a life that is full of abundance, overflowing with blessings. He also reveals who the devil is—a thief, killer, and the destroyer of lives. However, the devil wasn't always the destroyer. In the beginning he was a beautiful archangel who lived in Heaven with God. What happened? The devil rebelled, saying he would be exalted above God. That day, without even a battle, the Ultimate Authority proved no one will ever be exalted above Him. The Bible says the devil and one third of the angels fell to earth like "a bolt of lightning." Now he despises the things of God, and he is out to destroy everyone he can.

However, as a child of God, we have no reason to fear him. Why? Because on the cross Jesus already paid the price for us to be free of him and we have been given the same authority over him that God has over him. When we **know** we have that authority…he knows he is powerless. This is why he does everything he can to keep people ignorant of their rights and how to use them. The Bible says he is the father of lies. Most of us can tell when someone is outright lying to us. So how does he get away with it so successfully? He deceives us by using some of the truth in what he says. Just like when he came to tempt Jesus in the wilderness he said, "If you are the Son of God, turn this stone into bread." Now just days before this incident, the sky had opened and the Father said aloud, "This is My beloved Son..." Both Jesus and the devil knew who He was, and Jesus could have demonstrated His power as proof of it. Instead, He spoke, "It is written," and then finished with the Word of God. The third and last time the devil tried to tempt Jesus he was the one who actually quoted the Word. However, he did his usual and twisted the meaning. Jesus quickly spoke the true Word, and the devil left Him. Defeated he was…defeated he still is today.

What if Jesus hadn't known the Word or questioned His rights as God's Son? The results would have been the same as when we're tested and we don't know who we are or our rights either. Do you know? Do you speak the Word? Even when the Son of God was tempted, He spoke the Word, and it defeated the devil. If Jesus, God's Son, needed to use the Word to achieve victory, why would we think we should do anything less? Don't be afraid. Jesus defeated the devil and his plans…so can you! Accept Jesus, the abundant life giver, and start to enjoy the blessed overflowing life He planned just for you.

AUGUST 3

> *"Then spake Jesus again unto them, saying, I am the light of the world: he that followeth me shall not walk in darkness, but shall have the light of life."*
> *John 8:12 (KJV)*

If you don't know who Jesus is or what He has done for you, this verse may be confusing. First, it's important for us to understand the events that led up to Jesus' statement. The preceding verses tell us the "religious" men of the day had brought a woman, who was caught in the act of adultery, to Jesus. The truth is they were trying to set a trap for Him by asking a question about the Law of Moses. This law stated the woman should be stoned. While they were presenting their case, Jesus was bent down, writing in the sand. After their persistent questions, He stood and said, "If any of you is without sin, then you throw the first stone." He bent down again and continued to write in the sand. The Bible says all her accusers left, one by one, the older men first. Jesus stood up and asked the woman, "Where are your accusers? Has no one condemned you?" When she saw they had all left she said, "No one." The Lord said, "Neither do I condemn you. Go now and leave your life of sin." In the above Words, Jesus then explained how to be freed from darkness—evil ways or a sinful lifestyle—not only for her, but for all of us, as well..."*he that follows me shall not walk in darkness, but shall have the light of the world...the light of life.*"

The Bible says there is now no condemnation for anyone who is in Christ. What does this mean? According to the Word, it means when we ask for forgiveness and turn from our wicked ways, God is faithful and just to forgive us. With His forgiveness comes freedom from feeling afraid, guilty or ashamed. Plus, when we choose to follow Jesus, we have the power to change our ways and not live in darkness as we once did. This is really good news, especially if you've tried to make changes on your own and haven't been real successful.

Jesus is the light of the world. He came to carry the burden and take the punishment for mankind's sin. He was a pure, holy sacrifice. He paid our debt and bought us back from this dark, evil world. You, too, can come out of your darkest crisis...if...you'll choose to follow Him. Don't be afraid. His love is forgiving, not condemning. There is no darkness—trial, problem, circumstance, situation, enemy or fear—that His light hasn't already conquered and overcome. Choose "THE" light. Follow Jesus, and you'll "see" the light, too.

> *"Now unto him that is able to do exceeding abundantly above all that we ask or think, according to the power that worketh in us,"*
> *Ephesians 3:20 (KJV)*

The *"Him"* in this verse is none other than God Himself. It states *God is able*, but it also reveals two other very important points. One, it explains His goodness to give us more than just what we need. He grants us "*exceeding abundantly above **all** that we ask or think.*" Two, it tells us how He does it…"*according to the power that worketh in us.*" There is usually no dispute God is able, but some still question whether or not He's willing. This is why it is so important to know what the Word says and for each of us to have a close personal relationship with Him. He is able, He's more than willing, and this verse tells us specifically how it's done. Once we understand this principle, it eliminates any fear of believing for the abundant blessing He promised us. It also eliminates the fear or suspicion that God only does things for a special, select group.

In the verses preceding this one, the Apostle Paul prays to the Father that we may come to know Christ. That by His Spirit we would be strengthened with power in our inner man. That we would know the length, breadth, depth, and height of the love that God has for us and that Christ would dwell in our hearts by faith. Paul prayed we would be rooted and grounded in His love, which passes all knowledge. Why does Paul want us to know these things? So we can be filled with the fullness of God. He also wants us full of the perfect love of God. Why? His love removes fear. Fear that keeps us from asking. Asking for what? The *exceeding, abundant* supply of God, which this verse states "we" control. All this works according to one thing…*the power that works in us*. What or who is this power? How does it work in me? Through the Holy Spirit the power is Christ, and Christ living and dwelling within you, the believer.

When Jesus lives on the inside of us, we have the same authority and power He did. God will do for us as He did for Him. This is how we open Heaven's doors. We accept His power and authority, and because He lives in us, we can operate in the same way Jesus did. We are rooted in the love of God. We use our faith and the fullness of God. We speak His Word, and we get the same results Jesus did. Aren't you ready for a change? Wouldn't you like to live fear-free? Don't you want to see some real power in your life? Don't be afraid. God's path for you is one of exceeding abundance. Accept it. Yield to it. Then "work" His great power which now lives on the inside of you!

AUGUST 5

"But you shall receive power—ability, efficiency and might—when the Holy Spirit has come upon you;"
Acts 1:8a (AMP)

Jesus gave His disciples final instructions before He ascended into Heaven to be with His Father. God's love is so great that He not only gave us His Son as our delivering sacrifice, but He also provided the help we needed after Jesus' work on the cross was finished. It is out of God's great love that the Holy Spirit, who is the third part of the Godhead, was sent to operate in us on earth. The Holy Spirit is a "He," a person, not an "it." He is also like God the Father and Jesus in the sense that He doesn't push or manipulate us into doing anything against our will. If we don't ask…He doesn't do.

When Jesus was leaving earth, He told the disciples He was sending another. Someone to teach, guide, and instruct them in all truth. He was to be their great counselor, their comforter, so no one would be lost or afraid. "He" was the Holy Spirit! They were told to wait in Jerusalem until He came upon them. The Bible says only 120 men and women obeyed. They waited for ten days in an upper room, when suddenly they heard a sound like a mighty rushing wind. Then cloves of fire appeared above their heads. They all began to speak in an unknown language. It's recorded there were visitors from all over the world in Jerusalem that day. They couldn't believe they were hearing all these different tongues and languages coming from the residents. Peter explained to the crowds what had occurred and then preached about Christ. Over 3,000 people accepted the Lord.

The Holy Ghost has been available to us since that time. He isn't for a select few. He is a gift from God to anyone who asks. We ask Jesus to come into our heart to be our Lord and Savior, and by our faith and the grace of God we receive this free gift. You also ask God to fill you with His Spirit. Believe you receive, and you will. Why is this important? If I already have Jesus, why do I need the Spirit, too? You can't receive the Spirit without first accepting Jesus, and the reason you need the Spirit is because He is the voice and power of God in the earth today. You need both. With the *Holy Spirit's power you'll receive ability, efficiency, and might.* Don't be afraid. This isn't some scary or spooky thing. He's called the "Holy" Spirit because He is Holy. If you need help cleaning up some unholy area or changing the destructive patterns that take you nowhere, then you already know you need real power to be able to overcome. Ask God to fill you with the Holy Spirit. He's all the power you'll ever need for every victory.

AUGUST 6

"And Jesus came and spake unto them, saying, All power is given unto me in heaven and in earth."
Mathew 28:18 (KJV)

This was one of the last statements Jesus made to His disciples before He went to be with the Father. Why was it important for Him to speak it and the disciples to hear it? Because when Jesus went to the cross, died, and went to hell, the Bible says He made an open display of the devil while He was in hell. This means the devil was forced to parade around in 'his' own domain like a captured criminal, humiliated and defeated. The devil also had to hand over the keys to death which Adam had given up through sin. Jesus' sacrifice paid the debt of sin and reversed the curse of the law of sin and death.

Jesus told His disciples all power in Heaven, earth, and now under the earth had been given to Him. He wanted them to know anyone who believes on Him would have that same power. The word power means authority, and now that they were God's adopted sons, He instructed them to go into every nation and preach the good news of the Gospel. They were to baptize people in the Name of the Father, the Son, and the Holy Ghost. Jesus told them to lay hands on the sick, and they would recover. He must have known devils were able to enter a person or He wouldn't have said to cast them out. He made it clear they now had all authority, too, and He expected them to use it.

The truth is He expects us to do the same. He paid a tremendous price so we could have victory in this life. He didn't suffer and die so the devil could trick us into thinking we are powerless against him. Jesus cleared up any doubts about our authority when we were accepted into the beloved and made joint heirs with Him. When you know you have the same authority as Christ to obey God and to do even greater works than the Lord did, it takes the fear out of the process of our daily routines. Have you accepted the Lord and you are now adopted into God's family? If so, did you know you have the same authority as Jesus? Are you prepared to use it? Don't be afraid. Stand up to the devil's lies. You know when you hear them…they bring confusion and strife…they're degrading, intimidating, fearful, and hurtful. When you hear these lies, rebuke him in the Name of Jesus. Tell him the truth. Speak God's Word…he'll leave you in exactly the same manner that he came…defeated!

AUGUST 7

> *"Teaching them to observe all things whatsoever I have commanded you: and, lo, I am with you always, even unto the end of the world. Amen."*
> *Mathew 28:20 (KJV)*

In His final statement to the disciples Jesus assured them He would be with them, *even until the end of the world.* Some religious theologians would have us believe the things Jesus spoke to His disciples were only for them. They argue that healing and the other gifts died when these men died. However, if this is truly the case, then what they are really saying is Christ died so that eleven men could have freedom, authority, wholeness, and the victory. And if this is true, then where does that leave the rest of the world?

It's obvious the Words and commands the Lord gave to those who walked with Him weren't just for them. Jesus picked the twelve, but the Bible also says He chose and sent out another seventy. When they returned from doing what they'd seen the Master do, they boasted about how the demons were subject to them. How were they able to heal and cast out devils if everything had only been for the twelve? Christ did not come for the few, but for the entire world. I know the power of God to heal did not die with the disciples because on two different occasions I've been miraculously healed. I have also seen God do miracles in the lives of others. If the laying on of hands for healing died when the disciples died or even in Jesus' day, how did these miracles occur? It seems mankind is afraid of what it can't logically or scientifically explain.

But this verse addresses an even greater fear for people and that is the fear of being or ending up alone. Jesus' Words in this verse comfort and dismiss fear for anyone who battles with feelings of loneliness. Maybe you don't have family or friends you can depend on in difficult times? Maybe you've never had anyone you could really trust or believe? Jesus said, "*He would always be with you.*" Not just when things were going good, not just for a special, select few, and not just for a season. He said, "*Until the end of the world.*" Then He finished it with "*Amen*," which means "so be it." God never intended for any of us to go through life alone. Maybe you've even thought about ending your life because of loneliness? Who would care anyway? You feel like you'd be better off and so would everyone else if you were gone? These are lies from the devil. Who cares? God cares because He loves you and He sent His only Son to prove it! Don't be afraid. He has your answers. Trust Him. <u>You are not alone</u>! He always has been, and He always will be right there with you...until the very end. He promises!

AUGUST 8

> *"Having predestined us into adoption of children by Jesus Christ to himself, according to the good pleasure of his will."*
> *Ephesians 1:5 (KJV)*

Through the Apostle Paul, God spells out His original plan to adopt us as His sons and daughters. This plan is fulfilled when we accept Jesus and His sacrifice on the cross. Webster's Dictionary states the word predestined means, "to destine, decree, determine, appoint, or settle beforehand." This verse should prove without a doubt God's intentions from the beginning. His plan was and always will be to receive us back unto Him as His own. Why does He do this? Because it is His *good pleasure…His will.* When did He decide to do this? The Word says beforehand. He chose us before the foundation of the world. In other words, He knew man would fall to sin, but He also knew Jesus would be willing to leave Heaven as God and come to earth as a human, His Son, to pay the price. It was all part of His will, His great unconditional, unfailing love that He has for us as His very own children.

I've heard, in some cases, adoptions can be challenging. The success is founded on many things. The opinions of the parents, grandparents, siblings, and even the adopted children themselves, if they're old enough to have a say, can be a huge factor during the adjustment period. When there are already other children in the home, whether they're adopted or not, jealousies and competition can create a strifeful environment. Every individual has a part to play in the outcome. In the end, the child may never be fully accepted, feel like they are at "home," or really belong. However, this is not the way it is with our Father. What He does for one He does for us all. He doesn't even show partiality to His own Son Jesus for He has given us the same rights and privileges He gave Him. What a Father!

Maybe you were adopted? Or maybe you never knew your father. Maybe your dad was never around to do things with you? Maybe you had the best dad in the world? Regardless of the type of father you had or if you even had one, God wants to be your Father, and He wants for you to be His child. He has made a way for you to enjoy His goodness and plans for your life. Don't be afraid… especially of God your Father. No natural parent could love you as much as He does. Let Him into your life, and receive the greatest love you've "never" known. *It's His will…His good pleasure…*and it's been His plan from the very beginning of time.

> *"But God, who is rich in mercy, for his great love wherewith he loved us, Even when we were dead in sins, hath quickened us together with Christ, (by grace ye are saved.)"*
> *Ephesians 2:4-5 (KJV)*

"***But God, who is rich in mercy,***" is quite an understatement. We know mercy is undeserved favor, compassion or lenient treatment. Here is a God who could have wiped us all out years ago for our disobedience, but instead, because of His *great love and grace* offered us His own Son's blood so we could be spared... we could be saved. How could anyone think God isn't good or He doesn't love them? The Apostle Paul would have been someone who truly knew the undeserved favor and compassion of the Lord. He could have testified God was more than lenient with him, and while Paul was dead in sin—killing other Christians and rejecting God's Savior to mankind—Jesus had already died to set him free.

This is what this verse means to us, too. While we were dead in our sins—dead meaning spiritually disconnected from God and ignorant of needing a Savior—God loved us and set a plan into place to save us. We don't have to be afraid of what we've done or even how many times we've done it. God's plan of redemption has already made a way for us to be made new. You might be thinking, "Well I've never committed murder or done anything really bad. Basically, I'm a good person." This may be true, but the Bible states we all have sinned. This means we need to be redeemed from that sin, and we can't save ourselves. We need a Savior. This verse confirms before we were aware of the Lord He knew us and was willing to die for us, so the very moment we receive what He has done for us our sins are washed away. We are made new.

When Paul was knocked off his animal and he realized he was talking with the Lord...the very One he rejected to believe had come, died, and was resurrected... can you imagine his fear? At the same time Paul was also blinded. I believe God allowed this for several reasons. 1) He wouldn't be able to focus on his surroundings. 2) He would have to look inward. 3) He'd confess and come clean in his heart about his sins. 4) He'd then believe and accept the Lord, which is exactly what happened. A few days later Paul's sight was totally restored. This one act alone demonstrates the loving and forgiving power of God. Are you afraid God could never love or use someone like you? Are your sins many? Nowhere in God's Word does He say Jesus died for those with just a few faults. Don't be afraid. God loves you and *quickened you together with Christ*, but only you can decide to believe. Have you been blinded to the truth? Or "*By grace have you accepted Him and ye are saved?*"

> *"For by grace are ye saved through faith; and that not of yourselves: it is the gift of God: Not of works, lest any man should boast."*
> *Ephesians 2:8-9 (KJV)*

This is the best news yet. The Gospel is the good news of Christ. God could have made it difficult by including restrictions, regulations, specifications or requirements in order for us to receive His plan and the blessings of salvation. He could have played favorites, but He didn't. Instead, He offers salvation as a gift to all who will receive it by faith, and it's a free gift at that. Why would God be so generous with something so valuable? Because the Bible says He is rich in mercy toward us. He loves us. He also didn't want anyone—at any time—for any reason—to think it was achieved because of their own doing. Why? Because God knew the devil would lie and try to create fear that for "whatever reason" you didn't qualify.

One of the most disappointing things we can experience is to apply for something, go through all the motions it takes, and then right at the end find out we don't qualify. It's worse if we miss out due to a technicality, but at this point it might as well be by miles. What difference does it make? If you don't have the goods...you don't have the goods. It's like boxing. You work out, keep yourself in shape, and the day of the fight you weigh in at more than you should. Or you train for years with only one shot at winning an Olympic medal, and you fall short. How devastating are these moments.

The same would be true for us if God had made His gift available to only the rich, or the extremely talented, or the good looking, or highly educated, and so on. His gift wasn't exclusive, but all inclusive. God is not trying to keep us out of the family. There is no race, no age limit, no unaccepted marital status, no job requirement, no educational training, no cover charge, no "any" thing that keeps us away from Him. You won't have to compete for it, work for it or try to earn it, *lest any man should boast.* He says to come to Him just as you are. There are absolutely no restrictions when coming to the Lord. You may be covered in tattoos, have multiple body piercings, blue or pink hair. The truth is God loves you the way you are. I saw a T-shirt that on the front read, "Body Piercing Saved My Life." The back was a picture of Christ on the cross. The Bible says, "He was pierced for my transgressions, my iniquities, my sins." Don't be afraid. Salvation is a free gift. It's yours by faith for the asking. It's the best and most lasting decision you'll ever make...it's for-ever-lasting.

AUGUST 11

"And lo a voice from heaven, saying, This is my beloved Son, in whom I am well pleased."
Matthew 3:17 (KJV)

One of the lies the devil uses to deceive people is Jesus really isn't the Son of God. The devil has even tried to confuse some Bible scholars and theologians to confess Jesus was a good man, teacher or a prophet, but the Son of God is still questionable. Why would the devil try to weaken or steal the identity of Jesus? Because if he can place doubt in our hearts and minds about whether or not Jesus is who the Bible says He is, then we would be afraid to believe any of God's Word. Fear and faith don't mix. If Jesus isn't really the Son of God, then who paid for my sins? Were they even paid for or am I still separated from the Father? What if I have believed a lie all along and none of this really exists? The devil's intentions are to create questions, doubts, unbelief, and fears that all of this is a well made up story tale.

The truth is the things that were recorded in God's Word about the ministry of Jesus were witnessed by not only the twelve men that walked with Him everyday, but by the multitudes of people who followed Him, as well. However, the real proof is in an event like the one in this verse. When God the Father spoke, He did it audibly, so that all men could hear. The prior verse says, "And Jesus, when he was baptized, went up straightway out of the water and lo, the heavens were opened unto him, and he saw the Spirit of God descending like a dove, and lighting upon him." Then God spoke aloud and introduced His beloved Son. Now if you had been there that day and were the slightest bit skeptic, you might have wondered if you had really heard a voice. I mean the water could have been noisy, the trees could have been rustling, maybe you just thought you heard something. But how do you explain the skies opening up to the Heavens? Or you see a bird coming down to sit on Jesus? These men witnessed an event like they had never seen before. They didn't just shrug their shoulders and walk off like this was a common everyday occurrence. You know they discussed what they saw and what they heard, too, amongst themselves, just like we would have.

That day God spoke loud and clear to all, so there would be no question about His Son, His beloved Son Jesus. He shared with the world He loved His Son, and He was pleased at the life Jesus had lived in preparation for what He had come to earth to do. Are you afraid to make a commitment to the Lord? Maybe the devil has tried to fill your mind with doubts about His true identity? This verse more than confirms that Christ is the Son of God, and if this is true, then all the rest must be true, too. Don't be afraid. Jesus came out of love and the Father's request for YOU…to save YOU…from your sin and its penalty. Only believe!

> *"Filled with compassion, Jesus reached out his hand and touched the man. I am willing, he said, Be clean."*
> *Mark 1:41 (NIV)*

A man with leprosy approached Jesus. He dropped to his knees and begged Him saying, "If you are willing, you can make me clean." Jesus answered Him with the same words He is saying to all of us today... *"I AM WILLING."* The Bible tells us the leprosy immediately left; he was made clean. There are places in the world today where leprosy is still very common. Leprosy is a chronic disease that forms nodules or sores on a person's body. They enlarge and spread, leaving those areas numb to feeling with eventual paralysis, the muscles deteriorate, there is loss of life in these particular areas, and limbs, fingers, and toes literally fall off. It eats away the flesh and brings death with it. It is a feared, dreaded, contagious disease.

In Webster's Dictionary one of the definitions for leprosy is, "a morally or spiritually harmful influence." Keeping this definition in mind, it becomes obvious that the life threatening effects of leprosy aren't just limited to a physical disease. Everywhere you look today you see the evidence of the enemy's attacks against our moral values which has a direct affect on our spiritual well being, too. From the provocative, sexually explicit TV sitcoms and commercials, to the magazine covers that report the latest dirt on one's character or women with very little clothing, to the music that spews out sex, suicide, racial hatred or destruction in a way that sounds "cool," to the video and computer games that promote violence and death in order to win, and to the movies…where do you even begin? Leprosy is a modern day disease, but the Word makes it clear, regardless of the enemy's attacks, we can be clean and are made holy through Jesus Christ.

Maybe there has been a form of leprosy that has attached itself to you? Addictions? An unholy lifestyle? The devil is subtle, and he works just like this disease does by first inflicting you with something—thoughts, fears, pain, etc. After awhile, if you don't deal with it, you'll become numb to it, too. This is a dangerous spot because death is soon to follow. Maybe not always physical death, but usually you just feel dead inside. Or maybe you wish you were dead? The leper said I know you can make me clean, but will you? Jesus proved that day He's not only able, but willing to heal our infirmities. Do you want to be made clean? Are you ready to let go of the thing that's been eating away at you? Don't be afraid. Whatever it is…turn to Him and ask. He is the only One who can make it right, and "*He will*" make you clean.

AUGUST 13

> *"As soon as Jesus heard the word that was spoken, he saith unto the ruler of the synagogue, Be not afraid, only believe."*
> *Mark 5:36 (KJV)*

Jesus and His disciples crossed the lake by boat. As they landed large crowds gathered around them. A synagogue ruler by the name of Jairus ran up to them and asked Jesus if He would come and lay His hands on his little girl who was sick and dying. Even though Jesus started to go with him to his home, the crowds continued to follow. In fact, the Bible says, the crowds were pressing in on Him. Suddenly Jesus stopped and asked, "Who touched me?" The disciples looked all around, and then asked, "With this crowd thronging you, how can you ask who touched you?" At that moment a woman came and fell at Jesus' feet. She explained that for twelve years she had been ill with an "issue of blood." The doctors had taken all her money, and she only grew worse. But she heard about Jesus, and as she forced her way through the crowd she kept saying to herself, "If I can touch His clothes, I will be made whole." Jesus said to her, "Daughter, your faith has made you whole. Go in peace, and be free of your suffering."

At that exact moment the report came to Jairus his daughter had died, and he shouldn't bother the Master any further. Jesus instantly turned to Jairus and quoted the above verse...*Don't be afraid, only believe.* When they arrived at Jairus' home, Jesus sent the mourners away. He took Jairus and his wife, Peter, James, and John into the bedroom with Him. Then, He took the little girl by the hand and told her to "get up." She got up and walked around, totally healed. Jesus told them to give her something to eat.

What has you so afraid? Remember, fear and faith can't work together. The devil brings fear. It's God who brings life and goodness. Only you can decide. Whose report will you believe? Can you hear Jesus saying, "*Don't be afraid... only believe.*" The woman and the parents of the young girl saw the power of God move in their lives because they believed. Maybe you're like the woman with the issue of blood. Maybe you have "issues," too? Are you sick in your body? Are you afraid you could die? Are you over your head in debt? Do you live in shame of past failures or heartaches? Regardless of your issue, you can be made whole. Jesus is still saying to every one of us today, "*Don't be afraid... Only believe,*" and right now He's commanding you to "get up" from your situation, just like He did the little girl. Take His hand. Speak the Word. Use your faith, and believe. Your faith shall make you whole, too.

> *"Give, and it shall be given into you; good measure, pressed down, and shaken together and running over, shall men give into your bosom. For with the same measure that ye mete withal it shall be measured to you again."*
> *Luke 6:38 (KJV)*

In this verse Jesus gives us the key to how we are to live. In the previous verses He helps the disciples understand how important it is to do things God's way, instead of how the world does it. The Lord wanted to impress upon them this principle..."whatever you do...it will come back to you." We are not to judge, so we won't be judged, we don't condemn others, so we won't be condemned, we are to forgive, so we will be forgiven. We are to give, and when we do, we can expect to receive. When you do things God's way, you are assured of your reward. It allows you to live free of fear, regardless of how your present circumstances may look. According to the Word, the present is only temporary which means it is subject to change.

Why did God, in this verse, go into such detail about the results of our giving? Because God is a giver and we are created in His image. It's interesting when I hear people pray for God to "take" sickness or "take" their addictions or "take" their "whatever." The truth is God doesn't ever take anything from us at all—good or bad. It's true, He does want us free of bondages, but it's God's nature to give. Some may think, "Well, God knows what I mean." This is also true. However, there is power in <u>your</u> words, and God is moved by <u>your</u> faith. If you're expecting Him to take it, then what's your part in it? Do you need Him to take it because you aren't truly ready to surrender that part of your life to Him? When <u>we</u> freely <u>give</u> up our cares—<u>He</u> is able to <u>give</u> us what we really need in return...true freedom.

This verse encourages us to give by teaching us God's math. He always adds or multiplies. Whatever amount or measure we give, we can expect even greater blessings in return. Remember, we're blessed to be a blessing! Maybe things have been tight for you financially, and you're afraid to give? Or maybe you've been giving, but you don't feel you've been blessed accordingly? Now the devil has tried to convince you giving doesn't work? Has fear stopped you from helping those in need? Don't be afraid. God's Word works. The Bible says the Word won't return void; it will accomplish that which it is sent forth to do. Keep obeying God. Give in faith. You shall receive...*running over!*

"And do not [for a moment] be frightened or intimidated in anything by your opponents and adversaries, for such [constancy and fearlessness] will be a clear sign [proof and seal] to them of [their impending] destruction; but [a sure token and evidence] of your deliverance and salvation, and that from God."
Philippians 1:28 (AMP)

When Paul wrote this in a letter to the church at Philippi, he was in chains in prison. He should have been singing the blues. Instead, He wrote this word of encouragement. Paul wanted them to know his imprisonment had actually helped further the Gospel. How could this happen? Well, in those days the guards were called Centurions, and they were part of the king's elite staff. Many times it has been asked about Paul's situation, "Who really was the prisoner—Paul or the guard?" Why? Because Paul continued to teach and preach the entire time he was chained to the Centurion. Many of them, after hearing the truth of the Gospel, were saved. They would then go back into the palace to share the good news of Christ with the others living there.

Paul's desire was for the other believers to understand they had nothing to fear. Can you imagine, "nothing to fear," coming from a man who was very much aware he could lose his life at any time? But Paul wasn't afraid, even in light of the torment or punishment, and it wasn't an act. He simply had no fear of the outcome because of his total confidence in knowing where he was going if something happened. However, he hadn't lost sight of his mission or purpose. He was going to keep on preaching. Paul's testimony is powerful. Under pressure and the roughest conditions He knew and trusted the Lord. The same is true for us today. When the world sees that we aren't shaken by the terror all around us, it will be a sign to them, also. You won't have to worry about anyone seeing you sweat—because you'll be fear-free.

This verse confirms we don't have to be afraid of anything. That means "no" thing, not even one thing the devil throws your way or tries to keep stirred up in your household. You have the victory! What has he been lying to you about? Are you afraid? Quit looking at your circumstances…LOOK UP! We no longer have to walk by what we see. Faith walks by the Word and what the Spirit of God tells us. Don't be afraid. God has offered you His divine covenant of protection. It never expires. Take it, and live fearlessly.

AUGUST 16

> *"So then faith cometh by hearing,*
> *and hearing by the word of God."*
> *Romans 10:17 (KJV)*

God never keeps us guessing or in the dark about how He works. If it takes faith to please Him, and nothing changes without faith, you can see why He wants us to know all about it. He also knows the devil comes to steal our faith by attacking us with fear. Even now the enemy lies with, "You can't have faith like God... who do you think you are? Don't you know it's only those who are called to ministry that have it? Even if you do have it, you'll never have enough for this problem or that circumstance." Have you ever heard any of these lies about your level of faith, and why it can't work?

God makes it clear we can't and won't have the "God kind of faith" we need for our trials without hearing the Word. Why do we need to hear? So we will know what God has to say about the specific trouble we're facing. Just believing God exists isn't the kind of faith it takes to bring about the exact changes your marriage, health or finances may need. It's true, you must first have faith in God, but then you need His specific Word of instruction for your situation. You can't tell cancer or major health issues to go, prosperity to increase, and the devil to cease his actions against you and your family if you don't know what God says about it or the authority and power He's already given you to use in overcoming them.

This is where the Word comes in. It is our instruction manual. The Bible says, "My people perish for a lack of knowledge," and the Word is the knowledge they lack. One of the definitions of the word "wisdom" is to know what to do with the knowledge you have. Jesus gave us the Holy Ghost to instruct us and guide us into all truth. If you didn't know the Word, would you know all the Holy Spirit's supposed to do? Would you know you have authority over the devil? I didn't, even though I was raised from a baby in the church. In fact, they even failed to mention the devil was still active in today's world. This is why it's vital you go to a church that teaches the whole truth...the whole Bible.

Faith comes by hearing the Word. Are you still struggling with areas? Are you coming up short of the victory? Be honest...where is your faith? Faith and fear can't operate together. You can't be afraid in one area, and then think faith will work for you in another. Don't be afraid. If you've been afraid...repent. Ask God to forgive you. You can "build up" your faith, and see the mountains move in your life, too. Just get into the Word, and continue to hear...hear...hear...hear.

> *"Behold, I give unto you power to tread on serpents and scorpions, and over all the power of the enemy: and nothing shall by any means hurt you."*
> *Luke 10:19 (KJV)*

Jesus spoke this verse to His disciples and the seventy-two other men He sent out to do the work of the Gospel. When they returned, they rejoiced that the demons had submitted to them in Jesus' Name. Upon hearing this Jesus told them their true rejoicing should be that their names were written in Heaven. The Word tells us when we give ourselves to the Lord we receive salvation, and our names are then written in a book in Heaven. On the final Day of Judgment all those who have their names in that book will receive everlasting life. All those who don't have their names recorded there are cast into hell where there is torment and gnashing of teeth. The devil works at faking people out by having them believe that even "if" there is a hell and they end up going there, it will be like one big ongoing college 'spring break' kind of party. In other words, he has painted a picture that hell is fun. This is not God's description of hell, and the Word says He can't lie. But the good news is it's the Father's desire that none would perish. You can choose God's great plan, accept the Lord Jesus Christ, and change your final destination.

Jesus gave us power over the devil and every deadly, harmful thing, so we could walk in peace and victory. This authority isn't temporary, and it isn't just available for those called to deliverance ministries. Christ knew all of us would face the devil in our everyday routine. And don't buy the enemy's lie that if you don't bother him, he won't bother you. I've had people tell me they told the devil this and he agreed. But the next thing they knew, literally all "hell" had broken loose in their house. I would say to them, "You know he is the father of lies. Why would you think you could believe him?"

It's much easier to use your God given authority, and never give the devil an opportunity in the first place than it is to have to regain your ground. If he knows you have a weak spot, he will set you up again and again, hoping you will fall for the same bait. If this is the case, get someone you can trust to help you, someone you can be accountable to, and someone who will pray for you. In every circumstance you have been given power for victory because you have power over the enemy's power. Don't be afraid. If you belong to the Lord, He has already given you all authority. Use it, and *nothing by any means shall hurt you.*

> *"And these signs shall follow them that believe; in my name shall they cast out devils; they shall speak with new tongues; They shall take up serpents; and if they drink any deadly thing, it shall not hurt them; they shall lay hands on the sick, and they shall recover."*
> *Mark 16:17-18 (KJV)*

Jesus gave His farewell statement to the disciples in this verse. However, He wasn't just giving them their marching orders. He was also making it clear that through His Name and authority they could do all things. They didn't have to be afraid. "Don't fear…Use My Name…Do as I did while I was with you." Now it needs to be clear, Jesus is not telling them to play with snakes or to drink deadly, poisonous fluids as some sort of ritual to prove His power. All He is saying is "if" they experience an attack of any deadly, dangerous substance—in His Name—they would not only be spared the consequences, but the terror that comes with it.

Once, when the Apostle Paul was about to be carried by ship as a prisoner to Rome, he told the captain they shouldn't sail that day. The captain didn't think Paul knew anything about boating, and he decided to sail anyway. A terrible storm came upon them. After fourteen days of fearing for their lives, an angel of the Lord appeared to Paul and told him it was God's will for him to testify in Rome. So even though the ship would be lost, he and the crew were going to be saved. Paul told the crew what the angel said, and it came to pass. When they got close to an island, they all swam to shore. While Paul was building a fire a snake jumped out of the wood and bit him on the hand. Paul just shook it off. The natives thought this man truly is guilty. Even though he survived the shipwreck, he will now die because of the snakebite. However, when Paul continued to preach the Gospel to the natives and went about doing the Lord's business, many were saved and healed after witnessing the power of God.

Paul believed what the Lord said. When we believe, we are guaranteed the same results. Are you feeling like someone has shipwrecked your life? Everything is upside down? Maybe you even feel like you are about to go down for the last time? Life's events can sting and bring pain…almost like you've been bitten. But we, through Christ, have the power to shake them off. Don't be afraid. Believe God's Word. Do what Paul did…shake off the enemy's weapons when they come against you, in the Name of Jesus. *Believe, take action, and signs shall follow.* There is always victory for the believer.

"Submit yourselves therefore to God. Resist the devil, and he will flee from you."
James 4:7 (KJV)

James, the writer of this verse, was the brother of Jesus. His purpose in writing was to help teach Christians how to be like Christ. He felt if we had real faith, we would show it. The book of James gives us practical advice on how to deal with anger, quarreling, controlling the tongue and our words, boasting, no patience, prayer, and favoritism. These are only a few of the areas the devil will try to use against us so we won't look like or act like the One we love and follow.

Years ago a comedian used to dress up as this wild female character. One of the famous lines from his act was, "The devil made me do it!" Everyone laughed, but in reality it isn't funny. First of all, the devil can't make you do anything you don't want to because as a child of God he has no control over you. Yes, he will try to tempt you, and he will target your weakest areas. However, this verse makes it clear **<u>if</u>** *we are submitted to God*, we will have the power to resist. When *we resist...the devil has got to go!* The key is we must first submit to God. The word submit is not a popular word today. It conjures up negative emotions, especially if you've been taken advantage of by someone in authority. It also isn't popular if you like to be the one in control. Webster's Dictionary says submit means to, "yield oneself to the authority or will of another; to defer to or consent to abide by the opinion of another." God's love makes it easy for us to submit to following His ways. Why? You can trust Him. His love isn't abusive or controlling. Instead, His love is fulfilling and affirming.

Are you trying to resist, but it seems nothing is fleeing? Or maybe you are failing the same temptations on a daily basis? Do you believe you can be free? Or are you feeling weak, powerless, and afraid? Don't be afraid. If you can't stop thinking lustful thoughts that lead to action…submit your eyes and ears to hearing only what is pure and lovely. Turn off the TV, internet or movie going and submit your hands to serving God. If you can't stop spending and keep yourself in debt…submit those credit cards to God, and get rid of them. If you are sick in your body…submit everything you eat by changing your eating habits to the Lord. God's Word doesn't lie. If He says you can resist, then you can, but there is only one way…Submit. Don't be afraid. Trust God. He loves you. You can submit to His authority. When you do, you'll overcome even your greatest temptations. God promised it!

> *"And they overcame him by the blood of the Lamb, and by the word of their testimony..."*
> *Revelation 12:11a (KJV)*

John, one of the disciples, wrote the book of Revelation as the result of a vision God gave him while he was exiled on the island of Patmos. Even though this book is filled with symbols and imagery, there is one major theme that is made very clear...JESUS CHRIST IS LORD, and He rules over every thing and every one. It is not the plan of God for us to be overcome by anything. That includes the devil.

The "him" we overcome in the above verse is the devil. This Word teaches us there are two weapons we can use that will defeat the devil every time. The first is the blood of the Lamb. We know this refers to Jesus. He became the sacrificial offering we needed for sin. His "innocent" blood was shed on a cross. This paid the way for us to be free of sin. It also delivered us from the curse of the law, which came upon man because of sin. When something is overcome it has no power. The Lord wants us to know that when He defeated satan, He stripped him of his power. When we use the Name above all names, Jesus, and remind the devil that Jesus shed His blood for us to overcome our situation, satan has to bow to the authority of Jesus and His Almighty power.

The second part of this verse has to do with us and our testimony. It's not only what Christ has done for us, but what He continues to do on a daily basis. It's how we are changed by His power. Being able to overcome isn't merely by our word. It is the combination of what Christ has done for us working together with our faith through the shed blood of Jesus. It doesn't matter what the devil throws your way...he is overcome...he is defeated with the blood and our testimony.

Maybe you aren't feeling like an overcomer? Maybe your trials have you scared and discouraged? Are you "spiritually" applying the blood to the core of your situation...the devil's tactics? Don't be afraid. The devil is powerless against the blood, and he knows it. I say, "Look devil, you know that I know, you are powerless, and by the authority that Christ has given me through His blood and Name—I command you to stop your activities against my_________." Then I fill in the blank with my family, finances, health, work, etc. You can do the same. Use your authority. Turn your "sad story" or test into a "powerful testimony." You'll have one because with Jesus you're always an overcomer!

"If we [freely] admit that we have sinned and confess our sins He is faithful and just [true to His own nature and promises] and will forgive our sins (dismiss our lawlessness) and continuously cleanse us from all unrighteousness—everything not in conformity to His will in purpose, thought and action."
1 John 1:9 (AMP)

John, the disciple Jesus loved, wrote this verse. John truly had a revelation of the immensity of God's love and His forgiving, cleansing power. Webster's Dictionary defines the word immense to mean, "supremely good or excellent; marked by greatness, especially in size or degree; transcending ordinary means of measurement." John allowed himself to experience the great and excellent love of God, which is available to all of us, and there is no doubt God's love transcends the ordinary.

This verse eliminates the fear of having to be "perfect" to please God. The Word tells us to walk by the Spirit because this gives us the power to not fulfill the lust of the flesh. However, if we slip up and fall, this verse alone reconciles us back to that right standing relationship with the Father. God's great love keeps the door open for all who have gone astray to have a clear cut path back into fellowship with Him. This totally wipes out any fear that our position with God can never be restored. Unfortunately the problem is sometimes we don't want to admit our sin or we still feel God's punishment will be too much for us. We let fear keep us from doing the one and only thing that will change our circumstances. The devil loves to make us believe God won't forgive us, "not this time" or "not again." After all, how many times can you expect God to forgive you? The truth is if there had been limits to forgiving us, the Bible would have stated it. John knew if we were sincere—truly experienced a change in our heart—when we asked God to forgive us, He would do it each and every time.

When the disciples asked Jesus how many times they were supposed to forgive their brother who sinned against them, Jesus replied, "Seventy times seven." This is recorded to be in one day. If God expects us to forgive one person who wrongs us up to 490 times in one day, then how could He not offer the same forgiveness to us? Don't be afraid. When you do wrong…don't wait…run to the Father. Repent, and get the newness and confidence you need in knowing that you've been restored to a right relationship. It can only come from God's loving, forgiving, cleansing power.

> *"He said to them, Because of the littleness of your faith—that is, your lack of firmly relying trust. For truly, I say to you, if you have faith [that is living] like a grain of mustard seed, you can say to this mountain, Move from here to yonder place, and it will move, and nothing will be impossible to you."*
> *Matthew 17:20 (AMP)*

In this verse Jesus explains the importance of having "now" or *living faith*. The verses prior to this one tell about the disciples not being able to cure a boy of epilepsy. The dad was at the end of his rope because his boy would throw himself into the fire and deep waters. Jesus rebuked the demon that was in the boy, and he was instantly healed of the disease. The disciples asked why they hadn't been able to cast out the demon. Jesus told them they had too little faith.

We have the same problem today. We've let doctrine and tradition dilute the Gospel until faith is a thing of the past. But faith is the key to releasing our problems. If you don't believe healing is for today...why would you need faith for your body to be whole? If you thought it was pious or holy to be poor, even though it keeps you from giving to the work of the Gospel...why would you need faith for prosperity? If you believe you're no good or undeserving, then when your spouse leaves, you lose your job or your kids won't listen…why would you need faith to change your surroundings? If life has treated you pretty good, and you're proud that you are a "self-made" person…why would you need to have faith in God for any reason?

Faith isn't new. People have faith in their favorite football team. They believe they will win the Super Bowl or their baseball team will win the World Series. You can have faith or trust that your new car won't break down and leave you stranded. There are different types of faith. However, in this verse, Jesus informs us of "true" faith—the "God kind of faith," and it doesn't need to be some huge thing. If your trust is firmly planted in the Lord and His Word, then your faith can be the size of a mustard seed, which is one of the smallest seeds, but produces one of the largest trees. The truth is even though it may be small, God <u>requires</u> faith from us. When we speak with it, He meets every request with His mountain moving power. Don't be afraid. Faith comes by hearing and hearing by God's Word. Are you ready for a change? Do you need a mountain moved in your life? Then I have just one last question for you. GOT FAITH? It pleases God. Use it, *and nothing will be impossible to you!*

"Jesus said to her, Did I not tell you and promise you that if you would believe and rely on Me, you should see the glory of God?"
John 11:40 (AMP)

Jesus spoke these Words to Martha who is the sister of His good friend Lazarus. Mary and Martha had sent word to Jesus that His friend was sick and close to death. However, Jesus stayed where He was to minister for two more days. In the meantime, Lazarus died. When Jesus returned to Bethany, He found the sisters and many of the other Jews weeping and mourning. Martha went out to meet Him. When she saw Him she said, "If you had been here he would not have died." Jesus assured her *if they would believe they would see the glory of God.* Martha went back to the house to get Mary, and they all went to the tomb where Lazarus was buried. Jesus gave the order to roll away the stone, but Martha tried to argue that the body would now stink, since he had been dead for four days. Jesus then reassured her with the Words in the above verse. They rolled away the stone. Jesus lifted up His eyes and said, "Father, I thank you that you have heard me. I knew that you always hear me, but I said this for the benefit of the people standing here, that they may believe that you sent me." Then in a loud voice He said, "Lazarus, come out." Lazarus, wrapped in his grave clothes, came out of the tomb. Jesus told them to free him, and let him go.

This testimony is just one of many that demonstrate to us the power of God. His love assures us that we don't need to worry or be afraid of life's darkest trials. God is the Ultimate Authority, Jesus is His only begotten Son, and He died and rose again so we could live free…without fear. His Word is the final authority in every problem or situation you're facing. If you're thinking, "You don't know how long I've been dealing with this thing. It might as well be dead. There is no reviving it, and now this mess stinks, too," then you need to hear the message Jesus gave to Mary and Martha again. "Did I not promise, if you would believe in Me and rely on My Word, that you would see the Father move on our behalf?"

What's stinking in your life? The very thing that died, and now you're afraid to believe for again? What has the devil lied about and told you will never happen? Maybe you feel like Mary and Martha, if the Lord had intervened at the time of your crisis, your dream wouldn't have died either? Now there is no way this can be resurrected. We all have areas that seem to be too-far-gone, even for God to change, but the Lord is encouraging us to not limit Him. Believing and exercising our faith is what changes every "stinking" thing in our lives. Don't be afraid. It's not too late for you or your miracle. Rely on the Word. Say "come out" to your dead thing. You'll see God's Glory in your own life and circumstances, too.

"MY LITTLE children, I write you these things so that you may not violate God's law and sin; but if any one should sin, we have an Advocate (One Who will interceded for us) with the Father [it is] Jesus Christ [the all] righteous-upright, just, Who conforms to the Father's will in every purpose, thought and action."
1 John 2:1 (AMP)

When John wrote this verse he wanted it to be clear, God knew we were going to sin, and because of it we were going to need an advocate or someone to defend us. However, this doesn't give us a license to sin. The truth is when you become a member of the family of God, you don't want to sin anymore, and it's disappointing when you do. This verse states when we are in trouble or sin, we should never hesitate to run to the Father. In other words, we don't need to be afraid to come to Him with our mistakes.

According to Webster's Dictionary, the word advocate means, "one that pleads the cause of another; one that defends or maintains a cause or proposal." God picked the best defense attorney of all time when He chose Jesus. He has been, and even at this very moment is still pleading our cause by defending us to the Father. His intercession for us never stops! So when we make a mistake, the Father is already prepared to forgive and restore us when we ask. He picked His own Son, Jesus Christ—*the all righteous-upright, just*—to be our defense attorney. Why? Because the Word says the devil is the accuser of the brethren. So when the devil tries to accuse you and says, "Look God, look at what your child has done," Jesus turns to the Father, who is seated right beside Him and says, "Your Honor, Dad, this child has repented! My blood now covers them!" God then says, "Innocent…Case dismissed!" Now this might seem too good to be true, but the whole salvation plan is too good to be true, too. This is how much God loves you. If you still want to disagree and place yourself under your own "punishment program" that is your choice, but this is not God's best. Nor is it His loving plan of grace, mercy, and forgiveness He has already prepared for us.

Have you been too afraid to approach God for forgiveness? Do you argue with yourself about whether this is really true? Can God really be this loving and forgiving? If you can't accept God's Word about this part, are you sure you've accepted it at all? All of the Bible is God's Word to us. All means all. The Word says God is not a man who lies. Don't be afraid. God put the plan into place. Turn to Jesus…He'll turn to the Father. He's your best defense. Believe it! Receive it!

> *"Therefore if any man be in Christ, he is a new creature: old things are passed away; behold, all things are become new."*
> *2 Corinthians 5:17 (KJV)*

This verse states when we accept Jesus as our Lord and Savior, *we are in Christ.* This means we are born again. At this time our spirits are new. Our sins are washed away. We become clean by the blood of Jesus, and our old ways that kept us in bondage are loosed so we can be free in Christ. Now whether you were really, really bad, you got away from God or you hardly did anything wrong at all, the truth is—all have sinned and need a Savior. Accepting Christ changes our past sin. He totally wipes our record clean.

For *any man* who has already made this decision, we know this is good news. However, there may be times you still feel like doing some of the 'old things.' Why? When we *become new* it doesn't change the outer man. If you were thin, did you become fat? Did you become bald if you had hair? The outer man isn't changed. Neither is your soul—your mind, will, and emotions. It's your spirit that's been made new, and now you have God's power within you to overcome temptations. So how do you stop old habits or bad behavioral patterns? You have to renew your mind to God's Word, which changes your thinking, which changes your actions. The Word is what changes us. Jesus said, "Man cannot live on bread alone, but on every Word that comes out of God's mouth." The Bible says, "IN THE beginning was the Word, and the Word was with God, and the Word was God." We must know the Word, and use it, to see the changes we desire.

The Bible says we have the power of life and death in our tongue, and we will eat the fruit that comes from it. In other words, what you speak—good or bad—will bring certain consequences. One of the definitions of consequence is the importance with respect to power to produce an effect. When Jesus gave us all authority it included power. I realized years ago my past words had brought the life I was living in now. I quickly changed what I was saying. I began to replace even the good talk with the Word because it is the only thing that can change me and my circumstances. Are your trials today the harvest of words you've sown in the past? Words like, "He'll never get off drugs...She's never been faithful...If it's going to happen to anyone, it will be me...They'll never finish school or get out of the streets...My mom and my sister both had cancer, it's just a matter of time before I get it, too." Replace your words with God's Word. It's the key weapon against any crisis the devil attempts. Don't be afraid. You can win your battles. Change weapons. Use the "right" words...His Words! *Old things will pass away*, and you will soon see "*new*" victories in every area of your life.

"In Him we have redemption (deliverance and salvation) through His blood, the remission (forgiveness) of our offences (shortcomings and trespasses), in accordance with the riches and the generosity of His gracious favor, Which He lavished upon us in every kind of wisdom and understanding (practical insight and prudence.)"
Ephesians 1:7-8 (AMP)

These verses guarantee for every believer a complete life with no limitations on the favor God desires to give them. This complete life is void of fear because of what Jesus did on the cross. Why should we fear when we know that *"In Him,"* all these magnificent benefits belong to us?

Webster's Dictionary defines *lavish* as, "expending or bestowing profusely; expended or produced in abundance; marked by profusion or excess." Webster also defines profuse as, "a pouring forth liberally: extravagant; exhibiting great abundance: bountiful; implies pouring forth without restraint; a rich and splendid abundance; unstinted or unmeasured excess." We are told in these verses His riches and the generosity of His favor are unmeasured, marked by excess, poured liberally, without restraint, and exhibits a great abundance for us to have wisdom and every practical insight needed to manage our lives in complete success. Do you see God has already given you everything you need, through Christ and His Word, to defeat the devil and every other crisis—every time? Why should we be afraid? The enemy's lies should no longer even faze us.

The key is for us to know what the Word says. If we don't know it and suffer because of it, can we blame God? If you do everything necessary to teach your child about safely crossing the street and they still choose to do it their way and get hurt…whose fault is it? You love your child. God loves His, but He won't force us to read or study the Word. Maybe the devil has lied to you and said you won't be able to understand it? You know if you hear those words, it's not God. It's only the enemy trying to deliver a spirit of fear. If a delivery person tries to drop off damaged goods at your door, do you have to accept it? No, you don't! And you don't have to accept every piece of damaged goods (lies) the devil tries to bring your way, either. These verses confirm *God gives us all wisdom.* In fact, *He lavished every kind of wisdom and understanding upon us.* Don't be afraid. As you've read the pages of this book, haven't you been able to understand God's Word so far? Give fear no place. Receive the *gracious favor* and every other provision *God has lavished upon you.* It's there for your every need!

> *"Making known to us the mystery (secret) of His will—of His plan, of His purpose. [And it is this:] In accordance with His good pleasure (His merciful intention) which He had previously purposed and set forth in Him."*
> *Ephesians 1:9 (AMP)*

The Apostle Paul wants us to understand that it was always God's intentions to make His will and plans for us known. "Guessing" the direction we should go is not the way God wanted us to progress through life. He lavishes His wisdom on us. Not to be controlling or dictatorial, but to clearly demonstrate His love in choosing a path that each of us would not only enjoy, but a path that would allow us to reach our own level of success, to reach our called destiny. Wouldn't you like to be on an enjoyable and successful path? Your path to destiny? Is this the path you're on now?

The problem is we hear people say, "God works in mysterious ways." This is simply not scriptural. When Paul uses the word *mystery* here, it is because God hadn't openly shared with the world His complete plan for Jesus. Why? Because if the devil had known he was about to be defeated…forever…he wouldn't have crucified Him. However, this verse confirms, God always had a plan, and the plan was "*in Him,*" Christ Jesus. The plans of God are available for all to see. God has always foretold every event that was going to happen…Noah and the flood, the destruction that was coming to Sodom and Gomorrah, the birth—death—and resurrection of Jesus, and now His soon return to us again as King.

God also sent His prophets to tell each king if and when to go into battle. God told one king to have the singers march in front of the army. Their praises caused the enemy army to turn against themselves. Even today the Lord sends us prophets. The Word of the Lord has always been available to His people. The Bible says, "Eye has not seen and hear has not heard, but God will tell you about these things beforehand." Does this sound like a mysterious God? The enemy tries to make us believe we are out here on our own or "You never know what God is going to do." This is just not in the Word. The Bible also clearly states God doesn't withhold any good thing from those who walk uprightly. Daily wisdom and direction from costly errors would be a "good thing." Yes? Are you asking? Listening? Don't be afraid. When situations catch you off guard, do you think God is surprised? Do you think He wrings His hands over what to do next? Ask for His will…His plan. Ask to know Jesus. *In Him* is the answer, and in His time He will make all things known to you.

AUGUST 28

"In Him we were also made [God's] heritage (portion) and we obtained an inheritance; for we had been foreordained (chosen and appointed beforehand) in accordance with His purpose, Who works out everything in agreement with the counsel and design of His [own] will."
Ephesians 1:11 (AMP)

Once again our benefits are confirmed. When we are "*in Him*," we are inheritors of His promises and will. If there were ever doubts about God wanting you to become His child or about what belongs to you because of that decision, this verse should settle it. God foreordained your coming into His Kingdom, which means you were chosen and appointed…beforehand. Now you might be asking, "Why me? What did I do to deserve this?" The truth is you didn't do anything. None of us did. It is simply the plan of God by His grace. If acceptance had been received because of who we are, our backgrounds, and so on, then the work of Christ would have had conditions or restrictions. God's love is unconditional. This means NO restrictions. He set this plan—*His will by His own design and counsel*—into place, and it all works together for His ultimate purpose.

Jesus and the cross were not an after thought in the plans of God. He didn't wake up one day and accidentally discover Adam had sinned. He didn't run His hands through His hair, pace across the throne room or go for a drive in His chariot around Heaven trying to figure out what He should do now. He already had the plan in place. The Bible tells us when Adam sinned he hid from God because he was afraid. God came down to the garden to talk with him and spend time with him daily. When Adam wasn't there, God asked, "Where are you?" We know God knew where Adam was, but what God was really asking Adam was, "Did Adam know where he was?" In other words, did Adam know his sin had separated him from the Father? Is God asking you the same question today, "Where are you?" He sees you, too, but do you know where you are? Have you let sin separate you from your Heavenly Father?

We are no different than Adam. When we sin or if we have sinned, we also want to run and hide from God. We're afraid. But God didn't destroy Adam, and He won't destroy us, either. God chose you…beforehand. Long before you were born God chose and appointed you. Accept His wonderful plan through His Son, Jesus. You don't have to be afraid of God, and with Him on your side, who or what else could cause you to fear? Don't be afraid. *By His own design* He's already worked it all out…just for you!

"In Him you also who have heard the Word of Truth, the glad tidings (Gospel) of your salvation, and have believed in and have adhered to and have relied on Him, were stamped with the seal of the long-promised Holy Spirit. That [Spirit] is the guarantee of our inheritance—the first fruit, the pledge and foretaste, the down payment on our heritage—in anticipation of its full redemption and our acquiring [complete] possession of it, to the praise of His glory."
Ephesians 1:13-14 (AMP)

The Holy Spirit is the deposit or *down payment of our heritage, the guarantee of our inheritance*—our victory. *We have heard the Word of truth, the glad tidings, and the good news of the Gospel.* Jesus, the Son of God, was crucified, He died, and was buried. He was resurrected and is now interceding for us at the Father's right hand. We receive God's plan of salvation by repenting and accepting Jesus as our Lord and Savior, but this is only the beginning of our inheritance.

When Jesus foretold of His death and what they would do to Him, the disciples wanted to stop it. After He was crucified, resurrected, and was about to ascend to Heaven to be with the Father, again they wanted to stop Him from leaving. Jesus told them it was better for Him to go, but He was sending another…the Holy Spirit. The Holy Spirit would be their comfort and guide them into all truth. Jesus calls the Holy Spirit a person…"He" not "it." The Holy Spirit is the third part of the Godhead or Trinity. He is the power of God. When God speaks, the Holy Spirit does what He says. In the beginning when God said, "Let there be light," the Holy Spirit brought it to pass. He is also the One who raised Christ from the dead. However, we can't limit His purpose to just the power. We need to know Him and develop a close relationship with Him, also.

The Holy Spirit is a real person. He doesn't have a body because He is a Spirit, but He lives on the inside of us, just like the Lord does. However, one of the most important things He does is to speak to us about what He hears the Father saying. When you ask God for direction or wisdom, the voice you hear that answers your questions is the Holy Spirit on the inside of you. Are you hearing what God is saying? It's the Father's will that you do. If you don't think you hear from God then ask yourself, "Do I know the Holy Spirit?" If you don't…you can. Don't be afraid. If you ask Him to come in and fill you, He will. You'll also find He is the sweetest, closest, and wisest friend you'll ever know.

> *"But when He, the Spirit of Truth (the truth-giving Spirit) comes, He will guide you into all truth—the whole, full truth. For He will not speak His own message—on His own authority—but He will tell whatever He hears [from the Father, He will give the message that has been given to Him] and He will announce and declare to you the things that are to come—that will happen in the future."*
> *John 16:13 (AMP)*

God's plan for His family is a complete one. He wants us to know the future. He wants us to know what is coming, so we will be prepared and equipped. Why? Because He knows "human" nature is to worry or to be afraid when we don't know or understand what's happening. However, He wanted only the best for His own children. So once Jesus ascended to Heaven, how was He going to make His Presence available to us on earth? He accomplished this by sending the Holy Spirit. While Jesus was on earth He was confined to a mortal body. Unless He was physically in your city, you couldn't be with Him. But today, all believers anywhere in the world can have the Spirit of God with them.

The Holy Spirit carries the messages from God to His children, but He doesn't knock us down to get our attention. He is a gentleman just like the rest of the Trinity. We ask, use faith, and then believe for our answer. The following verses tell us the Holy Spirit will Honor and Glorify Jesus. And Jesus said He, meaning the Spirit, would take what was God's and reveal or disclose it to you. Since everything God has belongs to Jesus, He can give the Holy Spirit exactly what He wants declared or transmitted to you for whatever you need. God never intended for us to be alone or to be in the dark about the upcoming events in our lives. This verse, along with many others, just confirms how important it is to the Father that we know about *the things that are to come—that will happen in the future!*

Is your life in shambles because you didn't seek the will of God? Are you dealing with areas that are way out of your control? It's not too late. The enemy would love for you to believe you have gone too far...it is past the "point of no return." Just for the record, that's not in the Bible, either. Don't be afraid. God always has a plan, and He can make a way out of no way. I've seen Him do it countless times. When you ask, the Holy Spirit delivers, reveals, discloses and transmits everything you need for change...AND...during your most difficult times, He will supply you with all the comfort you'll ever need to get you through.

"And in that day ye shall ask me nothing. Verily, verily, I say unto you, Whatsoever ye shall ask the Father in my name, he will give it you. Hitherto have ye asked nothing in my name: ask, and ye shall receive, that your joy may be full."
John 16:23-24 (KJV)

In these verses, Jesus gives His disciples further instructions about what they should do and say after He goes to be with the Father. When He says that "*until now you have asked Me for nothing,"* He is referring to their time together for the past three and a half years. During this time traveling and ministering their wants and needs were provided for by Jesus. Contrary to some teachings, Jesus was not poor. It takes money for one person to travel, let alone the twelve disciples and all the others who went with them. Jesus had taken care of everything for them, but now that was about to change. His instruction was once He goes to the Father they should…1) Ask the Father for what they want or need. 2) Ask in Jesus' Name. 3) After they ask, they will receive from their Father in Heaven.

These are the same guidelines for our asking today. We ask the Father for what we need or want, and we do it in Jesus' Name. Then, we use our faith, and believe we receive. Jesus said when we do these things, we will receive, and He tells us why…*so our joy would be full.* God loves us, and He is such a giver. He wants us to live a happy and fulfilled life. As parents, don't you want the same for your children? "*Whatsoever you ask*"…also proves that They haven't narrowed down the asking to only cover our needs. If there had been restrictions to His instructions, doesn't this seem like the appropriate time to mention them? The truth is God hates lack, and He hates the fear that comes with it. Why? Because His Son already paid for lack and the heartache it causes when He went to the cross. Poverty and lack were part of the curse of the law of sin and death, which Jesus destroyed at Calvary. Now you can see why the Father isn't pleased when He sees us struggling or going without, especially if it's because we simply haven't asked.

God is faithful to His Word. The Bible says God doesn't lie. So when we read Jesus said for us to *ask in His Name and the Father would give it*, then we have no excuse for not asking. Don't be afraid. The Father loves giving "good" gifts to His children. It not only makes our joy full, but it's just as pleasing to the Father. Just ask, in Jesus' Name, and you shall receive!

SEPTEMBER 1

> *"In that day you will ask in my name. I am not saying that I will ask the Father on your behalf. No, the Father himself loves you because you have loved me and have believed that I came from God. I came from the Father and entered the world; now I am leaving the world and going back to the Father."*
> *John 16:26-28 (NIV)*

Before Jesus was betrayed, crucified, resurrected, and ascended He spoke plainly to His disciples about what was about to happen. He wanted them to know the Father loved them because they accepted and loved Him. And even though Jesus is now seated at the Father's right hand to intercede for us, He isn't begging Him to be good to us. In fact, these verses make it clear that *He won't ask the Father for anything on our behalf* because the *Father, out of His own great love*, already wants to give to us.

Once we allow ourselves to have a relationship with God our Father, and we experience His love to us, why would we be afraid of anything? If God is for me, then who can be against me? The Bible says, "no one." Even though man and the devil may try, the attempts will be futile. When John writes about his life with Jesus, we also get a clear picture of Christ and His relationship with the Father, the disciple's relationship with the Lord, and now what our relationship as a believer can be with both of Them. Jesus said, "If you've seen Me, you've seen the Father." They also witnessed the wondrous miracles, love, and compassion Jesus showed everyone, especially the sinner. The Word proclaims He came to save the lost.

Right now you may be feeling lost. Maybe you don't know the Lord. Or you know Him, but you've lost the joy or confidence you're supposed to experience as a believer. You're feeling tired, weary, and now fear says "nothing will ever change." Don't believe it! This is not God's plan for His children. Stop and take inventory. Are you praying and asking God in faith? Then do you stand and believe you receive? Is there unforgiveness or bitterness in your heart toward anyone? Are you speaking the Word or your problem? Are you thanking God in the midst of your trial or are you complaining like the children of Israel? Have you opened the door to fear? Do you just know "about" God or do you really know Him? The Bible says, "This too," or whatever the trial is, "Shall pass." Don't be afraid. If needed, repent, and make a change. Remember—NO FEAR! Faith stands firm. Trust God. He loves you, and He will deliver you out of every trial.

SEPTEMBER 2

> *"I have told you these things so that in Me you may have perfect peace and confidence. In the world you have tribulation and trials and distress and frustration; but be of good cheer—take courage, be confident, certain, undaunted—for I have overcome the world.—I have deprived it of power to harm, have conquered it [for you].*
> *John 16:33 (AMP)*

Jesus has already defeated every trial, thought, fear, addiction, divorce, bankruptcy, and any other problems life may throw at us. He has triumphed over them all, and the Bible says we are more than conquerors through Christ. How can this be? How can we be more than Christ? He was the One who paid the price...He took the beatings, was spit upon, lied about, falsely accused, tormented, persecuted, and crucified in our place. BUT—He was also victorious. He conquered death, hell, and the grave. He reversed the curse for us. Through His shed blood on the cross, when we accept and believe on Him, we receive the same reward or inheritance as a child of God. We, too, can have a relationship with the Father now and a place in eternity later. This makes us more than conquerors because we have received all the benefits without doing anything. Christ did it all.

In the verses prior to this one, Jesus had shared with the disciples all the things that were about to happen to Him. He told them in advance so they wouldn't be afraid. They could have His peace. He is saying the same thing to us today. We, too, can have *perfect peace and confidence.* We can have His peace...nothing missing, nothing broken, nothing lacking, total wholeness. He knew how frustrating the world would be, and yet, He said peace belonged to us. How can we experience this kind of peace when it seems all hell has broken loose around us? The first thing we need to do when things get tough is check our faith level. What's changed? Did the problem grow that much bigger? Even so, when did God become that much smaller?

The truth is you've let fear into your life. If you find yourself angry, frustrated or tormented, the root is you're afraid of the outcome. You've got to let go of the fear, and let God do what <u>only</u> He can do. He can handle His part, and you can do yours by staying in the Word and using your faith. What does the Word say about your trial? *Jesus said we would have trials in this world, but to be of good cheer, He had overcome the world.* Don't be afraid. Keep speaking the Word, take courage, and be confident of your victory. Jesus already overcame. *He deprived the world of all its power so that nothing*—not one thing—*could harm you.* He conquered the world so we could be more than conquerors!

SEPTEMBER 3

> *"If you live in Me—abide vitally united to Me—*
> *and My words remain in you and continue*
> *to live in your heart, ask whatever you will*
> *and it shall be done for you."*
> *John 15:7 (AMP)*

John writes to us what Jesus shared with them regarding the importance of first having and then keeping a close relationship with God. We cannot be successful in our endeavors without God. It's His daily input that keeps us from making the wrong moves that can turn out to be so costly. Can you relate? Is there an area you wish you'd had His wisdom…beforehand? This verse confirms it is vitally important to stay hooked up or *abide in the Lord*. Webster's Dictionary defines the word abide as, "to wait for; to endure without yielding; to bear patiently; to accept without objection; to remain stable or fixed in a state; to continue in a place." In other words, Jesus instructed His disciples to wait on Him; to be patient and to endure without giving up; to accept the plan without complaining or backtalk; to stay fixed, and then to continue, so they could remain in God's plan.

In the verses before this one, Jesus gives the example that He is the vine and the Father is the gardener. He describes the necessary steps that must be taken in order for the vine or the branch to remain healthy and continue to produce the maximum amount of fruit. Jesus went on to say that any branch which doesn't bear fruit, the Father cuts off, and even those that do bear fruit must have regular pruning in order to stay productive. Jesus also said He is the vine, and we are the branches. Whoever chooses to live in Him—then He will live in them. Once this happens, this person will now be able to bear much fruit. However, if we choose to live apart from Him, we can do nothing.

Examine your life. Are you bearing fruit? Do you feel like your life has purpose? Are you going somewhere? Or are you in the same place you were ten years ago? Maybe there are some areas in your life you need to cut out or have pruned? Jesus said we can do nothing apart from Him. Where is your relationship with Him? Do you even have one? The Father wants to provide and will grant us whatever we wish when we ask, but there must be a relationship. Don't be afraid. Don't let what you have or have not done keep you from the Father. He loves you, and it has always been His desire to be close to you. Just accept… abide…remain…ask…and you will receive!

SEPTEMBER 4

> *"Let not your hearts be troubled: ye believe in God, believe also in me."*
> *John 14:1 (KJV)*

In this verse Jesus reassures all those who already believe in God that it's right they should also believe in Him. There are troubled hearts around the world who still want to dispute or argue about the man called Jesus. Is He really the Son of God? Jesus knew what was about to come. He also knew some of the early church leaders were not going to accept Him. They were looking for a conquering king. The truth is they weren't the generation to see the Conquering King...WE ARE! The world will soon see Jesus, as King, when He returns.

However, this verse also speaks about our daily turmoil or problems. There will always be situations, events, and circumstances that can cause our hearts to be worried, anxious, and troubled. What is the prescription for a troubled heart? *Believe in God...believe also in the Lord.* Why? They are the only Ones who can change your situation and heal a broken heart. Jesus says there is a "way" we can live in this world and not be troubled by all the things happening around us. This "way" destroys fear, and it comforts us with the truth we are loved. This "way" believes in Him.

Is your heart heavy? Are you carrying the cares of your family or work, and it feels like the cares of the world, too? Has the weight of it all gotten to be too much? Jesus said to trust and rely on Him...*to believe in Him.* When you are in fellowship with Him, you know how much He loves you. He knows the only way for you to get rid of heaviness in your heart is to give it all to Him, and once you get rid of it, don't take it back. Let Him do what only He can do, and in the meantime, you do your part by speaking the Word and thanking God for the victory.

Jesus has given you all power over the enemy and every problem that is trying to talk to you right now. Did you know your troubles have a voice? Like when that medical bill asks you, "How are you ever going to pay this?" Or that pain or symptom in your stomach or lower back says, "I wonder if this is an infection or what if I need back surgery or what if it's cancer?" Oh, yes, your troubles will tell you all kinds of things, but they will never line up or agree with the Word, so you can't listen to them. Every ache and pain isn't the "C" word, and every bill doesn't have to mean financial ruin. Don't be afraid. If Jesus said, *"Let not your heart be troubled,"* then it's possible. "Let" means it's your choice. Do you want peace? Then give up your troubles. *Believe in God* who loves you. *Believe also in Him* for total peace and rest.

"And whatever ye shall ask in my name, that will I do, that the Father may be glorified in the Son. If ye shall ask any thing in my name I will do it."
John 14:13-14 (KJV)

These verses assure us that whatever we ask, if we ask for it in the Name of Jesus, the Father will do it. Asking is an important issue. Jesus says it numerous times, and here He repeats it, back to back. In the verses prior to these, Jesus answers the disciple's questions about the Father. He told them if they saw Him, they had also seen the Father. He wasn't doing things or saying things out of His own will, but of the will of the One who sent Him. Jesus said when He spoke it was the Father who told Him what to say. Jesus asked them to believe Him when He said, "He was in the Father and the Father was in Him," and if they were having a hard time with that oneness, then at least consider and believe the evidence of the miracles they'd not only witnessed, but had participated in, also.

Why was it so important the disciples understood this oneness? What did they need to see about His relationship with the Father? First and foremost, the key to understanding how anything works between God and us is through relationship. This is why Jesus kept emphasizing He and the Father are one. But what benefit is this to us? How does this impact my life? The answer lies in truly being able to grasp what Jesus meant when He said, "He didn't do or say anything the Father didn't tell Him to do or say, unless He heard the Father tell Him." This is so important for us to understand because people think Jesus said and did what He did because He was still God while He was on earth. But the truth is He gave up His Deity to come to earth. He was a man, just like you and me. Why is this crucial to our understanding? Because if Jesus hadn't been "just a man," listening and doing what the Father told Him, how could we believe we could have the same power to do not only what He did, but even greater works as the Bible states? This statement allows us to see and fully understand the source behind the miracles. We can also see where wisdom for all situations, safety, protection, and all sufficiency for every need originates. Jesus was the earthly extension of the Father, and our example of how our relationship with Them works. They were still connected…one…and it was as if God was doing it Himself.

Today, Jesus wants us to be the earthly extension of Them. Our receiving has nothing to do with our abilities, gifts or talents. It is based on our relationship with Him and the Father. We are to be one with Them. We also ask, listen, and then obey. This verse states we can ask for any "thing," not just a need. God meets needs, but He wants to do so much more. Don't be afraid. God wants us blessed. He told us how. Ask, in Jesus' Name. He will do it, and we will receive!

SEPTEMBER 6

> *"This is love: not that we loved God, but that he loved us and sent his Son as an atoning sacrifice for our sins."*
> *1 John 4:10 (NIV)*

John had truly learned how to accept the love of the Lord. He had a great revelation of this love and how it was an overflow of love from the Father. God first loved us, and that love was so great He was willing to sacrifice His only Son in order to make a way for us to be restored back to Him. The Bible clearly states there is no fear in perfect love.

In the Old Testament, only the Priest was able to take the sacrifice into the Holy of Holies, and offer it to God. This sacrifice was in the form of an animal, and it only covered their sins for one year. The Priest went into this Holy place with fear and trembling. If his life was not repentant or clean, he could die instantly. The other Priests, who waited in the inner court, tied a rope around the Priest's leg before he entered the Holy place, just in case he didn't come out. They knew they couldn't go in without possibly dying, too. So if needed, the only safe way was to drag the body out. God changed all that when He chose to send His only Son to be our sacrifice. Jesus was pure and sinless, but He didn't just cover our sins. He completely and totally wiped them away. When we repent and ask Him to come into our hearts, we are washed clean, as though we had never sinned.

The willingness to die for another is without a doubt the highest definition of love, especially when all the rewards or benefits go to others. There are those today who feel they are willing to die, and they believe it's for others, but if they create some horrendous crime or bring death and destruction in the process, who or what others are truly benefited? The truth is there is no benefit, and it isn't God's way. *God is love*. God is also a giver…the giver of an abundant life! The devil is the one who takes, kills, steals, and destroys. When we witness these acts of terrorism, vandalism, and violence being done by someone who is willing to die, who do you think is really behind the attack? The Word's clear…it's the devil working in or through people that have bought his lies of deception.

The truth is God loves you, and even if you have made mistakes or caused major chaos and destruction, Jesus still died for you. He doesn't like what you've done or maybe you're still planning to do, but He has never stopped loving you. If you will accept the greatest sacrifice of all, Jesus Christ, your sins can be forgiven and washed away, too. Don't be afraid. God is love, and He first loved you. Let His <u>love</u> motivate you—not hate—not fear. We've all sinned. Make the decision to let *His atoning blood* cleanse you for good.

SEPTEMBER 7

"There is no fear in love—dread does not exist; but full-grown (complete, perfect) love turns fear out of doors and expels every trace of terror! For fear brings with it the thought of punishment, and [so] he who is afraid has not reached the full maturity of love—is not yet grown into love's complete perfection."
1 John 4:18 (AMP)

God's love is hard to accept because it seems too good to be true. Most people have never experienced a love like the Father's. The love we've come to know is very conditional. It has qualifiers. "If" you love me...you will do this or go here or buy me that, and "if" you don't…there could be punishment or unpleasant consequences. When John writes *there is no fear in love*, he speaks of the Father's love. When you truly get a revelation of this kind of love, with no conditions or restrictions, you'll be fear-free, too. This freedom will roll over into every other area of your life. You won't be afraid if you hear a bad report of health, finances, family problems, job concerns (a bad job to no job), storms in the natural or storms against you in the spirit. There is no fear in His perfect love!

This verse also talks about us maturing, and in that maturity we would come to "know" the complete and perfect love of Christ. You know love is powerful. If you've ever fallen in love with someone, you can hardly stay away from them. Their love for you is like a magnet that draws you closer and closer. They can consume your thoughts and affections. Christ's love for us does the same thing. I've heard it said His love for us was so strong that nails weren't needed to hold Him on the cross. His love alone would have been powerful enough to hold Him there. This powerful love is what He has for you. "Knowing" you are loved and accepted gives you confidence and "joy" unspeakable during your trials.

God has worked out every detail of your life in advance, and He has given you the tools to put it all into place. Plus, you can have peace and joy while you're doing it. Now if your life is in a mess you might be wondering, "What tools?" The tools He's given you are HIS NAME and the power of attorney to use it against any attack. He's given you HIS WORD, and when you speak it, angels will be dispatched to do the work. Use YOUR FAITH, it pleases God, and it moves His mighty hand when you ask, and you have HIS LOVE, which is perfect and casts out all fear. Don't be afraid. He is working it all out. Just receive His perfect love for you. It will expel every trace of terror, erase your deepest fears, and bring you hope, joy, and confidence for the victorious future He has planned for you.

SEPTEMBER 8

> *"We love him, because he first loved us."*
> *1 John 4:19 (KJV)*

Many times when someone who has just accepted the Lord gives their testimony they will say, "And then I found the Lord." The truth is He was never lost…we were. An even greater revelation is, if God had not loved us from the very beginning, and gave us His Son, and Jesus hadn't been willing to pay for our sins by becoming our sacrifice…we still wouldn't be in the family of God. All of this is what allows us to be free of fear and the attacks of the devil.

Several years ago I took in a stray cat. She had been mistreated, and as a result didn't like to eat in the same room with my other cat. When it's meal time and I have her dish ready, she looks to see if I'm coming with her food. Then she starts her journey. She finally picks a spot. When she stops, I sit the food down, and she eats. Now I realize this is a bit much, but many times as I am following her to make sure she gets what she wants, where she wants it, I've heard the Father say to me—"isn't this exactly what I've done for you?" I do it for her because I love her, and He's done it and is still doing it for me for the very same reason. Maybe you've been mistreated? Maybe you've never been treated like you were special? Maybe you've never known true love in your entire life? Well, you can. This verse confirms He has always loved you.

Now using my cats to teach me about His love seems a little extreme, but at that moment when I feel the love for my pet, I can also feel the love He has for me as His "pet." His love was there long before I realized it. He had put people in my path to share the good news of the Gospel, He had sent the Holy Spirit to 'woo' me to Himself, and He had protected me from danger and self-destruction while I was still doing my "own thing" in the world. If He would do all this before I knew Him, what would keep Him from showing me the same kind of love after I became His child? Nothing…and nothing will keep Him from showing you that same love, either.

If you have come to know the Lord in a personal way, you already know what He did to provide and protect you in your past. You've experienced His love. However, if you haven't made the decision, <u>don't put it off.</u> He has loved you and has been waiting for you long before you were born. Don't be afraid. His love is pure and unconditional. Once you feel His love, you will want to follow the truth in this verse and love Him, too.

"For everyone born of God overcomes the world. This is the victory that has overcome the world, even our faith. Who is it that overcomes the world? Only He who believes that Jesus is the Son of God."
1 John 5:4-5 (NIV)

These verses talk about accepting the plan of God for your life by receiving the salvation message of Jesus. When you do, you are an overcomer, but there is only one way this overcoming power is available to us. We must believe Jesus is God's Son and then become born again. This verse boldly states, *"For everyone born of God overcomes the world."* What exactly does this mean? How are we able to overcome the world? We overcome it with the knowledge that death is not the end for us as believers. Death, and the fear of it, is the end for people who don't know the Lord. The Bible says when Christ died on the cross, went to hell, got the keys, and arose from the dead, He defeated death. While the Holy Ghost was resurrecting Jesus from death to life, the devil knew He was going to have to hand over the keys of death that came through sin to the King of kings and the Lord of lords, Jesus Christ.

Believing Jesus is God's Son, creates a confidence that removes the fear of dying for the believer. We know where we're going, and we also know we'll be united with other loved ones who believed. This is a comforting thought. God wants His family to be with Him. Why wouldn't He want us to be with ours? The Bible says death has been swallowed up in victory; death and the grave have lost their sting. This means death, even though the outer body perishes, can't hold our spirit after we die. We have overcome death through the blood of Christ.

However, His blood doesn't just give us victory over death. It also gives us victory over the things of this life. We don't have to wait until we die to get our "heavenly" inheritance. Do you receive an inheritance on earth after you die? No, you get it after someone else passes away. Jesus died and left us an inheritance. The good news is He arose from the dead. He is alive and at this very moment is interceding for us with the Father. If your relative left you millions of dollars in their will, but you never went to claim it, whose fault would it be if you lived poor and alone? God has a rich inheritance for the saints…you and me. But if we won't receive what belongs to us, whose fault is it? We can't blame God for living sick or broke. He left us health, wealth, and wholeness in His will. Don't be afraid. Receive your benefits. Be of good cheer. He overcame, and with Him, so will you.

SEPTEMBER 10

> *"Do not be seized with alarm and struck with fear, little flock, for it is your Father's good pleasure to give you the kingdom."*
> *Luke 12:32 (AMP)*

Throughout the New Testament the Bible refers to the "Kingdom of God." Jesus used many parables to describe it. To all who had ears to hear, He taught the Kingdom was likened to a mustard seed, a net cast down into a lake that catches all kinds of fish, a treasure hidden in a field, the yeast a woman mixes into her flour, and many other things, as well. After each example, He explained to them how these items and the Kingdom were the same.

In the New Testament we are referred to as sheep. We are the sheep of His pasture. In Psalm 23 it says, "He makes us to lie down in green pastures, and He leads us beside still waters." This is one of the major roles of a shepherd. Every day he searches for the greenest pastures and the best watering holes for his flocks. If a natural shepherd knows to do this, how much more would the Great Shepherd do for us to meet our daily provision? In this verse Jesus makes it clear the Father will provide, and He tells us why. It is because He loves us and *wants to do it out of His good pleasure.*

This verse and others were given to us to eliminate fear, alarm or terror. In Webster's Dictionary by the word alarm it says, "See fear," and it means, "a sudden sharp apprehension and fear resulting from the perception of imminent danger." Most of what we say, feel, and do is the result of how we perceive a situation, but we can't always base things on what we see or how we feel because the enemy's scheme is to trick us or to deceive us. Remember, fear stands for False Evidence Appearing Real. Why does the devil's plan always try to scare us? Because he knows fear and faith don't mix. It's like water and oil. Do the devil and God mix? Not at all. Faith is from God…fear is not!

The other issue this verse clears up is that the Kingdom is for everyone. He has one plan, and it's for all mankind. If you accept His Son, who paid for your sins on the cross, then you will have a place in the Kingdom of God. Don't let the enemy lie to you. The qualifications for getting into Heaven have nothing to do with your works. It's all about Jesus. So *"little flock,"…Don't be afraid…or seized with alarm.* Let Jesus be your good Shepherd, and you'll see all of the Father's good pleasures.

"Fear not; I am the first and the last: I am he that liveth, and was dead, and, behold, I am alive for evermore, Amen; and have the keys of hell and of death."
Revelation 1:17b-18 (KJV)

John, the writer of these verses, had been exiled on the island of Patmos. On the Lord's Day he heard a voice like a trumpet which told him to write down everything he saw and heard. Then he was to send it to the seven churches in the cities of Ephesus, Smyrna, Pergamum, Thyatira, Sardis, Philadelphia, and Laodicea. When John turned around to see who was talking to him, he saw seven golden lamp stands. Among them was someone like "the Son of man." John goes on to describe what Jesus looked like, and at His appearance, John fell over as if he were dead. Jesus laid His hand on John and spoke the Words in these verses. The Lord then commissioned John to write about what he saw and the things which were to come.

John knew Jesus. He knew the events surrounding His life before and after the cross. Yet, Jesus felt it was necessary to assure John he had nothing to be afraid of, and He stated for the written record who He really is—*I am the first and the last.* He was the first to die for man's sins, and He would be the last. He had paid the price in full. He restates for the record, "*I am he that was alive, was dead, and behold, I am alive for evermore.*" This was obvious to John since he walked and ministered with Him for three and a half years. Jesus also confirms He has the victory over death, hell, and the grave by announcing—"*I HAVE THE KEYS.*" Jesus wasn't martyred or murdered like other Christians. He willingly gave His life to be our sinless and flawless sacrifice. Now, He is exalted above all, and He lives and reigns for evermore.

When we, as children of God, truly understand the power that was first given to the Lord, and now to us, we will quit feeling afraid or sorry for ourselves because of our situation, and do something about it. We've already been given everything we'll ever need. On the cross Christ did all He needed to do for our victory. Now it's up to us to take what belongs to us and defeat every enemy that tries to come against us. Aren't you ready to "kick the devil" out of your situation? Wouldn't you like to taste victory? Don't be afraid. God, living on the inside of you, is so much bigger than any trial you're facing. He's got the keys—He's already paid for your victory—TAKE your authority, and USE IT!

SEPTEMBER 12

> *"And it shall come to pass, that whosoever shall call on the name of the Lord shall be saved."*
> *Acts 2:21 (KJV)*

In the forty days between Jesus' resurrection from the dead and His ascension into Heaven, He appeared to over 500 people. On the day of His ascension, He told them to go to the upper room and wait for power to come upon them. Only 120 of the 500 obeyed, but God is always faithful. On the tenth day of their wait, which is now called the Day of Pentecost, those 120 men and women received the gift of the Holy Spirit. It was a life changing experience because when the Holy Spirit came upon them, they all started speaking in other tongues or an unknown language. The crowds below heard this and were astonished.

The Bible says there were God-fearing Jews from every nation present in Jerusalem that day. When each of them heard their own languages being spoken from this central location, they were amazed and bewildered. They asked one another, "Aren't these Galileans? How is it we hear them declaring the wonders of God in our own languages?" Some wondered what this meant. Others thought they were drunk. Peter assured them they were not drunk, since it was only about nine o'clock in the morning. He then preached the message of Jesus and all that they had witnessed. When the crowds heard what he said they asked, "What shall we do?" Peter said, "Repent, and be baptized in the Name of Jesus Christ for the forgiveness of your sins, and you will receive the gift of the Holy Spirit." They accepted his message and were baptized. The Bible records about 3,000 *called on the Name of the Lord,* and they *were saved* that day.

You don't have to be afraid God's plan doesn't include you. Jesus completed the mission of all missions, and because of it, we can complete ours. All we are asked to do is to believe on Him, ask for forgiveness, and then we are assured of being saved. Saved from what? Any and every evil, disruptive, devastating thing this world has to offer, including death. With Jesus, we know we can not only have the good life now, but we can also confidently live knowing that we will have even a better life after we leave earth and go to live with Them in Heaven. Are you afraid of what the future may hold for you? Do you know you have a great home awaiting you? Jesus said my Father has many mansions which I will go and prepare for you. Don't be afraid. You can be sure of your future with the Lord. In fact, this may be the only sure thing we'll ever be truly able to count on in this insecure world. To secure your future…just *Call on the Name of the Lord, and you'll be saved.*

"And the angel said unto them, Fear not: for, behold, I bring you good tidings of great joy, which shall be to all people."
Luke 2:10 (KJV)

Luke, the writer of this verse, was not one of Jesus' disciples or followers. He was a physician, a highly educated man. So why would a doctor want to write about the life of someone he never even met? In the first four verses of chapter one, Luke expresses the reasons he wrote. He wanted to give an orderly account of the life of Jesus. Luke went to Mary, Jesus' mother, to get all the personal and intimate details of His birth. He investigated Jesus' daily activities by speaking to eyewitnesses about the miracles, signs, and wonders, and he talked with all the disciples. Luke states he investigated everything, from the very beginning. He wanted to write about it, so that no one would doubt or be uncertain regarding the Lord and what He did for mankind.

In the verse above, the story goes like this—a decree came from Caesar Augustus that a census should be taken. Joseph, the husband of Mary, needed to travel to Bethlehem to register. Mary was pregnant and near her delivery time. When they arrived in Bethlehem, they discovered the town's inn was already full. However, the innkeeper had compassion on them and let them stay in his barn. Later that night Jesus was born. They wrapped Him in swaddling clothes and laid Him in a manger. That night there were shepherds in the fields around the same country watching their flocks. Suddenly an angel appeared to them, and the Glory of the Lord was all around them. They were told the good news in this verse. A Savior had been born—Christ the Lord—and this was a sign to them. They would find the baby in a manger. They were then afraid and bowed to the ground. Suddenly, a multitude of angels appeared and praised God by saying, "Glory to God in the highest, and on earth peace, good will toward men."

God's plan to restore us and bring peace to the world was at last in place. It was a joyous time for Him and for what He was bringing to the world. It was good news then and the best news offered to mankind today...the glad tidings and joy of eternal life. Jesus was born, so He could die, and with His death and resurrection, He gave back everlasting life to anyone who asks. Don't be afraid. Do you know Jesus? Do you have peace? His peace—nothing missing, lacking, or broken—and good will are for all. He fulfilled the Father's plan of peace—not fear—for all people, and that means you!

"For this is my Father's will and His purpose, that every one who sees the Son and believes and cleaves to and trusts and relies on Him should have eternal life; and I will raise him up [from the dead] at the last day."
John 6:40 (AMP)

God makes His plans and purposes known, so there is never any question, fear or doubt about what He wants for us. This verse brings total confirmation that *it's the Father's will and purpose for everyone* to be saved or have eternal life. Jesus, His Son, paid a high price for us, and God doesn't want anyone left behind. He wants us all to be with Him on the last day. However, we cannot enter the family of God without coming to the Lord first. We also cannot fulfill the plan of God for our lives individually without coming to the Lord.

Becoming one of God's children also qualifies you for blessings now. In the book of Deuteronomy, Chapter 28, God decrees the blessings of His covenant. If we obey Him, He said all this belongs to the child of God. He tells us we are blessed in the city and in the country—this covers location. He said the fruit of our womb—our crops, livestock and herds would be blessed—this covers any increase for provision. He said our baskets and kneading trough would be full—this covers our food and daily supply. He said we would be blessed coming and going—this covers divine protection. He said our enemies would be defeated…if they came from one way they would have to leave seven ways—this covers our peace…physical and emotional well being, and security…protection for our families. He said He would bless our barns and prosper whatever we put our hand to—this covers our employment and businesses. He said He would establish us as His holy people, and others would look at us and be afraid—this covers divine favor and fortunate events. He said He would grant us abundant prosperity—this covers our finances. He said He would see to it there was always rain for abundance, and we would lend and not borrow—this covers being debt free.

With these promises, why would you choose to live away from God? Or be afraid? Sick? Poor? Defeated? Choose, and then, obey God's plan. He said *eternal life is for everyone who sees the Son and believes, trusts, and relies on Him.* Don't be afraid. This means you can have the good life now, and when your natural body dies, your spirit will instantly *be raised up to be with the Lord.* God's love and plans are always complete…both now and later.

*"All scripture is given by inspiration of God,
and is profitable for doctrine, for reproof,
for correction, for instruction in righteousness:
That the man of God may be perfect,
thoroughly furnished unto all good works."
2 Timothy 3:16-17 (KJV)*

These verses alone should remove any fear that the Word of God is only the opinions of man. One Bible translation says the Word is God breathed. Knowing and believing it is the inspired Word of God allows us to not only trust it, but to be able to take it literally. This is why and how it becomes good or useful to us for correction, training in righteousness, and for teaching.

Many today, even biblical scholars, want to argue about the authenticity of the Word. They tear it apart by looking at it from the Greek and Hebrew, an historical view, and then they try to analyze it or explain it from every angle. However, dissecting the Bible isn't like dissecting a frog. When you start the frog is dead, and when you finish the frog is dead. But the Bible is alive, and it should still have life left in it when man's intellect is through. If it doesn't, then it has been made to be of no effect. The Bible says to not add or subtract from the Word, and it also says God's Word will not come back void. This means it will accomplish what it has been sent to do. The Bible says we're to study the Word to show ourselves approved. Why? So we will be trained to know what the Word says in order to be equipped in every battle or storm. Why? So when the devil tries to scare us with his lies, we'll know the real, uncompromising truth. The Word says the truth makes us free, but to be free you have to first know the Word or truth.

Jesus repeatedly said if you have ears to hear...hear, and if you have eyes to see...see. He knew they had both. What did He mean? He was referring to the Spirit. The Holy Spirit in us gives us the ability to see and hear God, not just in the natural, but now with new eyes and ears of the Spirit. This is necessary in order for us to understand God because His ways aren't like our natural ways. When we're attacked, don't we want to get even? Jesus said to turn the other cheek. He also said to love our enemies and to pray for those who intentionally hurt or use us. Is this what you feel like doing? God wants us to use His inspired and breathed Word to instruct, guide, correct, and to profit us. This is possible if we'll see and hear from Him by His Spirit. Is His Spirit living on the inside of you? Do you see and hear without using your natural senses or common sense? God isn't common. Why would His ways seem right to us? Don't be afraid. Let His Word thoroughly perfect or mature and equip you for every good work.

SEPTEMBER 16

"Since, therefore, [these His] children share in flesh and blood—that is, in the physical nature of human beings—He [Himself] in a similar manner partook of the same [nature], that by [going through] death He might bring to nought and make of no effect him who had the power of death, that is, the devil; And also that He might deliver and completely set free all those who through the (haunting) fear of death were held in bondage throughout the whole course of their lives."
Hebrews 2:14-15 (AMP)

It is evident, by the numerous verses throughout the New Testament, God knew people were going to be afraid of dying. It's for this reason He emphasizes what His Son did. Jesus' death and resurrection gives us power and freedom over fear and the challenges life brings…if we accept Him. Now, if you haven't made the decision yet, you might be thinking, "It's only believing, and then confessing with my mouth. How can that really change anything?" This may be all you do in the natural, but this isn't just a natural thing. You are allowing your spirit to be reconciled to His Spirit. You'll be able to communicate directly with Him. Tell me you don't think this will make a difference in your decisions or where your life could go from here?

These verses confirm that God sent Jesus in the flesh, as a human, and He walked and talked with mankind while He was on earth. He wasn't a ghost, flying from place to place. His needs were like ours. He ate and slept, and He wept for the lost. After His resurrection, He ascended to Heaven to join the Father. This is why He sent the Holy Spirit, so we can still communicate and be one with Them.

The Bible says we can know for sure where we are going after we die. We can settle it for all eternity. Choose Jesus and Heaven or don't choose, and go to hell. I don't mean to be offensive, but thinking you won't go to hell by "not" making a decision is a lie. The devil always makes us feel like we have plenty of time to decide. Then he works day and night to kill, steal, and destroy lives so the time runs out. Don't be afraid. You can be sure of life after death through Christ. Your spirit will be joined to the very Spirit who created you. Death will no longer be a weapon the devil can use to scare you or your family. Remember, God loves you, and it's because of this great love that He always tells us what to do beforehand. God's road map to Heaven is specific. It has very clear cut directions for a very clear cut reason…He wanted no one to be lost!

"Are not the angels all (servants) ministering spirits, sent out in service [of God for the assistance] of those who are to inherit salvation?"
Hebrews 1:14 (AMP)

This verse is important to the believer, the heir of Christ's work on the cross, because it helps us better understand that we need to put God's servants, the angels, to work. As the world has become more open to "spiritual" things, the knowledge of angels has also awakened. Unfortunately, according to the Bible, some of the information isn't always accurate. God's Word is very clear about everything. He never left holes or gaps because He knew the devil would jump at the chance to try to fill them in with his lies and deception.

In the first and second chapters of Hebrews, God spells out the role of the angels. He makes it clear they are not our path of escape. In other words, they have no "saving" abilities. God has not given His dominion or authority over the world to angels, but to His Son and all those who believe on Him. The verses prior to this one prove this point. God said "nothing"—not the angels or anything else would be above the Lord. Verse 13 asks which of the angels did God say would sit at His right hand or He would make their enemies a footstool for their feet? And it also asks when did God tell any of the angels He would make them His Son or He would be their Father? God's Word says Jesus is His Son. When we accept Him, we become *inheritors of salvation.* His authority is now ours...even over the angels. In the Psalms it says when God made Adam, all of Heaven watched, and the angels wondered who is this man or the son of man that God would be so mindful of him?

As God's children we need to recognize our authority and use it. We need to send the angels or ministering servants out to do His work on our behalf. How do we do this? When we use the Word they go into action. The Bible says they harken or take action to the voice of God, which is His Word. If you want to see things change, command the angels to minister to you according to the Word of God and to_______, then fill in the blank with the Word you need for your circumstances. Angels are our warriors, but we are warned to not worship them. Don't be afraid. Both angels and man worship God, but through the *inheritance of salvation*, we now have the same privilege Jesus has...to know God and to call Him our Father.

"And I will ask the Father, and He will give you another comforter (Counselor, Helper, Intercessor, Advocate, Strengthener and Standby) that He may remain with you forever. The Spirit of Truth, Whom the world cannot receive (welcome, take to its heart), because it does not see Him, nor know and recognize Him. But you know and recognize Him, for He lives with you [constantly] and will be with you."
John 14:16-17 (AMP)

John writes these comforting words, which Jesus spoke to the disciples, so we would be comforted, too. Just before Jesus went to Heaven to be with the Father, He told the disciples about the things that were going to happen. Naturally, they didn't want Him to go. They loved Him. They had spent every day with Him for over three years. But the real truth is they were also afraid. They had left everything to follow Him. If He went away, what would they do now?

The Lord knew their thoughts. This is why He told them to go and wait in the upper room until they received power from on High. This power was the Holy Ghost, the comforter Jesus had assured them *He would ask the Father to give* to them. The Holy Ghost not only came upon all those who were in the upper room, but He is still with us today. He's the same Holy Spirit who counsels and guides us into all truth. The Bible says He is our constant companion…our comforter. In the Greek, the word comforter is "*Paraclete*" and it means "the one called alongside to help," or our advocate. The Father sent Him to stand by us, to strengthen us during our battles, and to calm our fears in our daily walk.

God also assigned the Holy Spirit as the Spirit of Truth to communicate and impart to us what is true or valid. He teaches us truth because He is truth. He teaches us the truth about the Lord, the Bible, and He teaches us about ourselves. This is a vital part of our relationship with Him, especially if we have hidden areas of hurt in our heart or an area of sin we can't seem to get under control. It is the Holy Spirit who shows us the root of our problems, and then helps strengthen us to make the necessary changes. Do you fight with getting free of drugs, alcohol, anger or other lusts of the flesh? Or maybe you have a spending problem? Did you come from an abusive past, and now you're abusive? Don't be afraid. Your past doesn't have to control your future. You don't have to live powerless any longer. This verse confirms you can "know" the Holy Spirit… the truth…the power *who is constantly with you.* Welcome Him into your daily routine, and watch your life turn around.

"Such hope never disappoints or deludes or shames us, for God's love has been poured out in our hearts through the Holy Spirit, Who has been given to us."
Romans 5:5 (AMP)

The hope the Apostle Paul writes about here only comes from the peace we have with God through the Lord Jesus Christ. We know as human beings we are not perfect or righteous, but we also know that Jesus, God's Son, was. When we have faith in the Lord and what He accomplished for us on the cross, we are freed of the power of fear and sin, we are given a new life, and we are restored to a right or holy relationship with God. The Word says because we have believed—have faith—we're justified. I've heard it said the definition of justified is "just as if I'd." Just as if I'd what? Just as if I'd never committed the crimes or was guilty. The shed blood of Jesus washed all the guilt and shame of sin away. Now you can see why *His hope never deludes* or leaves room for fear or *disappointments.*

God loves you. It's His perfect love that removes all fear. The Holy Spirit is the very One who makes the love of the Father real to us. The Holy Spirit, being the Spirit of Truth, assures us of the promises of God. He gives us revelation when we read God's Word. The Bible says the promises in God's Word are "yes" and "amen." This means if God said it, He will do it, and we can believe it. His promises aren't for a few or for someone else, and they aren't for just one time or for some of the time. They are for all of us, every time we use them. The word amen means, "So be it." God is saying to us in every one of His promises... YES, I'LL DO IT...SO BE IT!

Have you given yourself permission to receive God's love? Or are you still feeling afraid, guilty, or ashamed of your past mistakes? Maybe you don't believe you deserve God's love? Maybe you're afraid to even "hope" for a better life? This is why Paul wrote to us about being justified through faith. This man admits to being the greatest of sinners. He had been responsible for killing some of God's chosen men. Don't you think guilt and shame tried to talk to him? What do you think Paul felt he deserved? But the truth is Paul let himself receive God's love and forgiveness...SO CAN YOU! Don't be afraid. Don't let fear, guilt, and shame lie to you or deceive you about God and His unfailing love. He gave you the Holy Spirit to reveal His truth. Receive God's hope, for *such hope never disappoints or deludes or shames us*, and let the Holy Spirit make God's love real to your heart, today!

"Do not fret or have any anxiety about anything, but in every circumstance and in everything by prayer and petition [definite requests] with thanksgiving continue to make your wants known to God."
Philippians 4:6 (AMP)

The Apostle Paul was a man who could have given in to feelings of being anxious. The Lord was calling him to preach the Gospel, and yet, every time he turned around he was back in jail. How was he supposed to carry out God's mission for his life from jail? We all have similar questions about our futures. How am I supposed to pay all these bills with my income? What will people think if they knew my past? How will I ever get this job done on time? The problems and questions are the same: How? When? Who? What? Where? Why? God never said this life would be easy. In fact, He said we would have tribulation in this world, but to be of good cheer because He had overcome the world. You may be thinking, "You just don't know how bad it is." You're right, I don't, but your Father does. The moment the "how bad" and the "what to do," blues set in, we've already eliminated God's provision as the answer. When we hear ourselves asking, "What am "I" going to do," we leave the door wide open for the devil to come in and fill us full of fear and doubt. Why? Because "I," by myself, never could do it!

You knew before you ever opened the statement that came in the mail the money wasn't there to pay it, right? Why ask yourself or think about the inevitable question? Instead, why don't you speak the Word? Say, "My God supplies all my needs according to His riches in glory by Christ Jesus." Remind the devil that you're a tither and a giver. Say, "God rebukes the devourer on my behalf." Why don't you remind yourself you are an overcomer? Say, "The greater One lives on the inside of me." Why don't you tell the devil he's defeated? Say, "What is impossible with man is possible with God." Speak the promises of God. This is how you change your finances, health or any other area. Ask the Holy Ghost for wisdom and truth about the specific action you need to take. He will guide you. How do I know? God's Word promises it.

Paul doesn't tell us to not be afraid or anxious about anything, and then sit in his jail cell biting his nails. Do you bite your nails? Or maybe you toss and turn night after night? Are you known as the family worry wart? Our trials should never be the gauge to our peace. Don't be afraid. If you need freedom from your troubles just speak the Word, and make your wants known through prayer with continual thanks and praises to God for His goodness. You'll see results!

"And God's peace [be yours, that tranquil state of a soul assured of its salvation through Christ, and so fearing nothing from God and content with its earthly lot of whatever sort that is, that peace] which transcends all understanding, shall garrison and mount guard over your hearts and minds in Christ Jesus."
Philippians 4:7 (AMP)

The Apostle Paul's life has become our example for many reasons. If he could have peace in the midst of his multiple beatings, shipwrecks, persecutions, imprisonments, and so much more, then we can have peace, too. How? We serve the same God he did. We have the same promise of salvation through Jesus Christ. We can also call on the Holy Spirit, our helper, for wisdom to show us how to handle every detail of life when it brings us torment and fear. This is "how" we can have peace.

Jesus told us He was giving us His peace, and this wasn't the peace the world knew. The world bases its peace on happiness or its surroundings, but the joy and peace the Lord talks about comes from within. It has nothing to do with our "outside" situations, good or bad. The "peace" Jesus spoke about comes from the Hebrew word Shalom. It means nothing missing, nothing broken or nothing lacking. It means being totally whole. You can see why Jesus would say this is not the peace the world knows. Unless you know Him, it is impossible to know true peace.

However, when you receive His peace, it will amaze you. You can look at your circumstances and laugh because your confidence is in the Lord and God's Word. Just as this verse says, *it is a peace that passes all understanding, and it guards your hearts and minds*. Why do we need our hearts or minds guarded? Because the first place the enemy attacks is our mind. The devil brings fear in the form of questions he knows we don't have answers to, and once we accept the challenge of trying to come up with an answer, he moves the fear from our heads straight to our hearts. That's when heaviness or despair sets in. Maybe you've been feeling that heaviness? Maybe you're at your breaking point? The problems just keep playing over and over in your head like a broken record? Don't be afraid. Throw that old recording away. Replace it with truth. Put God's Word on continuous play. Peace is part of God's covenant package. It belongs to you. Isn't it about time you decided to receive it? Choose His peace, and watch your joy return.

SEPTEMBER 22

> *"[Not in your own strength] for it is God Who is all the while effectually at work in you—energizing and creating in you the power and desire—both to will and to work for His good pleasure and satisfaction and delight."*
> *Philippians 2:13 (AMP)*

In my life there have been many times I've asked myself, "How or why did you ever agree to do this?" After the assignment was completed, and all was well, I knew I hadn't been the one to complete the mission. I never could have done it on my own. *It was God the entire time energizing and creating in me the desire to do His will and to work toward His good pleasure.*

Many missionaries in unreal situations have testified to the same. Sometimes they couldn't even tell you how the project was completed. They just knew God had supernaturally strengthened them because it was His will for the job to get done. Now you might be thinking, "Well that's great if you're in ministry or working for the Lord, but what about me? I'm a mother of five, or a dental hygienist, or a car salesman, or a city employee." The truth is God has called us all to be His vessels of light in different professions, but the fact still remains, regardless of who you are or what you do, aren't there times when you could use some help? Don't you need wisdom for raising your kids? What about making your sales quota every month? Or how about some more energy, just so you can get through those trying days?

God will provide what we need when we need it, if we ask Him. I was in commission-based, outside sales for many years. At one job I had a new territory. Everyday on the way to work I prayed for wisdom and asked the Holy Spirit to direct me to the customers who needed my products. I always met my monthly quotas. However, there were a couple of times when I would have been short and by thousands of dollars. So in my prayer time, the night before the last day of the month, I reminded the Lord He said in His Word, "Everything I put my hand to would prosper." I had been diligent to work and put my hand to it. I then asked for wisdom to know exactly who to call, what products I should offer them, and at what price. Both times, when I got to work the next morning, I knew exactly what to do. By noon I was at my quota. *Not in my own strength*, but God all the while was working in me to will and to do His good pleasure. He will do the same thing for you. Do you need help? Are you afraid to ask God or just too proud? Both are the work of the devil. Don't be afraid. Ask Him. Let God strengthen you and work His will and good pleasure in your life, too.

"This was so that by two unchangeable things [His promise and His oath], in which it is impossible for God ever to prove false or deceive us, we who have fled [to Him] for refuge might have mighty indwelling strength and strong encouragement to grasp and hold fast the hope appointed for us and set before [us]."
Hebrews 6:18 (AMP)

God wants to prove beyond a shadow of a doubt He does not lie. If He said it in His Word, it is true. Verse 17 states it was His desire to show the heirs of His promises the unchanging nature of His plans and purposes, and He wants to demonstrate this in such a manner that we would be convinced. How was He going to convince us? He explains in the above verse there are two ways: His promises and His oath. He more specifically states, in verses 13-16, that men may swear on someone higher than themselves to end disputes with a confirmation of an oath, but since there is no one higher than God, He would swear an oath to Himself.

So how do we inherit God's promises, plans, and purposes for our lives? The key is to believe first, and then receive. I've heard it said, "We must adopt the policy—if God said it, I believe it, and that settles it." But there is one more step. We must live it as if it were so. We can't speak the Word to our mountain, and then in a few hours, days, or whatever length of time fear and doubt starts to appear, change our confession from the Word to what we see. Faith doesn't work by sight. It is calling those things that aren't as though they were. If you find yourself wanting to confess your pain or your failures again, your faith has weakened. Don't be afraid. It happens to all of us. It's right then we need to strengthen our faith. How do we do this? The Bible says faith "comes" by hearing the Word. It's strengthened the same way.

What have you been doing in your prayer time or have you even had any? How much time have you spent in the Word? The enemy will keep us busy or distracted so we don't have time or we're just too tired when we do find the time to read the Word. But the Word is our spiritual food. Your body would be weak if you went for a few days without natural food. How do you think your spirit feels with a snack once or twice a week? Learn to make time for God. Know what He has promised you in His Word. This verse confirms *in Him* there is refuge, an inner strength, and encouragement. It's *in Him that we can hold fast to the hope that was appointed and set before us,* so we can know victory!

SEPTEMBER 24

"[Now] we have this [hope] as a sure and steadfast anchor of the soul—it cannot slip and it cannot break down under whoever steps out upon it—[a hope] that reaches farther and enters into [the very certainty of the Presence] within the veil, Where Jesus has entered in for us in advance..."
Hebrews 6:19-20a (AMP)

Verse 18 encourages us to hold on to the hope that has already been appointed or set before us. This appointed hope is God's own Word or promises to us. In other words, we can count on what He says because God, who swore an oath on Himself, can't lie. The above verses refer to *hope* as an anchor for our soul, which is our mind, will, and emotions. An anchor is an important part of a ship. Although it is very small in comparison to the size of the ship, it is able to maintain reliable support, stabilize, and firmly hold the ship from drifting off course, which could cause damage to itself and others. It offers a stable, steadfast hope to the Captain and all those aboard that it will do what it is designed to do.

Many times we may feel like our ship in life has gotten off course or even worse we're shipwrecked. We're just floating aimlessly. We may even try to use faith, but when the trauma is so great or has occurred for a long time, hopelessness appears. Now, you're not sure about any of it. Don't feel alone. The truth is, when our answers seem to be delayed, we can lose both our hope and faith for the outcome. Why? We're afraid God won't do what He said He would. The devil is right there to confirm your worst fears…it won't happen for you, and the Word "or faith" doesn't work. The enemy knows his best weapon is fear, but God's weapon is faith. Now do you see why the devil does all he can to steal and attack your hope? It steals your faith, too.

God gave us hope as an anchor for His promises. If an anchor can hold a huge ocean liner in place, our hope can hold our faith in place against the major attacks of life. Have you felt like you tried standing on God's Word? Maybe you're afraid to hope and believe again? Did you work faith or did fear do a work on you? The enemy will launch a vicious attack when we start to hope and use faith. Why? When hope and faith show up, he knows it's all over for him. In these verses God assures us *hope is sure and steadfast,* and when we step out on it, this anchor cannot slip or break down under the weight. Don't be afraid. The Word says, "*Now...we have this hope...*" This means "*Now*" you can have yours, too. Get rid of fear. Use your hope…your faith…and still receive your miracle.

> *"For out of His fullness (abundance) we all received—all had a share and we were all supplied with—one grace after another and spiritual blessing upon spiritual blessing, and even favor upon favor and gift [heaped] upon gift."*
> *John 1:16 (AMP)*

Webster's Dictionary defines the word full as, "complete: meaning all that is wanted, needed or possible; containing as much or as many as possible, not lacking in any essential; it implies the presence or inclusion of everything that is wanted or required by something or that can be held, contained or attained by it." When God says out of "*His fullness*," He is really saying He has everything we need or want. He is not lacking in any essential, and in His Presence there is joy, grace, favor, gifts, and every spiritual blessing.

This verse reveals we all have an opportunity to share in *His fullness*, if we'll receive it. God doesn't have a "Fortune 100" club in Heaven. In fact, when God established the original covenant with Abraham, He made it clear that anyone who believed and trusted in Him, followed and obeyed His laws, would be wealthy. It was promised too many times in the covenant contract God gave to us in Deuteronomy 28. God's intentions from the beginning were to bless His own. Think about the garden He gave to Adam. It was filled with every kind of fruit-bearing tree, plants, fish, and birds, all the animals, and then He made Eve so Adam wouldn't be alone. Adam was also given dominion over every part of it. All he had to do was manage it. What did Adam know about managing? What had he done to deserve all of this? Nothing…and that's exactly what we've done. It is what Christ did for us that allows us access to God's benefits.

Most times when people have a hard time accepting the wealth or over abundance of God, it is from fear that stems from a guilty conscience. Their own shortcomings compared to God's perfect righteousness has them looking for punishment instead of forgiving love. Wrongdoing or sin distorts a person's view. This is why God sent His best, His Son, to remove our sin and shame. He wanted us to receive all *His fullness*. The truth is when you accept the Lord, if your heart is truly transformed and your mind is renewed to the Word, fear will no longer be able to lie about you not deserving to receive God's fullness. Don't be afraid. He's the beginning and the end, and His plan is still the same… abundant blessings…heaped upon His own!

SEPTEMBER 26

"But when the time had fully come, God sent His Son, born of a woman, born under law, to redeem those under law, that we might receive the full rights of sons."
Galatians 4:4-5 (NIV)

God wanted all of us to be reconciled back to Him. We do not qualify for any of the blessings without belonging to the Father. For example: If you were born in a country like England or one that is ruled by a Monarchy, a King or Royal Family, you wouldn't automatically qualify to inherit the Royal family's possessions. The only way, other than marriage, to receive what belongs to them as rightfully yours is through adoption. The same principle applies for us to receive our inheritance from "THE KING." God's Royal Family adoption plan is through His Son, Jesus, and it offers us the ability to *receive full rights as His sons.*

When Jesus was born on earth of a woman, the Bible says He was born under the law. This was the "law of sin and death." It came into place on the earth after Adam sinned. When Jesus fulfilled the work of the cross, He paid for the sins of mankind from Adam...until the end. Just because you weren't born then doesn't mean it's now too late. He didn't just die for the sins that had been committed before that time. The Bible says He looked ahead in time and died for all of mankind's sin that was to come, too. His perfect blood was the ingredient God needed to redeem us back to our original state of perfection, which is a sinless life. His perfect blood bought and paid for us to have the same freedoms Adam had been given and to restore us to the legal position of being sons and daughters of the Most High God.

The Bible says we are joint heirs with Christ. We are adopted into the family of God. I know this is hard to believe. God knew this would put the natural mind on tilt because of our works or earning mentality. Fear and religious spirits would ask, "How could you possibly think you deserve the same as or would be equal to Jesus?" The truth is we don't deserve it, and we aren't equal in the natural. It's only through His Spirit. This is why we don't qualify on our own. We can only come to the Father through believing in His Son and all that He did for us on the cross. Don't be afraid. God repeatedly speaks about His plan of adoption, not only in this verse, but many others. Will you receive His plan? Will you accept Jesus and gain the greatest Father anyone could ever have? He loves you, and He wants to call you His own. Go ahead. Your rights and inheritance as His child await you.

> *"Because you are sons, God sent the Spirit of His Son into our hearts, the Spirit who calls out, 'Abba, Father.' So you are no longer a slave, but a son; and since you are a son, God has made you also an heir."*
> *Galatians 4:6-7 (NIV)*

Once again God clarifies our rightful position in His family. He sent the Holy Spirit to confirm and to seal it in our hearts by living within us. It's the Spirit who gives us the ability to call out to our Father, but the term is actually more endearing than Father for "*Abba*" means Daddy. Abba is a close, intimate, affectionate term for daddy. You see, it is God's desire for us to be so close to Him that it would only be natural for us to call Him Dad.

Now, if you've had a dysfunctional relationship with your natural parents this is probably one of the most bazaar statements you've ever heard. Or maybe you didn't think it was possible for you to be intimate or personal with God? How is it possible to have intimacy or closeness with someone you can't see or touch? I would try to correlate it to when a loved one goes to a distant land for business or war. They may be gone for months or even years. You don't see them, nor are you able to have physical contact with them, either. Does your love for them change? Does your position or relationship with them change? Hopefully the answer to both questions is no.

Our love and our relationship with God shouldn't change, either. The way God prevents this is by sending His Spirit to dwell on the inside of us. He lives in our hearts. The Holy Spirit keeps us stirred up when we read the Word or when we pray. He gives us confidence that our Daddy is right there, which allows us to feel His Presence. He also directs and guides us into all truth, and the biggest truth is no one could love you more than your Heavenly Dad. This love casts out any and all fear. If you didn't have an opportunity to have a relationship with your natural father, this may seem awkward, but I encourage you to accept God's offer. His love is powerful. It fills voids and gaps, past hurts, emotions, and wounds that have been there for years. Only the gentle touch of pure unconditional love can minister that kind of healing. Were you hurt in the past? Did your earthly father disappoint you? Maybe he was never there for you? Don't be afraid. The Bible says God won't ever leave you. His Word also says, "He loved You first, before you loved Him." He chose You, remember? He called You to be His son, an heir. Isn't it time you joined the family, and accepted the greatest, most loving Dad, ever?

"For in Him the whole fullness of Deity (the Godhead), continues to dwell in bodily form—giving complete expression of the divine nature. And you are in Him, made full and have come to fullness of life—in Christ you too are filled with the Godhead: Father, Son, and Holy Spirit, and reach full spiritual stature. And He is the Head of all rule and authority—of every angelic principality and power."
Colossians 2:9-10 (AMP)

The Apostle Paul wrote these truths as a warning to the church in Colosse. He didn't want them to be taken captive by deceptive philosophy, which depended on man's traditions or the basic principles being taught by the world. False teachers had come to the Colossians with angel worship and orders to follow special rules, traditions or ceremonies. In these verses Paul brings direct correction to make sure they all understood that *Jesus is the fullness of God.* He is the "Supreme" Authority. His power is over every power, both demonic and angelic, and because *He lives on the inside* of them the *fullness of Deity* rules through them, as well.

Today, it is vital for us to recognize the same thing. We are to walk in the same authority and speak with the voice of God. This is the power we need to move the "mountains" in our lives. Why or how are we able to do this? It's because of Jesus, who is the *fullness of Deity,* and who lives on the inside of us. The Bible says the fullness of the Godhead dwells in Jesus richly, and if the Godhead or Deity is in Him and He lives in us, then this means the Godhead has to be in us, also. The Father and the Holy Spirit dwell in us, too. Does this make us a god because they live in us? No, absolutely not! We are not gods. Satan wanted to be God…remember what happened to him?

It is because of the Spirit and the gift of God that they live in us. But the most significant factor is the authority it gives us as a believer. Do you understand when you speak you have the same authority as Christ or the Godhead? Now, when the Bible says you have the power of life and death in your tongue, do you understand where this power comes from? Don't let the devil cheat you out of this truth by stealing your authority. Don't be afraid. The key to changing any situation is speaking God's Word. When you know you are speaking with Their Authority, you can expect things to change, and you'll leave no place for fear. There is no problem or trial too big for you to demand to change. You just need to remember…You are in Him…AND…HE IS IN YOU!

"And you, being dead in your sins and the uncircumcision of your flesh, hath he quickened together with him, having forgiven you all trespasses; Blotting out the handwriting of ordinances that was against us, which was contrary to us, and took it out of the way, nailing it to his cross; And having spoiled principalities and powers, he made a show of them openly, triumphing over them in it."
Colossians 2:13-15 (KJV)

Verse 13 makes the connection between spiritual and natural death. *Dead in your sins* refers to being spiritually dead because of Adam's sin which separated us from God and put us under the curse of the law of sin and death. Under the old covenant, men were circumcised as a physical reminder of their covenant with God. Paul now explains that circumcision in the flesh is no longer required. Once you accept Christ, a spiritual circumcision takes place in your heart.

The rest of these verses continue to confirm what Christ did for us on the cross and the benefits we now have *in Him* as believers or partakers in the covenant. We're no longer guilty of our past sins or trespasses. There is no more fear about our wrongdoing or God's wrath in taking care of it. The Word says that *all trespasses and ordinances were nailed to the cross*, wiped away, blotted out, as if they never happened. Now they didn't literally take legal documents or paper ordinances and nail them to a piece of wood to get rid of them. Instead, God's only Son was nailed to the cross, and although He was sinless, God put the sins of the entire world—past, present, and future—upon Him. While on the cross, the Bible also says, "Surely He bore our griefs and sorrows, he was wounded for our transgressions, and bruised for our iniquities, the chastisement of our peace was upon Him, and by His stripes we are healed." Jesus completed God's plan. This is why Jesus' last Words from the cross were, "IT IS FINISHED!!!"

However, God's final blow to defeat the devil—forever—came while Jesus was dead in Hell. The devil thought he had won the ultimate battle. God had different ideas. On the third day God said, "NOW," and the Holy Spirit raised Jesus up from the dead...HE WAS ALIVE! It was then Jesus spoiled or ruined the powers of the devil. *Jesus made a show of them openly* or a display in hell over satan's defeat, *triumphing over them*. Christ paid for sin, sickness, poverty, the curse, and then defeated death, giving us a life, both now and forever with the Father. Don't be afraid. All of this was done for you. Accept the Lord, and have all your trespasses blotted out. Now *in Him*, you'll have all power over the enemy, too!

"It was God (personally present) in Christ, reconciling and restoring the world to favor with Himself, not counting up and holding against [men] their trespasses [but canceling them]; and committing to us the message of reconciliation—of the restoration to favor."
2 Corinthians 5:19 (AMP)

Webster's Dictionary states reconciliation means, "to restore to harmony or friendship." God personally made Himself available to us through Christ, so our sins could be forgiven, and we could be restored back to a place of friendship with Him. God came to the garden each day to be with Adam. They were friends. But after Adam sinned, those times together stopped. This isn't what God wanted, but God is Holy and sin isn't. Sin separates us from God. On earth if a child does something wrong, a parent can appropriately punish them, and when it's all over, they can hug them and continue on with their relationship. It didn't work that way for God. If He had touched or hugged Adam after he sinned, Adam would have been destroyed. Holiness and sin don't mix. This is why it was imperative that God send His Son to earth. It was the only way the *world could be restored to favor*, closeness, and the friendship status we were originally designed to have with our Father.

Did you know you could have a personal relationship or be friends with God? I'm sorry to say that some don't teach this fact. It's true, they may teach Christ was born, died, resurrected, and sits at God's right hand, and they may even teach our sins are forgiven, but this is where the benefits end. Their teachings would still have us believe that we are no good and unworthy to receive anything from God, let alone His best. Our position is to beg at His feet for any crumb He may hand out because we sure wouldn't want to ask Him for anything from our lowly state. This teaching is fear based, man-made doctrine, and God weeps over it. It is nowhere in the Bible. The hard truth is when we do not accept **all** that Christ did for us on the cross…we're still rejecting the cross. This means Jesus died in vain. Do you think this is the teaching or kind of faith that pleases the Father?

Your sin, sickness, peace, prosperity, past curses, and punishment were paid for …cancelled! If you paid your traffic ticket, would you continue to ask the judge what more you could do to make it right? Of course not, and we don't have to beg God, either. Don't be afraid. God doesn't want you afraid of Him or anything else. This verse confirms, *in Him*, we have God's favor. Do you want it? He loves you. His plan and message has always been one of reconciliation or to be your friend. Accept His friendship…you'll soon find there's nothing like it.

> *"For our sake He made Christ [virtually] to be sin Who knew no sin, so that in and through Him we might become [endued with, viewed as in and examples of] the righteousness of God—what we ought to be, approved and acceptable and in right relationship with Him, by His goodness."*
> *2 Corinthians 5:21 (AMP)*

The Apostle Paul confirms to the believer that through their relationship with the Lord, they are restored. They are *the righteousness of God*. God never wanted a separation between man and Himself, but this is what sin brought. Under the old covenant the Ark of the Covenant housed the Glory of God and was located in the Holy place in the temple. No one was allowed in the Holy place except the Priest, and then it was only to perform the sacrifice. This sacrifice involved two perfectly flawless animals. One of the animals would be killed. The Priest would then put its blood on the top of the Ark between the two angels. This place was called the mercy seat. If God accepted this first sacrifice, then the second animal was taken out to the wilderness and released as a sign to the people that their sins for another year had been forgiven. They escaped the punishment they deserved …the animal was their "scapegoat." However, the animal sacrifices never did away with sin. They only covered them for another year.

God's Son, Jesus, by the Holy Spirit was born of a virgin. This was absolutely necessary because it broke the sin bloodline which came through an earthly man's disobedience. Jesus lived a sinless life. He had no imperfections, so He was the acceptable sacrifice the world needed. This verse verifies Jesus, *Who knew no sin,* would become sin, which means the sins of the entire world came upon Jesus. He became our scapegoat, but He didn't just cover sin, and it wasn't for only one year. He removed all of our sin, once and for all. When we accept what He did for us *by His goodness*, we escape our penalty and become *what we ought to be, approved and acceptable and in right relationship with Him!*

If God loved us enough to replace our sin with *His goodness*, why would we be afraid of Him? Or afraid of anyone else? Or why would we believe or be afraid of the lies of the devil? The Bible asks if God is for you, then who can be against you? Do you see what a lie fear is? Why would God continue to repeat, over and over again, that through Christ we're forgiven or that we're restored to a *right relationship* with Him or that we have *His goodness* and *His favor*? Why? He wants us to not only know about His love, but to actually feel His love to us. He wants us to receive His perfect love, which not only will fill us, but remove all fear and bring us continual victory.

OCTOBER 2

"Looking away [from all that will distract] to Jesus, Who is the Leader and Source of our faith [giving the first incentive for our belief] and is also its Finisher, [bringing it to maturity and perfection]. He, for the joy [of obtaining the prize] that was set before Him, endured the cross, despising and ignoring the shame, and is now seated at the right hand of the throne of God."
Hebrews 12:2 (AMP)

If the Apostle Paul had stayed focused on either his past or how his current situation looked, instead of staying focused on the Lord, he never would have completed what God called him to do. Why? Both were extremely distracting, and both could have been huge instigators of fear. He, as well as many others, rejected Jesus as the Son of God and their Messiah. In fact, Paul had been one of the worst, becoming a zealous killer of the followers of Christ. How could God use him? Why would God even want to use him? And now that God was trying to use him, how could Paul preach the Gospel from jail? Trying to answer the "how and why" questions is one way the devil distracts us. What is the enemy using to distract you? If you had to pick whether you live in the past, present or future, where would it be? Does the enemy still bring up unpleasant events from your childhood? Do your actions still reflect behavioral patterns you've had since you were young? Why does the devil only remind you of the past, bad, hurtful things? Because his plan is to kill, steal, and destroy your future.

The truth is if we can't get beyond our past hurts and rejections, we can't live in the present, and if we don't live in the present, we will never have a future. The devil, years later, is still trying to steal and destroy your life. So, how do you get out of the past? How do you erase the "emotional" cancer that eats at you every second of the day? How can you move from a place of 'being stuck?' There is only one way. *Looking away from all that distracts and looking to Jesus.* This verse confirms He is our Source—both the Author and Finisher—of our faith. Maybe you think, "That sounds too easy. You don't know all I'm dealing with." It's true, I don't, but He does. He knows exactly what will heal your scars and bring wholeness to every area. Even if what you experienced was truly horrible, why let the devil still use it today to keep you miserable and defeated? Don't be afraid. Make the decision…**Let go** of the past. Jesus took all your pain and shame to the cross, so you could have a bright and hopeful future. He's already made a way for you to live in the present. Even *now He's seated at the right hand of God*, working for you. Look to Jesus. He alone will perfect your faith for victory.

OCTOBER 3

> *"For the law of the Spirit of life in*
> *Christ Jesus hath made me free*
> *from the law of sin and death."*
> *Romans 8:2 (KJV)*

When Christ bore our sins on the cross, He delivered us from the law of sin and death, which came upon the earth because of Adam's disobedience. This freedom from the old law has many benefits, but the most significant is we no longer need to be afraid of our past sins or our death in the future. Because of the cross, Christ restored us back to the law of the Spirit of life. This is the Spirit of God, the Spirit of truth. It is His Spirit which brings to us the power and presence of Almighty God.

When we reject God, we live under the influence of the law of sin and death. We can try to do the right things, but we won't have much success. Why? It's because the nature or will of mankind under this law is to sin. However, the Bible says when we accept Christ, by the Spirit we are made new creatures…the old man has passed away. Our outward man doesn't physically change, but now, because the Spirit of life lives on the inside of us, we have the ability to not sin. The Spirit gives us the strength and the desire to want only the things of God. He is the One who helps us renew our minds to the Word by instructing us in the truth from the Word, and He helps us to stay on a righteous path. We're delivered from fear of failing God and ourselves. The sin nature no longer has dominion over us. We don't have to sin, and that brings great freedom.

We also don't have to be afraid that we are powerless against the enemy, which at times may include our own wills and secret desires. Does this mean we will be perfect or never sin again? Probably not…the devil will still try to tempt us and remind us of all our past wrongs. However, if we renew our minds to God's Word and ways, we now, through His Spirit in us, have the power to move beyond our old thoughts, lusts, and weaknesses. Remember, the devil will still try to condemn you, deceive you, attack you with guilt and shame, and distract you from the things of God. However, verse 1 of this chapter states, "There is **no** condemnation for those who are in Christ Jesus." Why? Because once we let Jesus redeem us back to the Father, even if we mess up and sin again, we know the Word says we can repent, ask God for forgiveness, and He is faithful and just to forgive us. All this is possible because of what Jesus did in setting up the law of the Spirit of life. Is the devil still trying to condemn you? If you're *in Him*, you're forgiven. Don't be afraid. *The law of the Spirit of life through Christ Jesus has already made you free.* Just accept it, and look toward your bright future.

OCTOBER 4

> *"But the fruit of the Spirit is love, joy, peace, longsuffering, gentleness, goodness, faith, meekness, temperance: against such there is no law."*
> *Galatians 5:22-23 (KJV)*

The *Spirit* this verse refers to is the Holy Spirit, and He dwells in us when we accept Christ and God's plan of salvation. Jesus sent the Holy Spirit so we wouldn't be alone. He also gave Him to us as our counselor, comforter, and guide. He's called the Spirit of Truth, and He leads us and guides us into all truth. Because He lives on the inside of us, the Word says our spirits will also be able to bear witness to the truth when we hear it. This is what allows us to not be deceived when the enemy tries to lie to us.

However, as you can see from the above verses, all these other very needed character attributes are a part of the Holy Spirit, too. When He lives on the inside of us, the fruit is available to us, also. Why is this important? Well, if you were in a legal battle, wouldn't you want to have an attorney right beside you to turn to for help? Or wouldn't it be nice to know you'd have the answers to any question that might arise in the courtroom? You can. The Holy Spirit is right there with truth and guidance. What if you have a hard time controlling your temper? Wouldn't you want the Holy Spirit with temperance, which is self control or discipline, right there for you to call on, too? If the enemy were attacking your mind with tormenting thoughts, wouldn't it be reassuring to know that you don't have to succumb to them because you already have the fruit of peace living on the inside of you through the Holy Spirit? Do you see what I mean?

If you're dealing with anger, addictions, long time abuse from a spouse or relative or maybe your spouse or a loved one is seriously ill and it requires your constant attention...whatever the problem, complete success is not possible without the help of the fruit of the Spirit living in you. The fruit is available and will produce when used. You may not have known or even felt like this was available to you, but it's true. However, there is only one way this is possible to us. We must accept the Lord and the Holy Spirit into our life. The fruit of the Spirit keeps us walking on the path God has chosen. He gives us the ability to break familiar self-destructive patterns and to make better, healthier decisions for victorious living. Don't be afraid. Jesus knew we needed the Holy Spirit to help us live free of bondages. This Word assures us when *we live utilizing the fruit of the Spirit, there is no law*—weapon or force—*that can come against us* and be successful. We can now live our lives knowing that all the help we need to overcome is right here, within us...He's the precious and powerful Holy Spirit.

OCTOBER 5

> *"But I say, walk and live habitually in the (Holy) Spirit—responsive to and controlled and guided by the Spirit, then you will certainly not gratify the cravings and desires of the flesh—of human nature without God."*
> *Galatians 5:16 (AMP)*

The only way we are guaranteed victory from the sinful nature of man is through Christ and the Holy Spirit, which He sent to live in us to help us. It's only through the Spirit in us that we are able to live by God's rules, rather than by the sinful desires of our flesh. I've met people who were afraid to give their lives to the Lord because they had repeated, unresolved sin in their life. I have also counseled those who were saved and filled with the Holy Ghost, but had the same problem. Why is this? The answer is the same for both...without the help of God and the Holy Spirit, neither will be able to change the desires of the flesh. The truth is when any of us reach that crucial moment of decision, if we're not drawing on the Holy Spirit for the power and strength we need, there is no way we'll overcome. We may hate how we feel afterwards because the enemy will instantly bring guilt and condemnation, but the problem still exists because at the moment of attack, when those improper thoughts start to come, we don't immediately call on the Holy Spirit, who is already present, to assist and deliver us.

The truth is when we get desperate enough, we make changes. I've heard it said, "Anything we can tolerate...we won't change." If our past sin issues stem from old habits, then we have to replace them with new ones. This is where the Holy Spirit will guide you into all truth. He lives in you. Do you think He doesn't know you? Do you think He doesn't know how you feel? Do you believe He can offer you a substitute for that fleshly craving? A holy replacement? He is the "Holy" Spirit. With Him, you'll know exactly what you need to correct.

The first time the Lord asked me to move, I not only didn't want to move, but I didn't want to move to the city He had selected. I discussed it with Him, but I knew this was His plan. So I asked the Holy Spirit to change my heart. I gave Him permission to change my desires, so I would be willing to follow Him. It was only a few days later that I realized I was so excited about moving I could hardly wait for the appointed time. The Holy Spirit helps us do what we can't do on our own. He gives us the power to live by His Spirit and deny our flesh. Maybe you still have "fleshly" battles? Are you struggling with the same issues, lusts or desires from years past? Don't be afraid. Nothing is too difficult for the Spirit of God. Give Him permission to change your heart. Renew your mind and thoughts to God's promises. You'll discover, with Him, you can truly be free!

OCTOBER 6

> *"I do not ask that You will take them out of the world, but that You will keep and protect them from the evil [one]."*
> *John 17:15 (AMP)*

The Apostle John writes the Words of Jesus in this verse. Jesus states plainly there is one in the world whose ambition and intent is to do evil. Webster's Dictionary defines evil as, "the fact of suffering, misfortune, and wrongdoing; something that brings sorrow, distress or calamity." Most of us understand evil because we've experienced it, but Jesus tells us we don't have to be afraid of the "*evil one,*" who is the devil, because He has asked the Father to protect us.

Maybe you've already gone through an attack of the evil one in your life? When you were young? Or your trauma was from someone you loved and trusted? Does your life keep spiraling downward, and it doesn't hold any real meaning? Maybe you've even considered ending it? Jesus told us trials and tribulation would come in this world, but we could be of good cheer because He had overcome the world. The devil's ammo is to create such devastation through injustice that we become victims…victims of our circumstances and victims of our environment. Why is this dangerous? Because it takes us from an offensive position or a conqueror to the defensive, and eventually it produces the ultimate fear—you'll never be able to change or get out of your past.

The truth is you can't change the past…this is why the devil tries to keep you there. However, YOU CAN CHANGE YOUR FUTURE! Today, with God's Word, you can live in the present and be "more than a conqueror through Christ." You are not a victim! YOU are the VICTOR! Jesus confirms in this verse *God does not take us out of the world.* God doesn't take life. He gives it. The Father protects and keeps us from the evil one. Why? Because He knows the devil is a taker…the evil one who came to kill, steal, and destroy. If you've gone through sorrow, wrongdoing, distress, calamity, pain and suffering then you know the torment the devil brings. Don't be afraid. God loves you. He protects and provides for His own, and you can be free of grief and sorrow because Jesus paid for you to have these freedoms when He died on the cross. He promised we would have beauty for our ashes, and joy for our tears. He is not only the giver of life, but a "new" life that is filled with covenant promises for great abundance. He has a great and victorious plan for your life, and it can begin, even today.

OCTOBER 7

"So that they all may be one [just] as you, Father, are in Me and I in You, that they also may be one in Us, so that the world may believe and be convinced that you have sent Me."
John 17:21 (AMP)

If there was ever a fear that God did not love us or Jesus did not love us or that Their plans did not include us being with Them, this verse should settle the matter. When Jesus died for us, He did it so we could have what He had with the Father. We would not only be heirs of God, but joint heirs with Jesus. The Bible states we are now the adopted sons of God. However, this isn't like in an earthly family where the natural birth children may become jealous of the new sibling. Jesus isn't afraid to share His inheritance with us. In fact, He agreed to die so that we could be one with Them, and we can also celebrate all God had planned for those who believed God sent Jesus.

Being one…that's true intimacy. The Bible says when you get married the two become one flesh. This first act is part of the covenant that takes place the wedding night as they consummate their marriage, but the covenant does not end there. There are days, weeks, and many years to come that the two live as one... loving, sharing, trusting, sacrificing, protecting, respecting, forgiving, encouraging, the list goes on. Getting to know someone intimately in order to be 'one' involves spending time with them. It also includes valuing one another. Although marriage is an important covenant to God, it was the second covenant God introduced. The first covenant was the one He made with mankind. His plan for us from the very beginning was to be intimate, connected, and one with Him.

Jesus said He never did or said anything unless the Father told Him. The key to His success was He learned to abide in God. He stayed hooked-up by the Spirit, so He could do and see things God's way. We should take heed to the same lesson. To be one with Them is to stay hooked-up to the Holy Spirit, too. How do you do this? You surrender your ways, your plans, your thoughts and desires, and you take on those of the Father. He knows you better than you know yourself. We've all proven this at different times when we've really worked or strived to gain something we really desired, only to find that after we achieved it, the final sensation wasn't all that! The real question is who or what need was the object falsely trying to replace or fulfill in us? God knows what's best for us. When we stay hooked-up to the Spirit, we're glad to follow His plans, instead of our own. Don't be afraid. God loves you. His desires or plans won't have you chasing after unfulfilling things. When you allow yourself to become one with Them, you'll not just hope God's Word is true, but by the Spirit, you'll be convinced of it!

OCTOBER 8

> *"I have given to them the glory and honor which You have given Me, that they may be one, [even] as We are one:"*
> *John 17:22 (AMP)*

The Apostle John writes what Jesus said about giving us His glory and honor; the very glory and honor the Father had given Him. Why would we, as earthly men and women need glory? Or honor? The truth is when God created man, the Bible says he was clothed or covered in glory. Neither Adam, nor Eve, realized they were naked until they had sinned. This separation from God caused the glory to leave. However, because Jesus fulfilled the Father's plan, this glory and honor belongs to us again. We can forever be one, reconciled, and restored to our original place with Them.

When we have a true revelation of all that has been given to us because of Christ's willingness to die on the cross, we have no need to fear the things of this life. I don't mean we are to ignore our present position or minimize the trials that come our way. The devil's days are numbered, and because of this he is at it full throttle, but he cannot and will not defeat you. When you accept what Jesus did for you and make Him your Lord, you have the same glory and honor He has, you are now a son of God, His child. The Bible states God is a just God. With this being so, how could He not offer all His children the same reward or inheritance?

Webster's Dictionary defines glory as, "praise, honor, or distinction; a distinguished quality or asset; a great beauty and splendor; the splendor and beatific happiness of heaven; a height of prosperity or achievement." And the word honor means, "homage, reverence, deference, respect and esteem shown to another; profound respect mingled with love, devotion, awe; yielding or submitting to another's judgment or preference out of respect." All of this is what Jesus offers us. Why? Because God not only wanted His children to honor one another, but the glory and honor on us would be a witness to the world. This is vital to our fulfilling the plans of God. He is a God of love, and because He has given us His Spirit to live in us, He expects us to walk in love and forgiveness to others, as well. Understanding and operating in this love and oneness is important if we are to be one with Them. Don't be afraid. His glory and honor are great assets, a height of prosperity and achievement, love mingled with respect. Receive it… give it…and be one with Them.

"I in them and You in Me, in order that they may become one and perfectly united, that the world may know and [definitely] recognize you sent Me, and that you have loved them [even] as You have loved Me."
John 17:23 (AMP)

Many times it is hard to truly comprehend the love of God. We may know it in our heads because the Word tells us, but we may not feel it in our hearts. If you "grew up" as a child in the Christian church, then one of the first things you were taught was "Jesus loves me, this I know, for the Bible, tells me so." Many of us, at different times in our lives, have had people tell us they loved us, but their actions told a different story. Maybe you can relate? Now, out of fear, we find it hard to believe God could love us, either.

God knew the trouble we would have in accepting His unconditional love for us because of the natural love that exists here on earth. But He makes His love clear to us through His Word by continually repeating it. God not only tells us in His Word, but He gave the most complete and total demonstration of His love when He sent His Son to die for us, <u>while we were yet sinners</u>. When you read the Word and talk with God daily, the Holy Spirit confirms His love. You can <u>feel</u> His love, if you'll let yourself. Only we can determine how close we'll let someone come into our lives here in the natural, and we do the same thing with God. Are you guarded or have you built walls because of past relationships? I encourage you to lay down anything that might stand between you and the Lord. His love is deep. It's pure and genuine, and it flushes out hurts and heartaches. His love will fill your heart with joy, peace, and His perfect love drives out fear.

God's plan and command to us is to love one another and to be *perfectly united.* Why? So through us the world will also see and know Their love. This won't happen if we don't have God's love in us. Without His love, human nature wants to criticize and judge. It's competitive, cold, calloused, selfish, and it's not willing to help those in need. It's unable or unwilling to show compassion or unconditional love to others. The Bible says if we do not love our fellow man, then the love of God is not in us. Is the love of God in you? Or are you guilty of some of the unlovely characteristics mentioned above? Don't be afraid. We know God loved His Son, and God really does love you, too. This verse confirms Jesus' desire that we receive His love, believe He was sent of God, and walk in unity as one family. They are love. They are one. Let's unite in love, so we are one, also. Allow yourself to receive Their love. Then it will flow out of you for the whole world to see. Their love will change your world!

"Father, I desire that they also whom You have entrusted to Me [Your gift to Me,] may be with Me where I am, so that they may see My glory, which You have given Me—Your love gift to Me—for You loved Me before the foundation of the world."
John 17:24 (AMP)

When Jesus made this statement to His disciples, He removed their fear of the future by assuring them that one day they would all be together again. It was God's promise and gift to His Son that we would go where Jesus was going. In this verse we hear the Lord's love and desire to be with us and the love of the Father expressed when Jesus refers to us as the "*Father's love gift to Him.*" But this verse does more than remove fear about where we are going and who we will be with in the future. It states for the record that God already had this plan in place before He formed *the foundation of the world.* When Adam sinned and died spiritually, it brought separation between God and man. It also brought physical death to the earth. God's original creation wasn't designed to die, but the Bible says the wages of sin is death. Now that sin existed on earth, the life span of mankind began to decrease as rapidly as sin increased.

God was not caught off guard by sin, and this verse proves it. Jesus said He knew *His Father loved Him before the foundation of the world.* How could this be? He wasn't even God's Son, yet. He hadn't come to earth, died, was resurrected or anything at this point. However, God knew what was going to happen, and He already had this plan in place. The Bible says God also knew each one of us before the foundation of the world. He knows the end from the beginning. The reason this is so important is because it removes every worry and fear that we are "unimportant," an after thought or an accident. God knew and wanted each one of us. He also knew the circumstances surrounding our births. Now if He knew all this, do you think He doesn't know where you are or what you're dealing with today? He also knows He wants you to be with Him and His Son for eternity. God made all the decisions for you…beforehand. That is, all but this one. Only you can say "yes" to Jesus and His ultimate plan.

Don't let the enemy lie to you that no one loves you or you're all alone. God loves you, and He doesn't want you to be afraid. God's a planner. He always has been, and this verse proves it. Don't be afraid. Before He created the world, He already had you and your well being on His mind. He had the perfect plan for you then, and He still has a perfect plan for you now. Say "Yes" to Him and His plan. Jump on in. You'll be pleased to discover it's quite the plan!

OCTOBER 11

> *"I made Your name known to them and revealed Your character and Your very Self, and I will continue to make [You] known, that the love which You have bestowed upon Me may be in them—felt in their hearts—and that I [Myself] may be in them."*
> *John 17:26 (AMP)*

Jesus was very close to the time of His betrayal when He said this to His disciples. This verse, plus countless others, confirms His love for them, the Father's love for them, and His desire that they would be together again. Jesus knew after the soldiers came to take Him away how frightening it would be. Peter tried to follow, until some of the people recognized and confronted him about being with Jesus. Yes, Peter denied He knew the Lord, but the sad truth is the rest of the disciples didn't even have the courage to see what was going on. They were shut up in a room—afraid—trying to figure out what they were going to do now. And yet, in this verse, Jesus was trying to prepare them to not be afraid because He had already revealed to them the available love of the Father, and they would never be alone.

Today, this verse does the same for us. When we accept the plan of God and realize through the Spirit of God that Jesus and the Father live and dwell within each of us, it gives us a confidence and a boldness to attack fears and problems. There is shalom peace—total wholeness—and power available to handle each and every trial the devil brings our way. We don't have to sit back and take it. The love Jesus felt from the Father is being passed on to us through Him, and now His perfect love is *felt in our hearts*. It is this love that stimulates and encourages us to follow and obey the Lord's commands.

When fear scattered the disciples they were powerless. Fear does the same thing to us. The devil knows there is strength in numbers and unity. This is why he brings division, not only in the world, but he also starts fights over doctrine and religious ceremony between believers. He knows this weakens and keeps us divided. The Bible asks, "How can two walk together unless they agree?" Has he tried to bring confusion and division to your life? Let God's love be in you, so it will pour out of you. The love and acceptance Jesus demonstrated is the Father's character and nature. It will have a powerful effect on all those with whom you come in contact. Don't be afraid. With Jesus in you, you can walk in the perfect love of the Father. Want your worries and fears to go? Remember, it's His perfect love that casts out all fear!

> *"Who wants all men to be saved and to come to a knowledge of the truth. For there is one God and one mediator between God and men, the man Jesus Christ, who gave himself as a ransom for all men—the testimony given in its proper time."*
> *1 Timothy 2:4-6 (NIV)*

In this verse Timothy explains God's desire...*He wants all men to be saved.* Timothy also confirms what the others have written, and that is we needed a mediator to restore us back to the Father. There is only one way to the Father, and that way is through Jesus, His Son. *Jesus is the testimony* of the goodness of God and His plan to buy us back. *He was our ransom and now our mediator to God.* Webster's Dictionary defines the word mediator as, "to bring accord out of by action; to interpose between parties in order to reconcile them; to reconcile differences." Jesus is the go-between for God and us. He brought us into one accord with Him because of His action on the cross. His shed blood brought reconciliation and became the bridge that closed the gap between God and man. Although it's a spiritual bridge, once you crossover, it becomes real to you. You won't see it, but when the heart is transformed, you definitely feel it.

Why does God continue to repeat His divine plan of salvation? Because it all just "sounds" too easy. Some struggle with how one man could die for all the sins of the world. The truth is it goes back to Adam...the one man who brought death into the earth through sin. If one man brought the fall, then why couldn't one perfect man bring the fix? Jesus remained pure and sinless, which qualified Him to be our sacrifice...and...it wasn't easy. The punishment He bore for us was horrific. He was stripped naked, beaten beyond recognition, His beard was plucked out, a crown of thorns was jammed into His head, and He was whipped 39 times because they knew 40 lashes brought death. After the beating, the flesh on His back hung in pieces like sliced meat. He was spit upon by over a hundred men. He was humiliated, shamed, and then expected to carry His own cross. He was nailed to that cross, suffered, and hung there for six hours before He died.

The Bible says, "He endured it for the joy that was set before Him." What was the joy? You and I. Jesus did it because He loves us. He did it so we would have access to the Father. He did it so we would have the power to overcome fear and death. He paid the price so we could be free from sin and bondages. Don't be afraid. Isn't it time you *came to the knowledge of God's truth* and desire? Let Jesus be your mediator through life. Let Him be your Lord, and you'll be saved.

OCTOBER 13

> *"Christ hath redeemed us from the curse of the law, being made a curse for us: for it is written, Cursed is every one that hangeth on a tree:"*
> *Galatians 3:13 (KJV)*

When the Apostle Paul wrote this he wanted believers to understand and accept that they could now have a life of total freedom and victory because of what Christ did for all mankind on the cross. Because of sin and the fall of man the law of sin and death brought curses upon the earth. Deuteronomy 28, verses 13-68, describe these curses. They covered everything from your location, housing, family, business, your coming and going, plagues, pestilence, famine, terror, being overtaken by countries and nations, and being made to be slaves. The curse included every form of sickness and disease, from the itch to tormenting life-eating illnesses, which meant you could go mad and lose your mind, go blind or be oppressed with no one to rescue you. It would come against your finances and poverty would come upon you. Your plants, vineyards, and every seed planted would fail from worms, locusts, and other devouring pests. You could pledge to marry a woman, but another man would take her. You could have all kinds of accidents. Do you get the point? Nothing about the curse was pleasant, and it affected everybody. No one was exempt, in any area of life.

The good news is Christ abolished the curse for us when He went to the cross. He not only took our sin, but the Word says He became sin which was the original curse. This verse confirms He removed the fear of the curse from us forever. When the Word says *everyone who hangs on a tree is cursed*, the tree it refers to is the cross. This is how criminals were punished, and even though Jesus was pure and sinless, He was crucified the same way. He fulfilled every requirement to deliver us and set us free. He gave us an abundant, fear-free life.

Now when the devil tries to bring symptoms of sickness, disease, poverty, lack, an unfaithful spouse, a failing business, stress, accidents, rebellious children, pressures, depression or oppression...YOU DON'T HAVE TO RECEIVE IT! Tell him, "This ______ (whatever illness or foul condition has tried to plague you) is under the curse of the law, and according to Galatians 3:13, Jesus delivered me from every curse. The curse is reversed. So devil, I rebuke ______ in Jesus' Name, and I'm no longer buying or receiving your lies." Don't be afraid. The devil knows he has no authority to persist or pursue, and if he tries to continue with the problem, just remind him again of the truth. Then keep thanking and praising God for your victory. *Jesus has already redeemed you* to BE FREE!

"That the blessings of Abraham might come upon the gentiles through Jesus Christ; that we might receive the promise of the Spirit through faith."
Galatians 3:14 (KJV)

The Apostle Paul describes how we are eligible to receive God's blessings. The original covenant God established was with Abraham, and it was for the Jewish people. Until the time of Jesus' ministry and death, God's Word had only been taught in the synagogues, but now God told them His message wasn't just for the Jews. It was also for the gentiles. The Bible tells us the gentiles were non-believing people from every tongue and nation. This verse confirms God's love is for all people. It is His desire that all men are saved, and now, because of their faith in Jesus Christ by the Holy Spirit, anyone can receive the same original blessings that God promised Abraham.

Faith, or believing the promises of God, is how we receive the blessings. God's covenant with Abraham promised him natural earthly blessings, and he was very wealthy, but it also promised him the hope of eternal life. They knew their Messiah was coming, and one day, He would deliver them out of the bondage of the law of sin and death. God has never broken His promises in the covenant, and through faith we not only have every earthly blessing God promised Abraham, but we can also receive the eternal blessing Christ bought for us through His shed blood.

Christ came to save the world. The Bible says, "That God so loved the world that He gave His only begotten Son, that whosoever believes in Him shall not perish, but have everlasting life." We don't have to be afraid Jesus won't accept us because of our nationality, gender, age, past failures or anything else. Regardless of the limitations the world may have tried to put on you, His blood knows no boundaries or prejudices. No matter what or who has rejected, abandoned, mistreated or abused you in the past, His Word confirms He will never, by any means, ever turn you aside or turn away from anyone who comes to Him.

Don't be afraid. If He loved you, when you were a sinner, why wouldn't He love you now as His child? You'll never have to question whether He loves you. Whatever has kept you afraid, whether it's events from your past or fear of an unknown or unsure future, Christ is the only One who can give you peace in the midst of it and deliver you from it. Use your faith, and by the Spirit receive His love, hope, and joy. Walk fear-free, and enjoy the blessings of your covenant with Him.

"[The Father] has delivered and drawn us to Himself out of the control and the dominion of darkness and has transferred us into the kingdom of the Son of His love,..."
Colossians 1:13 (AMP)

Paul encourages the church at Colosse with the good news that they are delivered and drawn back into the loving arms of God. Sin cost mankind the privilege of being able to have intimate fellowship with God. We also lost our rights, so the authority and dominion man had over the earth and everything that was on it was surrendered to the devil...or the power of darkness. Since this was never the Father's plan, *He has delivered and drawn us to Himself* once again because of what His Son, Christ Jesus, did for us. As a result the Bible says we can now go boldly into the throne room of God.

When Christ defeated the devil and was victorious over death, hell, and the grave, He delivered us out of the kingdom of darkness. This means we are delivered out of the devil's control or dominion. However, even though satan no longer has any authority over us, his main attack is to still bring fear and to steal our most valuable possession...our "rights" and "authority" as a child of God. How does he do this? In several ways...by lying about what really belongs to us as the redeemed of the Lord, by bringing the curse of the law back on us through sickness, guilt, shame, and poverty, and by working to distract us to keep us from utilizing the Holy Spirit within us which provides us with the power to live in the fullness of God. The only way satan can be victorious is if he deceives us into believing his lies. Even though the devil is the thief, he can't "take" your victory. However, if you don't know your rights, he won't have to take it because you'll end up giving it to him.

The truth is satan is defeated! Regardless of the lies he wants you to believe, his control over darkness no longer has any power over you. God has delivered you from darkness, fear, and the torment of this world that the devil inflicts through disasters, terrorism, a sluggish or bad economy, disease, famine, and any other form of oppression that screams doom, gloom, and despair. Have you received His delivering power? Do you know your rights as a child of God? Did you know that God has transferred you, which means He moved you from one place to another? This also means He knows where you were in order to transfer you to where you are. Don't be afraid. You can walk in the fullness and victory of being transferred into His light...*transferred into the kingdom of His dear Son...the kingdom of His love.* As His child, use your God given rights and authority, and really live your life victoriously.

> *"In Whom we have our redemption through His blood, [which means] the forgiveness of our sins."*
> *Colossians 1:14 (AMP)*

God just never quits relaying the message that through Christ we are forgiven. And yet, so many still suffer and are tormented with thoughts that God not only doesn't love them, but He absolutely…couldn't possibly…even remotely… consider forgiving their sins. The Bible tells us we are special to God, but this is a form of "special" in the reverse. Do you think you or your sins are so bad, so wicked, that the blood of Jesus isn't powerful enough to take care of it? Where in the Word does it say the blood only covers certain sins? Jesus bled in seven places to cover our every need, but even if there had only been one drop, it would have been more than enough.

Lies, guilt, and shame are from the devil, and they will distort your thinking. The Bible is full of people who killed, cheated, worshipped false gods, lied, were disobedient, and rebellious in the ways of God. But the moment they repented and asked God for forgiveness, it is recorded He forgave them—every one—every time. Don't let the devil steal the joy that comes when you get clean and washed of your sins before God. You may not like confessing them at first, but when you start to experience the freedom and joy that comes when you do, you will want to run to God when things occur.

Do you have unconfessed sin in your life? Who are you really trying to hide it from because you know God already knows? The Bible tells us if we judge ourselves, then we won't be judged. In other words, if we confess and ask, then all God has to do is forgive. If we don't confess, then God has to judge us and punish us accordingly. He is a just God, and as the Supreme Authority, He must bring justice. Don't be afraid. God's "forgiveness" program is a lifesaver. Maybe you're embarrassed or ashamed because you have to ask for forgiveness for the same sin? God didn't put a limit on how many times you can ask. Just ask, rejoice, get rid of the guilt, and rejoice all over again. Shame is from the devil. Draw on the Holy Spirit on the inside of you to help you overcome your temptation. He knows the answer to your problem, and He is there to help you, if you will let Him. I'll say it again…Don't be afraid. God knew about your problem before you did. That's why He sent Jesus to the cross…just for you…just for your problem. Make the decision to accept the power of His shed blood, and finally receive the best gift anyone could offer you…total forgiveness.

"But God's free gift is not at all to be compared to the trespass—His grace is out of all proportion to the fall of man. For if many died through one man's falling away—his lapse, his offense—much more profusely did God's grace and the free gift [that comes] through the undeserved favor of the one Man Jesus Christ, abound and overflow to and for [the benefit of] many."
Romans 5:15 (AMP)

In this one verse the Apostle Paul sums up what happened to mankind because of the sin of one man, Adam, and then explains the benefits that were restored through the one *Man Jesus Christ.* When this verse talks about *many dying because of one man's falling away,* it is retelling the events of Adam's disobedience. This not only brought sin and immediate spiritual death or separation from God, but it also unleashed natural death onto the earth at the same time. This earthly death brought fear with it.

After Adam and Eve ate the food the devil offered them, they lost their spiritual connection and intimacy with the Father. Instantly, they knew everything had changed. For the first time they were afraid. They realized they were naked, and they covered themselves with leaves. When Adam accepted the devil's plan, he gave up the authority God the Father had given him on earth. Fear and death were satan's gifts. When God came to visit His family they were already so afraid, they were hiding from Him. Sin and holiness don't mix. Adam and Eve didn't like their new position of separation, but neither did God. He loved them and wanted to talk and walk with them each day. Can you imagine God Almighty coming and sitting with you or wanting to hang out with you every day? The truth is He still does, and because of Christ's sacrifice, He is now able to be with us once again.

This verse confirms God's great love for His family by *His free gift* to mankind in His Son Jesus. His sacrifice is so much greater than the fall or trespass of man, that it can't even be compared. This verse says, "*His grace is out of proportion.*" Are you separated from God? All mankind has sinned, but you don't have to let your sin keep you from the only One who has ever loved you and accepts you for who you are. Don't be afraid. Receive God's overflow of grace and favor for you. Choose His free gift Jesus, and choose real life.

> *"Once you were alienated from God and were enemies in your minds because of your evil behavior. But now he has reconciled you by Christ's physical body through death to present you holy in his sight, without blemish and free from accusation—if you continue in your faith, established and firm not moved from the hope held out in the gospel."*
> *Colossians 1:21-23a (NIV)*

The *alienation* this verse describes came about because of sin. Sin and an evil mindset separate us from God. But God sent His only Son to die for us. Christ's death brought us reconciliation with the Father. It was His *physical body*, blameless of sin, that was sacrificed for everyone's sins. The Bible says they plucked out His beard, stuck thorns into His head, He was spit upon by 100 men, His body was whipped 39 times until His flesh was hanging like raw meat, He was beaten beyond recognition, He was nailed to a cross, and hung there for six hours until He died. It's His death that allows us *to be presented holy in His sight, without blemish and free from accusation*. Jesus paid the cost. He took our punishment. The crimes that were against us are now totally forgiven.

This is why Jesus has been exalted to the right hand of God, and His Name is above every other name. The Bible says that named or unnamed, Jesus is the Highest Name. Why is this important? The enemy would like for us to believe because there aren't exact medical terms or names for some of the new diseases listed in the Word, it's not covered. What a liar! When we use the Name of Jesus in combination with the Word, there is no weapon the devil can use to defeat us. We don't need to be afraid of him because his power has already been broken.

Every place Christ's body was broken and He bled was for our healing, wholeness, forgiveness of sin, and the curse to be removed. He restored full liberty to us, so we can live in divine health, just like Adam did in the garden. Today, medical science reports that every known disease fits into 39 main categories. Jesus was whipped 39 times. Just a coincidence? Isaiah prophesied, "By His stripes we are healed." 2000 years ago Christ paid for your healing and deliverance, plus every other need you have. While He hung on the cross, He asked God to forgive those who had done this because they didn't know what they were doing. Don't be afraid. Aren't you ready to receive freedom from life's accusations? Wouldn't you like to know you could be presented to God *holy in His sight, without blemish, and free from fault*? You can. Just accept Him and what He has done for you, and then hold on to your hope and faith in the Gospel.

"[For my concern is] that their hearts may be braced (comforted, cheered and encouraged) as they are knit together in love, that they may come to have all the abounding wealth and blessings of assured conviction of understanding, and that they may become progressively more intimately acquainted with, and may know more definitely and accurately and thoroughly, that mystic secret of God [which is] Christ, the Anointed One."
Colossians 2:2 (AMP)

The NIV says this is Paul's purpose and prayer. He wants us to be encouraged in our hearts, united in love to one another, overflowing in all we need, assured we can know the fullness of Christ's riches, and also have an intimate knowledge of Him. When we have these things, we'll know *that mystic secret* or the mystery of God, which is summed up in the person of Jesus Christ, God's Anointed.

I know this seems simply put when you are trying to live and walk out all of the above. When the devil strikes at you...and he will...God wants our hearts to be encouraged. Why? It's because the enemy tries to steal your hope which brings despair, heaviness, and fear. Ever been heartsick? Heartbroken? We all have, so how do we stay encouraged and remain hopeful in the midst of crisis? There is only one way, through Jesus Christ. We remind ourselves of what He did, which makes us more than overcomers. The Word says we can have unspeakable joy. Have you experienced this kind of joy? It's available to you through Jesus. God wants us to walk in love toward each other. Why? Because God is love, and if the Godhead dwells in each of us richly, then we have no excuse for not loving and helping one another. He wants us to know and understand Him and His knowledge. Why? Because His ways are higher than ours, and He can't teach or help us change from our old destructive patterns if we don't know His ways. How can we know anyone intimately if we don't spend time with them?

God wants us to know Him. He doesn't work through mysterious ways. The only *mystery is Jesus Christ,* and in reality it is a mystery how one Man, Jesus, His Anointed One, could have done it all? And why would He be willing to do it? And who am I that He would do it for me? Loving and saving someone who doesn't deserve it may be a mystery to us, but it was always God's plan. Don't be afraid. Do you have what the Apostle Paul prayed for in the above verse...hope, joy, peace, knowledge, and intimacy with the Lord? It's available, if you'll accept it. God has already designed a unique path for you to reach your divine destiny. Just believe *in Him*, and get ready for your future.

> *"In Him all the treasures of [divine] wisdom, [of comprehensive insight into the ways and purposes of God], and [all the riches of spiritual] knowledge and enlightenment are stored up and lie hidden."*
> *Colossians 2:3 (AMP)*

Paul writes plainly about all wisdom being *in Him*, the Lord Jesus. His purpose is so that no one will be deceived by false doctrines, traditions, persuasive, fine-sounding arguments or attractive speech. Paul wanted the truth of the Gospel revealed, and the truth is all wisdom and spiritual revelation is found in the Lord Jesus Christ. When Jesus ministered to the crowds He spoke in parables, which is a story within a story. Afterwards, He would explain to the disciples the deeper meaning. Jesus wasn't trying to speak in riddles. He was training them to listen with spiritual ears and to look with spiritual eyes. God's ways are not our ways. If we are going to walk in the fullness of what God has for us, we have to learn to ask and rely on the Spirit of God within us. The Holy Spirit relays what God wants to say to us.

Many times, if I hadn't asked the Holy Spirit or He hadn't told me, I would have never chosen to do or go the direction I did. But He's always right. Maybe you're thinking, "God never talks to me." The truth is He's always talking. Are you listening? Years ago a friend came to visit me. On the way to dinner I had to make a quick stop. When I was returning to my car, I heard the Holy Spirit say, "Don't let them drive." Usually I'm thrilled to hear what the Spirit has to say, but not this time. It was Friday evening, I'd had a rough week, we were just minutes from the restaurant, and since discussing their driving skills usually ended in an argument…I ignored the Spirit. At an intersection, only two blocks later, an oncoming car, in the turn lane, failed to yield. My friend plowed right into him. Both drivers said the same thing, "I never saw you." The sad part was…I had seen him coming. I knew he was going too fast to stop when he pulled into the turn lane. If I'd been driving, I would have stopped. We wouldn't have collided.

Long story short…if I had obeyed the Holy Spirit, the accident wouldn't have happened, and I wouldn't have lived for many years in constant pain with limited mobility in my body from the injuries. My car was never the same, either. Haven't you heard that "still, small voice" at times, too? After the fact, you've even thought or said, "Something was telling me to_____." That "something" is the Holy Spirit. This verse confirms *all insight into the ways and purposes of God are in Him.* Don't be afraid. God wants you to know. ASK for wisdom. LISTEN to the directions. Then, OBEY! It's a fail proof plan!

> *"HOW GREAT is the love the Father has lavished on us, that we should be called the children of God! And that is what we are..."*
> *1 John 3:1a (NIV)*

John called himself the disciple Jesus loved. He continually spoke of his relationship with the Lord. The truth is Jesus didn't love him anymore than anyone else, but John allowed himself to receive His love. Jesus said the Father was in Him, and He was in the Father. Since John felt Jesus' love, he also felt God's love. This verse says the *Father lavishes His love upon us*. The word lavish means to utilize or produce in extreme abundance. Our Father God has an abundance of love, and He is quick to shower it upon us.

Besides, the Father IS love. It isn't just what He does. His love for us from the very beginning included being close to us and enjoying times of fellowship together. Now this may seem unusual or strange to you if you've never heard or been taught the truth about God. He isn't the "One" way out in the universe somewhere. Nor is He the "Big Guy" or the "Man Upstairs." He doesn't carry a club, and He isn't waiting to clobber you with it. He is your Father, and He wants a relationship with you. You can hear and know His voice through the Holy Spirit, and this intimacy allows you to share your heart and open yourself up to His trust, direction, and extreme love.

His love is the most wonderful thing you will ever experience. It is genuine, never demanding or controlling. He is a giver, and when He gives us His love, it is life changing. It produces a confidence and a peace in us that leaves no room for fear. The Bible says if God is for us, then who can be against us. Have you found out He's really for you? Do you spend time with Him? Can you feel His love? If you don't, then you need to. You'll find His love is perfect. The Bible says this perfect love casts out or gets rid of fear. Maybe life has dealt you some real tragedies. Maybe even now you're afraid of losing your job, spouse, home, health, car or children? If you're afraid of anything, you have a "love deficit." When you truly understand and receive the abundance of love the Father wants to lavish on you, His child, things will pale in comparison. You'll know, regardless of how things look, He will provide the answer. Don't be afraid. The Father has more than enough love to remove all fear and fill you with the confidence you need. You are HIS child...AND...nobody loves you like your Father.

OCTOBER 22

"[And indeed] the Lord will certainly deliver and draw me to Himself from every assault of evil. He will preserve and bring [me] safe unto His heavenly kingdom. To Him be the glory forever and ever. Amen—so be it."
2 Timothy 4:18 (AMP)

When the Apostle Paul wrote this in a letter to Timothy, he had been going through much adversity. Many who were helping him preach the Gospel had now deserted him. When Paul went to trial, no one supported him. Another man, who opposed the message, spoke against him and brought much damage and harm. It appeared in the natural he was alone and fending for himself, but Paul knew God had promised to never leave or forsake him. Regardless of what it looked like or how he felt, Paul knew he didn't have to be afraid because the Lord would rescue and deliver him from every weapon or assault the evil one had planned. Paul knew the Lord would be faithful to lead him to a place of safety, and Paul was prepared, even if it meant dying and going to Heaven.

All of us have faced difficult times. You may be in the heat of a battle right now. Has someone you loved and trusted betrayed you? Maybe at your darkest hour the one you counted on the most for support deserted you, too? Maybe the one, who committed to be with you until death do you part, has left? Rejection is one of the most painful emotions we have to deal with, but it is real, and it happens a lot. People are fickle, and the more problems they have, the less likely they are to help others. The enemy knows this. That's why he keeps piling on the problems. Problems will keep you focused on yourself, distracted, and unable to help others in real need.

However, the Lord made a way so none of us have to be loaded down, over-burdened, and stressed out. He said, "Come unto me all that are burdened or heavy laden and I will give you rest." He also said to, "Call on Him in your time of trouble and He would deliver you out of them all." Paul did this. He learned he could count on the Lord. How did he learn? He spent time with the Lord, stayed in constant prayer, and trusted the Holy Spirit for wisdom and comfort. Paul wasn't afraid. If people did things that weren't trustworthy or reliable, he didn't blame God or put Him in the same category with the others. He believed the Word and stood on God's faithfulness. So can you! Don't be afraid. Call to Him. *He will deliver you from every assault of evil,* and you can also count on Him to *preserve and bring you* to a place of safety, too.

> *"Fight the good fight of faith; lay hold of the eternal life to which you were summoned, and confessed the good confession [of faith] before many witnesses."*
> *1 Timothy 6:12 (AMP)*

In this verse the Apostle Paul encourages Timothy to use his faith. The persecutions were mounting against the believers, especially Paul, who faced hardships in prison and in preaching the message of the Gospel. However, Paul didn't want others to look at his or their own circumstances. He wanted them to stay focused on what they knew, confessed to be true, and then to continue to stand in faith.

The Bible tells us every Word that was written in the Bible is the inspired or God breathed Word. What did Paul mean when he said we need to *fight the good fight of faith*? If God would give us rest, deliver us out of our trials and tribulations, heal and prosper us, then who, what or why would we be fighting? Why would we need to do anything? The truth is all we need to do is what the Word says. However, many Christians still live somewhat defeated lives by sitting back, waiting on God to do it all. God has already done all He is going to do because of Jesus. He gave Him all authority, and now Jesus has given us the same authority. God isn't moved by need. If He were, the whole world would be fixed. He's moved by faith—our faith to command things to change. We do our part...God does His.

The Bible says, "Faith is the substance of things hoped for and the evidence of things not seen." Just hoping God will do something to change our situation isn't enough. God expects us to do something with our hope. So what do we do? We add faith to it. We speak the Word and believe God that what we have asked and hoped for is done, right then, when we prayed. This is using faith...believing the unseen thing is already seen and finished. If you've ever done this, then you know it goes against everything in the natural. Your mind battles with it, your natural sight says this isn't real, and your body may say it still hurts. The enemy attacks you with fear...it's foolishness to believe. You have now entered the fight. You not only have to fight against the situation, but your own natural senses. Faith and common sense have nothing in common. You fight the *good fight* because the ways of God are good, they are right. Don't be afraid. When you stand and stand and stand in faith, you will see the victory. FAITH WORKS. It pleases God, and it will produce the results you need to see for successful living.

"For the grace of God that bringeth salvation hath appeared to all men."
Titus 2:11 (KJV)

When you become familiar with the Word of God, you understand there are reasons He repeats certain things over and over. God knew some would struggle with what was said or who was saying it. He also knew because of the goodness, kindness, and forgiveness He continually offers, people would even question whether it could really be true. However, the Word teaches us God's grace is His unmerited, unearned, and undeserved favor. It is not only His covenant blessings, but it is also the forgiveness of sins because of His Son's sacrifice. I've heard it said the acronym for GRACE is: G—God's
R—Riches
A—At
C—Christ's
E—Expense

God offers us every blessing and adoption into His family by becoming His very own child through Jesus, and He offers it to every one—every where. God keeps repeating this message because there are still those who do not believe they can receive His grace for their victory because of their past actions, their past or present illnesses, their past financial failures, and so on. In other words, they don't believe God's Word or promises. They have let the devil and life's choices lie to them about who God really is. God doesn't make decisions for each one of us based on His mood, our past, or our works or good deeds. He is stable. The Bible says God never changes. He is the same yesterday, today, and forever. Why would this be important for us to know? Because for years the devil has tried to tell people the Bible was only for those people who lived back then. It isn't for us today. It isn't relevant to us today. It's too "old fashioned." If you knew the Word would defeat you, wouldn't you do all you could to discredit it? Wouldn't you lie about its contents, too?

However, the real truth is the Bible is our handbook for daily living because God's principles are still the same. Remember, He is the same yesterday, today, and forever. By this we are confident that if it worked for them…it will work for us. Have you had a hard time believing God's Word is true? Do you know what keeps you from receiving His promises? It's fear. Fear—it's just too good to be true. Fear—you've already blown the plan. Fear—He couldn't have meant you. Fear—you _________! What are you really afraid of? If Christ, while hanging from the cross, could forgive those who crucified Him before He died—He will forgive you, too. Don't be afraid. Accept His wonderful grace. Receive Jesus as your Lord and Savior. His plan of salvation truly is for all.

> *"Who gave Himself on our behalf that He might redeem us (purchase our freedom) from all iniquity and purify for Himself a people—to be peculiarly His own—[people who are] eager and enthusiastic about [living a life that is good and filled with] beneficial deeds."*
> *Titus 2:14 (AMP)*

The events of the Lord Jesus Christ and what He did to redeem us back to the Father is continually preached throughout the Scriptures. Why? Because it is the foundation of our faith, our hope, and it is the good news of the Gospel. We would have no relationship with God or be entitled to any of His promises if Jesus had not gone to the cross as a willing sacrifice. He chose to lay His life down. Jesus was crucified, and His death is paralleled to that of a lamb going to the slaughter because a lamb never makes a sound or struggles; it just lies down. Jesus is referred to as the lamb that was slain before the foundation of the world. God had a plan—Jesus the lamb—in place to pay for Adam's sin before he ever sinned.

Jesus' sacrifice paid for us to have the fullness of the blessings of God: health, financial prosperity, social well being, spiritual enlightenment, and the forgiveness of sin. He not only cleanses us from all unrighteousness, but He purifies us so we can have a relationship with Him. We belong to God. We are His people. The Bible says we are a peculiar people. This doesn't mean we're to act in a strange way or to be "flaky" over spiritual things. It simply means we don't do things the way we used to. We don't think or operate the way the world does anymore, which may seem totally "peculiar" or unusual to those who are around us or to those who knew us before this transformation took place.

His sacrifice is the foundation for us to walk free of sin. It allows the Godhead to live in us, which gives us power to speak to things and expect them to change. The delivering and staying power to say "No" to evil desires, "Yes" to serving God, and being enthusiastic about helping others. Are you still having a hard time leaving the old behind? Even when you know it's destroying you? Then you need the purifying power of God. Don't be afraid. It comes through accepting, believing, and confessing His Son, Jesus Christ. Once this is done, you must believe He has forgiven you, but you also must forgive yourself. You are washed clean, purified. Receive it. Then replace the old thoughts and ways of your flesh with joy and *eager enthusiasm for living a life that is good and filled with beneficial deeds.* You'll be amazed at how much brighter your future will appear!

> *"For we do not have a High Priest Who is unable to understand and sympathize and have a fellow feeling with our weaknesses and infirmities and liability to the assaults of temptation, but One Who has been tempted in every respect as we are, yet without sinning. Let us then fearlessly and confidently and boldly draw near to the throne of grace—the throne of God's unmerited favor [to us sinners]; that we may receive mercy [for our failures] and find grace to help in good time for every need—appropriate help and well-timed help, coming just when we need it."*
> *Hebrews 4:15-16 (AMP)*

The Bible clearly states Jesus is our High Priest. He walked this earth as the son of man and the Son of God. He experienced every kind of emotional torment and temptation the devil offers, just like everyone else does. Oh, yes, the devil tried to tempt Jesus, too. The Bible tells of many situations when both satan and demons spoke directly to Jesus, and Jesus spoke back. This should be our example, too. You can't defeat the devil with your mouth shut. If Jesus spoke the written Word to defeat him—then we need to use His Words, too.

The Bible is explicit, regardless of the devil's attempts, Jesus never sinned. We know He couldn't have and still remained the blameless sacrifice God needed to reconcile us back to Him. The truth is most people don't think about Jesus having the same opportunities to feel and react to circumstances in the flesh as they do. But this verse confirms that He did. Otherwise how could our High Priest be able to *understand and sympathize with our feelings?* When we face trials and fear tries to grip our heart, He also recognizes those feelings. However, He didn't give in to fear or anything else because He chose to walk by the Spirit, not the flesh. We can make the same choice. We can receive what Jesus has done for us, and *then fearlessly, confidently, and boldly draw near to the throne of grace.*

Through Jesus we have God's unmerited grace and favor. We can expect mercy not only for our failures, but in other times of need, too. Don't be afraid. God wants His children comfortable in coming to Him. He has the *appropriate help* for your every trial. He is not only *on time* with the help, but you will find He has always been there, just waiting for you to come to Him.

> *"For the Word that God speaks is alive and full of power—making it active, operative, energizing and effective; it is sharper than any two-edged sword, penetrating to the dividing line of the breath of life (soul) and [the immortal] spirit, and of joints and marrow [that is, of the deepest parts of our nature] exposing and sifting and analyzing and judging the very thoughts and purposes of the heart."*
> *Hebrews 4:12 (AMP)*

God's Word is alive. This is why the Bible says the Word is God breathed and inspired. It may have been man's hand that put it to paper for our benefit, but these individuals were like God's secretaries. A secretary or administrative assistant doesn't think up the content of the letters they write. They only type what the person in authority gives them, and it is done verbatim. This is what the writers of the Bible did, too. They took down God's Word exactly as the Holy Spirit gave it to them.

What does it matter if the Word is alive? Or it has power? How does that benefit me? Well, if you were in major combat, would you want to use a BB gun or an automatic weapon? We both know you'd want what has the most power. Why? It's the most effective. As a child of God your words have power. The Word says there is power in the tongue to bring life or death—choose life. God's Word is powerful, and it's eternal. The Bible says, "Heaven and earth will pass away, but My Word will never pass away."

This verse describes the purpose of the Word. It's sharp—it gets to the point. Like a two-edged sword, it cuts out of our life what is harmful to us, and it cuts out the plans or attack of the enemy. The Word discerns what we think, our attitude, emotions, desires, and all the key issues of our heart. Why is this good? Because when life has not treated us fairly, we have a tendency to lie to ourselves as a defense mechanism. Have you ever told yourself, "I don't care?" or "It doesn't matter what 'they' say or do or think?" The truth is you do and should care. But once you start lying to yourself, you won't be capable of discerning the truth. However, God's Word can. When you read it, you'll feel the Holy Spirit talking to you about things. At that point, you'll be able to make the changes. Don't be afraid. God's Word is powerful. It's your weapon. Just as you would make sure your gun is loaded and ready, load the Word into your heart, mind, and mouth. Then, when the enemy comes, just fire away!

"But because Jesus lives forever, he has a permanent priesthood. Therefore he is able to save completely those who come to God through him, because he always lives to intercede for them. Such a high priest meets our need—one who is holy, blameless, pure, set apart from sinners, exalted above the heavens."
Hebrews 7:24-26 (NIV)

In the Old Testament God called the Levite tribe to be the Priests, and as good as they may have been in fulfilling God's purposes in the temple, they have all died. *But because Jesus lives forever, he has a permanent priesthood.* In other words, Jesus is not only alive today, but He will live for eternity. The Old Testament Priests had to offer yearly sacrifices, not only for their own sins, but for the sins of the people. But Jesus, by offering Himself as our sacrifice, paid for our sins once and for all. Under the old law the Priests were still men who were sinners, but our High Priest is Jesus, God's Son—*One who is holy, blameless, pure, set apart from sinners, exalted above the heavens.*

Jesus is at the right hand of the Father this very moment. Do you know what He's doing? He's talking to the Father about you. He's bridging the gap between God and you, so you can boldly enter God's throne room. The Word says He intercedes for us. Webster's Dictionary defines the word intercede as, "to intervene between parties with a view to reconcile differences: mediate." Jesus is your mediator. Why? He doesn't want you to be afraid. He doesn't want you to be afraid that your sin will keep you from the Father, and when there is no fear of your past sins, you will be confident that He will meet your every need.

Jesus has been exalted above the heavens as our High Priest. *Therefore He is able to save completely those who come to God through Him.* The good news is He meets all your needs—because He is holy…you are holy, because He is blameless…you are blameless, because He is pure…you are pure, because He is set apart from sinners…you are set apart, because He is righteous…the Bible says we are the righteousness of God in Christ, because He is exalted above the Heavens…the Bible says, "We are no longer of this world, but we are seated in heavenly places with Christ Jesus." Don't be afraid. Christ was our substitute. He substituted His goodness for our filth. He substituted His purity for our sin. He substituted His freedom for our guilt and shame. Isn't it time you let go and let *such a high priest meet your needs,* too? Wouldn't you like to know you have someone who is mediating or intervening on your behalf? Just call on the Lord Jesus. He is and always will be your High Priest…forever.

> *"And having an high priest over the house of God; Let us draw near with a true heart in full assurance of faith, having our hearts sprinkled from an evil conscience, and our bodies washed with pure water. Let us hold fast the profession of our faith without wavering; (for he is faithful that promised.)"*
> *Hebrews 10:21-23 (KJV)*

Because Jesus is our High Priest and He reigns over the house of God, we can boldly enter the throne of grace. We can be assured that our faith and the profession of it will keep Heaven's doors open. This verse speaks of our hearts being sprinkled from an evil conscience. What was it that was so powerful that only a sprinkle could remove a sinful conscience? It was the blood of Jesus. His shed blood on Calvary washed every part of us.

When the devil comes to kill, steal, and destroy, he uses the same ammunition on everybody. First, he tempts you with fleshly desire to get you to agree to do something. After it's done, he subjects you to guilt, shame, and fear, which troubles the heart. The Bible says as a man thinks in his heart, so is he. In other words, if our hearts are unstable or they're emotionally beat up, then the rest of our actions will demonstrate this, too. The Bible also says out of the abundance of the heart the mouth speaks. You cannot stay in faith if your heart condemns you. At that point, whatever comes out of your mouth will be fear, doubt and unbelief. A guilty conscience condemns, and satan knows it. Sin is heavy, and you will break under the weight of it. This is the devil's plan. But Christ defeated the devil with His shed blood.

It is faith in Jesus...*It is a true heart in full assurance of faith* in the power of the Gospel that gives us total trust and reliance in God's faithfulness to do what He promised. Aren't you ready to get rid of your past failures? Don't you want to draw near to God? Do you know what Jesus did for you on the cross? Have you accepted Him? Are you holding on to His truth? *Your profession of faith?* Don't be afraid. He traded His goodness and greatness for our ungodliness, so we could be made clean. Don't let fear keep you from receiving the fullness of the faith. Hold fast without wavering to the Word, receive all God has for you through Jesus, your High Priest, and watch Him be faithful to His promises.

OCTOBER 30

> *"And we know that all things work together for the good to them that love God, to them who are the called according to his purpose."*
> *Romans 8:28 (KJV)*

How can all things work for good? What good can come from the misery and torment I'm in? What good comes from an illness, lost job or increasing debt? These are tough, painful situations. We've all been there at different stages in our lives, and maybe some of us have been there more than once. However, the Word says the Lord will deliver us out of our every trial.

When God uses words like trials or tribulation, it should be clear to us that even with the Lord in our life and on our side, the devil isn't going to give up. But this verse confirms, regardless of what the devil tries to throw at us to destroy our families or us, God is working all the time to turn the situation around. If we belong to Him and love Him, we can't lose. We know God has a plan for us, and when we have surrendered our will to His will and plan—then we are confident we will complete it. Yes, there will be storms along the way. A perfect example of this is when Jesus told the disciples to take the boat and go to the other side of the lake. He then went to another part of the boat and fell asleep. A major storm came up, and water filled the boat. The disciples thought they were going to die. Fear gripped them, so they woke Jesus saying, "Lord, do you not care about us that we should perish?" Jesus got up, rebuked the wind and the water, and they became peaceful. He then asked the disciples, "Where is your faith?"

The disciples' circumstances appeared overwhelming to them, and yet, the Lord was right there with them. They let fear of what they saw cause them to believe something that was not true. Are you doing the same? Where is your focus? What storms have made you think it's all over? Isn't Jesus right there with you, too? Then where is your faith? If He isn't with you, ask Him to come into your heart. Surrender your life and trials to Him. Maybe, like the disciples, you have a relationship with the Lord, but you have let fear of what you're looking at become greater to you than His power. Have you forgotten that He's in your boat? His Word promises *He will work <u>all</u> things out for your good.* Don't be afraid. Use your faith. Love God. He loves you. Look up, and believe. Only the Lord can restore you or your situation. This means He will make things better than they ever were before. You just have to use faith, and trust Him to do it!

> *"For whom he did foreknow, he also did predestinate to be conformed to the image of his Son, that he might be the firstborn among many brethren. Moreover whom he did predestinate, them he also called: and who he called, them he also justified, and whom he justified, them he also glorified."*
> *Romans 8:29-30 (KJV)*

The Bible clearly states God knew us before the foundation of the world. It also says He saw us before we were ever formed in our mother's womb. Why is this important? Because these verses remove any fear-based theory about you being an accident or that life just happened to evolve by an outer space collision or it came from the developmental progression of an animal. The truth is…"IN THE BEGINNING WAS GOD." He created everything, including us, *before* the very beginning. This is God's way…to do things beforehand.

This verse confirms we are predestinated. What exactly does that mean? Webster's Dictionary defines the word predestinate as, "to foreordain to an earthly or eternal lot or destiny by divine decree; fated or determined beforehand." The NIV states it like this, "For those God foreknew he also predestined to be conformed to the likeness of his Son, that he might be the firstborn of many brothers." God, in His foreknowledge of all life's events, without fail, guides the destiny of all those He foreknew to be just like His firstborn Son, Jesus. "*For whom he did foreknow*" are reassuring Words to us that His plan of salvation is for everyone. We all can have this path as our destiny. Why? Because He's already made it clear He knew each of us *before* the foundation of the world… *before* we were ever formed in the secret, hidden places of our mother's womb.

However, this Word also confirms that *those He did predestinate*, you and me, *He has also called, justified,* and *glorified*! Now you might be asking, "What does all this mean?" It means we have the ability to conform ourselves into the image of His Son, and to live as Christ did. His blood made us worthy, righteous, justified. He bore or paid my penalty, but it's credited to me "just as if I'd" never done it, and He did the same for you. This restored us to a right standing position with the Father, which also qualifies us to be glorified with Him. Our loving Father made sure we were going to be taken care of from before our birth to after our death. Don't be afraid. By now it should be completely obvious how much He loves you. "*For whom He did foreknow, He also….*" God has always had a plan…just for you. Receive it!

NOVEMBER 1

> *"What shall we then say to these things? If God be for us, who can be against us?"*
> *Romans 8:31 (KJV)*

In this verse, when the Apostle Paul asks, "*What shall we then say to these things*," he's referring to the original plan God established for all of us to live by. Everything goes back to His great plan…the plan that predestined, called, justified, and glorified us. The plan that guarantees He loves us and confirms He was fully aware of us beforehand. The plan He already had in place when Adam gave into sin and disobeyed. The plan He offered for His Son to be the sacrifice for the world's sin and punishment. The plan Jesus followed and successfully completed. The plan that raised Jesus from the dead and gave Him victory over death, hell, and the grave. The plan that seated Jesus at the right hand of the Father, so He can intercede for us daily. The plan that offers us everlasting life. The plan that allows us to rule and reign with Him in His Kingdom. The plan that has Him coming again, soon, to take us home to Heaven. What can you say to a plan like this? This is Paul's point in this verse…what can you even begin to say?

God is a planner, and by now, it should be evident to all…it is quite the plan. If God would have prepared this complete and "total" program for you and me, beforehand, then how could we not believe He would be there for us today? How could we wonder where He is, or if He sees us, or if He really cares about our circumstances? The truth is when we find ourselves afraid, frustrated or questioning God about His higher ways, it should be a sign to us we don't know or esteem Him like we should. It should be a warning signal to us that we still haven't received the depth of His love for us, either.

When you struggle with feelings of fear and doubt, and we all have at times, you might want to ask yourself…"If God, before the foundation of the world, could have put this masterful plan in place for my good, then what am I worried about today? *If God is for me, then who can be against me*? If God is for me, then why should I be anxious? If God is for me, then who or what should I fear?" Knowing God is for us is why we believe no weapon formed against us can prosper. It is the confidence we need to carry out His business throughout the earth. So when man disagrees with us or tries to cause strife, we can ask ourselves, "What can they do against a Mighty God?" Don't be afraid. Now you know what to say to all these things. The attacks against you will be powerless because His plan is still working for your benefit. His plan, established beforehand, for your victory!

NOVEMBER 2

> *"He who did not withhold or spare [even] His own Son but gave Him up for us all, will He not also with Him freely and graciously give us all [other] things?"*
> *Romans 8:32 (AMP)*

God the Father gave up His only begotten Son so we could be free of fear, sin, the works of the devil, trials that come to steal our peace and joy, and to deliver us from the negative effects of the curse. The Bible says Jesus came to not only give us life, but life more abundantly. Now you may be thinking, "How does this happen when He's no longer on the earth? What can He do for me now? Don't I have to wait until I get to Heaven for my blessings?" Let me ask you, "What blessings do you think you'll need in Heaven?" In Heaven there is no worry or fear, no debt, lack or poverty. There is no sickness, disease or death. There is no crime or destruction, no lying, cheating, anger, depression, stress or any other trial that causes torment. It is a pain free, tear free, joy filled place where love abounds. Heaven is "need" free.

When a verse like this is written, it is because God wants us to know He is willing and able to make all grace abound to us—HERE ON EARTH. All grace for every need we have and more. Why? So we will be able to give to His work and every other charitable work that will establish and further the preaching of the Gospel. God knew we were going to need His plan on earth. Earth is where our needs exist. Earth is where the devil ruled, but it was only for a limited time, and his time is up. We are in what the Bible calls "the last days," and because of it we are about to see God pour out His Spirit and blessings like no other generation before us has ever seen.

This verse sums up the love of God. If God was willing to give up His Son, and Jesus was willing to bridge the gap for all mankind, and the Holy Spirit is now willing to live in us as our helper and comforter, then why wouldn't God give us the "*other*" things we need when we ask? The truth is He will. He freely gave before we asked, and He will continue to freely give when we ask. Are you still afraid to accept Christ and what He did for you? Or maybe you've received salvation, but you've also bought the devil's lie you have to "hold on" until you get to Heaven to receive God's fullness? The enemy is trying to steal and cheat you out of the goodness God has for you today. Don't be afraid. His Word doesn't lie, and this verse confirms it. He freely gives, so you can freely receive all His benefits, both now and forever.

NOVEMBER 3

"Who shall bring any charge against God's elect [when it is] God Who justifies—Who puts us in right relation to Himself? (Who shall come forward and accuse or impeach those whom God has chosen? Will God, Who acquits us?)"
Romans 8:33 (AMP)

It is apparent Paul understood the answer to these questions is "no one," and he wants to make sure we…as God's children…*His elect*…understand it, too. It was Paul's mission to preach the good news of the Gospel, but it was also important his listeners clearly understood certain facts. Facts like…only Jesus was perfectly righteous and by no other means are we made holy or righteous. Facts like…only by accepting and believing in the Lord and His work on the cross are we restored to that right standing position with God. Facts like…we need faith which comes by hearing the Word and believing Jesus is the Son of God who came, died, and rose again. Facts like…it is only by God's grace, through faith in Jesus, that we become a new person, spiritually. Paul also taught that because of all these things we should live our lives as Christians or like Christ and be holy and pleasing to God.

So when Paul asks the above questions, he is prompting the reader to think about what God has already done for them. When we were guilty in our sins and didn't even know it, God rescued us for all eternity. If God is for you, then who can be against you? And if God has chosen you, then who would even attempt to accuse you? Even if they did, how much weight would it carry anyway? This verse states it is God who justifies. Remember this means—just as if I'd—never committed the sin. God is our judge, and He does the acquitting. Webster's Dictionary defines the word acquit as, "to pay off; to discharge completely (as from an obligation or accusation.)" Any guilt, shame, accusation or charge against us has already been paid for through God's Son, Jesus, and now we've been discharged of all obligation and accusation because of it.

Has someone accused you? By what authority? Are you "justified" in the Lord? When the Supreme Judge of the Universe is for you, there is no need to live afraid. God has put us into a right relationship with Him again, and neither the devil nor man can impeach, accuse or tear down God's elect. Don't be afraid. God chose you. He is for you! Isn't it comforting to know the Judge is your Dad?

> *"Who is there to condemn [us]? Will Christ Jesus, the Messiah, Who died, or rather Who was raised from the dead, Who is at the right hand of God actually pleading as He intercedes for us? Who shall ever separate us from Christ's love? Shall suffering and affliction and tribulation? Or calamity and distress? Or persecution, or hunger, or destitution, or peril, or sword?"*
> *Romans 8:34-35 (AMP)*

Paul continues in these two verses with questions that challenge our faith. Why? Because when troubles attack us from every angle we are challenged by the same questions. However, the answer for some is to blame someone else for their hardships. Unfortunately, many times it's God who gets the blame, right along with everyone else. Paul states for the record it isn't God or Jesus Christ who causes these distresses. In fact, Paul makes it clear. As God's child or the elect, They are on our side…Jesus, constantly playing the role of Attorney, pleading our case and interceding for us, while God the Father is seated as Judge, ready to dismiss every accusation with an acquittal.

Paul goes on to ask, "What then could possibly separate us from the love of Christ?" He lists some pretty devastating circumstances. If anyone would have first hand knowledge of persecution, hunger, calamity or distress, suffering, affliction, tribulation, perils, and the sword, it would be Paul. This man continually experienced major adversity in delivering the freeing message of Jesus Christ. And yet, through all of this Paul never quit feeling God's love. Nor did he lose sight of the promises, which God fulfilled.

Maybe you don't feel God's love for you? Maybe you still battle with a guilty conscience? The truth is there is no condemnation for those who are in Christ Jesus. So, *Who is there to condemn you*? If you've repented before God, He makes it very clear…it won't be Him! And if He isn't the "*Who*" that's condemning you…isn't it time you quit? Don't be afraid. God's Word is specific, and it's straight to the point. Look up the verses on God's love for you and start to speak them over yourself everyday. Remind yourself throughout the day how valuable you are to God. The Bible says, "You're the apple of His eye." You'll soon see and believe the effects of hearing the truth in His Word, and the truth is… nothing, not one thing, can separate you from God's love...ever!

"Yet amid all these things we are more than conquerors and gain a surpassing victory through Him Who loved us. For I am persuaded beyond doubt—am sure—that neither death, nor life, nor angels, nor principalities, nor things impending and threatening, nor things to come, nor powers, Nor height, nor depth, nor anything else in all creation will be able to separate us from the love of God which is in Christ Jesus our Lord."
Romans 8:37-39 (AMP)

Paul states *we are more than conquerors through the Lord Jesus Christ.* Why? Because when Christ gave His life for us on the cross at Calvary, He paid for our every victory, and now, He lives in us. When Paul refers to "*all these things"* he is talking about persecution, distress, calamity, suffering, hunger, affliction, and tribulations, which Paul was more than qualified to speak about. Yet, he had already experienced that regardless of his trials, he would be victorious...an overcomer...more than a conqueror.

The Bible says Christ in us is our hope of glory, and Christ lived in Paul. We can have Christ living in us, which becomes our hope, too. All His fullness and love are available to us. Paul experienced more hardships than most, and yet, he never wavered in his faith. How did this happen? What gave him such determination to carry out the plans of God? It was two things. He loved the Lord Jesus with all his heart, and he allowed himself to receive a heart full of love from God through Jesus. Paul wasn't afraid of what was to come. The Bible says perfect love casts out all fear. It was God's perfect love that Paul accepted and then received that brought him perfect peace and rest. Yes, even in the midst of all he was going through, Paul had peace.

Are you at perfect peace and rest? Or are you looking at what is to come? How high, deep or wide is it? How threatening is your distress or calamity? Do you know God's perfect love removes any and all fear in the midst of your troubles? Paul knew Jesus said He and the Father were one, and He wanted us to be one with Them, also. How could we be one with Them and not only feel the love They have for one another, but also feel the love They have for us? It would be impossible. Don't be afraid. Take your eyes off of your situation or what is to come, and look to Him who loves you. Nothing *in all creation will be able to separate* you from His love. It's His perfect gift to you, and it never fails!

"And she shall bring forth a son, and thou shalt call his name JESUS: for he shall save his people from their sins. Now all this was done, that it might be fulfilled which was spoken of the Lord by the prophet, saying, Behold, a virgin shall be with child, and shall bring forth a son, and they shall call his name Emmanuel, which being interpreted is, God with us."
Matthew 1:21-23 (KJV)

Matthew was one of Jesus' disciples. He had been a tax collector. One day Jesus saw him sitting in his tax booth and simply said, "Follow Me." Matthew got up, left his things, and followed Him. He walked with Jesus every day for over three years and was an eyewitness to His life and the miracles. In the verses prior to these, Mathew testifies that just before Mary, Jesus' mother, was about to marry Joseph, an angel of the Lord appeared to her. The angel told her God favored her among women, and she would have a child through the Holy Spirit. Mary agreed to God's will. Afterwards she told Joseph. Now Joseph was a righteous man who didn't want to publicly disgrace Mary, so he thought he would divorce her after they were married. But an angel of the Lord appeared to Joseph in a dream and told him to not be afraid to take Mary as his wife because what is conceived in her is from the Holy Spirit. The angel confirmed *Mary would have a son*, and they were to *call Him Jesus* because *He would save His people from their sin.*

In over 330 verses in the Old Testament the Prophets not only foretold Jesus' coming, but also every detail of His death. God made His purpose clear from the beginning. Jesus was sent on a mission of love to save God's people—to save "us" from our sin, death, and destruction. However, He also fulfilled another purpose in coming which was to bridge the gap between God and mankind, again, so we could have fellowship with our Father God. Verse 23 clearly states His purpose by saying *you will call Him Emmanuel*, which means *God with us.*

God wants us to know He isn't "out there" somewhere, but through Christ, He is right here—with you. He's right here…right now…right in the midst of your everyday needs. Maybe you're feeling it's just you and the world? Maybe you've never had anyone you could rely on to be there? The angel instructed Mary and then Joseph to not be afraid. Today, the angel would tell you the same thing. Don't be afraid. God loves you. No matter what you're facing, you can be assured through His promises, you aren't alone…God is always with you.

> *"For with God nothing is ever impossible, and no word from God shall be without power or impossible of fulfillment."*
> *Luke 1:37 (AMP)*

When the angel of the Lord appeared to Mary, Jesus' mother, and told her she was going to have a child, Mary asked how this could be since she was a virgin. The angel explained that the Holy Spirit would come upon her, and the power of the Most High would over-shadow her. He also told her the Holy One born would be called the Son of God. Then the angel told her Elizabeth, who was Mary's relative, was also six months pregnant. This, too, was a miracle because Elizabeth was old in age and had been barren. The angel told Mary *with God nothing is ever impossible.*

This is quite a statement. However, as I think back on the amazing things I've seen God do in my own life it just confirms we serve an awesome God. Many times I've heard the Holy Spirit tell me to do something, and I was glad I was sitting down at the time. "You want me to do what? Go where? This is way out of my league." But as I asked Him for the details, He explained to me the "how to" just like the angel told Mary. And if my faith started to weaken during the journey or I needed encouragement along the way, the Holy Spirit would remind me of a verse in Isaiah which asks, "Was it not you who dried up the sea, the waters of the great deep, who made a road in the depths of the sea so that the redeemed might cross over?" This verse is such a comfort to me because in remembering what God did for His people to bring them into their destiny also reminds me of what God has promised me…*and no word from God shall be without power or impossible fulfillment.* These verses boost my faith and remove any fear or unbelief that tries to come against me. If the Lord can make a "sidewalk" or road in the middle of the ocean for them—then He can do what I need, too!

After it rains the smallest puddle has sticky, soggy ground under it. Even after the water dries up, the ground itself stays wet for awhile. How many feet or miles would the ground have been wet under the Red Sea? God didn't just part those waters so His people could go through mud and muck to get across. They walked across on <u>dry</u> ground. If God would do that for His people then…then He'll do whatever it takes for you and me, His children, now. Are you looking at something that's too big for you? Do you feel like you're wading through mud just to make it? Or maybe you're stuck? Don't be afraid. Look to God's Word for your answers. This verse confirms there is both power and purpose in His Word. Use it! Use your faith, and you'll see the *impossible fulfillment* of your situation, too.

"No temptation has seized you except what is common to man. And God is faithful; he will not let you be tempted beyond what you can bear. But when you are tempted, he will also provide a way out so that you can stand up under it."
1 Corinthians 10:13 (NIV)

Many times the devil brings fear on an individual by telling them they are the only one going through their trials or they are the only one that feels this way or they are the only one that________, and so on. When temptation comes—and it will—it is the same weapon the devil has been using since the beginning. When he came to Eve he tricked her by asking, "Is this really what God said?" The devil is still deceiving people today with the same lies, "Are you sure you're hearing God? That's not the way God would do it! God couldn't possibly love someone like you. Go ahead—who's going to know?" Adam also bought the devil's lie, and we've all paid for it since then.

The Bible makes it clear that temptation doesn't come from God. He can't be tempted, nor does He tempt us. Temptations come from the devil, our own lusts, and selfish desires. However, God is still so good and faithful to us that He never lets the devil *tempt us beyond what we can bear.* What this really means is as His child, when we know what the Word says, take our authority, and use our faith regarding a matter, the enemy will never get the victory over us. Trials may come, but we won't be defeated.

The only way the devil can get control of us or the situation is if we give it to him. If we give in to the trap or swallow the bait he sets for us, we can fall into temptation because it fulfills our own evil lusts. Or when we see the "schemes" of the enemy, and we don't use the weapons God gave us—like His authority, Jesus' Name, the Word, and our faith, then we can also fall into temptation. In every situation, regardless of the circumstances, God has made a way of escape. You don't have to be afraid of temptation. He's given you the "Holy" Spirit, who dwells on the inside of you. There is no place you can go that He is not right there. When you "feel like" or you're being tempted to compromise your righteousness…you must stop, right then, and call on the Holy Spirit to give you wisdom and the strength you need to provide your way out. Have you fallen into the devil's trap? Don't be afraid. You don't have to stay trapped. Repent. Call on the Name of the Lord. He'll provide a way out. Ask the Holy Spirit to help you, and then, obey God! Resist the devil, and he and his temptations will flee.

"Now thanks be unto God, which always causeth us to triumph in Christ, and maketh manifest the savour of his knowledge by us in every place."
2 Corinthians 2:14 (KJV)

The AMP translation says, "Thanks be to God, who in Christ always leads us to triumph as trophies of Christ's victory." Everybody loves a winner and when we are adopted into God's family, we are winners. Not because of who we are, but because of who He is in us. Christ is our leader, and this verse confirms *He always causes us to triumph*, to achieve overcoming success. You may be thinking, "I don't feel like an overcomer? How is God able to cause things to always work out?" There is only one sure way to success…FOLLOW and STICK WITH GOD'S PLAN! Most of us have learned if you want to change anything—like your eating habits or exercise—the worst thing you can do is start, quit, then start, quit, then start again. Any professional will tell you the key to success is to stay with the program. God's path to victory is the same. He's given us great weapons for battle—His authority, His Word, and the power of Jesus' Name, but we have to keep using them with our faith. God's plan for us always works—*always leads us to triumph*—when we work His plan.

Do you need help? Would you like for Almighty God to show up on the scene? Then, in addition to using faith with your weapons, you must keep an attitude of thanksgiving and praise. The Bible says God inhabits or visits the praises of His people, not their complaints. I know this is difficult when you feel like you can't go through another day or you can't deal with one more medical test or you can't work with your boss or…the list goes on. But the Bible says the joy of the Lord is our strength. God said He would give us joy, and it would be unspeakable. Our thanks, praise, and joy give God an arena to work in. When the devil launches his greatest attack and you've still got your joy, you're singing and praising God, he won't stay. Fear leaves, and you'll see the victory.

Your victories make you a witness of the power of God, and you become Christ's trophies. People want to be around you. They want what you have, inner peace and joy. Before you ran a race, if you already knew you were going to win, wouldn't it make a difference in your confidence level? Don't be afraid. You're running God's race. You can have the same confidence because in Him you're guaranteed to win. Every lap…you'll beat the devil…every time.

"What agreement [can there be between] a temple of God and idols? For we are the temple of the living God; even as God said, I will dwell in and with and among them and will walk in and with and among them, and I will be their God, and they shall be my people."
2 Corinthians 6:16 (AMP)

Even if we fully understand God's plans and desires, it can still seem overwhelming. I mean, think about it, the God of the Universe wants to dwell on the inside of us, and He wants to make our bodies His home on earth—His temple. God says, "*I will walk in and with and among them, and I will be their God, and they shall be my people.*" With this knowledge, what crisis, trial, circumstance or situation could cause us fear? The Godhead, with all power and authority, is right here—in us. Who then could be against us?

Have you ever found yourself face to face with a bully? And at just the right moment someone showed up to come to your defense? Now you may be too old for the school bully, but when the devil shows up, huffing and puffing with a negative report and your name's on it, your first reaction is to feel the same way. You get that sinking feeling in the pit of your stomach. Fear, despair, and discouragement become like weights that hang from your neck and shoulders. These natural, physical responses to tragedy and drama are always fear based. This is part of the curse Adam brought on the earth when he sinned. However, Jesus became the curse for us and broke the power of the law of sin and death. This means if we belong to Christ, we are new creatures. We don't have to operate solely in the natural or by the flesh any longer. We have the power to operate by the Spirit of God who lives in us. The Holy Spirit gives us the power to conquer our natural feelings and emotions and bring them into agreement with what the Word of God says about our situation.

The Bible says we're to get rid of every thought or imagination that tries to exalt itself above God and to stop every thought in obedience to Christ. This means if it isn't what God says, then we stop thinking it and believing it. Don't be afraid. When the devil says you'll never get a job or a raise, you'll get rid of that lie because the Word says your promotions come from God, and He gives you the power to get wealth. If he tells you he's going to kill you…laugh. With our promise of eternal life, you can't threaten God's child with the fear of death. Just remember, God lives on the inside of <u>you</u>. He's not afraid. Why should you fear?

> *"And I will be a Father to you, and you shall be My sons and daughters, says the Lord Almighty."*
> *2 Corinthians 6:18 (AMP)*

God takes His position of being a Father seriously. The Bible says every time one person gives their life to Jesus and comes into the family of God, all of Heaven stops and rejoices. Think about it…the angels stop worshiping God and rejoice over your decision to become a part of the family. Why? Because they know how much it pleases God. His plan from the beginning involved being an active participant in our life. He likes communication and fellowship with us because He loves us, and when you love someone, you want to spend time with them. You want to know how their day went and everything else. Now, even though God already knows all of this, He still wants you to feel comfortable in sharing your most intimate thoughts and feelings with Him. You can talk to Him, just like you would your best friend.

One night while I was in prayer, several years after I came to know the Lord, I heard a voice say to me, "You know My Son very well, but you don't know Me at all." I realized I was talking with God the Father. I told Him, "I didn't know I could know You. I thought I just prayed to You, but I was to have the relationship with Jesus." He then said, "I created mankind to have fellowship with Me." I told Him I didn't know how to have a relationship with a father because my dad died when I was young." (Like He didn't already know this!) He said, "You had a wonderful father. If he was here today and you had a problem, wouldn't you be able to meet with him and tell him all about it?" I said, "Yes." He said, "And if he didn't have all the answers, wouldn't he call someone or research it in order to help you?" I said, "Yes." Then He said, "And would he say he might tell you the answer right then or maybe in a day or two or he would tell you whenever he felt like it?" I said, "No, he wouldn't." Very adamantly God said, "Neither will I, and I won't need to call anyone because I have all the answers. If you come expecting an answer from Me, just like with your dad, you'll get one."

This conversation changed my life. All those years the devil lied to me about being fatherless. I had to make up for a lot of time. I wanted to know what God thought about everything. I asked—He told me. For whatever reasons, if you grew up without a dad, you don't have to be fatherless any longer. Don't be afraid. God had always wanted to be my Father, and He wants to be yours. Will you let God be your Dad? Trust me when I tell you, "Your life will never be the same."

NOVEMBER 12

"And God is able to make all grace (every favor and earthly blessing) come to you in abundance, so that you may always and under all circumstances and whatever the need, be self-sufficient—possessing enough to require no aid or support and furnished in abundance for every good work and charitable donation."
2 Corinthians 9:8 (AMP)

God is able to make all grace abound to us. Grace is His unmerited favor. We didn't do one thing to deserve His goodness or favor, except—accept His Son, Jesus. When we make Jesus the Lord and Savior of our life, we are entitled to the grace of God because we are now heirs of His Kingdom.

The original covenant God established with Abraham brought many blessings. He owned a lot of land, much livestock, and He had many servants. In fact, when his nephew Lot had been captured and was being held hostage, Abraham gathered 318 trained men that had been born in his own household to go with him to free Lot. There was a time when he was offered money and possessions from one of the kings, but Abraham refused them. He didn't want anyone to say that man had made him rich. His blessings were from his covenant with God. The Bible says we are heirs of this same covenant through Christ.

God intended for us to be wealthy, but not just for our own selfish desires. We're blessed to be a blessing. God doesn't expect us to live in inadequate housing or not be able to drive our car of choice. However, He does expect us to tithe and give into every charitable work, which furthers the truth of the Gospel through preaching, teaching, and healing. God cares about the poor. He cares about your 'single parent' neighbor who struggles to feed the kids and keep the lights on. He cares about the elderly or widow who can't keep their yard up or house painted. God has made His riches available to us, so we aren't bogged down with the fear of lack or "not enough." This verse confirms *He has already made His grace and favor come to you in abundance.*

Do you call on His grace? Are you expecting favor? Do you use faith and speak to your area of insufficiency? Don't be afraid. His blessings are for everyone. This verse assures us it is God's will and plan for us to have what we need—in abundance—all sufficiency in every area. Accept God's plan of grace, and experience His divine favor. Don't wait to join His family. You'll become an inheritor in the greatest covenant of blessings, too.

NOVEMBER 13

*"As for those who seemed to be important—
whatever they were makes no difference to me;
God does not judge by external appearance—
those men added nothing to my message."
Galatians 2:6 (NIV)*

The Apostle Paul had dealt with many men both for and against the Gospel of Jesus. He found there are always those who want to use their position or appearance to persuade people toward their own mission. Paul was not intimidated or impressed by either, good or bad, and he makes it clear, neither is God. God never looks at the outward part of man. Instead, He looks at the intent of a man's heart. The devil can use our appearance and our abilities, or the lack of them, to bring fear. He tries to get us to play the comparison game. If "so and so" has the looks, brains, right background, etc., then they will always come out on top. We'll create handicaps for ourselves if we try to compare. In the world you hear "man" referred to as body, soul, and spirit. However, the Bible refers to us as spirit, soul, and body. What's the difference? The world works toward being important...beautiful...changing the outward appearance to impress others or to feel fulfilled. But God prepares and changes the heart. He works from the inside out. The Word says the outward man perishes daily, but the spirit of a man lives forever, that is if He has accepted God's plan of salvation.

Jesus told a parable about three men. Their master gave each of them talents, according to their own abilities. One man got five, another two, and the third man received one talent. When the master returned from his trip, he asked each man what they had done with their talents. The man with five doubled his, the man with two doubled his, but the man with one had buried his talent out of fear, so he wouldn't lose it. He gave the one talent back to his master and was rebuked for not using what he had. The one talent was taken from him and given to another. Fear will keep us from receiving all God has for us, too. The devil will try to tell you—you aren't good enough, you can't make a difference or who do you think you are? The enemy's purpose is to keep us focused on the outer man and our shortcomings. The Bible says <u>we can do all things through Christ who strengthens us</u>. This doesn't sound like it takes much qualification on our part. Don't be afraid. If God has given you one talent—don't bury it. Your one is just what is needed, and it's as important as the two, five or ten. Be faithful to what you've been given. Don't compare. God knows your heart. That's what really matters to Him.

> *"For we are God's [own] handiwork (His workmanship), recreated in Christ Jesus, [born anew] that we may do those good works which God predestined (planned beforehand) for us, (taking paths which He prepared ahead of time) that we should walk in them—living the good life which He prearranged and made ready for us to live."*
> *Ephesians 2:10 (AMP)*

The Bible says God is the potter and we are the clay. This verse supports this by stating we are *His handiwork...His workmanship.* The potter doesn't create any two vessels the same, and neither does God. Our fingerprints prove this. God has always had a rich plan, *which He prepared beforehand* for each one of us based on our own individual uniqueness. His plan is thorough. It accomplishes what He desires, so we can *live the good life.* It brings us more success than any plan, of our own design, could ever bring.

When we accept the Lord, the Bible says we become new creations. This is when our transformation begins. Life would be so much easier if we knew about these things from birth or at least at a young age. However, I was twenty-seven, married and divorced before I surrendered my life to the Lord for Him to do what He wanted with me. By that time this vessel not only had some nicks and cracks, but a few bumps that needed major sanding. I know that sounds painful, and some of it was, but it was my own fault. I needed healing from deep emotional wounds that had come from living my life, my way.

Why did it take me so long to give my life to the Lord? I bought the devil's lie that God's plan was boring, unfulfilling, and I was afraid to trust Him. Now, after walking with the Lord all these years and following His "great" plan, I can't believe I listened to the devil. Does this mean that bumps don't pop up anymore? No, I'm still a work in progress, and the devil does his part to bring offense and division. But when opposition arises, I know God loves me, and the Bible says what the enemy means for harm, God will turn it to good. His Word isn't just for me...it's also for you. Maybe you've bought the devil's lies? Are you afraid to trust God? Are you afraid to accept His plan for your life? Don't be afraid. God beforehand—predestined you to a plan of love, *to walk on a path that was prearranged and made ready for the good life.* Trust the potter to shape and mold you ...become *His handiwork.* You will be transformed into the most glorious vessel He's recreated you to be in Christ Jesus.

"Draw nigh to God, and he will draw nigh to you."
James 4:8a (KJV)

James, the brother of Jesus, writes this to confirm that God, under no circumstance, ever turns anyone away who comes to Him. God doesn't beckon us and the Holy Spirit "woo" us into accepting the Lord, and then the moment we say "Yes" this loud voice says, "I object." When you move close to God, He doesn't look through a book to see what you have or haven't done. He doesn't check your credit rating or whether you're single, married, divorced or remarried. It doesn't matter whether you have a GED, PHD, or a title at all. He doesn't verify you're employment or if you've ever worked a day in your life. This verse clearly states God's unconditional acceptance of us, and His unconditional love to us. When you come to Him, He will come to you.

The devil has used every lie in the book to keep us from God. When we choose life, as the Bible says, the enemy knows he's defeated. Oh, sure, he will continue to set his traps and tempt us with the things we once thought were enjoyable. But the truth is we aren't the same. When the Bible says we become new and the old man has passed away, it's true. Things that we may have desired before now don't seem to spark any interest. God washes away the old sin, and now, we can start new. We can start again.

What lie has the devil told you to keep you from coming near to God? Maybe he's told you God doesn't like drug addicts, and you know you can't quit? Maybe he's convinced you divorce is a sin, God hates divorce, and now hates you? Maybe you've killed someone, and you know the Bible says, "Thou shalt not kill," so there is no way God could come near to you? The foundation to these lies and any of the devil's lies is fear. He tries to make us afraid to believe God and to take Him at His Word. However, the Bible says God is not a man who lies, and the devil is the father of all lies. Now, who do you think you should believe?

God has loved you from the beginning. No, God does not like sin, but because of the blood of His Son, Jesus, which was spread on the mercy seat, God no longer sees the sin of those who have come to Jesus. He now sees us through the atoning blood of Christ. Don't be afraid. God's already done His part. Now He's waiting for you to make the next move. If you draw nigh or come close to Him—just the way you are—you can be totally and completely assured—He will come close to you.

> *"For He says, In the time of favor (of an assured welcome) I have listened to and heeded your call, and I have helped you on the day of deliverance—the day of salvation. Behold, now is truly the time for a gracious welcome and acceptance [of you from God]; behold, now is the day of salvation!"*
> *2 Corinthians 6:2 (AMP)*

Behold...or take heed and listen...the Lord is saying, "*This is the day of salvation.*" Why would the Lord be so bold as to declare that this is the day of salvation? He is declaring it because He knows no one knows the day or hour of their natural death. He also knows no man knows the day and hour of Christ's return, except the Father. Jesus Himself does not know. It's a huge gamble to wait. In fact, it could be the most fatal bet of a lifetime.

I ask you, "Why are you waiting? What do you think will happen if you accept the Lord?" Maybe you belong to a different religion? Will your family disown you? Maybe you could even face death or other persecution? Maybe you just don't think your life is that bad and you need a Savior? Whatever your reason or excuse, it won't stand up on judgment day. The Bible says on that last day the Book of Life will be opened. If you have accepted the Lord, your name will be written there. This means you will have eternal life with the Lord forever. If you haven't, then you will be cast into hell to suffer and be tormented for all eternity.

This shouldn't be a hard decision. God loves you, and He made a way of escape from this sinful world and your sinful past, so you could live in the bounty He has planned. This verse confirms *God's favor is ready to welcome us* when we come to Him. The moment we call, *He heeds our call.* Instantly He comes into our heart to change us and make us new. Is your life really so great that it could compare to the heavenly life God has planned for you? Is what you're doing so much fun that you would be willing to die for it? Go to hell and be tormented forever? God doesn't want us afraid, but hell should be feared. It is a real place, and anyone who has had a near death experience...went to hell and came back, reported hell was the most horrific place. They didn't really have the words to describe the pain, anguish, and torment they witnessed and even felt. You have a choice, but hell is not the Father's plan. Don't be afraid. Your Father loves you and wants you to be with Him forever. Behold—listen! Call on Him. He'll deliver you. He'll save you...TODAY!

> *"NOW FAITH is the assurance (the confirmation, the title-deed) of the things [we] hope for, being the proof of things [we] do not see and the conviction of their reality—faith perceiving as real fact what is not revealed to the senses."*
> *Hebrews 11:1 (AMP)*

The Bible says "faith" is what pleases God. It isn't the ability to quote half the Bible or to understand deep theological theories. Although knowing and understanding the Word is important, anyone who has walked with God for any length of time knows it only takes <u>One</u> <u>Word</u> from God to change your life, forever. When God gives you a Scripture to stand on or tells you through prayer what your next move is, that Word from Him is alive. That Word becomes a "Rhema" word or a "Now" word for your situation, and you can base and release your faith on it. You believe what you "know" to be true, by the Spirit, as opposed to what you can visibly see in the natural.

Maybe you're wondering, "How do you know if you're using faith?" There are several important things to know about faith. You need to know how faith comes, how faith works, and then how to release your faith. The Bible says <u>faith comes</u> by hearing and hearing by the Word of God. So in order to have faith, you must know what the Word says. You keep the Word of God before you in your eyes and in your ears. <u>Faith works</u> when you know what to do with it. Believing God can heal, just because He's God, isn't enough. Believing God will 'magically' make everything OK, just because you believe He's real or exists, isn't enough, either. If you "believe" a doctor can help with a diagnosis or treatment, but you don't ever go to see one, will you be helped? And if you "believe" the medicine they give you will work, but you don't take it, will you be helped? And they wouldn't give you heart medicine for a broken toe, would they? They're specialized in their help. So is God. We need to be specific with the Word we use for our particular need, too. Then we <u>release faith</u> by applying it to our current situation. We put the "Rhema" word in our mouth, we speak it out—continually, we believe it's done, and we don't change our confession until it's visible in the natural.

Faith is alive. It is a firm foundation, a conviction, a positive persuasion that what you hope for, believe, and have asked God for in prayer, will come to pass. Faith believes you receive it now…when you pray. Don't be afraid. Faith always defeats fear. Use your faith. It works, and it also pleases God.

"Do not, therefore, fling away your fearless confidence, for it carries a great and glorious compensation of reward. For you have need of steadfast patience and endurance, so that you may perform and fully accomplish the will of God, and thus receive and carry away [and enjoy to the full] what is promised. For still a little while—a very little while—and the Coming One will come and He will not delay."
Hebrews 10:35-37 (AMP)

This "*fearless confidence*" exists because of our faith. Faith in God, faith in His Son Jesus, faith that Christ died and was raised up, faith that He sits beside the Father in Heaven, and faith He is coming again for His family of believers. By faith we have confidence that because we have used or released our faith, believed, and obeyed Him, we will be rewarded. The Bible says God rewards those who diligently seek Him. What is this reward? It is the knowledge that on that final day we will be with the Father and our Lord, forever. We will reign with Christ over the earth because we are joint heirs with Him. I would say this is quite a long-term compensation package for being obedient in following His plan now.

However, there is a difference between confidence and arrogance. Many years ago the press criticized a famous athlete for his boasting or constant bragging. I'll never forget his reply, "If you can do it…it ain't brag." This guy truly was a gifted player and could do the stuff. However, it made me think of the promises of God. God can deliver the stuff, too. So when I believe and use my faith based on what God said He could do and not on what I think I can do…then I can have the same kind of confidence. I don't have to be afraid that this or that won't work. All I have to do is know what God says about it, believe it, and use my faith until it presents itself in the natural.

God hasn't changed, and neither has the Word. He is faithful to complete what He has started in each of our lives. This verse says there is a great reward for those who patiently wait for our Lord's return. Don't be afraid. The Old Testament had are over 330 prophecies telling of His first coming. There are twice that many in the New Testament about His return. Why so many? Well, even after it was prophesied, not everyone was ready or believed Him, and God wants to make sure this time we're prepared. He is coming back for a church without spot or blemish. If you are washed in His blood, this means you! Your faith will produce an eternal harvest. Hold on to it, and receive your reward!

"But Jesus immediately said to them:
'Take courage! It is I. Don't be afraid."
Matthew 14:27 (NIV)

Jesus sent His disciples to go across the lake in a boat without Him. He went up the mountain to pray and to be with the Father. Later, He joined them by walking on the water. When they saw Him they were afraid and thought they were seeing things. The Lord comforted them with the above verse. Then Peter said, "Lord, if it's you, bid me to come." It was the Lord, so He said, "Come." Peter got out of the boat and started to walk on the water to get to Jesus. The waves were high and rough. After a few steps, Peter looked down. Fear came over him. He started to sink. He cried out to the Lord for help, and Jesus instantly took his hand. They walked back on the water together and got into the boat. Jesus said, "You of little faith. Why did you doubt?"

Let's look at what really happened. Jesus gave Peter a command. Peter instantly obeyed, and God's power was there to hold him up to do what He had commanded. Peter took his eyes off the Lord to look at the seriousness of the circumstances that surrounded him. He sank. Jesus saves him. Then Jesus tells him why he failed…he began to doubt, and he used little faith. This is the same reason most of us fail today. Fear and faith can't operate at the same time. If you believe and speak the Word, but later in desperation claim "this will never happen," you've canceled out your faith. Remember, faith doesn't speak what it sees or feels. It speaks the truth. It only speaks what God says.

Peter is no different than most of us. However, he's the disciple that usually gets picked on because he was always shooting off his mouth. He tried to stop the crucifixion, and Christ had to rebuke satan from him. He told the Lord he would never deny Him, but he did it three times. He gets out of the boat and sank. But the truth is Peter was the only one who had the courage to make a move. He was the one the Father spoke to in identifying Jesus as the Christ, the Son of the Living God. He was the one who preached on the Day of Pentecost and 3000 came to the Lord. He was the one whose shadow healed the sick. Peter made major blunders, and yet, God forgave and used him mightily. Have you made so many mistakes you're afraid of God? Have you shot your mouth off and failed? Maybe you stepped out and now wish you hadn't? Maybe you're still failing because you won't follow God? Whatever the case…*Take courage. Don't be afraid.* Get your eyes back on the Master. Use your faith. He'll raise you up and position you for great things, too.

NOVEMBER 20

> *"But after that the kindness and love of God our Saviour toward man appeared, Not by works of righteousness which we have done, but according to his mercy he saved us, by the washing of regeneration, and renewing of the Holy Ghost; Which he shed on us abundantly through Jesus Christ our Saviour; That being justified by his grace, we should be made heirs according to the hope of eternal life."*
> *Titus 3:4-7 (KJV)*

The motivation for God's entire and original plan was love, kindness, mercy and grace. The Apostle Paul writes this to Titus who had traveled with him on an earlier missionary trip, but was now the leader of a church. It is apparent that mankind, both then and now, still want to do "works" for their salvation, but this verse confirms it is *not by works of righteousness, but according to His mercy.* God has a great benefit package for His children, both now and later. However, only we can decide our final destination for eternity—Heaven or hell.

We usually think of hell as being full of liars, cheaters, murderers, and basically the bad guys from earth. This is true in part, but an earthly crime is not what sends people to hell. The Bible says if anyone believes in his heart and confesses with his mouth that Jesus is his Savior…HE WILL BE SAVED!" We've all sinned, and this statement alone removes any fear that salvation is only for the good. Jesus came to save that which was lost. You and I are the lost. It's only God's kindness and mercy that offers us a washing and renewing by the Holy Ghost. This verse confirms how important the finished work of the cross is to each one of us because none of us could have "worked" hard enough to "earn" righteousness. Salvation is ours—a free gift—and it's salvation that gives us access to the Holy Spirit, and it's the Holy Spirit who gives us power to overcome sin and the other things on earth that try to destroy us.

The Bible says, once we're born again, sin no longer has dominion over us. Maybe you're afraid you can't live up to God's expectations? Or you think you need to wait until you can clean your act up? Don't be afraid. You can't work or earn righteousness, but you can be saved. You can be justified by His grace through Jesus Christ, the Savior. He not only makes you righteous, but you'll now become an *heir* of all the promises *according to the hope of eternal life.* Can you ask for more than that?

"This Jesus God raised up, and of that all we [His disciples] are witnesses. Being therefore lifted high by the right hand of God, and having received from the Father the promised [blessing which is the] Holy Spirit, He has made this outpouring you yourselves both see and hear."
Acts 2:32-33 (AMP)

One of the main differences between Christianity and other religions is the Christian's God is alive. However, Christianity isn't supposed to be a religion... it's a lifestyle...a relationship with Jesus Christ. When religion honors an earthly man as God, regardless of their greatness, they are still just men, and mankind dies. If religion honors an animal or a plant, although these may be alive, they have no feelings, nor can they relate to man's nature or needs. Other religions may honor a statue of stone, wood or metal. The question is "What difference does it make if the God you worship is dead or alive?" The greatest difference is you can't have a conversation or a close relationship with someone or something that can't respond to you or understand your needs.

Jesus Himself was limited to His earthly body while He was here. If you wanted to see or touch Him, you had to be in the same city or vicinity. But this verse confirms *the disciples were witnesses* to Christ being raised from the dead and His ascension into Heaven to be with the Father. Today, because of the Holy Spirit, we all have the same power that raised Christ within us, which makes God omnipresent. This means He is present every where at all times. When God said He was with us, He wasn't kidding. He is with us wherever we go, every hour of every day, all three hundred sixty-five days a year. God is also omniscient. This means He is all knowing. He has universal knowledge and insight into each one of our lives. Why is this important? Because it gives us our unique relationship with Him. We know He understands us and everything we're going through, too. But this isn't all. Our God is also omnipotent. This means He is not limited in His creative power. When I need Him to do a miracle in my life, it doesn't stop Him from doing miracles in a million other people's lives at the very same time.

Jesus was raised up by the Holy Spirit. He is alive and with the Father, and now, we can receive *the promised blessing, which is the Holy Spirit* to come and live within us, too. Don't be afraid. All the benefits of a living-loving God can belong to us when we choose God's plan. Let the Holy Spirit fill you, and you will complete your destiny and live a life that is filled with victory.

"But now the righteousness of God has been revealed independently and altogether apart from law, although actually it is attested by the Law and the prophets, Namely, the righteousness of God which comes by believing with personal trust and confident reliance on Jesus Christ, the Messiah. [And it is meant] for all who believe. For there is no distinction, Since all have sinned and are falling short of the honor and glory which God bestows and receives."
Romans 3:21-23 (AMP)

In these verses the Apostle Paul explains that God's plan of righteousness is revealed or known to man through faith in God's Son, Jesus Christ. Although this is separate from Old Testament law, the Prophets announced or attested over 330 times what was to come in the birth, death, and resurrection of the Lord Jesus. "He" is how we are made to be righteous. We personally believe, trust, rely, and have faith in what Christ, the Messiah, did for us on the cross. And since this verse states *all have sinned and fallen short of the honor and glory of God,* then we know His plan of salvation is for all, too.

For all those who believe, there is freedom and deliverance from every form of fear and evil. The devil will try to trick you into falling for the standard lies, but once you know the truth, it sets you free. Why is it important to know we're righteous? Because being righteous makes us holy and this puts us in a right standing position with God. Why is this important? Because it eliminates any fear that would keep us from marching straight into God's throne room for our personal and intimate times with Him. So now when the enemy says, "Who do you think you are? Or you don't qualify to be holy," YOU can laugh because YOU know the truth. The truth is, in and of ourselves we aren't and never would be righteous, but you know and have believed in the One who is.

Do you believe His Word? Have you asked for forgiveness of your sins and accepted the Lord? Don't be afraid. Through Christ you're restored to a right or holy position with the Father. The work has already been done...it's paid for... and nothing has the power to change it. Confidently trust and believe Him. His "Holy" Word says, "You are the righteousness of God in Christ Jesus." If God says it, all we have to do is believe it!

"[All] are justified and made upright and in right standing with God, freely and gratuitously by His grace (His unmerited favor and mercy), through the redemption which is [provided] in Christ Jesus. Whom God put forward [before the eyes of all] as a mercy seat and propitiation by His blood—the cleansing and life-giving sacrifice of atonement and reconciliation—[to be received] through faith. This was to show God's righteousness, because in His divine forbearance He had passed over and ignored former sins without punishment. It was to demonstrate and prove at the present time (in the now season) that He Himself is righteous and that He justifies and accepts as righteous him who has [true] faith in Jesus."
Romans 3:24-26 (AMP)

These verses sum up God's position…why it was necessary for Jesus to come, and why we need to believe in the Lord. When Adam sinned and death came upon the earth, God allowed the priests to sacrifice an animal to cover everyone's sin for one year. But no one ever paid for or was punished for the sin that first began with Adam, and then continued throughout the generations. The Bible says the wages of sin is death. Since God is just, someone was going to have to pay the price for us to be restored to a blameless, holy, right standing relationship with the Father. That someone was Jesus. His sinless blood was the propitiation or our substitute for the death penalty that came through sin. God's plan of redemption is free, and anyone who accepts it is not only restored or reconciled to fellowship with Him, but receives power over fear and the enemy.

It is important that we understand what happened to us and what God did to correct it. The Bible says we've all sinned, and sin separates us from God. He is holy. Sin loudly declares we're not. The devil uses this to lie and bring fear concerning our worth, purpose, and the ability to be loved. Sin brought death, but God wasn't going to let His own perish. So according to God's Word, which He cannot break, the punishment or price for sin had to be paid. Jesus' sacrifice made sure we were cleansed of our sin and our worth or righteousness was restored. Don't be afraid. Isn't it a relief to know when you accept Jesus everything you've ever done is removed? Don't wait. Accept Jesus. These verses confirm God will *accept, justify, and call righteous all who believe and have true faith in Jesus*.

> *"Now the Lord is the Spirit, and where the Spirit of the Lord is, there is liberty—emancipation from bondage, freedom."*
> *2 Corinthians 3:17 (AMP)*

For most of us, when we hear words like *bondage* or *emancipation*, we instantly think of slavery. Slavery isn't just a part of history. It still occurs in many parts of the world today. Webster's Dictionary defines slavery as, "drudgery; toil; submission to a dominating influence; the practice of slave holding." Bondage is, "the state of being bound by compulsion (as of law or mastery); captivity; servitude or subjugation to a controlling person or force." As you can see, slavery or bondage isn't just isolated to being someone's slave. Everyday many live with the same fears and "drudgery" that comes from being under the influence of a controlling, dominating person or force.

This verse states *where the Spirit of the Lord is there is freedom—liberty.* How can the Spirit of God bring freedom? The Spirit lives on the inside of you. He is the Spirit of truth, and the first truth you'll find is no matter what you do, good or bad, it has no bearing on who you are in Christ and what God has called you to do. God loves you...period. This love destroys fear—fear of what the devil may bring, and the fear of man. The world is caught up in titles: He's a doctor, she's an attorney, they're a teacher, etc. Depending on the profession and whether or not the world considers it a higher or lower status, it will try to determine your self-worth. You can literally be in bondage to your career. When the Spirit lives on the inside of you, you already know you're worthy. You are so loved and special that God sent His Son to die for you. Your worth is who He is in you. Now you can have joy and peace that no man, money, title or status can give.

The Spirit of God also has the power to deliver you from whatever "force" it is that's trying to control you—addictions, weight, pornography, anger, rage, credit card debt, an abusive relationship or maybe you're a shopaholic or a workaholic. Any of it can put you in bondage. Fear starts talking with, "It will never change ...you'll never be free." This is a lie. The truth—the Word says there is freedom, liberty in the Spirit of the Lord. Don't be afraid. Bondage is not of God. He sent His Spirit to live in us, to be with us, to make sure we have freedom, regardless of the battles we're facing. The Holy Spirit knows what you need. Seek the presence of the Lord, His Spirit...the Spirit of all truth, and discover peace, liberty, and true freedom for yourself.

"And He has said to me, 'My grace is sufficient for you, for power is perfected in weakness.' Most gladly, therefore, I will rather boast about my weaknesses, that the power of Christ may dwell in me."
2 Corinthians 12:9 (NASB)

The Apostle Paul directs us in how to handle those times when we're feeling frail or weak. Fear talks—and it always speaks negatively. It degrades, intimidates, and your physical body reacts when the lies start. Every excuse goes through your head from your background, education, gender, training, and so on. These areas, even if they do exist, are not handicaps to God. Paul wants us to understand when we're weak—don't have the skill, ability or seem unequipped in the natural—we are then forced to lean and depend upon the Holy Ghost to teach and instruct us. Paul learned when he was in over his head, it always turned out great because he trusted, prayed, and relied on God. It appeared as if he were strong. That's why *he would rather be weak and boast in the Lord*. He learned he could do all things through Christ who strengthens him. We will, too, if we won't be afraid to trust God.

Paul was taken to Heaven and shown many things. Afterwards, he was attacked three times by the same thing. Each time Paul asked God to remove it, but the Lord said, "*My grace is sufficient.*" Paul explains these attacks were a messenger sent from satan to torment and buffet him. In other words, this messenger was a tormenting devil. What's a tormenting devil? It's a devil, specifically assigned to steal your peace by whatever means possible. This demon was sent to harass Paul and to distract him from his mission. How did he do this? One way could have been to attack Paul's thoughts by reminding him of his past. What about his record as a killer? He brought death in the past, but now he thinks he can bring life through the Gospel? Even if people listened, who would believe him? Wouldn't they think he's unstable, losing his mind? After all, "Didn't you hate Christians, Paul, but now you say you love them?" This devil also stirred up hatred in the Leader's hearts, which brought major persecution. But through it all, Paul learned his past failures wouldn't keep him from fulfilling God's plan—God's grace was complete.

Maybe the devil is tormenting you about your past? Is he trying to distract you from God's plan? Don't be afraid. Even in your weakness, God will still turn evil to good. Call on His grace. It is sufficient. You'll find like Paul did that you'd rather *boast of your weaknesses, that the power of Christ may dwell in you*, too.

"We did not follow cleverly invented stories when we told you about the power and coming of our Lord Jesus Christ, but we were eyewitnesses of his majesty. For he received honor and glory from God, the Father when the voice came to him from the Majestic Glory, saying, 'This is my Son, whom I love; with him I am well pleased.' We ourselves heard this voice that came from heaven when we were with him on the sacred mountain."
2 Peter 1:16-18 (NIV)

Peter, Jesus' disciple, gives us the *eyewitness* account of their mountain top experience with the Lord. He makes it clear, no one "made up" what they heard and know in their hearts to be true. What an experience—hearing God's voice validating who Jesus was and that God was pleased with Him. How could you forget an incident like this one? The truth is you can't. This is exactly why God had witnesses. When the devil brings fear he always questions the truth. Think about it—doesn't it usually start with some kind of question, "What are you ___?" or "What if they___?" Eve was deceived by his question. Since he can't create anything new, he tries to use the same techniques on us.

When it comes to the Bible, people for generations have questioned the validity of the Word. Did this really happen? Aren't these just "stories" like our fairy tales? I mean, how could three boys be tossed into a fiery furnace and not only live, but come out without smelling like smoke? How does one spend the night in a hole in the ground with man-eating lions and live? How does a young boy kill a giant with a slingshot and one stone? Did Jesus really walk on the water? Was He really the Son of God? How does a virgin get pregnant? Did he hang on the cross? Was He truly raised from the dead? All these questions and more are clearly answered in the Word. The Old Testament verifies these testimonies through witnesses, and so does the New. The disciples, other men and women, all those who traveled with Jesus, and the historians of the day recorded the events. All supported the truth, the Word.

Satan is the father of lies. Why wouldn't he start the master of all lies by trying to discredit the Word? It's the Word that gives us our faith, and it's our faith in all of God's Word that empowers us to be delivered and defeat the devil at the same time. Don't be afraid. The Word of God is true...EVERY WORD. It is God inspired, God breathed to bring you abundant life, peace, and total wholeness.

"Above all, you must understand that no prophecy of Scripture came about by the prophet's own interpretation. For prophecy never had its origin in the will of men, but men spoke from God as they were carried along by the Holy Spirit."
2 Peter 1:20-21 (NIV)

Regardless of the man's hand that penned it, Peter clarifies once again for accuracy and the record that the Word of God is inspired by the Holy Ghost. The Holy Ghost is the voice of God in the earth. This is vital to the foundation of our faith, since faith comes by hearing the Word. If the Word weren't true—to be taken literally—then how could we build any kind of a firm foundation? Or if we could pick and choose the parts we liked and wanted to believe, then what makes one part more accurate than another? These verses and many others confirm the Word was carried to men by the Holy Spirit, and if He wrote it—He can also interpret it for us today.

The Holy Spirit is right here with us, waiting to guide us and instruct us in all truth. Why would we have to "figure it out" or be afraid when the original author is still available to tell us exactly what it means? Besides, when the prophets of old foretold the birth and coming of Christ they called Him their King, a deliverer. How could you "think up" a king and then have Him born in a manger in a stable? Or that He would be born to a virgin girl? How could you be as specific and detailed as Isaiah was in describing the beatings and punishment that would be inflicted upon Christ at the cross and how it would bring us the ultimate victory? How could David see the Lord seated at the Father's right hand and know He would one day be with Him, when the Lord hadn't even been born, yet, let alone resurrected? These men had no way of knowing future events except by the Spirit of God and the Father's desire to reveal them.

God's Word is living proof. He has never wanted us to be in the dark. He told us, from the beginning, His plan for us now and in the future. He gave us His written Word as our manual for life, and these instructions are easy to follow. Through His Son, Jesus Christ, He's defeated the devil and removed all worry, anxiety, and fear. Have you had questions about the Word? Has the devil tried to tell you, "You can't understand the Bible?" Don't be afraid. Talk to the Spirit…WHO KNOWS…and lives in you. Jesus sent Him to guide you into all truth. The good news is when you consult with Him, you'll have wisdom that applies to every area of your life.

"For I will give you words and wisdom that none of your adversaries will be able to resist or contradict."
Luke 21:15 (NIV)

Jesus warned His disciples of all the tragedies and perils of this life, especially for their obedience in following Him and His teachings. He prophesied things to come for them and for Jerusalem, even until the end of time. Although He tried to prepare them for the upcoming dangers, He also wanted to encourage them. The Bible says all things are possible with God, and when you know you have *His words and wisdom* for any occasion, it eliminates fear. Today, we have the same promise against our enemies.

How many times have you been in a situation and afterwards thought, "Why didn't I say this or that" or "If I could only think fast on my feet?" If you believe this verse, you can ask God to fill your mouth with *His words and wisdom,* and the Spirit of God will prompt you to speak what is needed in every circumstance. Now if you think fast on your feet, you might be thinking, "I don't need help. I always know what to say." Do you? You have never said anything, and then later wished you hadn't? Much damage is done everyday by words, especially those done in jest or kidding. The Bible is very clear we either bring life or death by what comes out of our mouth. Our words not only affect us, but they also affect all those we come in contact with, too.

In the many years I've counseled, one of the main areas has been to help people overcome the effects of what others have said to them, and to help them recognize the destructive behavioral patterns that were established because of it. Negative words create an atmosphere of death, doubt, and fear. Are you still recovering from words spoken over you as a child by your parents, another relative or maybe even your teacher? Do you still view yourself through the eyes and words of someone else? Do you now speak harshly or are even rude because of what past words have done to you? The enemy knows there is power in words and he's using them to destroy you. Don't be afraid. God's Word brings life, and it gives us faith to believe what He says. Words from your past have no power to talk to you today. If they don't line up with what God says, get rid of them. Speak God's Word. He will fill your mouth with the right words—life words—so you will always be prepared.

NOVEMBER 29

> *"Heaven and earth shall pass away,*
> *but my words shall not pass away."*
> *Luke 21:33 (KJV)*

Why would Jesus have thought it was important to give this Word to His disciples? What hope, comfort or encouragement did He believe this would bring to them? What does it really mean? In the short three and a half years Jesus taught and did the work of His Father, it is recorded only thirty-four days of it were spent ministering to the crowds. The majority of His time was spent with the disciples, teaching them the words and ways of God. He wanted them trained and prepared to continue preaching the Gospel after He finished His Father's business and ascended to Heaven to be by His side.

The Bible says, "In the beginning was God, and the Word was with God, and the Word was God." It also says when God, through Jesus, came to earth, that the Word was made flesh and dwelt or lived among us. The Word is God living among us today. Do you now understand if the Word "IS" God that when you use it, there is more than enough power to change any and every situation? When Jesus spoke this verse to His disciples, He wanted them to know when they used His Words and His Name, the same power was available to them for the same results.

The disciples did come to know and witness this truth. On one occasion Peter and John saw a man, who had been crippled since birth, being carried to the temple gate to beg for money. They walked over to the man and told him to look at them. Then, because he was expecting money, they told him they weren't going to give him money, but they would give him what they had. Peter took him by the hand and said, "In the Name of Jesus Christ of Nazareth, walk." The man jumped to his feet and began to walk. They spoke the "Word—God," used Jesus' Name, and the man received his miracle, which is what he really needed. Money wouldn't have delivered him, but the Word made flesh was enough to free him of this infirmity.

The Words of God are as powerful today as they were in the beginning. They are God, and this verse confirms *they will never pass away* because God will never pass away. When we speak them in faith, in Jesus' Name, we can expect the same results. Are you crippled? Financially, emotionally, physically? Don't be afraid. God is faithful to His Word, and He will bring it to pass. It worked then—it will work again. Use it. Believe it, and receive your miracle.

NOVEMBER 30

> *"While we look not at the things which are seen, but at the things which are not seen: for the things which are seen are temporal; but the things which are not seen are eternal."*
> *2 Corinthians 4:18 (KJV)*

One of the ways the enemy steals our joy and peace is to keep us focused on the things around us. Why? Because if we stay focused on what we see, whether the circumstances are positive or negative, it takes our eyes off the Lord and the victory in His Word. We won't fulfill the lust of the flesh when we look unto the author and finisher of our faith, and we choose to follow the Spirit of truth's guidance. The devil knows this. That's why he creates such a huge disturbance in the natural as a "smoke screen" to distract you from doing what you know to do in the midst of a crisis. However, all of these circumstances are subject to change because they are only temporary. God's Word is permanent…forever.

In this verse the Apostle Paul instructs us to stay focused on what has true or lasting value. He wants us to see there is a greater goal, a greater plan, and this plan isn't temporary. It doesn't bring satisfaction for just a moment. It brings fulfillment for a lifetime and beyond. Whether you're being beaten and living in jail, like Paul, or you're just trying to raise your kids in today's society with all the evil influences, God's plan offers you hope and a confident assurance that you are and will remain victorious.

Where is your focus? Is it on the things of this world? Be honest. Have your problems become your main agenda or topic of conversation? Or are your sights set on the riches of the eternal? Don't let the devil distract or keep you buried in your day to day activities. Jesus gave us His peace…nothing missing, lacking, or broken. No one knew problems better than Paul did, but he also knew the benefits of believing for the greater goal—the lasting promise and eternal glory of being with our Lord and Savior. Jesus is our eternal goal. He is not only our hope for victory and overcoming power today, but for the future, too.

Stay focused on your eternal destiny, instead of the temporary distractions. Use your faith. It calls those things that are not…the unseen, as though they were… the seen. God's plan and Word are everlasting. Don't be afraid. Turn from the 'seen' thing in your life to the greater blessing of the 'unseen.' Faith uses spiritual eyes. It is "the sight" for sore eyes.

DECEMBER 1

> *"Jesus Christ, the Messiah, [is always]*
> *the same, yesterday, today, [yes]*
> *and forever—to the ages."*
> *Hebrews 13:8 (AMP)*

Jesus is our firm foundation. When we believe in Him, we receive a relationship with God and inherit His promises. He is our stability. God never changes, and this verse confirms Jesus never changes, either. Why is this so important? Because it's difficult to base beliefs and trust in someone or something that continually shifts or changes. Have you ever stood on something, and then all of a sudden you feel it shifting or start to give way? It's an unsettling feeling that affects your confidence or trust level. We all love and need to feel secure. God knows this about us. This is why He makes it clear in His Word, which never passes away, They never change.

How does having security or stability in our daily living really affect us? It removes fear. It allows us to base our peace—nothing missing, lacking, or broken—on what the Word says and not on what we see happening all around us. If the economy is bad, do you think God has any less power to perform His miracles? Do you think He worries about where or when the provision is going to come? The Bible says He owns all the gold and the silver, and He has cattle on a thousand hills. It doesn't say He owns them in just the good times on earth. Knowing this gives us confidence to trust God to be our source, regardless of the stock market, current economical status, or any other earthly signs.

There is comfort and absolutely no fear when you know what God has said, and since He can't lie, you know it will come to pass. His principles or spiritual laws work just like our natural ones do. Gravity is a law, and it never changes. Aerodynamics, a principle involved in aircraft lift off, never changes. Whether or not you believe in either law is irrelevant. They are natural laws that always work. We have the same assurance with God's supernatural laws. When we do our part, use our faith, and expect the Word to work, God gives us what we need for our specific situation.

Don't be afraid. He never changes, and His Word to us never changes. There is no better investment to put stock in than the Word of God. The Dow may change daily, but you won't lose by putting your faith in Jesus Christ the Messiah. He and His Word are solid—*yesterday, today, and forever—to the ages.*

> *"Jesus saith unto him, I am the way, the truth, and the life: no man cometh unto the Father, but by me."*
> *John 14:6 (KJV)*

When Jesus told the disciples about His going away, they became confused. He told them He was going to be with the Father in Heaven where there were many mansions. He said He was going to prepare a place for them. Then He would come back to get them, and they would go to where He had been. Jesus then said, "You know the way to where I am going." At that moment, in their confusion, Thomas asked the Lord how they were supposed to know "the way" to where He was going, when they didn't even know "where" He was going. Jesus went on to explain—"He" was "the way," and the "where" would eventually mean going to live with the Father in Heaven.

The Word doesn't lie, and it never changes. Jesus is still the only *way*, our path, which allows us to live in Heaven with God the Father. That's why He's called the "way-maker." Today there are many false, confusing theories about what happens "after death." They are not comforting or encouraging. Reincarnation is thought to offer new life in another body or life form. Why would you want to come back and let the devil torture you again? And even if you thought you would do things better or knew how to make the right decisions this time around, nothing would be the same. How could it be? Think about how different the times are just between the years you grew up and kids now. And how can you change your past if you keep coming back as a different person or animal? And what about the belief you must keep coming back until you get it right? Who decides what is right?

None of these are God's plan. How can you know for sure? Go to the truth—God's Word. It says it is appointed unto man to die "once." There are two places after death...Heaven or hell. God told us to choose life. This would mean to choose His plan—His Son, Jesus. Besides, none of these other theories create peace. We serve a God of love and peace. Do you want peace? No fear? Accept the truth. He has already gone to prepare a place for you, but He is also returning—one day soon—to take all those who haven't died back to Heaven with Him. Will you be ready? Don't be afraid. There is no more fear about the "what after" when you believe and receive Jesus. God's plan is complete. It is for us now and for all eternity. Do you want to spend your forever with God? Choose life and seal the deal...accept *the way*, accept Jesus.

DECEMBER 3

> *"I tell you the truth, anyone who has faith in me will do what I have been doing. He will do even greater things than these, because I am going to the Father."*
> *John 14:12 (NIV)*

Why did Jesus make this statement to His disciples? What was He really saying to them and to us about our faith and future plans? Jesus knew in His final days on earth He needed to be explicit about what was going to happen to Him and the effect this would have on the disciples. In the previous verses in this chapter, Jesus states He never did anything except what He saw the Father do, and He never said anything except what He heard the Father say. He and the Father were one. He wasn't just bragging about how close He and the Father were. He was pointing out if He could do, say, and have the power of God, that now through Him, they could also have the same power. He was giving them His authority, and He gave them hope—not fear—for their futures. Fear would send them back to their old lives, but faith would motivate them to continue with the great work of the Gospel.

In truth, Jesus said, "***anyone*** *who has faith in Him would not only do what He did, but would do even greater works.*" "*Any one*" means you and me. How is this possible? How could we do *even greater* works than the Son of God? Didn't He live victoriously? Wasn't He blameless? Didn't He teach, preach, cast out devils, heal all who where oppressed by the devil, heal every manner of sickness and infirmity, and raise the dead? Didn't He walk by the Spirit and lead twelve men, for over three years, who then took His message of the Father's love and salvation plan to the entire world? Yes, Jesus did all these things and much more, and yet, **He** said we would do more than He did.

The Bible shows us this is possible through the Holy Spirit. Jesus only ministered in the location where He was physically. Now, by the Spirit of God living in and working through us, He isn't limited to performing miracles in a few cities, through just a few men. When we have accepted Christ and have faith in God's Word, God can use *any one* of us to do exactly what Christ did in every city around the world—all at the same time! Jesus said signs and wonders would follow them that believe…lay hands on the sick, and they would recover. Why? We're letting the same power that flowed through Him now flow through us. Our results will be the same as His because the God He obeyed is the same God that lives on the inside of us through the Holy Ghost and our faith. Don't be afraid. *Have faith in Him.* You've been given all authority—His authority. Just use it!

> *"May Christ through your faith [actually] dwell—settle down, abide, make His permanent home—in your hearts! May you be rooted deep in love and founded securely on love,"*
> *Ephesians 3:17 (AMP)*

God knows the answer to our living successfully and productively is love. The world continues on a daily quest to find love. We look for it in people, our families, spouses, friends or other relationships, work, social activities, extra curricular events, and all the material "things" we've been told will bring us pleasure. We "love" food. We "love" sports, or movies, or our jobs, and so on. We want to be loved or be in love because it fills an emotional void. Or does it? What is it that causes mankind to continually search or chase after worldly things, even when we know they can't completely satisfy?

It's that deep, inner need to truly feel loved. The love the world knows cannot be compared to the kind of love God has for us. Worldly love is unstable and performance based. However, God's love is secure. He doesn't love us one day, and then, based on our actions, deeds or performance, not love us the next. Although sin separates us from our fellowship with God, His amazing love for us is never affected. The Bible says that nothing separates us from the love of God. The Word also says the love of God is shed abroad in our hearts. How does it get there? It's *through our faith in Christ's settling down, abiding, and making His permanent home in our hearts*, which allows us to become rooted and grounded in His love.

When Jesus taught the disciples about the Father and He being one, He wanted them, and now us, to understand it works both ways. We, too, can be one with Christ and the Father. Jesus said, "If we have seen Him we have also seen the Father." *Through faith, Christ lives, dwells, and abides in us*, and it's His desire the world would be able to see Jesus and the Father in us, too. How could they see Them in us? Through the evidence and power of Their unconditional love flowing through us. God's love is perfect, and now His perfect love lives in us. His perfect love...the love that casts out all fear. Don't be afraid. This verse encourages us to be rooted and grounded in love so that we may be secure, stable, fearless. God's love is genuine. It's the only love that will ever fill that void, deep emptiness, and emotional need. Will you open your heart to God's love? You'll find when *you're rooted deep in love and founded securely on love*, it's life changing, totally freeing, completely fulfilling, and fear removing.

> *"That you may have the power and be strong to apprehend and grasp with all the saints (God's devoted people, the experience of that love) what is the breadth and length and height and depth [of it];"*
> *Ephesians 3:18 (AMP)*

The Apostle Paul knew what it was to be loved by God. He had been responsible for the deaths of some of God's finest men, and yet, the Lord loved him and wanted him to fulfill the plan and destiny that was established for Paul before the beginning of the world. Paul also knew and used the power that was available to him because of this love. Perfect love—power—no fear! What Paul experienced then is the same power and love that eliminates our fears today.

This verse was part of Paul's prayer. He knew it was necessary for us to *have this power and be strong to apprehend, grasp or understand God's love.* Why was this so important to Paul that it became one of his prayers for the believer? Paul had learned for himself the most important thing to God is love. Why? It's because **God IS love**. Everything God does flows from love. He demonstrated His love to us from the very beginning by sending His only Son, who also demonstrated His love by being willing to come and fulfill the call. God's first and second commandments to us are to love Him, have no other gods before Him, and to love others as He has loved us. Everything hinges on God's love flowing freely in and through our lives.

The Bible says faith works by love. We cannot defeat the devil without faith, and faith doesn't work without love. Are you having some difficulty seeing your prayers answered? Have you truly examined your "love" walk? Are you short tempered or rude to people, even if they ask for it? How is your anger level once you get behind the wheel of your auto? Is there unforgiveness in your heart? We will stop the work and flow of God on our behalf if we don't forgive and love others, including loving ourselves. Paul's mission would not have been successfully completed if he had not *apprehended and grasped* God's love and forgiveness of his past. But Paul also had to forgive and love himself with the same love...God's love that now lived on the inside of him.

Has shame or guilt of your sins put you in a place of self-hatred? The Word says there is no condemnation for anyone who is in Christ. Are you disappointed with your behavior? Then be glad God's love for you isn't based on your works, but on the work of His Son on the cross. Don't be afraid. You can be strong in the Lord. You can *experience the breadth, length, height, and depth of His love.*

DECEMBER 6

"[That you may really come] to know—practically, through experience for yourselves—the love of Christ, which far surpasses mere knowledge (without experience); that you may be filled (through all your being) unto all the fullness of God—[that is] may have the richest measure of the divine Presence, and become a body wholly filled and flooded with God Himself!"
Ephesians 3:19 (AMP)

Paul continues his prayer for us in this verse. He wants us to know the love of Christ that *surpasses* our earthly knowledge. This is a love that is full and rich…a love that totally fills us with the *fullness of God*. "Where" do you get this love? There's only one place to receive this kind of love…from the Lord. "How" do you get this love? The only way is through a personal and practical experience with Him. Earthly or human love has boundaries and limitations in the love it expresses. God's love knows no limits or boundaries. This is why Paul writes it goes beyond head knowledge. It is deeper and more gratifying than anything we have ever encountered or experienced.

Now you might be thinking, "This isn't possible. How can God fill or flood our existence with Him?" The truth is, He can't and won't, if we don't ask Him. The only way we can ever expect to receive all the blessings and fullness of God is through His Son. When we believe in Jesus and confess Him as our Lord and Savior, the Bible says the old man passes away. Now our bodies don't physically die. This new creation is done by the Spirit. However, some things will "die" in the flesh because you will no longer have a desire to do them. Why? Because the natural man's inclination agrees with pleasing the lusts of the flesh because the "sin nature" takes the side of the devil. But once you choose to come into agreement with the life and plans of God by accepting Jesus, the "righteous nature" of God and faith changes your desires. The new man is now motivated by God's love and obedience…not fear.

Accepting Christ and developing a personal relationship with Him is how we come to "know" for ourselves the love, plans, and ways of God. We practically experience and feel Christ's love that now lives on the inside of us. Don't be afraid. You'll find that His love is life changing. Even though, at first, your mind may not totally understand it, your heart will be able to experience it. Make the choice to let the ever increasing, fullness of God's love fill you to *His richest measure of divine Presence*.

> *"Now to a laborer, his wages are not counted as a favor or a gift, but as an obligation—something owed to him. But to one who not working [by Law] trusts (believes fully) in Him Who justifies the ungodly, his faith is credited to him as righteousness—the standing acceptable to God."*
> *Romans 4:4-5 (AMP)*

The Apostle Paul states we are not righteous because of who we are or what we do because our work or labor would be in vain. Work requires some sort of compensation, something owed in exchange of service. God's plan of righteousness is a free gift to us through His Son. It cost Jesus His life, a high price for our souls. He paid a debt He didn't owe; we owed a debt we couldn't pay. Paul reminds us that Abraham, our forefather, trusted and believed God, and it was his faith, not his works, that was credited to him as being righteous. His faith put him in right standing or *the standing acceptable to God.* The Bible says, "God is no respecter of persons." This means what He allows for one, He must allow for everyone. If He had allowed works to be Abraham's path to righteousness, then He would have been obligated to allow it for all of us, as well.

Why or what difference would it make to God how we become righteous? God is a 'just' God. If He had left it up to each individual, then how could a person with one talent qualify the same way the person with four talents could? What if you were wealthy, didn't have to work, and could spend your time volunteering or doing "good deeds" all day, everyday? How would you be able to distinguish their "righteous" qualifications in comparison to someone who works everyday and has no time to volunteer? God made it a free gift so no one could boast about their own accomplishments, and so no one could claim it was too hard, unfair or too difficult for them because of their past or current circumstances. God also knew it would stop the devil's lie in creating fear that it wasn't for them or it's not for everyone or it's only for a select few. With this "free gift" plan, God made sure no one would be afraid they didn't qualify.

Does it sound too simple? Is it hard to believe that after all you've done your sins could be forgiven, and you could be "right" with God? God made it simple... easy...because He loves you. If there had only been one person, Jesus would have died for that one, but it's God's desire we're all saved. Don't be afraid. Accept Jesus. *Trust, believe fully in Him.* When you do, you will be made righteous—*the standing acceptable to God*—too.

> *"Blessed and happy and to be envied are those whose iniquities are forgiven and whose sins are covered up and completely buried. Blessed and happy and to be envied is the person of whose sin the Lord will take no account nor reckon it against him."*
> *Romans 4:7-8 (AMP)*

The Apostle Paul knew the joy of having past sins wiped clean as if they never existed. He also knew how the devil likes to remind us of our past "no good" or "unworthy" status. Fear of our crimes, whether they are many or few, and fear that God will reject us because of them can keep us from turning to Him. But this verse confirms *Jesus will take no account of it or hold it against us.*

In Luke, chapter 7, the Word gives another example of Jesus' willingness to forgive. Jesus had been invited to Simon the Pharisee's house for dinner. A sinful woman heard Jesus was dining there. She went to the home with an alabaster box of expensive perfume which she broke and poured on the Lord. She washed His feet with her tears and dried them with her hair. The men at the table thought to themselves, if Jesus really were a prophet, He would know the reputation of this woman and send her away. Jesus, knowing what they were thinking, begins to tell the story of two men who owed money to the same money-lender. One owed a large amount and the other a small amount. Neither of them had the money to pay, so the money-lender canceled both of their debts. Jesus then asked, "Which of these two men do you think loved the most?" Simon answered, "The one who owed the most." Jesus said, "This is correct." He went on to say, "When I came into your home, Simon, you didn't offer Me any water to wash My feet, and yet, this woman washed My feet with her tears. I wasn't offered a kiss of welcome, and yet, this woman hasn't stopped kissing My feet. I wasn't offered any oil for My head, and this woman has poured expensive perfume over Me." Jesus then turned to her and said, "Your many sins have been forgiven because you loved much—your faith has saved you; go in peace."

Have you let your faith save you? Can you love much? The Lord says to you no sin, regardless of how big or how many, can keep you from receiving His love and blessings. Don't be afraid. Through Christ, your past sins are *forgiven, covered up, buried*, no record of wrongdoing is held against you. Ask, and you will receive His forgiveness. You, too, will be *blessed, happy, envied*!

DECEMBER 9

> *"Beloved, I wish above all things that thou mayest prosper and be in health, even as thy soul prospers."*
> *3 John 1:2 (KJV)*

It has and always will be God's plan for His children to prosper. God established His covenant with Abraham who the Bible tells us was so wealthy the world envied him. But God's promise wasn't just for Abraham. It was also to his heirs—Isaac, Jacob, and the rest of the lineage. Today, for most, blessings are usually associated with money. However, you could have more money than you know what to do with, but if you can't get out of bed because of an illness, what good is the money? Or what if you have a powerful anointing to teach or preach the Gospel, but you don't have a car, food, place to stay or money to go anywhere? How much good could you do? God wants us to prosper, and this includes every area of our lives.

The soul is our mind, our will, and our emotions. If you are so beat up from past abuses that you still live in the past…how can you fulfill your destiny for tomorrow? Many think that new circumstances will change their attitudes or feelings about their current status…if I could have a better job, if I could be single again, if I could only find a spouse, if I had gotten a better education, if I could ______. All these things may add or make life more interesting for a period, but sooner or later your feelings or emotions will rise to the surface again in your new situation just like they did in the old. The truth is we can't completely and totally prosper and be in health in our outer man until our inner man is healthy. God always works from within.

So, how do we get healthy in our mind, will, and emotions? God made provision for us to live a well balanced life by renewing our minds to His Word through His Spirit. The Holy Spirit will search your heart and show you the things you'll need to adjust. He will reveal things about your past and comfort you at the same time. He will bring the healing power of God to chase away the fears of yesterday and help you get into your present. It is impossible to move into your destiny or plan when you're still holding on to unhealthy problems or habits from the past. Maybe you're afraid of what's ahead? Fear that the future will hold nothing different than the past is the catalyst that keeps us bound. Don't be afraid. This verse confirms *Beloved, ABOVE ALL THINGS,* My plan for you is that every part is prosperous, made whole, and in good health. This is and always has been God's plan for you. Receive it, and enjoy the true meaning of the good life!

> *"I am the Alpha and Omega the Beginning and the End, says the Lord God, He Who is and Who was and Who is to come, the Almighty—the Ruler of all."*
> *Revelation 1:8 (AMP)*

After Jesus appeared to the Apostle John, who was exiled on the island of Patmos, John wrote the book of Revelation. Jesus revealed knowledge to John about Himself, seven different churches, and what was coming to the world for believers and nonbelievers alike. In this verse Jesus states He is the *Alpha* and the *Omega.* These are the original Greek words, Alpha, which means the beginning, and Omega the end. In other words, the Lord *was* here before the world began, He *is* alive and lives within us now, and He *will come* again as our reigning King. This is important because it forms a strong foundation of trust and confidence in our relationship with Him that is stable and permanent. In an ever-changing, unstable, insecure world this is crucial in restoring peace to our lives because it eliminates fear. We know we're never alone. *The Ruler of all* was, is, and always will be with us.

If He was here from the beginning, then He has also known you from the beginning, and if He knew you then, He knows you now. The truth is He knows everything about us. He knows us better than we know ourselves, and He also knows our end…our destiny. This is why we must trust the Lord to lead us. His leading helps us to overcome any obstacles that would stand in the way of us reaching our God given destiny. Did you know you could be an obstacle to your own future? Past hurts, poor decision making, and self-destructive behavioral patterns can keep us from reaching our destiny. If you've been a victim, you'll think like a victim, and you will continue to make decisions that will keep you in this same pattern. These decisions become habits, good or bad. It's not where you want to be, but subconsciously it's where you're comfortable.

Do you find history repeating itself? Do you think life keeps rotating the same vicious cycle in your life? This is the pattern of a victim, **but you can break this cycle.** How? You must change the way you think, so the old habits will change. How do you change your thinking? You renew your mind to what God says in His Word, and you let the *Alpha* and the *Omega* have the final say in the decisions in your life. Don't be afraid. Jesus, *the Almighty—the Ruler of all* has been with you from your beginning, and now, if you follow Him, He'll be with you until your end.

DECEMBER 11

> *"The world and its desires pass away, but the man who does the will of God lives forever."*
> *1 John 2:17 (NIV)*

Have you ever looked at an old photo of you or a family member and laughed at the clothes or hairstyles? We all have. If you can remember back to that time in your life, you probably had to fight with your parents to wear your hair that way or maybe you even argued with them about the clothes you wore. Styles change and along with it our desires and tastes. I remember how ugly I thought tie-dye clothing was when my generation was wearing it. I never dreamed it would be fashionable again. The very things we "must have" today become foolishness to us tomorrow. We lust after the newest and latest kind of electronic toy or device, and the day we buy it, it's already outdated. The world is constantly changing, and we are supposed to change with it. But just like the "big" handheld calculators of the 1970's and the first computers have passed away, we know there will be a time when we will pass away, too. The Bible says it is appointed unto man to die once. However, there is a way we can leave our earthly body and still have life. This way is through Jesus Christ.

Many individuals think about retiring, traveling, doing things they didn't have time to do while they worked. When retirement time comes, sometimes they do what they've planned, but more times than not, they don't. The number one reason is one of the parties becomes too ill to travel. The expected and hoped for end doesn't turn out to be what was expected at all. However, God's "end" is the ultimate retirement. There are no surprises, and there is no fear in losing the exterior house because the inner man, our spirit, will live forever. Although the new location will be fantastic, the biggest benefit is we will be with Him. We don't have to be afraid of where we are going or where we'll "end" up, and we can also rest in knowing all our loved ones who have accepted the Lord will be there, too.

Don't you want to live with God? Wouldn't you like to know "for sure" you are going to Heaven? The Bible says you can know for sure if you "repent of your sin, believe on Jesus, and confess Him with your mouth to be your Lord and Savior." Don't be afraid. Accepting Jesus is the will of God, and this verse confirms *the man who does the will of God lives forever*. So, when the things of this world pass away, including your body, you'll be rejoicing because you'll be forever living with Him.

"Don't be deceived, my dear brothers. Every good and perfect gift is from above, coming down from the Father of the heavenly lights, who does not change like shifting shadows."
James 1:16-17 (NIV)

James, the brother of Jesus, addresses practical everyday issues we all experience in life. When bad things happen, even people that give no thought to God want to blame Him for the crisis or tragedy. God is then bombarded with questions like, "Why" or "How did this happen." But the biggest question is, "Why didn't You do something to stop it?"

In 2001, when the tragedy hit our nation, the cry that went up across the land was, "Where was God in all of this?" A well known minister of the Gospel fasted and prayed for the Lord to reveal the answer to this question. The Lord told him He had spoken to every person in the towers that day, but there were three classifications of people. There were those who didn't know the Lord's voice because they had rejected the Gospel. When God spoke to them, they didn't recognize Him. Then there were those who knew the Lord's voice, but weren't always in the habit of following the Holy Spirit's leading. So they did their own thing, too. Then there were those who heard the Lord's voice and obeyed. We have heard countless testimonies of people who were nowhere near the property. Some will tell you they didn't know why they were late or they had to go somewhere or do something else first. However, that's what they felt like they were supposed to do. As it turned out, they were following the impression of the Holy Ghost living on the inside of them, and because of it they were kept safe and sound.

God is a good God, and this verse confirms that only those *good and perfect gifts* are what come from our Father above. He doesn't change. There is no variance. *He doesn't move and shift around like shadows.* When we know His position, it removes any fear the devil tries to conjure up against Him and us. He is stable, and He makes every provision we need. The key is, are we in a right relationship to hear Him? And when we hear…will we obey? Have you blamed God for your situation? *Don't be deceived.* He isn't the one who came to kill, steal, and destroy. You can't fight the devil without God's power and the work of the Holy Spirit. If God is for you, then who can be against you? Don't be afraid. God is for you. His plans for you are for good, not harm—for hope and a future—for peace, not fear. And *His gifts* to His children are always *good and perfect.*

> *"But—obey the message; be doers of the Word, and not merely listeners to it, betraying yourselves [into deception by reasoning contrary to the Truth]."*
> *James 1:22 (AMP)*

James not only lived with his brother, Jesus, but he was able to watch him on a daily basis, too. Jesus was a constant, excellent example. James learned how to deal with the practical issues of life that we all face. He also saw the key factor that kept people from living in victory. What is this key factor? It's faith. Why is faith a key to our victory? Because it gives fear no place, which means it gives the devil no place. James witnessed the biggest downfall to a person's faith is to not obey or do what the Word says. In other words, people may have faith because they are listening to the Word—faith comes by hearing—but they aren't releasing their faith or doing something with the Word after they hear it. The Bible says faith without corresponding action is dead. When we're in the heat of the battle and need our circumstances changed, using a dead work doesn't cut it. We need the life and power of God working with us, on our behalf.

Do you have faith? Are you releasing it over your situations? Many Christians may hear the Word on Sunday mornings, but they don't think about God or what the Word says until they get back in church the following Sunday. God isn't just a "Sunday" or a "Wednesday night" Savior. If you don't let Him be a daily God to you, then you won't have the miracles or power you need on a daily basis, either. We didn't have to start training our troops after the September 11th tragedy. They were already trained and ready for battle. They weren't in the habit of cleaning their weapons only once a week, nor did they workout a couple of times a month to keep themselves in the best top physical condition. Everything is a daily process. Even when they weren't in direct combat fighting, they prepared everyday for battle. After 2001, when the devil struck and launched his initial attack against our country and then the world, they were ready.

Are you ready when the devil attacks you? The best defense is a strong offense. Knowing the Word and knowing what to do with it is how you stay on the offense. There is no fear when you know what to do and are prepared to do it. In fact, when you are on the offense, you will see the attack coming and can stop the devil in his tracks. Don't be afraid. And don't be deceived. *Be a doer of the Word.* It's your weapon, and it's the only defense that guarantees to keep you on the offense.

> *"But the wisdom from above is first of all pure (undefiled); then it is peace-loving, courteous (considerate, gentle). [It is willing to] yield to reason, full of compassion and good fruits; it is whole-hearted and straightforward, impartial and unfeigned—free from doubts, wavering and insincerity."*
> *James 3:17 (AMP)*

The wisdom from above is from our Father, and it is made available to us through the Holy Spirit. How could it be anything but *good, sincere, full of compassion, impartial, gentle, and with a whole heart* if it's coming from God through the "Holy" Spirit? The Bible says, "If any man lacks wisdom let him ask God and without reproach God will give it to him." This means God won't think we're stupid for asking. However, to receive your answer you must use faith and believe. The Bible says faith believes it "receives" when you ask and pray, not when you see or feel it in the natural.

Faith is that confident expectation, a sure foundation. When we use faith, we know God is all the while to will and to work His good pleasure in our life. In other words, He's answering our prayer. We have no fear because He is faithful to His Word. We can ask for clarity, so we know how and what to pray. We can ask for specifics on business deals. We can ask about medical reports and the action we need to take. We can ask God about everything. He has all the answers. When you know His wisdom is filled with compassion and every good thing, you won't be afraid to ask for it or to receive it.

Do you hear God's voice? Many have the impression that "if" or "when" God answers He's limited to three categories: Yes, No, and Maybe. However, this is not what the Word says. Many times the Lord wakes me up in the middle of the night to tell me something. He doesn't just say "Yes" or "OK," and then end the conversation. What if I'd been praying about more than one thing, which most of the time I am? Was I supposed to just guess which prayer He was answering? Dialogue takes two or more people. God talks in full sentences, and He uses more than one. We have conversations—I ask questions, He answers them—right then. Sometimes He even asks me questions. Sound like a relationship? You're right, and He wants the same with you. Don't be afraid. His wonderful, loving wisdom is for all those who ask. Why doubt or wonder or be in fear? He has your every answer…*pure wisdom from above*. Just ask Him.

DECEMBER 15

"That if you confess with your mouth, 'Jesus is Lord,' and believe in your heart that God raised him from the dead, you will be saved. For it is with your heart that you believe and are justified, and it is with your mouth that you confess and are saved."
Romans 10:9-10 (NIV)

The Bible makes God's saving grace to mankind clear in this one verse by telling us exactly what we must do in order to spend eternity with the Lord. First, He says, "*If,*" which means it's our decision. Then He says, "*YOU.*" This is important because it removes any fear that it might not be for everyone. It also assures us and guarantees that we all will have a future because it's not only blessings for this life, but the one to follow in Heaven with the Lord.

God works with mankind's heart and mouth. The Holy Spirit, who is also a free gift, lives on the inside of us in our hearts. The Bible says we are to guard our hearts and minds through Christ Jesus because out of our hearts flow the issues of life. There is only one place the flow can come out…our mouths. We all can relate to this, especially when we're angry, disappointed or heartbroken. Under certain pressures or situations it's hard to talk positively and the longer the trial…if we're not prayerful…it seems impossible. These negative thoughts and feelings are the result of a discouraged heart, a heart and mind that has not been guarded by the Word of God. The devil knows if he can contaminate our thought life, our hearts and mouths will soon follow. Why? Doubt and unbelief set in. Fear is now in operation. It becomes easier to talk about our mountain than it does to obey the Word and talk to it.

This is the reason we must not only believe in our hearts Jesus was God's Son, He died, and rose again, but we speak it. God's Word is alive, which makes it life changing. Anytime we speak the Word or truth, things are changed, including us. Science has proven we must hear something repeated seven times before we really know it, but if we hear it said with our own voice, it only takes three times. In other words, we are able to receive it and retain it quicker when it comes from us. Do you see the importance of "speaking" the Word to your situations and not the problem? Guarding your hearts and minds? Whatever your ears hear the most…that's what you'll eventually come to believe. Don't be afraid. You can change your confessions, but you must first make the right confession. It all starts with Jesus. *Believe in your heart...confess with your mouth*…and *you will be saved.*

> *"As the Scripture says, 'Anyone who trusts in him will never be put to shame.' For there is no difference between Jew and Gentile—the same Lord is Lord of all and richly blesses all who call on him, for, 'Everyone who calls on the name of the Lord will be saved.'"*
> *Romans 10:11-13 (NIV)*

"*Everyone.*" Do you realize this means you? It also means there is no past sin, background, gender, nationality or anything else that can keep you from receiving the Lord as your Lord. God's promises are for everyone. Nothing or no one can keep you from what God has prepared for you, except you! Only you can decide to *call on the Name of the Lord, and be saved.*

The biggest reason anyone rejects a relationship with the Lord is fear. We're afraid He won't really accept us. We're afraid of what friends or family will think or do? We're afraid He might ask us to do something or go somewhere. We're afraid we may have to give up something—like smoking, drinking or whatever it is we already know we shouldn't be doing—not because it's a sin necessarily, but it's killing our bodies. However, God never said in His Word to lay down all your sins and then come to Me. Nor did He say you make the changes—clean yourself up—then I'll see if you qualify for "My" Kingdom. The truth is He loves you just the way you are. Do you think what you are doing is a shock or surprise to Him? Do you think when the Bible says before the world began He already saw you in your mother's womb, that He wouldn't know you or your habits later on? He knew and saw everything you would ever do. He also knew everything you would ever even think about doing, AND HE STILL LOVES YOU!

He loved you enough to send help. Help from your problems, your enemies, and from yourself if need be. Before I got saved I had a sharp wit and a quick tongue. I was quite funny. However, most verbal jabs are usually at the expense of someone's feelings. When I accepted the Lord, I wanted my mouth yielded to His Words—bringing love, not hurt. With the Holy Spirit's help, renewing my mind to the Word, and guarding my heart, I've come a long way. But at no time during this process did I hear God say, "Don't come to Me until you clean up your talk." He loved me, and He had already made a way of escape for me through His Son, Jesus. Don't be afraid. You can have the same escape route. What God does for one, He does for everyone. Jesus is *Lord of all. Trust in Him ...you'll never be put to shame. Call on the Name of the Lord...you'll be saved.*

DECEMBER 17

> *"We know that we live in him and he in us, because he has given us of his Spirit."*
> *1 John 4:13 (NIV)*

Knowing there is a God and He created the universe is one thing, but recognizing that the same God is available to actually live on the inside of us...well, that's another subject. This concept is difficult to grasp. That is until you decide to make Jesus your Lord. Why? Because in the midst of this confession, you'll feel something happen...something spiritual takes place. You may be using your mouth and heart to ask and receive Him, but this isn't a natural or a physical event. There is a transformation that happens when you let go and surrender your ways and life to the Lord Jesus Christ. At that moment, by the Spirit, you've given God the OK to come and live in you. Instantly you feel different. You are washed clean of every sin. Nothing about you may have changed in the physical realm or on the outside, but you couldn't tell it by how you feel on the inside... lighter...happier...free from all your cares, and free from fear.

This is the promise of salvation. When the heaviness of past sins, failures, disappointments, mistakes, bad decisions, guilt, and shame are wiped away—totally forgiven and forgotten, forever—it is a moment you won't soon forget. God's immense love is fulfilling, satisfying, and every fear vanishes. You're complete and accepted. Now, your gratitude to Christ for what He paid for you to enjoy is overwhelming, and your love for Him is hard to describe. The hardest thing to comprehend is He was willing to do it. The Bible says He had the power to lay His life down, and He had the power to take it back up. His love for us, even while we were right in the middle of our biggest mess ever, was His motivating force.

The Bible also says we "now" know and also believe these things because the Spirit of God is the always present witness we feel on the inside of us. He directs and guides us into all truth, and it is the truth of God's Word that now bears witness with our spirit. It is the Holy Spirit who helps us understand the Scriptures and what God is saying to His people. Not only then, but what He is still saying to us today. It's what makes the Bible our handbook or instruction manual for everyday living. The Spirit confirms the truth for our lives, and He removes the fear of the devil's attacks to destroy us. Don't you need the Lord's wisdom? Love? Comfort? Don't be afraid. You can confidently *know* you can *live in Him*, and *He* can *live in you* through the precious gift of the Holy Spirit.

> *"If anyone acknowledges that Jesus is the Son of God, God lives in him and he in God. And so we know and rely on the love God has for us. God is love. Whoever lives in love lives in God, and God in him."*
> *1 John 4:15-16 (NIV)*

The foundation of God is love. Everything He has ever done was out of love because this is who He is. He sent His Son out of His love for us, and Jesus came and fulfilled the ultimate act of love by being obedient unto death to pay the price for our freedom, our victory.

The Bible, God's inspired Word, makes it clear They are one. *God lives in Him, and He lives in God.* The Word also makes it clear they are love, perfect love, and *whoever lives in love lives in God, and God in him.* It is crucial in our relationship with Them for us to understand just how great and powerful Their love really is. Jesus was asked, "Of all the commandments, which is the most important?" "The most important one," answered Jesus, "is this: 'Hear O Israel, the Lord our God, the Lord is one. Love the Lord your God with all your heart and with all your soul and with all your mind and with all your strength.' The second is this: 'Love your neighbor as your self.' There is no commandment greater than these."

Some theologians believe these two commandments now replace the original ten that God gave Moses. This isn't true, but when you *live in love* you won't be able to kill, steal, covet your neighbor's property or spouse, or disrespect your father and mother, either. Do you see the Lord Jesus Christ doing these things? We know the answer to this question is no, and because of the love in Them, which is now in us, we no longer have the desire to commit these sins, either. The Bible says we love because He first loved us. They are love. What else could They do but love us? Maybe you're thinking, "I know They're love, They're perfect, but I don't fit in." It's fear from our own failures that causes us to feel that way. God knew our sins. That's why this verse and countless others keep repeating *anyone* is a candidate. None of us are perfect, but HE is, and through our relationship with the Lord our sins are justified, forgiven, forgotten. Don't be afraid. All of this is a free gift, *"so we know and rely on His love for us."* His love that now lives on the inside of you. His love is perfect, and perfect love removes all fear.

> *"And this is the confidence that we have in him, that, if we ask any thing according to his will, he heareth us: And if we know that he hears us, whatsoever we ask, we know that we have the petitions that we desired of him."*
> *1 John 5:14-15 (KJV)*

Once you've asked the Lord to be your Lord and Savior, there is an inner knowing, a feeling of confidence, an inner belief that strengthens your faith to stand on God's Word and to not back down in the face of opposition. Faith gives you courage, the confidence to stay the course, regardless of what you see, hear or feel in the natural. When you know the Lord in an intimate, personal way, you receive peace, closeness, and the ability to trust what He says to you, even when everything around you is screaming, "You must be crazy to believe this."

God hears every word we speak, and when we cry out to Him, He is there to do what needs to be done. This verse confirms God hears our prayers or petitions. When we present our desires, *according to His will, He hears us.* This verse also confirms *if we know He hears us*, then we can be sure *He will also answer us.* Why would you need to be afraid if you knew God would hear you and answer your prayers? You already know how much He loves you, and He wants to give you good gifts. The Bible says the plans He has for us are to prosper us and not to harm us, they are to give us hope and a future. The Bible says every good and perfect gift comes from our Father, who doesn't shift and change like shadows, and our promotions are from Him, too. His plan or will for our lives is one of wholeness, success, victory.

When you ask for anything according to His plan or will, He grants it. Don't let the devil keep you from asking for the things you want and need. Your kids ask you for what they want and need, don't they? Do you think it strange when they do? No, it's just part of you fulfilling your role as their parent. God feels the same way. He is still our Father, and it hurts Him when we think we can do it without Him. Have you been afraid to ask? Maybe you were taught He's too busy for you? Maybe you haven't received His love for you, yet? Don't be afraid. He loves you and desires to help you. Follow His plan and directions. Ask. Use your faith. Believe you receive when you ask. Then, thank Him for it until you see the victory. *And this is the confidence that we have in Him*...you will see it!

> *"Praise be to the God and Father of our Lord Jesus Christ! In his great mercy he has given us new birth into a living hope through the resurrection of Jesus Christ from the dead, and into an inheritance that can never perish, spoil or fade—kept in heaven for you, who through faith are shielded by God's power until the coming of the salvation that is ready to be revealed in the last time."*
> *1 Peter 1:3-5 (NIV)*

God's plan is complete. It not only covers every part of our past, but it also provides protection for us today, tomorrow, and throughout time until we reach our glorious future. It is God's great mercy, love and compassion that created this plan and the great love of Jesus to carry it out. The Bible says, "Jesus, who was in His very nature God, did not consider equality with God something He had to hold on to or retain, but he made Himself as nothing, a servant, a slave, in that He became a man born of a human being. He humbled Himself even further and became obedient even unto death, the extreme death of the cross. Therefore God has exalted Him to the highest place or position of honor and has bestowed upon Him the name that is above all names. That is the name of Jesus and at that name every knee will bow both in heaven, on earth, and under the earth and every tongue will confess that Jesus is Lord to the glory of God the Father."

Jesus' love is overwhelming. He didn't mind leaving His position as God and coming to earth as a man to suffer and die in order that we could be reconciled to the Father. Jesus did it all to give glory to His Father, God. And now we reap the benefits of a *"new birth*" experience *that is a living hope.* Jesus is alive. This is why our hope is living. We also reap the benefits of our Father's inheritance, which never fades or passes away. It is forever, eternal, kept in Heaven, just for us. And we reap the benefits of having faith made available to us, so we can use it to be *shielded by God's power* against any obstacle the devil would try to bring against us. The Bible says no weapon formed against us will succeed. How could we be afraid when we have this kind of a benefit package within reach? Don't be afraid. God made His salvation plan available to all mankind, everywhere, on every continent and island. Are you ready to receive your benefits? Believe and confess Jesus. Your inheritance, which never perishes, is waiting.

DECEMBER 21

> *"But as it is written, Eye hath not seen, nor ear heard, neither have entered into the heart of man, the things which God hath prepared for them that love him. But God hath revealed them unto us by his Spirit: for the Spirit searcheth all things, yea, the deep things of God."*
> *1 Corinthians 2:9-10 (KJV)*

This verse clearly states that God never intended for us to have to guess at the plan for our lives. Our future is too important to Him. After all, He gave His only Son to secure our destiny with Him, forever. If He had a detailed plan for that, why would He leave us hanging now? He won't. God's ways are higher than our ways. This is why our eyes haven't seen, our ears haven't heard, and it hasn't entered into our hearts. It is for this reason He sent the Holy Spirit to live in each of us. He directs and guides us down the right path. The Bible says He is our comforter, counselor, and guide. He knows the truth. He is God's voice to us, and He tells us what the Father is saying. He reveals the very nature of God to us. He helps us understand the truth of the Word, and He searches our hearts and reveals to us those hidden truths that keep us from getting free of past hindrances or distractions.

All God's power and wisdom is available to us when the Holy Ghost dwells on the inside of us. Why would we let what we see in the natural affect what we believe? Or be afraid? The natural only produces symptoms. We can't deny the facts, but this still doesn't make our circumstances the truth. If they don't line up or come into agreement with what God says about the way it should be…then they have to go. Facts are temporary, subject to change. However, the truth never changes. God's Word is the truth. The Bible says God is the same yesterday, today, and forever. He is the Word. The Word is God's manifested presence to us. It is permanent, everlasting.

Are you still wondering what you were created to do? Are you searching for your purpose or destiny? The Bible says God has a plan for your life…a good plan. And He went a step further by sending the Holy Spirit to reveal it to you. Have you asked God to fill you with the Holy Spirit? He is a free gift just like salvation. Don't be afraid. This is still part of God's plan in making sure we would be provided for in every area. The Holy Spirit is for every believer—anyone who asks. Are you an "any one?" Then ask and receive your personal guide to the deep things of God and your ultimate destiny.

DECEMBER 22

> *"My sheep hear my voice, and I know them, and they follow me."*
> *John 10:27 (KJV)*

One of the biggest lies of the devil is, "You can't hear God's voice." You can see why this would create fear. How can you follow someone if you can't see or hear them? I've counseled for many years, and this is one of the main questions I'm asked, "How do you know if it's God's voice? This verse confirms it is God's will we hear His voice. Why? So we can clearly follow Him. The devil lies to bring confusion, but God's Word brings clarity to every area. God gave us His Word so we would have an accurate sounding board, a basis for truth which produces stability. It's like the instrument a piano tuner uses. It gives the main tone or sound to which all the other keys are adjusted. What if this tool didn't exist? If the first key was wrong, all the others would be, too. Would you like to spend hours listening to this music?

God's Word is the tool we use to adjust our lives. It is clear, constant, never changing. His Word is the number one way He speaks to us—every Word is God inspired, God breathed. We need to know and stay in His Word. When I pray and ask God for information or direction about a matter, sometimes I feel impressed by the Spirit to read a certain chapter or verse. The answer is always right there. Another way God speaks to us is Spirit to spirit. This is where most people question God's voice. However, if your best friend calls, don't you know their voice? When you let Jesus become your best friend, you will know His voice, too. Once I was struggling with the outcome of what I believed God had told me to do. In frustration I said, "Lord, what's the deal?" At that moment, I heard God's voice in my spirit tell me to turn to a verse in Isaiah which said, "I am doing a new thing." I laughed and said, "OK, Lord, what do You want me to do now?" A detailed conversation followed.

God uses the Word, and then gives us more specific details when needed. Remember, He created us to talk with Him. He knew our hearing and following Him would be vital. Don't be afraid. "He" said "you" would know His voice. If you start to think, "I can't hear Him," it is one of two things. The devil is lying to you or you haven't gotten still enough to listen. Prayer is conversation. You talk, but more importantly, you listen! God knows your voice, and He wants you to know His. Ask. Listen. Then follow Him!

DECEMBER 23

> *"And be not conformed to this world: but be ye transformed by the renewing of your mind, that ye may prove what is that good, acceptable, and perfect, will of God."*
> *Romans 12:2 (KJV)*

Paul wrote this to encourage believers to not think or act like the world, regardless of how they may have been trained, but instead, to renew their minds or their thinking patterns to the Word. Why? Because when God's Word is applied, it brings freedom, deliverance, and change to our behavior. A renewed mind gives you the ability to lay down bad habits, fears, and anything else that could keep you from being in God's perfect plan or will.

All action comes from a thought first. Are you having difficulty in an area? Drugs? Over spending? Over eating? Most addictions start by "thinking" this will be the "quick fix" to the problem, but now the fix has become part of the problem. Has fear told you, "You'll never get free?" The only way to break unfruitful habits, which are the result of unmet emotional needs, and get free from the same old rut is to change your thought process. The only way to do this is to conform your thinking to God's Word, ways, plan, and His will. Would you like to know and live in God's perfect will for your life?

This verse tells us how…we renew our minds to His Word, His ways. We must depend on the Word and the Spirit of God to show us and lead us into all truth. This only comes when we renew our minds to God's wisdom. We allow His Word to transform our way of thinking to His way of thinking. Years ago I saw a watch I really liked. I asked God if I could buy it. He said, "No." Several weeks later I saw it again. I asked a second time, but the answer was the same. I can truthfully say I never gave that watch another thought. Several months later, during prayer and one of my regular conversations with the Lord, He said, "Go today, and buy the watch." When I arrived at the jewelry store, I found they were having a closeout sale. The watch was 86% off the original price. This was now God's will, and it was perfect. This verse assures us His will for us is *good, acceptable, and perfect.* I trusted His promises to me. Even when I heard "no," I still accepted His way and plan. Wasn't it better than mine? When you know how much God loves you and wants to bless you, then even if you hear a "no" or "not now" you don't feel rejected or mistreated. Don't be afraid. Wouldn't you like to know God's will for your life in every situation? You can, and this verse confirms when we *renew our minds,* we won't be conformed to this world. We'll not only be able to think like Him, but we'll be able to prove or know His will for our continued success.

DECEMBER 24

> *"Faithful is He Who is calling you [to Himself] and utterly trustworthy, and He will also do it [that is, fulfill His call by hallowing and keeping you]."*
> *1 Thessalonians 5:24 (AMP)*

Paul wrote this to the Thessalonians who, at the time, were suffering from much persecution. He didn't want fear to arise because of their circumstances and cause doubt or unbelief. He wanted them to be fully aware of the return of Jesus and to encourage them to wait. He assured them the One they believed in would always be faithful to His Word and promises. Today, through His Word and the Spirit, God still assures us **He is faithful!** Webster's Dictionary defines faithful as, "firm in adherence to promises or in observance of duty; steadfast in affection or allegiance; given with strong assurance or binding; true to the facts or standard." In other words, if God said it, you can count on it. The Bible also says His promises are "yes" and "amen." This means if we are praying according to His Word and will, His answer will always be "yes" or "so be it."

Why would this be important to us today? Let me ask you, "When was the last time someone kept their word to you? Is there anyone you can rely on 100% of the time?" In an ever changing world, stability and security are essential to a firm foundation. God is more than a 100% God. He can't lie, which makes Him bound to His Word. The Bible says everything will pass away, but not the Word of God. This is why we must know what it says. It holds the answer to every problem we will ever face. It is our sure foundation, and this verse confirms "*Faithful is He*" who is for us, steadfast in affection, strong in assurance, and true to His standard.

Paul said the One who calls you is faithful. He makes it clear. God won't let us down. The key is to not look at what the enemy is trying to do in the natural, but to stay focused on the Faithful One. This is our road to bypass fear and enjoy peace and success. He called you, and He is faithful to do it. Isn't it good to know you still have a bright future, regardless of the stock market, economy or even what the job market is doing? Doesn't it bring peace to know that you and your saved loved ones have a permanent home after death? And you will all be together again? Isn't it exciting to know Jesus is coming back, and it may be in your lifetime? Don't be afraid. Faith believes in the Faithful One who makes His plan clear. In the end, you won't be surprised, and you definitely won't be disappointed.

DECEMBER 25

"And let the peace (soul harmony which comes) from the Christ rule (act as umpire, continually) in your hearts—deciding and settling with finality all questions that arise in your minds—[in that peaceful state] to which [as members of Christ's] one body you were also called [to live]. And be thankful—appreciative, giving praise to God always."
Colossians 3:15 (AMP)

Christ's peace is the nothing missing, nothing lacking, nothing broken kind of peace. It means total wholeness in all areas of our lives. His peace stops fear when life's questions and trials surface. How? When we belong to Christ, we don't ever have to be afraid of the outcome. As a member of God's family you'll enjoy peace, rest, and even joy in the middle of chaos. How is this possible? Peace during chaos? Sounds like an oxymoron, doesn't it? But this verse tells us how. We first *decide,* and then, we *settle* it in our minds. Settle what? We settle any question, crisis, or situation that tries to exalt itself above a Mighty God. We settle it that God's ways are higher than ours, and He has all the "right" answers. We settle it that our minds will be renewed to what God says about our troubles—not what our boss, the TV newsperson, or the physician has to say. We settle it that we are Christ's. We belong to the Father, and He has promised us an abundant life that includes prosperity in our health, family, friends, and finances. We settle it that this peace leaves no room for fear. We settle it that we live by faith because faith pleases God.

The only way our mind settles these things is to stay hooked up to the Word. It literally becomes our lifeline. If you were in the hospital, would you let someone disconnect you from your source of power and life? The Word is our power source. It connects us to God. There is life in the Word, and if you are fighting death or the power of darkness in any area, you can't win without the constant application of the Word. So…have you settled it in your mind? Do you believe what the Word says? Are you ready for a little peace—*soul* (mind, will, and emotions) *harmony*? Don't be afraid. Once you settle these issues, you will live in the peace Christ has called you to live in, and as a result, you'll thank God. You'll praise Him because He is faithful. You'll be *thankful—appreciative* for His love, saving grace, and delivering power. You can let the peace that passes all understanding keep and guard your heart and mind in Christ Jesus. Just decide…then, settle it.

DECEMBER 26

> *"And let us not lose heart and grow weary and faint in acting nobly and doing right, for in due time and at the appointed season we shall reap, if we do not loosen and relax our courage and faint."*
> *Galatians 6:9 (AMP)*

The devil's plan of attack is to consistently bring trials against us in order to weaken us or to make us weary during the battle. Why would this strategy be effective? Because when we get tired, worn down or weary, we aren't as sharp or mentally alert. We even make silly mistakes that we wouldn't ordinarily make. The devil waits for these moments of opportunity to launch his attacks—dropping bombs of fear, doubt, and discouragement—hoping to distract us from God's will and purpose.

This verse tells us God knew there would be times we would feel weary or be discouraged. The devil's goal in bringing discouragement is to steal our courage. Courage is connected to faith, and faith is our confidence, conviction, and firm persuasion in the Word and God's ways. The truth is, all of the enemy's attacks work toward his ultimate attack, which is to steal our faith. When we use faith, along with the Word, he's automatically defeated...and he knows it! The enemy also knows if he can get something to go wrong, while we're doing our part in following the Lord, we can really become tired and weary in the process. Or if he can use someone close to us like a loved one or friend to come against us, we are even more apt to grow tired and lose heart. Maybe you've thought, "What's the point?" Or you've wondered why it seems you can't win for losing? These are clues the devil is close, and you need to get your "faith" shield up.

Did you know your faith is a shield against the devil? Are you aware God has given you a full suit of armor? The Bible says to put on the full armor of God so you can stand against the devil's wiles. We are to stand with the belt of truth buckled around our waist, the breastplate of righteousness, and our feet shod with the preparation of the gospel of peace. But above all, we are to take the shield of faith, which stops all the weapons of the devil, our helmet of salvation, and the sword of the Spirit which is God's Word, and stand against the devil. God has given us all we need to protect ourselves from weariness and defeat. Are you feeling discouraged? Do you feel like throwing in the towel? Hopelessness stems from fear. Don't be afraid. Keep your faith shield high. Guard your heart. For *at the appointed time*—your due season—*you will reap* God's reward. Even if it doesn't look like there is an end in sight, you can still be sure you will reap. How can you always be sure? His Word promises it!

DECEMBER 27

"You have made known to me the paths of life; you will fill me with joy in your presence."
Acts 2:28 (NIV)

God has always wanted His plan for His children revealed. It was and never has been a secret. Everything God does is done in the light. Anything else that is done in darkness is of the devil. Think about when most of the crimes happen…it's after dark. The first thing God created was light. The Bible says, "Jesus is the light of the world." If God does His work in the light and it's all good, why would we think He would want to keep us in the dark about the direction for our futures? Our families? Financial matters? Health issues? The truth is He doesn't. He made certain there would be a way we would know about things to come, how we can get on the right path, how we can stay on the right path after we get there, and how we can live without the torment of fear. How does He reveal or make these paths known? He does it through the Holy Ghost.

The Holy Ghost is available to us after we receive Christ. We receive Him by faith just like we did our salvation. We ask God to fill us with His power through the Holy Spirit. Jesus knew it would be crucial for believers to have the Holy Ghost. This is why He told them to go to the upper room and wait. Wait until they received power from the Holy Ghost as the Father had promised. So 120 men and women obeyed, and they waited for ten days. Then the Bible says, "There came a sound like a mighty rushing wind that came from heaven and it filled the whole house where they were sitting. Then they saw what appeared to be cloven tongues of fire that separated and came to rest on each of their heads. All of them were filled with the Holy Ghost and began to speak with other tongues." Jesus foretold this event to His disciples before He went to Heaven. He said men knew water baptism through John, but there was another baptism coming…the baptism of fire.

Don't be afraid. The baptism and power of the Holy Spirit is available to anyone who asks. We don't have to wait for it like they did. Once the Spirit came to earth, He's here to fill you with God's joy, presence, and fullness. Tongues or our heavenly language is the physical evidence the Spirit is with us. When we use our heavenly language the Bible says we're using our most holy faith. Why? It bypasses the mind. We may not always know what we're saying, but neither does the devil. We're speaking directly to God…Spirit to spirit. Let the Holy Spirit fill you. He'll *make known the paths of life* that God has in store for you.

> *"For [if we are] in Christ Jesus, neither circumcision or uncircumcision counts for anything, but only faith activated and energized and expressed and working through love."*
> *Galatians 5:6 (AMP)*

God is love. He demonstrated His love to mankind even while the law of sin and death reigned on the earth by sending Jesus to pay for our sins. But it didn't end there. Throughout the Scriptures, He continually expresses His unconditional devotion and love to us. This verse states that once we *are in Christ,* the only thing that *counts for anything* is when our *faith* is *activated and energized and expressed and working through love.* When the Bible tells us that without faith it is impossible to please God, and God IS love, then wouldn't this make sense? Our faith, the very thing we must use to fight our battles, get the victory, and then keep the victory must be rooted and grounded in love.

In this verse Paul also answers questions about circumcision. Under Jewish law, circumcision was man's fleshly reminder of his covenant with God. When the Gentiles accepted the Gospel, the Jews wanted them to be circumcised, too. Paul made it clear whether they did or didn't wasn't the issue. Paul believed when we receive the Lord, it is our hearts that are circumcised. There is a spiritual cutting away of the old. The Bible says all things become new. Paul just wanted them to stay focused on the real issue, which had nothing to do with religious tradition. The real issue is our faith. Faith that is propelled by action and fueled by love.

The Bible says, "Even if we can speak with the tongues of men and angels, and we can prophesy, and have the gift of understanding all mysteries and knowledge, and we have faith that moves mountains, and we give all we own to the poor or even be willing to die in flames—**but we don't have love**—it profits or gains nothing. We are as sounding brass or a clanging cymbal." Do you think God takes this love thing seriously? Why? Because He knows His "perfect" love casts out all fear. Not just some fear, some of the time, but all fear, period. We know fear and faith can't operate together. Fear is sin, and faith pleases God. Faith conquers fear and every other attack of the devil, but it must be activated by love. When was the last time you checked your love gage? Is it low? Do you need a minor tune-up? Or would those around you agree you need a total overhaul? Don't be afraid. With the Godhead or "LOVE" living in you, His love is available to flow through you to others. Just remember, love...plus faith...always equals victory.

> *"How God anointed Jesus of Nazareth with the Holy Ghost and with power: who went about doing good, and healing all that were oppressed of the devil; for God was with Him."*
> *Acts 10:38 (KJV)*

God anointed Jesus with the Holy Ghost and with power, and what did He do with this anointing? The Word says *He went about doing "good."* Do you see if we have a mental picture of the Godhead and it's not a "good" one, we have bought the lie of the enemy? Jesus used the power God gave Him to set people free by removing their fears that came from past bondages, curses, failures, and sin. He healed...**everyone**...that was oppressed, and He cast out devils. The word oppressed means to be unreasonably burdened, severe or overwhelming abuse in spirit or senses. It is a cruel and unjust use of power or authority. Doesn't this sound like the devil? The one who comes with a negative report of poverty, illness, fear, and death?

When the devil tries to oppress, he tells lies—like "You can't be healed" or "After 10 years of drugs, how could you quit or be delivered?" Maybe you were taught healing isn't for today? Or it's not for everyone? However, there is this truth to consider. If Christ dwells on the inside of you through accepting Him as your Lord and Savior, and God anointed Him with the Holy Ghost and power to heal and deliver, how is that same anointing and power not present and available to work on the inside of you, too? The Holy Spirit is given to us as a free gift, and it is through Him the fullness of the Godhead lives within each of us. How can that kind of power live on the inside of you and sickness and disease, lack, addictions, and an old sinful lifestyle have any place or authority? The truth is it can't. It's there because you have let fear lie to you that maybe you don't deserve the power, or you don't believe you have the same authority as Christ did, or you are subconsciously allowing your problem which is another way of fulfilling other deep emotional needs or desires. Whatever your reason...defeat in any areas isn't the will of your Father who loves you.

The Bible tells us it was the Holy Spirit who raised Jesus from the dead, and now He lives in you. He's the same power. Do you really think if He was able to raise the dead, He can't take care of cancer or other diseases, addictions, pornography, lusts, debt, unemployment or a troubled marriage? Don't be afraid. Nothing is impossible with God. He anointed Jesus. *God was with Him*, and God will be with you. Use your authority and the Word. Speak to your "mountain." Command the devil to go! And be free!

> *"Who said, Men of Galilee, why do you stand gazing into heaven? This same Jesus, Who was caught away and lifted up from among you into heaven, will return in [just] the same way in which you saw Him go into heaven."*
> *Acts 1:11 (AMP)*

The disciples asked Jesus when He would He be returning to them. Jesus said only the Father knows the appointed time. He then gave instructions for them to go to Jerusalem and wait in the upper room until they were filled with power, the gift the Father promised them in the Holy Ghost. He told them to be witnesses unto Him in Jerusalem, Judea, Samaria, and to the ends of the earth. At that moment, He was taken up to Heaven right before their eyes in a cloud that hid Him from their sight. Suddenly two men dressed in white stood beside them and spoke the above Words in this verse.

Jesus had previously said He was going to prepare a place. Then He would come back to take us to live in Heaven with the Father and Himself. God sent these two men to not only comfort the disciples, but to confirm the message of eternal hope—"Christ is returning." They brought an immediate reminder to mankind of their final destination. Why? Because God knew life as they knew it was about to change, and change produces fear. But the biggest fear mankind would experience is the thought they would never see their Lord again. If the devil deceived Eve, and then Adam about what God had really said, do you think he wouldn't try the same thing again? Maybe he'd try to confuse them with, "Did Jesus really say He was coming back? Or did He say He didn't know if He was coming back? Or did He say only the Father knows if He's coming for sure?" The truth is <u>He IS coming back</u>...only the Father knows <u>when</u>. The biggest question is, "Will you be watching? Will you be ready?"

The Bible says we are to be about His business until He returns. Are you a witness in your Jerusalem...family, neighborhood, workplace, community or city? Jesus said to be a witness. The way to do this is to show God's love, power, and blessings through our lifestyle. Do the people you know want what you have? Or are you as miserable and unhappy as they are? Do you really know the Lord? If you don't...don't wait to make Jesus your Lord and Savior. God's Word promises eternal life through Him. Don't be afraid. His Word is our assurance... *HE WILL RETURN...in just the same way in which* He left. Let's be watching, waiting for Him. Let's be ready!

DECEMBER 31

"For the Lord himself will come down from heaven, with a loud command, with the voice of the archangel and with the trumpet call of God, and the dead in Christ will rise first. After that, we who are still alive and are left will be caught up together with them in the clouds to meet the Lord in the air. And so we will be with the Lord forever."
1 Thessalonians 4:16-17 (NIV)

God didn't want anyone speculating about the end—"how" it would happen or even "if" it would occur. Why? Because uncertainty breeds fear and speculation can breed false doctrine. Paul repeats what Jesus told His disciples and the two men in white confirmed. He is coming back, and *we will be with Him forever.* We don't have to be afraid. God always tells us the plan beforehand. Both the Old and New Testaments confirm this truth.

God told Noah about the flood and asked Him to build an ark. Noah worked on the boat for 120 years, all the while telling people they could be saved. Even after the boat was finished and Noah, his family, and the animals got on board, the Lord left the door open for seven more days, so none would perish. However, the moment the doors closed, the rain started. Only Noah and his family believed God. They were saved. When the cities of Sodom and Gomorrah were about to be destroyed for their sexual perversions and sins, God sent two angels to warn Abraham's nephew, so he and his family could leave the city. Why? God keeps His Word, and He had a covenant agreement between Himself and Abraham. God always announces what He is going to do. He doesn't want us to be afraid.

The Old Testament prophets foretold over 330 details of Christ's birth and death, all of which came to pass exactly as recorded, and yet, people didn't believe Jesus was God's Son. The New Testament has more than twice the amount of prophecies about Christ's return. Wouldn't it stand to reason that if the Old Testament was one hundred percent accurate about what it prophesied that the New Testament would be just as accurate? Christ is God's Son. He was born to die, to pay for our sins, so we could have eternal life. This is no longer prophecy, but fact, and God is telling us the future again…"*For the Lord Himself will come down from heaven...*" It's true, Christ is coming, again, and He's coming soon, but you must accept Jesus as your Lord and Savior. He is the only way to the Father. Will you be ready? Will you listen to and heed God's warning? Don't be afraid. Only believe. Obey, and be saved through the power of His love and grace…forever!

SALVATION PRAYER

It is the will of God the Father that all mankind—every man, woman, and child, every race, tribe, nation, and tongue be saved. He made the way simple, so all could do it, and He gave us only one way, so we wouldn't get confused. This one way is through His Son, Jesus Christ. God sent His only begotten Son, Jesus, to come to earth, be born of a virgin, suffer and die for our sins. Because of sin, man could not be the sacrifice, but because Jesus was sinless, He could pay the price. He was crucified and died, and on the third day He arose from the dead—defeating the devil and bringing the keys of death, hell, and the grave up with Him. He ascended into Heaven and is seated at the right hand of God the Father where He intercedes for us every moment of the day. When we accept Jesus into our hearts, we no longer have to live in fear about anything…especially death. We no longer have to be afraid if we will go to Heaven or hell when our physical bodies die. The moment we die our spirits will be with the Lord in Heaven. If you would like to make Jesus the Lord and Savior of your life and receive all the benefits of a whole, healthy mind and body, financial prosperity, social well being, and an abundant life both now and later, then pray the following prayer:

> Heavenly Father, I come to You admitting that I am a sinner. I cannot save myself. I need a Savior. I ask You to forgive me of my sins and I declare to turn from my ways and follow Your ways. I believe Your Son Jesus died on the cross for my sins. I believe He rose again from the dead, so that I would be justified and made righteous through my faith in Him. I ask You now to come into my heart and to be my Lord and Savior. Thank you for washing away all my sins and making me brand new. I am Your child. I am now born again. Amen.

If you prayed this prayer to receive Jesus Christ as your Lord and Savior we would like to hear from you. Please contact me at:

Polly Harder
848 N. Rainbow Blvd. #479
Las Vegas, NV. 89107
www.dontbeafraid.info

THE BAPTISM IN THE HOLY SPIRIT

The baptism of the Holy Spirit is subsequent to salvation. It is also a free gift from God for the asking. Sometimes this experience is referred to as "the baptism of the Holy Spirit," "receiving the Spirit," or "being filled with the Spirit." They are all scriptural terms for the same experience. When we received salvation, we asked, and then accepted it by faith. It works the same way with the baptism of the Holy Spirit. We must use our faith to receive Him. When we receive, according to Scripture, speaking in tongues or another language other than our own is the first sign of being filled. The Word says He will give us utterance as we yield our tongue, but it is still our responsibility to speak it out. He does not take over. This is why we can stop or start speaking our heavenly language at will, and we can also sing in the Spirit when we desire. The baptism of the Holy Spirit accomplishes several important things in the believer's life. He strengthens and empowers our prayer life. It is His power in us that gives us the ability to overcome our sinful ways and live a Godly life, and His wisdom directs not only our own lives, but He gives us knowledge to help others so we can be a true witness for Jesus. The Bible also says when we don't know what to pray, the Holy Spirit will make intercession through us. He always knows what to pray. If you would like to be empowered by God on High and receive this gift, pray the following prayer:

> Dear Heavenly Father, I am asking you to fill
> me with Your Holy Spirit, so I can speak
> directly to You and be empowered to live
> a Godly Christian life. I know this is a gift
> from You, and now I yield myself to Your Spirit
> and by faith I receive Him. Thank you, Lord
> for Your goodness to me. Amen.

Now don't use your mind because this is a spiritual experience. Just speak those few syllables or sounds you heard and God will fill you and increase your language. The Bible says praying in tongues is using your most holy faith because it isn't contaminated by your own thoughts or ideas. It's you and God—speaking Spirit to spirit.

If you have prayed this prayer, we would like to hear from you. Please contact me at:

Polly Harder
848 N. Rainbow Blvd. #479
Las Vegas, NV. 89107
www.dontbeafraid.info

AMEN.

ABOUT THE AUTHOR

Polly Harder received the Lord Jesus Christ as her Savior as a young child. At age fifteen, God told her, "One day I'm going to ask you to do something for Me." However, because the church she attended didn't teach the salvation message or the gifts of the Spirit, Polly didn't know the power or authority she had in Christ Jesus. After living life "her way" for many years and suffering the consequences, she decided to call on God for help. The Lord directed her to a church where she heard for the first time that God wanted a personal relationship with her, He had a plan for her life, and how easy it was to get into the flow of His plan. It was then, at the age of twenty-seven, she realized the true meaning of becoming "born again." She experienced the realness of what it means to have Jesus Christ living in your heart. She also learned how to let God the Father become the father she grew up without, since her father suddenly died when she was eleven years old. From that time until now, He has become more than a friend to her. He has also become the Supreme Authority in every area of her life. It was at this point her exciting journey began.

However, walking with the Lord and learning His ways is a process. Since that time, because of her close, personal relationship with the Lord, Polly has learned what it means to "let go" and "let God." She has let go of the past baggage and fears in her life, and instead, has let God show her how to live by His ways…to "live" by faith. She knows the difference only He can make. She has discovered the truth and power that is found in His Word will change any circumstance, and beyond any doubt she can testify He is faithful to see that His Word comes to pass. She has allowed God to move in miraculous ways on her behalf.

Polly has owned and managed several companies. She has also worked in the areas of training, management, and counseling for several large corporations. In 1993, God's plan included starting Jordan House Ministries, Inc. Polly holds the positions of Director and President. JHM is a non-profit corporation whose vision is to help mentor individuals with their transition from an unproductive place in their lives toward the plans and purposes God has for them. Jordan House was named after the Jordan River. In the Old Testament everyone who reached the Promised Land first crossed the Jordan River. Jordan House Ministries does what is necessary to become the bridge, temporarily filling in the gap, so all those who want to crossover into what God promised for them will have the opportunity to do so.

Through effective communication, she uses her gifts to educate, train, and counsel. She also relies upon the gifts of the Holy Spirit through words of wisdom, knowledge, and the discerning of spirits. It's a combination of these skills that have empowered many to "crossover" to a new place of freedom and victory. Her precise direction and Biblical methods teach…you don't have to live afraid. You don't have to live defeated. You can live free of fear from your past, present, and future. This God given victorious lifestyle enables you to crossover from the "just barely existing" into living an abundant, more productive, fulfilling life!

Polly is available for both individual and group sessions. She develops and conducts seminars and training sessions for ministries and businesses. These programs are designed to improve individuals' communication skills and increase productivity. She is available for personal mentoring to aid individuals in discovering their purpose and destiny. If you would like more information regarding any of the sessions or if you would like to schedule a meeting time, please contact Polly at:

848 N. Rainbow Blvd. #479
Las Vegas, NV. 89107
www.dontbeafraid.info

Printed in the United States
93048LV00004B/79-138/A

9 780977 246076